Missing 411

• EASTERN UNITED STATES •

Berry Pickers
Sheepherders
Farmers

Unexplained disappearances of North Americans that have never been solved.

Copyright © 2011 David Paulides
All rights reserved.
ISBN: 1468012622
ISBN 13: 9781468012620
Library of Congress Control Number: 2011962091
CreateSpace, North Charleston, South Carolina

DEDICATION

Missing 411 is dedicated to every family that has ever suffered the disappearance of a loved one. There can be no worse fate than not knowing the whereabouts of a relative or friend. In every incident that was researched in this book, the amount of human sacrifice that was expended in the effort to find a son, daughter, father, brother, or friend was deserving of the highest esteem. The subsequent pain suffered if the person wasn't found stays with the searcher a lifetime—, it's something that he or she can't forget, something he or she doesn't want to forget.

I have personally had nightmares about several of the incidents described in this manuscript; they still haunt me today, but my nightmares pale in comparison to those of any family member who couldn't find a loved one.

To each and every one of you mentioned in this book, I dedicate this work to you and your family. May you find inner peace.

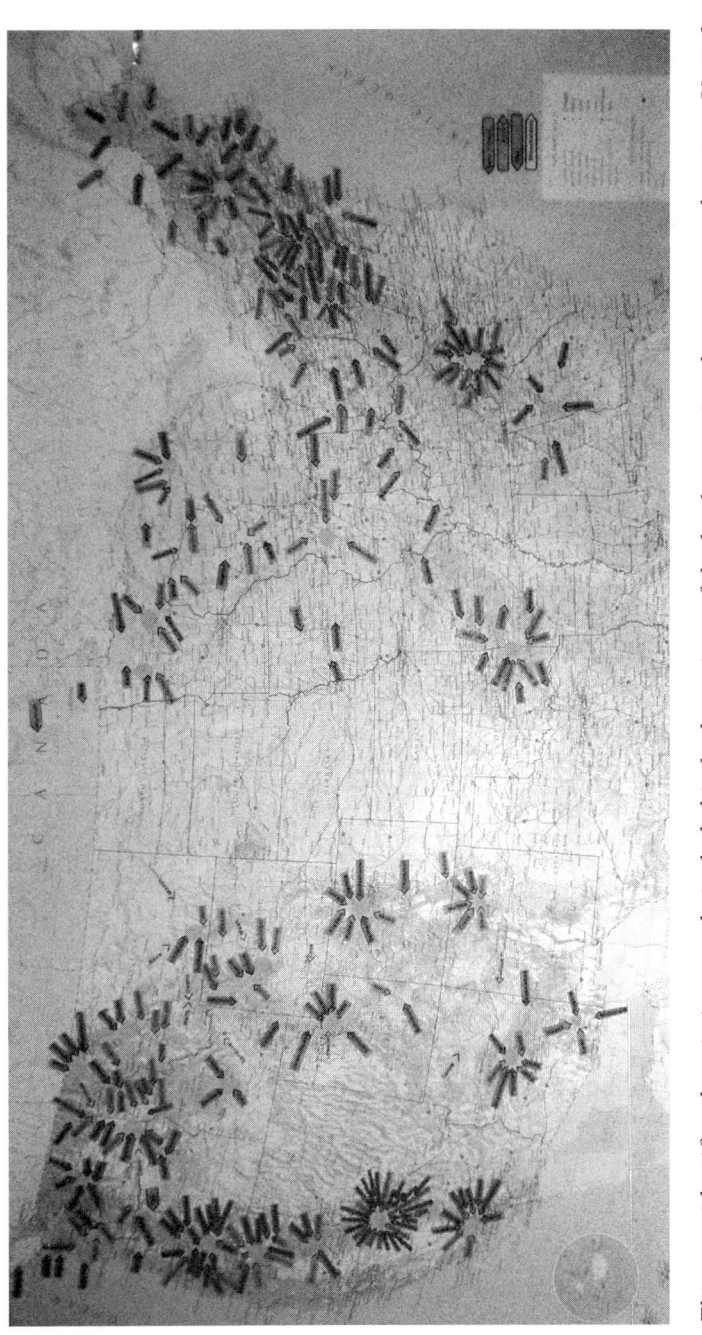

This map identifies the missing people included in both versions of the book, covering the eastern and western United States. The twenty-eight large dots on the map represent clusters of missing people. When you study the map, you can clearly see a defined area in the middle of the United States where there are no missing people fitting the book's criteria. This made it easy to decide where to split the versions of the book. Texas and Florida were not included in this study—I could easily write an entire book on many disappearances in these states–thus no marks on the map. The light-colored tabs represent females; the dark tabs represent males.

CONTENTS

Introduction · xi
    Clusters · xii
    Unique Factors in Disappearances · · · · · · · · · · · · · · · · · · xiii
Missing People · 1
Unique Groups of Missing People · 2
    Central Ontario · 2
    Berry Pickers · 8
    Sheepherders · 21
    Farmers · 26
Midwest United States · 34
    Minnesota · 34
    Wisconsin · 47
    Michigan · 54
    Iowa · 68
    Illinois · 69
    Missouri · 73
    Oklahoma/Arkansas · 75
Southern States · 95
    Georgia/Alabama · 95
Appalachians · 105
    Great Smoky Mountains · 105
    Ohio · 165
    Pennsylvania · 169
    West Virginia · 215
    Kentucky · 225

Northeastern United States · 232
- New England · 232
- Vermont · 264
- New Jersey · 277

Lists · 283
- Master List of Missing Children Under Ten Years · · · · · · · 283
- Analysis · 288
- Master List · 296
- Decade Breakdown of Missing · 307

Conclusions · 309
- Gaps in Time · 309
- Danger in the Woods · 310
- Screams and Yells · 312
- Bow Hunters · 313
- National Park Service · 315
- The Interview · 318
- DOI Recommendations · 320
- FBI Involvement · 322
- Next Steps · 328

Index · 331

ABBREVIATIONS

BIA	Bureau of Indian Affairs
DOI	Department of the Interior
FBI	Federal Bureau of Investigation
FOIA	Freedom of Information Act
NPS	National Park Service
SAR	Search and Rescue
USFS	United States Forest Service
FLIR	Forward Looking Infrared Radar

INTRODUCTION

I was originally led to this story by an off-duty ranger at a national park I was visiting. They informed me of a series of missing person cases at the parks that were not getting any visibility in the press, and they felt that there might be a series of similar cases at other parks. That one meeting set me on a three-year study of the missing people topic, which led to two books highlighting 411 stories.

The most interesting and fascinating portion of this study on missing people is the discovery of clusters of missing in various areas of North America. The clusters were indentified after years of research and hours spent while I studied maps. The following are the clusters that were identified in the eastern section of the United States:

Oklahoma/Arkansas Border
Hokit
B. Jamison
M. Jamison
S. Jamison
Cook
Krebbs
Jones
Jackson
McDonald
Hanson
Davenport
Hague
Reel
Lavies

Great Smoky Mountains NP
Haun
Gibson
Melton
Lindsay
Hearon
Ramsay
Toney
Martin
Auberry

Georgia/Alabama
Moore
Tankersley
Thompkins
Upshaw
Tippin
Thomas

Northern Illinois
Sweely
Chenoweth
Shackleford
Klamecki

NW Minnesota

Ayotte
Kelly
McQuillan
Long
Warner

NW Maine
Newton
Johnson
Brown
Hoover
Johnson
Renaud

New Hampshire/S. Maine
Lauro
McCarthy
Chapman
Abbott
Marvin

S. Vermont
Jepson
Herrick
Rivers
Davis
Weldon
Baker
Langer
Bishop

NE Minnesota

Sommerville
Bordwell
Coleman

N. Michigan
Ahtonen
Perry
Benjamin
Henegan
Hallaxs
Clewley

N. West Virginia
Kuhl
Shoemaker
Moore
McKinney

Pennsylvania
The entire state is a cluster

Notes on clusters:
   The northern Illinois cluster is the only cluster in both books in which everyone missing is a female.

Vermont is the only cluster that has a tight time frame surrounding all six missing people, just twenty-four years, 1926–1950.

The Great Smoky Mountains National Park and the surrounding region is an interesting study area because Native Americans originally settled it. Modern-day disappearances started in 1919, the latest occurring in 2008.

The entire state of Pennsylvania is a cluster, an amazing accumulation of juveniles who have disappeared under very similar circumstances.

Unique Factors in Disappearances

The factors I am describing relate to the entire study and not solely to this book. Many of these factors are evident in the eastern United States, while others are in the west.

As you read the story behind each missing person, you will start to hear a consistent theme that includes facts found in other disappearances of missing individuals. Part of the criteria I used for a missing person case to be included in the books corresponded to the number of factors included on this list that were evident in the story. Here are a few of the factors you will find in many of the cases outlined in this book:

Rural Setting – All of the missing people outlined in this project disappeared from a rural setting, not a city or downtown location. There were usually no witnesses, there was significant cover, and difficult terrain

Dogs – For some unknown reason dogs played a major role in many of the disappearances in the eastern United States. Many of the cases involve children following their dogs into the wild.

Bloodhounds/Canines Can't Track Scent – A very unusual trend I found in many of these cases was that expert tracking dogs were brought to the scene of the disappearance and were not successful at doing their job. The dogs were given the scent via a person's shoe or worn shirt, they were brought to the location where the person was last seen, and they either refused to track or couldn't pick up a scent. This behavior has occurred too many times to ignore, and it's not understood why this often occurs.

Disabled/Impaired – Several cases in the east involve disabled children who disappear. Initially, I believed that this was occurring because of the disability, but the more I read and understood about these cases, I think the numbers are too high for random occurrence. I don't understand why so many disabled children disappear, but the numbers don't seem coincidental.

Fever – I have had discussions with physicians about the children who return from being missing who have fevers. When they are examined, physicians noted in the articles can't find a reason for the fever, and the physicians I spoke with couldn't explain it. Only a handful of these incidents were described in articles, but I believe children returning with fevers had occurred many more times than noted. The condition wasn't told to the media, and it was handled as a normal medical anomaly.

Conscious/Semi-Conscious – One of the most unusual conditions found among missing people is being found in a conscious or semiconscious state. I understand that when people go missing for extended periods hallucinations can occur because of an absence of food and water, but these conditions are prevalent even when those factors do not exist. You will read about cases in which the missing are found unconscious, lying on the ground. When questioned later, they have no recollection of how they came to be missing. In some cases the missing person does recall the facts surrounding his or her disappearance, and the facts of those cases create fascinating reading.

Kidnapping – In several incidents law enforcement officials believed the victim was kidnapped. In many of the cases, the people returned in fairly clean clothes, and even though there was heavy precipitation, they were dry. The truly astonishing factor is that in many cases there was no shelter found, and it couldn't be explained why the victim was dry.

In several of the cases in which the word "kidnap" was used, law enforcement officials backed off their position, and it was never explained why. In hindsight, many of these cases occurred in a rural area, and the press or local sheriff may not have wanted to alarm the community.

Afternoon Disappearance – From the information gleaned from the project, the optimum time for a disappearance to occur is in the 2:00 p.m.–5:00 p.m. time frames.

Swamps and Briar Patches – Many of the missing are found in the middle or on the perimeter of a swamp and/or briar patch. Some rescuers have commented on the unusual location a child is found in and how they don't understand how he or she got there. These are not locations that people would casually visit.

Berries – The fact that berries and berry bushes play a continuous role in many disappearances is overwhelming. People disappear and are found in the middle of berry bushes. They go missing while they are picking berries, and some are found eating berries. The association between some missing people and berries cannot be denied.

Clothing Removed – In numerous cases cited, the missing person is found and at least one significant piece of clothing has disappeared. Sometimes people are found inexplicably naked. While this may sound like a minor issue, it often isn't minor once you read the facts surrounding the cases and understand how consistent the details are surrounding each incident. While searchers are scouring every inch of a quadrant from the point last seen until the missing is found, in many instances the clothing is never found. Some large pieces of clothing are never found. I know that some search manuals indicate that children do remove their clothing; the facts surrounding these cases do not seem to support that assertion, however, as it was extremely detrimental to their survival.

Missing Found in an Area Previously Searched – Another common factor found in many search and rescue (SAR) missions. Searchers find the missing person and later are adamant that the area in which the person was found had been thoroughly searched numerous times in the past. Sometimes the missing person is found on a major trail that searchers had used daily. SAR commanders are sometimes mystified by the the victim's location when found.

MISSING PEOPLE

As you read about these incidents, I want everyone to apply his or her own level of common sense to what is explained. Ask yourself these questions:
1. Could my child have accomplished what the child in the article allegedly did (walked this far, survived in this environment, etc.)?
2. Would my child ever do what the child in the article did?
3. Does this story even make sense?
4. Does it seem like someone is trying to manipulate the story?
5. Does there seem to be a consistency in the stories?
6. Could these events be related to one another?

I can almost guarantee that you will go back and read many of the stories a second and third time. Look at the terrain on "Google Earth" and see if you can notice any similarities in the locations of the disappearances.

I have included as many maps as I could afford in this book. The 411 cases included in both the Western and Eastern United States books *are not* all of the cases that fit this criteria. I guarantee there are more, probably many more. With the advent of the internet and better communications, the idea that more adults and children are missing in the Canadian North is a guarantee. The *New York Times* has done a great public service of making their articles before 1900 free for the public to view, and its coverage of the United States was fairly good.

I have included three special categories of missing people that are quite unique: farmers, berry pickers, and sheepherders. Again, I wasn't looking for a subcategory to include, these jumped out at me. Several of the missing berry pickers were young children that were momentarily left alone and almost seemed to vanish under their parent's supervision. Many of the disappearances occurred in very remote areas where there were no other cars or people present, yet there were indicators that these children may have been abducted, a very troubling and serious possibility that I'm sure law enforcement never adequately or thoroughly investigated.

Missing People

Central Ontario

This is a special section included in this book because the majority of people missing were hunters. The ages of the people missing in this area of Ontario is quite old and does not match the demographics of any other area of North America.

The center point for missing people in north Central Ontario is Timmins. There are seven people missing from within fifty miles of the Timmins City Limits. Readers should understand that you could travel two miles from downtown Timmins and be in a very remote and desolate area that has significant wildlife.

The disappearance of two men (Weeden/Newcombe), simultaneously from the Crown Game Preserve is a very unusual event.

List of Missing People from Ontario by Date:

Name	Date/Time Missing	•Age •Sex
Meryl Newcombe	10/29/59-Unk	•50•M
George Weeden	10/29/59-Unk	•63•M
Elizabeth Kant	10/16/72-Unk	•45•F
Vital Vachon	05/01/73-Unk	•56•M
Foster Bezanson	10/25/80-Unk	•64•M
Clayton McFaul	08/15/86-Unk	•59•M
John Clifford	10/10/87-Unk	•65•M
Dustin Rhodes	07/06/91-Unk	•64•M
Bernard Champagne	07/10/97-Unk	•80•M
Michael Linklater	07/13/03-Unk	•44•M

•• Refer to the chapter on "Farmers" for details on the Clayton McFaul disappearance.

Meryl Newcombe
Missing 10/29/59,
Chapleau, Ontario
Age at Disappearance:
50 years

George Weeden
Missing 10/29/59,
Chapleau, Ontario
Age at Disappearance:
63 years

Refer to the Weeden narrative for details on Mr. Newcombe.

George Weeden and Meryl Newcombe were at a hunting lodge that was owned and operated by Mr. Newcombe. They were hunting near the lodge when they failed to return from an outing on October 29, 1959. They were never seen again. They were last seen between mile marker 106 and 107 of the CPR Line.

George Weeden was an individual that was never going to walk or hike long distances. In 1941 George had been seriously injured in a train accident in which he sustained a broken back and debilitating injuries to his right leg. George Weeden had a very difficult time walking any long distances.

One of the largest provincial searches during the 1960's was conducted for these two men. There was a second search in the spring of 1960 after the snowmelt occurred, with searchers never finding one clue about what happened to the two men.

Case Summary:

The case of Weeden and Newcombe is highly unusual, very frustrating, and doesn't make much sense. The men were at a remote hunting lodge owned by Newcombe. These were seasoned outdoorsmen who were not going to walk far from their vehicle. They were staying close to the truck because of Weeden's injuries. Both men were undoubtedly armed because they were hunting. The men would not have been attacked by a bear; bears would have been hibernating in late October. Both men were hunting in the Crown Game Preserve, known for its outstanding variety of birds and mammals. The Ojibwe First Nations Tribe lives in the middle of this area and knows the variety of game that it offers. They have the freedom to hunt the area at times when others cannot. The weather in this area would have been very cold, snowy, and difficult to walk in. People would never hike long distances at this time of the year in this area.

The law enforcement officials conducted an extensive search in the spring after the pair disappeared and after the snow had melted and still could not locate the men. It may be plausible for one man to disappear in this region in late October; how two men disappear baffles my common sense approach to search and rescue.

Elizabeth Ann Kant
Missing 10/16/72, Adair Township, 73 Miles e/o Cochrane, Ontario
Age at Disappearance: 45 years
5'5", 160 lbs

Ms. Kant was with a hunting party in a desolate area approximately seventy-three miles east of Cochrane, Ontario. During the hunt, Elizabeth got separated from her party near camp #23 at Abitibi. This is an area near where the Abitibi River enters the lake and very close to Abitibi-De-Troyes Provincial Park. At the point that the party got separated was the last time anyone saw Elizabeth.

There was a large and lengthy search for Elizabeth, but she was not found.

Vital Vachon
Missing 5/1/73, Lucas Township near Timmins, Ontario
Age at Disappearance: 56 years
5'6", 158 lbs

The last confirmed sighting of Vital was as he departed a bush camp in Lucas Township near Timmins. A search of the bush camp and surrounding area failed to find any evidence of Vachon.

Foster Bezanson
Missing 10/25/80, Cochrane, Ontario
Age at Disappearance: 64 years
5'7", 149 lbs

The area surrounding Cochrane gets very desolate very quickly. It is surrounded by wildlife and has significant water sources very close to the city. The townships in this area of Ontario are not close to each other; there are long stretches of roadway without people, commercial services, or residences. Small farms do dot the landscape in this area.

Bezanson left the Abitibi Road 48 area near Cochrane to spend the day hunting. He was armed. Mr. Bezanson was last seen on Translimit Road 4 east to mileage 60, north 2 one mile on Abitibi Road 48. He was armed with a 30–06. This area of Ontario is fairly flat. When Bezanson failed to arrive home, a search was initiated. Mr. Bezanson was never found.

Several people are missing in the same region as Foster Bezanson under similar circumstances. No evidence of Bezanson was ever found.

John Samuel Clifford
Missing 10/10/87, Frederick House River, Ontario
Age at Disappearance: 65 years
5'10", 180 lbs

John Clifford was a sixty-five-year-old gentleman who loved the outdoors. He specifically enjoyed hunting and fishing the area around his residence in Frederick House, Ontario. On October 10, 1987, Clifford went missing near Floods Landing on the Frederick House River. This occurred in close proximity to the location where Foster Bezanson disappeared.

Clifford has been missing for over twenty years, and it is difficult to get information on his disappearance.

Dustin Rhodes
Missing 7/6/91, Timmins, Ontario
Age at Disappearance: 64 years
5'10", 220 lbs

Dustin Rhodes was staying at his rural cottage on Lake Gibson. On July 6, 1991 at approximately 11:00 a.m., it was discovered that Dustin was missing.

Lake Gibson is located approximately five miles south of Kettle Lake Provincial Park and fifteen miles east of Timmons. The cabin is located in a very rural area that is remote with woods and forests surrounding the lake. There is no evidence of Dustin's whereabouts.

**Four of the eleven people on this list in Central Ontario have disappeared in July.

Bernard Champagne
Missing 7/10/97, Val Cote, Ontario
Age at Disappearance: 80 years
5'6", 149 lbs

Bernard was an elderly gentleman living in a rear building at a rustic cabin on the outskirts of Val Cote. The owner of the cabin kept close tabs on Mr. Champagne and quickly realized he was missing.

A massive search of the area that included canines, helicopters, airplanes and a ground search never found any trace of Bernard. If Bernard did die in close proximity to the residence, odors from decomposition would alert the homeowners and Bernard's body would've been found, this did not occur.

Case Summary:

This is another case where readers need to take a breath and not be numb to these disappearances. Think clearly about how far an elderly eighty-year old man could get in the bush of Manitoba? How is it possible that Mr. Champagne was not found? Why would Mr. Champagne ever want to walk out into the bush? Even if the man was senile, how far could he really get when others are trying to keep track of him?

Michael Joseph Linklater
Missing 7/13/03, 6:00 a.m., between Cochrane and Moosonee, Ontario
Age at Disappearance: 44 years
5'6", 158 lbs

On July 9, 2003, Michael went to the Linklater hunting/fishing camp located between Cochrane and Moosonee. More specifically, the camp is located near mile marker 115 on the CN Railroad Line. Sometime on July 13 Michael disappeared while in the outdoors.

Despite numerous searches in the area, Michael has not been seen since 6:00 a.m. on July 13, 2003.

Chapter Summary

The age of the people missing in Ontario is striking. They are consistently older than people missing in almost every other region in North America except other regions of the same province. Why aren't there consistencies in the age of the missing?

Missing Berry Pickers

I included a section on missing berry pickers because it was a unique subset of people missing in the wild. The missing in this bracket are predominantly older, but there are eight under the age of ten, and the circumstances of their disappearance is quite troubling. Seven of twenty-one listed are missing from Canada, a significant percentage of missing berry pickers. Many of the places where these individuals went missing are very desolate but abundant with food source at the time. There never was a conclusion on what happened to these people except in circumstances in which a body was found. None of the berry pickers was found to be taken by a bear or killed by a bear.

Names of the victims were entered by the date they went missing.

Berry Pickers Listed by Date Missing

Name	Date Missing•Age•Sex•Location
Stephen Ford	08/05/1880•9•M•Pleasant Valley, PA
Johnnie Lembke	08/12/10•15•M•Elyria, OH
Eddie Hamilton	07/06/28•2•M•Elrose, Sask
Wesley Piatote	08/04/32•7•M•Nespelem, WA
George Wanke	07/27/35•58•M•Brightstone, MAN
Jack Pike	09/05/35•5•M•St. Norbert, MAN
Emma Steffy	07/18/39•75•F•Reading, PA
Simon Skogan	07/02/40•9•M•Winnepeg, MAN
Mrs. August Nelson	07/28/43•75•F•Drummond, WI
C. H. Bordwell	08/01/44•44•M•Keewatin, MN
David Feif	07/06/52•85•M•Rehoboth, MA
Gary Bailey	07/17/54•3•M•Knox, ME
Rose Jewett	08/11/57•95•F•Elk River, ID
Richard Craig	08/15/57•5•M•Goldendale, WA
Mabel Moffitt	08/10/66•55•F•Gilmore Creek, Alaska
Marcelene Cummungs	07/14/69•54•F•Newport, WA
Yehudi Prior	09/23/74•2•M•Vancouver Island
	**22 years without a berry picker missing
Szpak, Frank	09/23/96•68•M•Kirkland, ONT

Raymond Tunnicliffe   08/26/02•NA•M•Weyakwin, SASK
Luciano Trinastich   07/24/07•78•M•Timmons, ONT

Stephen Ford
Missing 8/5/1880, Pleasant Valley, Pennsylvania
Age at Disappearance: 9 years

There were few details about this disappearance. I found one *New York Times* article dated August 9, 1880.

Stephen was the son of John Ford who lived in Pleasant Valley, southeast of Pittsburgh. Stephen disappeared while he was gathering berries near his house. The boy had been missing four days when the article was printed, and searchers had not found him.

Stephen disappeared in the same area as two females, Bowers and Thorpe. Refer to the chapter on Pennsylvania disappearances for additional details.

Johnnie Lembke
Missing 8/12/1910, Elyria, Ohio
Age at Disappearance: 15 years

An article in the *Evening Telegram* on August 12, 1910 stated that Lembke was picking berries when something unexplained happened. They found his half full pail of berries lying on the ground, but no other indicators of Johnnie. The Vermillion River is adjacent to the land that Johnnie was on and the river was dragged for his body several times with no signs of the boy.

The article theorized that Johnnie may have attempted to run off another berry picker or had disturbed a hawk's nest. As best as I can determine, Johnnie was never located.

The hawk's nest is an unusual explanation for this incident as a fifteen-year-old boy is a large object for a hawk to carry away and consume. I've read many interesting conclusions to missing person cases, especially in older articles. Many of the explanations have no basis in reality but appear to be printed to offer some logical explanation to a very unusual event.

Eddie Hamilton
Missing 7/6/28, Elrose, Saskatoon
Age at Disappearance: 2 years

Mr. and Mrs. Freeman Hamilton from Elrose took their two-year-old son (Eddie) with them as they went berry picking just south of their hometown. They exited their car in the thick, berry-infested area and Eddie immediately walked off in one direction. The Hamilton's momentarily lost sight of the boy and never saw him again.

The area that the Hamiltons were in was flat ground for three miles to the south up to the White Bear Hills that surround White Bear Lake. There are three small lakes, all approximately one-half mile long and narrow. There are sets of hills on each side of the lakes and the bodies of water sit inside a small valley. These are the only hills anywhere in the vicinity of Eddie's disappearance.

Once Eddie was out of sight, the Hamiltons immediately started to call his name and search for him; they did not receive an answer. The parents searched the area multiple times and couldn't find the boy. The husband stayed in the area searching, and the wife went for help. The Royal Canadian Mounted Police (RCMP) quickly arrived, and before dusk a large search had started. The SAR had over 250 participants inside of twenty-four hours, with searchers working around the clock. Planes had been used for low flight passes in an effort to see ground movement, none was seen.

A July 13, 1928 article in the *Saskatoon Phoenix* noted that searchers had found "boot prints" and "heel prints" in one area AND the following: "There are footprints however in the vicinity but though the wheat fields and undergrowth for miles around have been thoroughly combed no further clue has been found."

The writer of this article is discerning because he made a definite distinction between the boot, heel, and footprint that were found.

Several articles stated that this search was the largest in the history of the province. It lasted for over three months, and nothing was found. No clothing in the brush, no other footprints, no witnesses, nothing. Almost two thousand people participated in the three-month effort.

On October 25, 1928, a traveling salesman was duck hunting three and one-half miles from where little Eddie Hamilton disappeared. The hunter was on White Bear Lake when he looked in the water and saw a small figure floating—it was Eddie. The body was retrieved, and the parents made a positive identification that it was Eddie Hamilton. The article in the *Winnipeg Free Press* made no mention of the condition of the body or the oddity of the find.

Case Summary:
If Eddie Hamilton were found in White Bear Lake, that little boy would have climbed over an 1800-foot mountain, walked down into a valley, and then into the water. There were many, many other small bodies of water in the area of the disappearance that he could have fallen into, but he didn't. The idea that a two-year-old boy could walk over three miles through thickets, brush, and over a mountain without ever hearing the frantic pleas of his parents is hard to believe—very hard to believe. The fact that he had to climb over mountains to reach the lake is something quite unbelievable for a two-year-old. You will find several notes in this book that describe small children supposedly hiking uphill when lost and later found at an elevation higher than where they went missing. It is the general belief among SAR leaders that children walk downhill when lost, not usually uphill, especially a two-year-old going 1800 feet uphill. A guidebook written to assist SAR commanders states that a one- to three-year-old child will be found 95 percent of the time on flat ground in less than a two-mile radius.

Wesley David Piatote
Missing: 8/4/32, Strawberry Mountain, Nespelem, Washington
Age at Disappearance: 7 years

Wesley was picking huckleberries with his mother and grandmother on Strawberry Mountain outside of Nespelem, Washington. In the late afternoon, the boy wandered a slight distance away from the women. The women heard the boy scream two times, and they became alarmed. Both women immediately searched for Wesley and couldn't find a trace of him. Within two days fifty men on horseback were looking for Wesley and could not locate the boy.

Please refer to the "Washington" chapter in *Missing411–Western United States*. There are similarities with this case and the disappearance of Jimmy Duffy. Duffy's disappearance near Wenatchee Lake was in the same general vicinity as this case, and both children disappeared in desolate locations. Both children made a loud sound or scream before they disappeared and were never found.

Jack Pike
Missing 9/5/35, St. Norbert, Manitoba
Age at Disappearance: 5 years
    Details about Jack Pike's disappearance can be read in the Minnesota State section.

George Wanke
Missing 7/27/35, Brightstone, Ontario
Age at Disappearance: 58 years
    On July 27 of 1935 the *Winnepeg Free Press* ran an article regarding Mr. Wanke's disappearance. The article stated that Wanke was from Beausejour and was traveling with twenty-four other residents from their city to Brightstone, an area known for berry picking. The group arrived and then agreed on a specific time to meet for the ride home. The entire group did arrive at the designated meeting location, except Wanke.
    Residents initially returned to Brightstone, and the next morning they drove back to their berry-picking spot with three truckloads of searchers. The search effort was in vain. Wanke was never found.

Emma Steffy
Missing 7/15/39, Reading, Pennsylvania
Age at Disappearance: 75 years
    Emma Steffy was a very strong woman. She left her residence adjacent to the Welsh Mountain Wilderness and hiked into the woods to pick huckleberries. A neighbor reported seeing her eight miles from her residence and asked if she needed a ride. She answered "no." She left her residence with her pipe, tobacco, sandwiches, and a bottle of coffee. After being seen by neighbors, Emma Steffy disappeared. Farmers and state police thoroughly searched the region for three days and were unable to find Emma. On the fourth day that Emma was missing she wandered into her residence with a torn dress and explained that she had hit her head badly. There were few details about Emma's three+ days in the woods.

Simon Skogan
Missing 7/2/40, 55 Miles North of Winnipeg, Manitoba
Age at Disappearance: 9 years

In early July of 1940, Simon Skogan traveled fifty-five miles north of Manitoba with his parents to visit the rural home of his grandparents near Tuelon. The area around the home was very wet and swampy, with farmland surrounding the vicinity.

On July 2, 1940 Simon went berry picking with his grandpa and disappeared. Local law enforcement was immediately called, along with military personnel but heavy rains hit the area immediately after Simon disappeared and this greatly hindered the search.. Eighty soldiers from the Canadian Third Division Ammunition Company stayed on the scene for over thirty days.

During the search for Simon, Indian trackers found some very unusual facts. A July 29, 1940 article in the *Windsor Daily Star* had the following:

A few days ago, however, Indians of the district reported traces of someone living on berries and sleeping in the woods. They even reported someone who ran away at the sight of them. Nearby residents said they often found their cows milked almost dry in the morning.

The search for Simon lasted over one month. There was even some conjecture that Simon was the one running from the searchers and living off the land. Over two hundred searchers assisted in the effort to find Skogan, including eighty soldiers. Professional soldiers could not locate the boy or whoever was living in the forest off the berries.

Simon was never found.

Mrs. August Nelson
Missing 7/28/43, Drummond, Wisconsin
Age at Disappearance: 75 years

Mrs. Nelson lived in a remote section of Bayfield County. She was partially disabled and had difficulty walking and used a cane. She left her residence and walked into the woods to pick blueberries. She never came back.

Bayfield County Sheriff Andrew Gidlof was assisted by fifty men who searched the region for Mrs. Nelson. After failing to find the woman, Gidlof stated that she must have wandered off and gotten lost.

**This is another case that makes absolutely no sense. A woman needs a cane to walk, disappears, and fifty men can't find her. It would appear that she had been abducted or searchers and neighbors would eventually smell a decomposing body. There was never any indication that animals may have attacked Ms. Nelson. I want readers to keep a mental note of the number of disabled individuals that go missing—it's abnormally large.

C. H. Bordwell
Missing 8/1/44, Keewatin, Maine
Age at Disappearance: Unknown

At the time of his disappearance, Mr. Bordwell was the chairman of the instrumental music department for the Keewatin School district. He went with his wife and a group of friends eighteen miles east of their hometown to pick berries. The group agreed on a time to meet for their return trip home. C.H. never arrived.

A search was conducted of the area where Bordwell was last seen, and he was not located.

Again, a healthy person disappears, is never found, and the search is terminated. I want all readers to take a breath here and realize this is a human life that was completely lost. Bordwell wasn't lost in the middle of the Atlantic Ocean. He was eighteen miles from his house. How does this happen? Why can't bloodhounds find certain people who disappear?

David Feif
Missing 07/06/52, Rehoboth, Massachusetts
Age at Disappearance: 85 years

David left his residence and went to a known huckleberry area. He did not come home, and searchers were called.

Bloodhounds tracked David's scent to a swamp area. A search of the perimeter area failed to produce any evidence of David's location. The community sent firemen, Boy Scouts, and volunteers who all participated in the hunt for David. I found two articles on this incident and could not locate anything that indicated David was ever found. You will read many accounts of missing people where swamps play a predominant role in where people disappear and where others are eventually found.

Gary Bailey
Missing 7/17/54, Spears Mountain, Knox, Maine
Age at Disappearance: 3 years

Mr. and Mrs. Kenneth Bailey had traveled from their home in Thorndike with their three-year-old son Bailey to Spears Mountain in Knox, Maine. The family was spending the day with friends picking blueberries. Spears Mountain sits next to the Frye Mountain State Management Area, fifteen miles east of Belfast.

Sometime during the day while the mother was with friends, Gary was being tended to by his blind father Kenneth. Somehow Kenneth lost track of the boy, and a search was initiated.

Articles state that five hundred searchers assisted in looking for Gary. The searchers included game wardens, state police, Boy Scouts, firemen, and volunteers. There was initially no evidence found during the first nighttime and early daytime search for Gary.

Approximately twenty-four hours after Gary disappeared, two searchers who had asked to join the hunt thought they heard crying. The searchers found Gary with scratches over his face but in generally good condition. A July 19, 1954 article in the *Sarasota Herald* had the following: "Searchers said the youngster was found on the opposite side of Spears Mountain from where he vanished, and his trail indicated he had passed over the top of the 1400 foot hill in his wanderings."

Another article stated that Gary was found three and a half miles from where he wandered away from his dad.

It's very hard to believe that a three-year-old boy would climb over a 1400-foot mountain and not just walk downhill. It's equally hard to believe that Gary could have covered three and a half miles of mountain climbing in twenty-four hours—at 3 years old!

Rose Jewett
Missing 8/11/57, 4:15 p.m., 10 Miles north of Elk River, Idaho
Age at Disappearance: 95 years

Friends and relatives of Rose took the elderly woman on a trip into the wild ten miles north of Elk River, Idaho. This region is very desolate with very rough roads in 1957.

Relatives established their camp on Thursday and at 4:15 p.m. on Sunday decided to head into the wild and collect huckleberries. The children left Rose in camp since her mobility was inhibited because of a stroke she had months earlier. Forty-five minutes after they left, the children returned, and Rose was gone. A five-day search by over fifty people failed to find any evidence of Rose.

Bloodhounds joined the search, and for three days essentially walked in a circle around the camp and stopped back at the camp road. They were useless. There was a belief by some that Rose caught a ride out of the area, but the children did not believe it.

On October 19, 1957, Rose's daughter offered a $300 reward for any information about her mother whether she was found alive or dead. It appears that Rose was never found.

Case Summary:

There was no blood or signs of an attack at the campsite. There is only one possibility in this case, abduction, period. The woman was 95-years old, recently had a stroke, and was disabled; she could not have walked away. The real question is who would be on a lonely dirt road in the middle of the Idaho wilderness who would want to abduct a 95-year old stroke victim? It seems unlikely that the suspect would be driving a vehicle or the family would have probably heard it on the rough dirt road.

Richard "Rickie" Craig
Missing 8/15/57, 10:00 a.m., twenty-five miles south of Mt. Adams, Washington
Age at Disappearance: 5 years

Richard a.k.a. Rickie Craig was with his parents picking huckleberries twenty-five miles south of Mt. Adams, Washington, in an area near Trout Lake. This location is approximately thirty miles north of Hood River and the Columbia River. The location where the family was picking berries is near the 2500-foot elevation.

On August 15 at 10:00 a.m., the family started to look for Rickie and couldn't locate him. The Craigs initially started to look for the boy by themselves and then went to the local Forest Service Office and asked for assistance.

Elmer Craig was a school principle in Harrah, Washington, and was on summer break when the family lost Richard. He was one of the main participants in the search for his son.

There were two full days of lengthy searches that included bloodhounds, law enforcement officials, and volunteers. The total number of searchers rose to six hundred by the second day. There were so many people looking for Richard that the Forest Service closed the Trout Lake area to all huckleberry pickers because they were getting in the way of the search effort.

At 5:30 a.m. on the third day Rickie was missing, a logging crew came into the SAR on their day off. The crew was three-fourths of a mile off Trout Creek Road and over five miles from the point that Rickie was last seen when they found the young boy. I made a monumental archive search for specific details of Rickie's condition, but little could be found. It was learned that the boy was missing one shoe and, according to doctors that examined him later in the day, they were fascinated by the phenomenal condition he was in for being in the rugged wilderness for over two days. They couldn't believe it.

Rickie never could say what he did in the wild for the two days or how he got lost, a common condition of many of the people who are found and later questioned about their ordeal.

Mabel Moffitt
Missing 8/10/66, Gilmore Creek, Alaska
Age at Disappearance: 55 years

Mabel and her husband Earl invited friends from their hometown of Fairbanks to accompany them berry picking, but the friends couldn't attend. The Moffitts drove to Gilmore Creek and were last seen at the RCA Gilmore site adjacent to the state highway.

When the Moffitts failed to return home, their friends reported them as missing. The state police immediately organized a search and on the first day found Earl Moffitt lying dead on the trail of an apparent heart attack. Mabel was eventually found two air miles from Gilmore Dome. She was rushed to the hospital and later released. Newspaper articles stated that Mabel had not been questioned about the incident and the details were not known.

Case Summary:

This case is interesting because one person in the group is found dead of an apparent heart attack, and the other is found alive two days later. What caused Earl to have the heart attack? Why wouldn't Mabel have walked back to the car and summoned help if she was able to do so?

Marcelene Cummungs
Missing 7/14/69, Monument Mountain, Washington
Age at Disappearance: 54 years

County Sheriff Deputies were searching the area near the Washington-Idaho border southeast of Sullivan Lake and in an area that overlooks Priest Lake in far northern Idaho. The deputies were looking for missing berry picker Marcelene Cummungs from Spokane.

Pend Oreille Sheriff Norman Cox was personally leading the search and had asked for assistance from Whatcom County and other law enforcement jurisdictions.

I could not find an article indicating that Marcelene was found.

**It's an interesting coincidence that Marcelene disappeared in this area as there are a series of missing women on the Washington/Idaho border near Coeur D'Alene that are described in "Missing 411-Western U.S." All of the women are missing in a rural environment with very few clues as to their disappearance.

Yehudi Prior

For details on the Yehudi Prior case refer to chapter in Vancouver Island, British Columbia (*Missing 411–Western U.S.*).

Raymond Tunnicliffe
Missing 8/26/02, Tracy Lake, Saskatoon, Canada
Age at Disappearance: 79 years

Raymond was from Saskatoon and left his residence for Tracy Lake to go berry picking. One of the last stops he made was at the general store in Weyakwin and advised the owner he was hiking to Tracy Lake. Tunnicliffe told the storeowner if she didn't hear from him in three days to notify authorities—well, she did.

The owner reported Raymond missing, and this notification started a two-week search. The RCMP used planes, canines, ground teams, everything imaginable to find Raymond. This quote in the 8/26/02 *Lethbridge Herald* by a family member regarding RCMP search efforts follows and describes their feelings and frustration: "There's absolutely nothing. We've almost narrowed it down to alien abduction because it's so clean."

Case Summary:

The quote in the *Lethbridge Herald* perfectly summarizes the feelings of many SAR teams when their efforts produce no results. It's understandable that search teams may not always be able to bring back a live body, but when they don't find footprints, clothing, blood, campsites, etc., it is truly mind-boggling what might have happened. I think it's also notable that Raymond went to the extraordinary measure of telling the storeowner about his trip and advising her to call authorities if he doesn't return. This action makes me wonder if he was expecting trouble.

Frank Szpak
Missing 09/23/96,
Kirkland Lake, Ontario
Age at Disappearance: 69 years

Frank left his residence to go blueberry picking in a local wooded section. When Frank did not return, the local RCMP conducted a massive search and could not locate him.

Luciano Trinaistich
Missing 7/24/07, Timmins, Ontario, Canada
Age at Disappearance: 78 years

Luciano had left his Porcupine subdivision home to go blueberry picking along Murphy Road east off of Highway 655. It was early in the berry season but Luciano went to see how the crop was doing. Law enforcement officials stated that a seven-kilometer area was covered as a grid search, intensive and thorough. A much larger area was covered by air, all without any success of finding Luciano. The area where Luciano disappeared has a long history of mining. The Boulan Reef mine was in that area and operating at the time but has since closed. The specific area where he disappeared is a known hot spot for berry pickers.

The search teams found Luciano's blue jeep Grand Cherokee and centered the search directly in that area. The law enforcement officials who worked Luciano's case became frustrated as was expressed by Opp Detachment Constable Marc Depatie, who stated, "I can't explain why we haven't come across this gentleman himself or some sign of what led to his disappearance."

It may be wise for Timmins area law enforcement officers to also look at the case listed just above this incident—the case of Frank Szpak. Frank disappeared eleven years before Luciano, but they both disappeared berry picking in relatively close proximity to each other. Both men were senior citizens, and both have never been seen again.

Is there some danger in senior-aged men berry picking in this region of Ontario?

Missing Sheepherders

Sheepherding is one of the occupations in which workers spend almost all of their time in the wilds. Many times these people are alone without another person for miles in any direction. They see the environment in a natural state without noise, machines, or other men.

The sheepherders main job is to ensure the safety of the flock and to supply them access to food and water. Predators are a constant threat to the sheep and the sheepherder must be constantly on guard.

The life of a sheepherder can be very dangerous as is exemplified by the list below.

**All of the missing sheepherders were males.

Name	Date Missing•Age•Location
Jack Wells	11/05/1901•NA•Red Lodge, MT
J. Mitchell	01/11/1909•NA•Grangeville, ID
Dewey Cook	03/02/42•25•Bitter Creek, WY
Al Owens	11/07/45•71•Ruby Lake, MT
John Koza	04/26/50•50-60•Acton, MT
Jerry Garcia	08/12/56•NA•Coconino Co, AZ
John Davis	08/26/56•72•Burbank, WA
Albert Cucupa	02/16/60•32•Zuni, NM
Frank Mean	04/21/66•55•Thermopolis, WY
Louis Sandoval	09/06/69•66•Dubois, ID
Greg Lewellen	08/03/73•66•Heber City, UT

Jack Wells
Missing 11/5/1901, Red Lodge, MT
Age at Disappearance: Unknown

Sheepherder Jack Wells was working for John Aier on Red Lodge Creek. Workers found Wells's body that was partly eaten by coyotes and badly decayed.

There was no clue as to the cause of Wells's death but law enforcement sources felt foul play was involved. The body was delivered to the coroner, but all involved suspected that something bad had happened to Wells.

J. Mitchell
Missing 1/11/09, Salmon River Breaks, Grangeville, Idaho
Age at Disappearance: Unknown

Searchers had been looking for Mitchell for over a week. The sheepherder was missing from his flock, and a search was initiated.

He disappeared in a heavy snowstorm and has not been seen since. Mitchell had been working for Mr. George Poe since early in 1908.

On January 17, searchers found the body of Mitchell under suspicious circumstances. The body was found at the bottom of a very steep hill near the Salmon River breaks. The body had a broken leg, skull, and wrist fracture.

There were no absolute answers about what happened to Mr. Mitchell.

Dewey Cook
Missing 03/02/42, 31 miles south of Bitter Creek, WY
Age at Disappearance: 25

Prior to putting sheep into an area, scouts go onto the range and find an area that meets the needs of the flock. Dewey Cook was scouting an area thirty miles south of Bitter Creek and just ten miles north of the Colorado border. Cook disappeared, and a search was initiated.

The original search lasted a week and searchers failed to find the man. I looked at an aerial photo of the area, and it's hard to understand why a comprehensive search did not find Cook. For a vast majority of the area, there is no significant ground coverage.

Two years after Cook disappeared, friends initiated another search of the area where Cook was last seen. Elias Gonzales, another sheepherder, found the skeleton of a man in the exact area where Cook was believed to have disappeared. A Logan, Utah, dentist positively matched the skull as belonging to Dewey Cook. There is very little other information available on the recovery of Mr. Cook's body.

This case is another example of a missing person's body is eventually found in an area that was thoroughly searched in the past.

Al Owens
Missing 11/7/45, 6 miles south of Alder, MT
Age at Disappearance: 71 years

Al Owens became lost while tending his flock in November of 1945. There was a massive search for Owens, and he was not immediately found.

Approximately fifteen miles from where Owens went missing, hunters found a skeleton in a ravine west of Ruby Lake., it was Al Owens. The coroner stated that he did not believe there was foul play involved. Fellow sheepherders felt that while Owens was lost, he might have been walking toward the city of Dillon, many miles to the west.

It's doubtful that Owens was lost to the point that he didn't know the difference between east and west. Dillon was west from his location, and safety was to the north. Why or how Al got completely turned around on his coordinates will never be known.

John Koza
Missing 4/26/50, Acton, MT
Age at Disappearance: 50-60 years

John Koza was working for the Herman R. Schroeder Ranch tending sheep at the time of his disappearance. The company hired search dogs that found his scent and tracked it to a large pond near the property he was working. At the pond the scent was lost, and the dogs went home.

On February 26, 1951 workers at the Schroeder ranch found a body believed to be Koza. No information is available on the condition of the body or the cause of death or if the body was confirmed to be Mr. Koza.

Jerry Garcia
Missing 8/12/56, Coconino County, AZ
Age at Disappearance: Unknown

Dean Nelson was the manager of the Dye Ranch that employed Jerry Garcia. Dean advised local law enforcement officers that the sheepherder was missing and requested assistance for the search.

Law enforcement officers from surrounding counties, U.S. Forest Service personnel, and state fish and game wardens all assisted in the search for Mr. Garcia.

As of August 14, 1956 the search had focused on Long Valley, and searchers were unsuccessful in finding Jerry Garcia.

John Davis
Missing 8/26/56, Burbank, WA
Age at Disappearance: 72 years

Davis was first reported as missing on August 26, 1956. A search of Davis's employer's ranch was initiated at that time. The search of the Hooper Sheep Ranch took two weeks, and searchers were unable to find Davis.

A witness states that he saw a strange object in the field in January under a pile of snow. The witness felt that what they saw was another sheep and ignored the object. The witness went back to the object that they observed and found it was the body of John Davis.

When John Davis's body was located, witnesses found something very strange. An article in the *Walla Walla Union* for February 19, 1957 stated, "Officers said that Davis's clothes were in a pile near the body." Law enforcement officials stated at the time that there was no evidence of foul play. The body was found on February 18, 1957.

It would be very interesting to interview law enforcement officers who were at the scene of John Davis's body. I would like to understand how officials believed that Davis's clothes came off his body. If law enforcement didn't believe anything suspicious was associated with a naked body in the middle of a field, I'd like to understand their thinking. I could not find any reports or articles that clarify this finding.

It should be noted that John Davis disappeared just fourteen days after Jerry Garcia vanished in Arizona, is that a coincidence?

Frank Mean
Missing 4/21/66, Thermopolis, WY
Age at Disappearance: 55

Frank Mean went to check on his herd twenty-five miles west of Thermopolis and was scheduled to be back at a specific time, but he never arrived. Law enforcement officers checked the surrounding hills and were unable to find any indications of Frank Mean's location.

Albert Cucupa (AKA Charlie)
Missing 2/16/60, Zuni, NM
Age at Disappearance: 32 years
    Albert goes by two last names, Charlie and Cucupa. Albert was tending a flock of sheep in the Nutria area when the region was hit by a heavy snowstorm. Zuni Tribal Police and Bureau of Indian Affairs Officers searched for nine days and could not locate the herder. Searchers were able to find Charlie's sheep but were unable to locate him.

Louis Sandoval
Missing 9/6/69, Fremont County, Dubois, Idaho
Age at Disappearance: 66 years
    A herd of sheep was being tended in the Bear Creek Basin, fifteen miles northwest of Dubois. Sandoval's horse rode into camp without the man, thus alerting other herders that he was lost or injured. The foreman of the L.U. Sheep Company reported the missing person to Fremont County Sheriff C. A. McDougall. A search was initiated in the rugged region, but Sandoval was never found.

Greg Lewellen
Missing 8/3/73, Bench Creek, Heber City, Utah
Age at Disappearance: 66 years
    It's always good to end a chapter on a strong story; this is definitely a very strange story.
    In 2002, during the Olympic Games, I spent time in Heber City, located in a small valley just a short drive east from Salt Lake. It's a gorgeous spot surrounded by large mountains and many ranches and farms.
    In early August, 1973, Greg Lewellen was tending sheep in Wasatch County in an area twenty miles east of Heber in Bench Creek. Lewellen had just arrived back from a short vacation in Nevada and had reestablished his campsite.
    On August 4, 1973, friends went to speak with Greg and found very strange circumstances at the camp. Greg wasn't at the location, and shouts for him went unanswered. Friends searched the immediate area and found his flashlight 250 yards out from the camp in the middle of a field. The dishes were not clean and his bed appeared as

though he had been sleeping in it. Both of Greg's dogs were missing. The night they discovered Greg missing they found one of his horses hobbled and another tied to a nearby tree.

Three days after Greg disappeared, his two dogs returned to camp. Search parties had been scouring the area and had not found any evidence of where he might be. According to Wasatch County Sheriff Floyd Witt, "What happened to Mr. Lewellen is a complete mystery."

Case Summary:
Readers need to think about the scene that was left behind and analyze the clues. It would appear that it was dark, probably late, and Greg was in his sleeping bag. Something caused him to get out of his bag and walk with his flashlight 250 yards out toward the flock. At that 250-yard marker, something dark happened. Whatever caused Greg to get up was happening close to camp because he didn't take his horse—or maybe the horse was spooked. His firearm was found under his bedroll and was not disturbed. Greg was never found, and no blood or tissue was ever located around his campsite. Because law enforcement didn't find blood or tissue, it must be deduced that Greg left voluntarily, which is very doubtful, or he was abducted.

North American Missing Farmers

Missing farmers in North America represent a specific group of the missing person phenomenon that needed to be included in this book. The majority of the individuals listed in this chapter who went missing were working alone on a farm. The missing people knew their farms like we know our front and backyards, yet they simply vanished. They knew the landscape and topography well, as did their families. They knew the nooks and crevices like the back of their hand. Farmers and families know the land well because it is their work place and home. They knew the dangers associated with certain areas and certain work, but after all those years and all of that experience, these intelligent people inexplicably vanished.

It's difficult to imagine what could have gone so horribly wrong that families and neighbors couldn't find the vast majority of these hard-working people. I've included in this section of the book a spattering of farmers who went missing and were later found dead. I believe that the stories behind how they died may tell us valuable information about the ones that were never found.

Finding historical archived articles about missing farmers is a difficult task. The missing are usually listed in a small, regional newspaper and their stories are rarely reported in the national news. Without a national database of these regional papers, finding information about a small town farmer who goes missing isn't an easy task. I will make a prediction at this point. I predict that once this information is nationally released, once people know that there are many others who have lost loved ones under identical scenarios, hundreds of families will come forward describing similar incidents, losses of loved ones, and a perplexing scenario that defies conventional explanation.

Farmers are the backbone of North American labor. Without an all-out effort on the part of law enforcement to find these people, to explain what exactly happened, to actively keep their cases open and continue the investigation, I believe that this scenario will continue to replicate itself, and great people will continue to go missing.

These incidents did not occur in places the victim rarely went. They occurred in places where they went daily. The families knew their land in intimate detail because many of the farms were in the family for centuries. There was no place to hide, no place to escape—this was home. The evidence from these cases indicates one thing: the victims were coerced into leaving their farms or were abducted from their land. No other explanation fits.

Missing Farmers List by Date

Name	Date Missing•Age•Location
Riley Amsbaugh	07/25/1902•55•Campbell Mills, OH
E. C. Jones	11/12/1903•NA•Webster City, IA
Edward Gerke	06/11/18•NA•Tomah, WI
**Bernice Price	03/22/23•NA•Awhanee, CA
William Pitsenbarger	08/07/31•61•Hoaglin, OH
Clarence Clark	10/17/32•62•Palermo, NY
Mr. Bell	08/31/36•62•Winnepeg, Canada

Leroy Williams   03/16/51•64•Ackworth, IA
Ralph Stutzman   08/17/52•46•Lagrange, IN
John Sweet   10/26/53•NA•Galatia, IL
Louis Blair   08/05/56•26•Provost, AB
                        ••••30-Year Gap In Time
Clayton McFaul   08/15/86•50•Havelock, ONT
**Only female on list

Summary of List
Readers should note the number of farmers missing in the ages 55–64 because it's very odd to have that many missing in that age range. It's also highly strange that there is a thirty-year gap of missing farmers between 1956 and 1986.

Riley Amsbaugh
Missing, 7/25/1902, Campbell Mills, Ohio
Age at Disappearance: 55 years

Newspapers described Amsbaugh's disappearance as "mysterious." Riley had breakfast and then headed into the fields to work. He was a man of habit and was expected back at his house for lunch, but he never returned. Witnesses had seen him in his cornfield and at a berry patch eating berries at 10:00 a.m., but few other details were available. The local sheriff did join the search and stated that seventy-five people had scoured the woods looking for Riley. No clues have been found.

This case wasn't placed in the berry-picker section because he was primarily farming at the time. It is interesting, however, that articles specifically stated that witnesses had seen Riley in a berry patch.

E. C. Jones
Missing, 11/12/1903, Webster City, Iowa
Age at Disappearance: Unknown

The *Pocahontas County Sun* newspaper describes another "mysterious" disappearance of a farmer on November 12, 1903. E. C. Jones was a man married only a month when he kissed his new bride goodbye and headed into his cornfield to work. At three p.m., Jones had not returned from the field so his wife requested one of the assistants to search the farm for Jones. The assistant found Jones's team "wandering the field with one tug broken and one ear of corn in the wagon box." A search by the local community failed to find any sign of the young farmer.

Edward Gerke
Missing, 6/11/1918, Tomah, Wisconsin
Age at Disappearance: Unknown

Gerke got a 6:00 a.m. start to his chores and went into the field Sunday morning to work his newly purchased land on Bear Creek. He didn't return for lunch, and the family became concerned. Midday Sunday the family went into the field and found Edward lying in a ditch in his pasture with a broken neck and sand in his mouth. They also thought that some of his clothes had been partially burned. Tomah Police were called and investigated the case; they were completely baffled about how Edward's neck was broken or how he got sand in his mouth. The case was turned over to Monroe County officials in Sparta who were to conduct an autopsy and further follow-up.

The coroner reported that lightning possibly caused Edward's death but there was never conclusive proof as to how his neck was broken.

Bernice Price
Missing, 03/22/1923, Awhanee, California
Age at Disappearance: Unknown

Ms. Price was a new wife living at the J. J. McGurk ranch near Awhanee. She was staying with her husband at the ranch when she mysteriously disappeared Monday night. The ranch sits at the foothills (2400-foot elevation) of the Sierra Nevada Mountains. Searchers believe she may have walked into the woods and become lost. Price was never found.

William Pitsenbarger
Missing, 8/7/1931, Hoaglin Township, Ohio
Age at Disappearance: 61 years

On August 7, William walked across his cornfield wearing his overalls and a straw hat enroute to do chores. When William didn't return to his residence at the end of the day, a search ensued. The SAR continued to intensify as the days and weeks went on. On August 31, a searcher pulled the cover off a well near an abandoned cabin on the Fronefield Farm approximately one-half mile from the Pitsenbarger residence. Inside the well searchers saw something odd twenty-five feet down. A recovery party pulled the deceased and decomposing body of William from the well.

The body was intact, but there was a slight discoloration on the right eye. He was wearing the same clothing as when he disappeared, except his straw hat was never located. Witnesses stated he was a very reliable man who had a successful farm. The coroner decided not to conduct an autopsy and ruled his death as a drowning. The coroner felt that William looked into the well, hitting his head. The well cover miraculously fell back into place.

Clarence Clark
Missing, 10/17/1932, Palermo, New York
Age at Disappearance: 62 years

The headlines of the *Syracuse NewYork Times* read, "5-Day Search in Woods For Strangely Missing Farmer Yields No Clues."

Clarence Clark lived on a Palermo Farm with his wife and eighty-three-year-old father, Gould. Clarence and Gould worked the livestock daily and were a very close father and son. After Wednesday's dinner, Clarence went into the livestock yard to check on the herd and then went to take a walk around the swamps that surround his property. This was the last time anyone saw him.

Sergeant Lawrence Fox of the New York State Police led a five-day search with over one hundred volunteers. The searchers covered the farm, dense woods, and adjacent swamps without finding one clue where Clarence might be. Searchers were mystified at the lack of tracks in the area and the complete lack of any evidence.

Mr. Bell
Missing, 8/31/1936, Winnipeg, Canada
Age at Disappearance: 62 years

Mr. Bell went missing from his remote farm outside of Winnipeg. He was 5'5" tall, weighed 125 pounds. His house and barn were searched, and everything appeared normal at each location. Nothing seemed to be removed from Mr. Bell's property. Mr. Bell was wearing overalls when he disappeared. A massive search of the adjacent area by RCMP failed to find any evidence of his whereabouts.

Leroy Williams
Missing, 03/16/1951, Ackworth, Iowa
Age at Disappearance: 64 years
 Williams was living on a farm three and one-half miles outside of Ackworth. Leroy was feeding stock and doing chores when he disappeared after he went outside in a heavy snowstorm. When Williams failed to return to the residence, authorities were called.
 Police brought bloodhounds that searched for hours and found no trace of the farmer. Sheriff Jack Taylor asked for volunteers to arrive at the farm and assist in the search. Searches did continue, and no clue as to Leroy's whereabouts could ever be found.

Ralph Stutzman
Missing, 8/17/1952, Lagrange, IN
Age at Disappearance: 46 years
 Stutzman was a hard-working father and farmer. He lived on his ranch with his wife and thirteen children. The day Ralph disappeared he was working the ranch. The children did their chores, and he told them that he'd play with them after he chased down a group of cows that had somehow gotten loose. That was the last time the family saw Ralph.
 A massive search of the farm and surrounding region failed to find any clue as to where he went. All of Ralph's clothes and property were accounted for in the house. Law enforcement officials were baffled as to where he might be. There was never any explanation about how his cows got out.
 **There are a few examples in this chapter in which farmers and ranchers respond when livestock gets loose. It is while the men are looking for the stock that something happens and they don't return. Is there a pattern to this?

John Sweet
Missing, 10/26/1953, Galatia Township, Illinois
Age at Disappearance: Unknown

John Sweet had a busy day when he disappeared. He went into town and sold a load of corn, bought groceries in Harrisburg, and returned to his home. He came into the house, left the groceries and his billfold of cash, changed clothes, and went to the back of his barn to work on a tractor. He also told his wife that he was going to repair a pigpen that had been damaged (somehow) and retrieve several of his pigs that had wandered away. This was the last time anyone saw John.

Relatives notified authorities, and seventy-five different local farmers arrived on their tractors to search the area. Nothing was found. Oil marks were found on a barbed wire fence leading away from the property, indicating that John may have worked on the tractor and then gone over the fence for some reason. John was not a small man. At 240 lbs he would not have wandered far without the tractor.

An intensive search failed to find any evidence as to what happened to John Sweet.

Louis Blair
Missing 8/5/56, Provost, Alberta
Age at Disappearance: 26 years

Blair was a bachelor who maintained a large wheat field on his farm just ten miles west of the Saskatoon border and twelve miles north of Provost. The area is dotted with hundreds of small lakes and rivers.

On Sunday, August 5, Blair left his house early in the morning and headed into his field. He was never seen again. Regional RCMP completed a three-day search by 150 men and canines without finding a trace of the man.

Clayton McFaul
Missing 8/15/86, Havelock, Ontario
Age at Disappearance: 59 years

Clayton got an early start the day of his disappearance. He told family that he was going onto the family farm to do his chores, but he never returned for lunch. The family called local law enforcement.

Law enforcement determined that Clayton was extremely punctual about his mealtimes, and he was not the type to be late. He was a small man in stature, 5'3", 141 lbs, and balding.

Several searches of the surrounding countryside failed to find any evidence of Clayton.

Anthony Holland
Missing 6/21/2009, Cordell, Oklahoma
Age at Disappearance: 51 years

Holland owned an eighty-acre ranch southeast of Cordell. He returned home after attending a gun show and then left again to check on his ranch. He never returned. His truck was found one mile from Vanderwork Lake near a remote section of his ranch. His keys and wallet were inside the truck, and his cell phone was found on the ground a short distance from the truck. Tracker dogs were brought to the truck but were unable to locate any scent and could not track.

The area of Cordell Oklahoma has a very interesting landscape. There are no fewer then 35 bodies of water within five miles of downtown Cordell. The most notable lakes and dams are the Boggy Creek and Calvary Creek Watershed and Oknoname Reservoir. The area to the west of Cordell is quite swampy while to the east is mostly farm fields. The area where Anthony disappeared has many farms and several scatterings of large bodies of water. There are no cities of similar size as Cordell for fifteen miles in any direction.

I know that you can exclude robbery as a motive in the disappearance of Holland as his keys and wallet were clearly visible inside his truck.

Extensive searches were made of the area without developing any evidence of where Anthony may have gone.

MIDWEST UNITED STATES

Minnesota

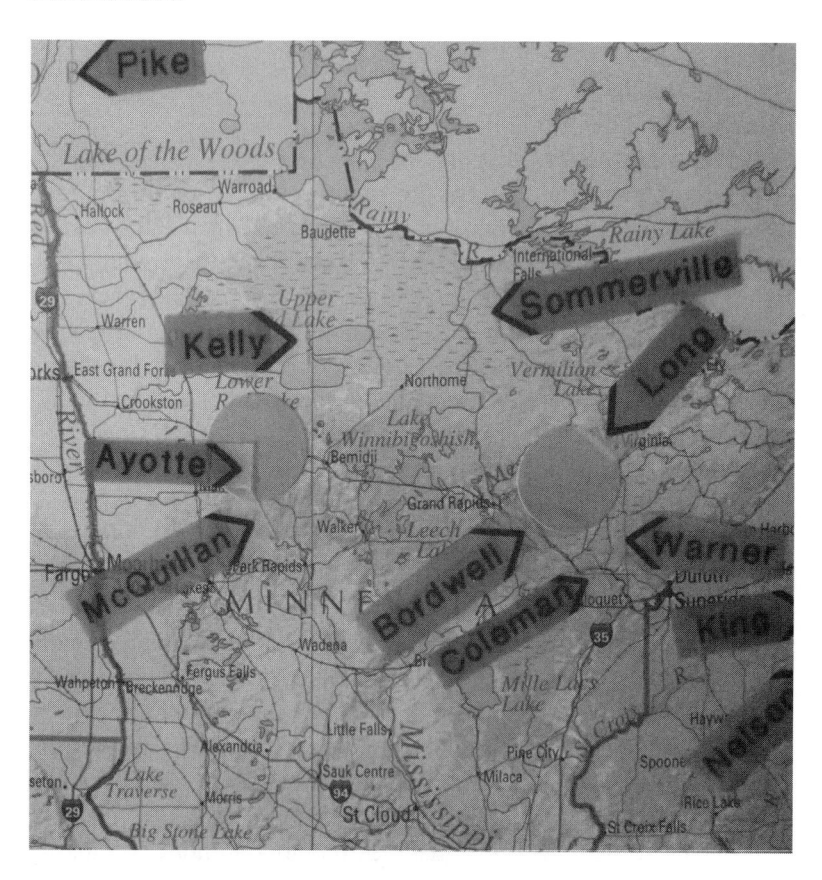

Missing People in Minnesota by Date
Name	Date Missing•Age•Sex
Jack Pike	09/05/35•5•M
••C. H. Bordwell	08/01/44•NA•M
Larry Coleman	08/20/49•3•M
Earl Somerville	11/03/57•48•M
John Long	04/10/63•58•M
Milda D. McQuillan	06/17/75•71•F

Kevin Jay Ayotte 09/30/82•3•M
Leeanna Warner 06/14/03•5•F
Kory Kelly 10/16/06•38•M
••Details on the disappearance of C. H. Bordwell can be found in the chapter "Berry Pickers."

Jack Pike
Missing 09/05/35, St. Norbert, Manitoba
Age at Disappearance: 5 years
**This case is included in this section because of its proximity to the Minnesota border.

The Pike family took a trip from their residence in St. Vital Manitoba to the area near St. Norbert to pick blueberries. The family exited the car and started toward the patch. Jack Pike ran through the bush and was out of sight only a few minutes when his mother heard something very unsettling. Mrs. Charles Pike gave an interview on September 7, 1935 to the *Leader Post* and she stated: "He screamed as if he were terrified, the scream seemed to be choked off in the middle." The mother ran the one hundred yards toward the scream and found nothing. The husband arrived, and they both scoured the area and didn't find the young boy.

The family was on the grounds of the Trappist Monks Monastery and somewhat near the Red River. The family called the police, and a search was initiated.

The search for Jack Pike lasted four days and was called the largest search in the history of Manitoba at the time. Over two thousand searchers went through the river, riverbanks, bush, trees, and the grounds, and they found nothing.

On the fourth day, a man was searching on the opposite riverbank and found Jack Pike under a bush, unconscious but still alive. The boy was rushed to the hospital where the doctors gave him stimulants, and his father gave him blood. At one point the boy awoke and stated, "Hi daddy." It was felt that Jack was going to survive, but in an unfortunate turn of events, Jack died hours later.

Searchers were confused how Jack could have made his way across the river to hide under a bush, a bush they felt was way too far from where he disappeared. Many were amazed that the boy had made it that far and survived that long. It had appeared that after four days without water or food Jack had died of either exposure or dehydration.

Authorities were concerned about the fact that it sounded as though Jack had been abducted, but they could not find any additional evidence or suspects.

Larry Coleman
Missing 8/20/49, McGregor, Minnesota
Age at Disappearance: 3 years

Mr. and Mrs. Kenneth Coleman from New Brighton Minnesota took their three children and headed for their parents' farm in a rural location in McGregor, Minnesota. The farm sat to the southeast of Duluth in one of the most rugged areas of the state.

After the family settled into the rural environment, the grandparents asked the children to go with them into the back of the farm and help collect pine cones. All agreed that would be fun. As the group of five was searching the back of the farm, somehow little Larry (three years old) disappeared from view. The grandparents couldn't believe he got away from them that quickly. The grandparents called Kenneth and his wife, and the entire group searched for the young boy. The group was screaming Kenneth's name, but there was no answer. The family decided they needed additional assistance and called the sheriff.

Aitkin County Sheriff Hjalmar Hulin responded to the call and immediately started to enlist the assistance of locals and also requested the National Guard. The first night there were hundreds of volunteers scouring the farm and surrounding forests for the small boy. Within days over one thousand people were at the farm searching and 260 National Guard Troops were marching through the woods. Helicopters, ground troops, canines, all were searching for little Larry.

The search continued to expand into the swampy exterior portions of the farm. This area was thick with underbrush and swampy ground. Much of the area was deep with water and thick with mosquitoes. One of the searchers brought his Labrador into this area and to the edge of a large swamp and the dog started to whine. It was an odd behavior, and searchers thought it might be a clue. The sheriff stated that everyone would focus their efforts in this area. After two weeks of exhaustive and nonstop searching, Larry Coleman was not found.

Larry's case was stagnant until Sunday, November 13, 1949 when a hunter found a piece of strange clothing in the bushy swamp area two miles from the Coleman's grandparents' farm. Game Warden Ray Wilkes ordered a complete search of the area, and two days later Larry Coleman's body was found in the middle of a swamp not far from where his clothing was found.

No newspaper articles were found on Coleman's cause of death.

Case Summary:

This story is another of the long series of cases in which a very young child disappears from a rural setting. In each scenario, the child is able to make a long journey to a dangerous place and then dies without his clothing on his body. The child is found in an area already covered during a prior search.

Many factors contribute to this being a very unusual case. First, Larry disappeared almost in the presence of his grandparents and brother and sister. Nobody heard or observed him leave the area. Larry did not respond to frantic calls. A search was conducted without finding evidence of the boy's location. The boy was later found in a swamp, a consistent theme in children that go missing in the wild.

Factors:
- Rural setting.
- Loss of clothing.
- Found in swampy environment.
- Disappears almost in the presence of relatives.
- Walks long distance.
- Dogs don't track scent or refuse to track.
- Victim doesn't respond to his name being called.
- Found in area already searched.
- Victim did not drown.

Keep track of the above elements in future cases you read to understand how many cases are very similar.

Earl Somerville

Missing 11/5/57, Loman, Minnesota
Age at Disappearance: 48 years

Earl Somerville was a logger employed by the Clayton Peterson Logging Camp eighteen miles southwest of Loman, Minnesota. On November 5, 1957, Somerville left the camp and headed into a swampy area to hunt grouse. He was never found. Authorities from the United States and Canada searched the border area, and they had assistance from employees of the Minnesota and Ontario paper companies.

Temperatures in the area of the search at night got down into the twenties. Searchers felt that Somerville could survive a few days because of his experience in the woods.

Weeks after Earl disappeared, some searchers continued to look for the man. It appears that he or his remains were never recovered.

John Long
Missing 4/10/63, Ely, Minnesota
Age at Disappearance: 58 years

John Long was a logger working at the Tomaro Timber Company near Echo Trail. On April 10, 1963, John was going to take a hike along the Moose River to watch spawning fish. He took his .22-caliber rifle with him for protection. When John failed to return by the following day, fellow workers went to the river and searched, but they couldn't find him. The workers returned to their camp and notified law enforcement.

The local sheriff organized a four-day ground search of the river area and also had planes fly the Moose River. Searchers couldn't locate John.

Milda Dahl McQuillan
Missing 6/17/75, Ponsford, Minnesota
Age at Disappearance: 71 years

Milda was driving her 1968 two-door, pea-green Dodge on East Bad Medicine Lake Road on the outskirts of Ponsford when she was last seen. Milda was reported as missing two days after she was last seen. Friends called law enforcement, and the sheriff started a search.

Milda's vehicle was found abandoned approximately one hundred feet off East Bad Medicine Lake Road in a heavily wooded setting. Deputies searched the area around the car and found nothing suspicious.

The area where Milda disappeared is very rural with hundreds of lakes in the surrounding area. There is a special historical marker on the road where she was last seen driving.

I could never find any articles indicating that Milda was ever found or why the road where her car was found had such an unusual name.

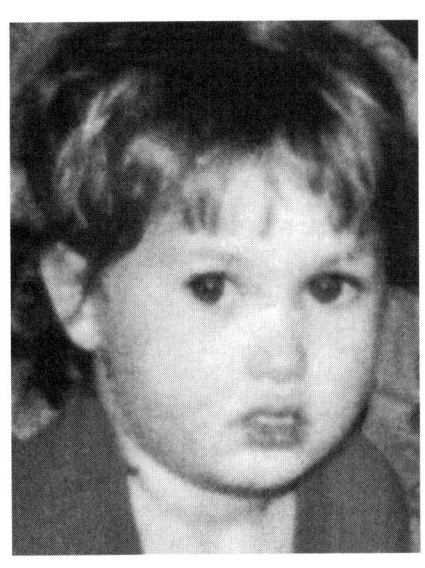

Kevin Jay Ayotte
Missing 9/30/82, Sugar Bush, Minnesota
Age at Disappearance: 3 years
4', 50 lbs, blue eyes, blonde hair
**Hearing Impaired

On the afternoon of September 30, 1982, Kevin Ayotte was inside his family's summer log home. The residence was in a very rural area near Sugar Bush, Minnesota. Kevin was in an upstairs bedroom the last time his mother saw him. She stepped outside the cabin to do some chores and left Kevin with his older brother. When she returned to the upstairs room, Kevin was gone.

The cabin is approximately forty miles east of Fargo, North Dakota, in a region with hundreds of lakes and creeks. The area of the cabin is only forty miles south of the Red Lakes Recreation Area and twenty miles west of the Paul Bunyan State Forest. The area has Little Sugar Bush Lake and the Callaway State Wildlife Management Area.

The cabin owned by the Ayottes is in Beltrami County, and their sheriff's department responded and orchestrated a nine-day search for Kevin. Hundreds of searchers participated in checking the bogs, swamps, creeks, and rivers of the area, all without finding any trace of the boy. Sheriff Dwight Stewart stated at the end of the search that they feel Kevin wandered outside and was playing with his dog when he disappeared. The sheriff did not cite any evidence about why he felt that Kevin wandered away.

Case Summary:
This case is a very strange case in an area where multiple strange disappearances have occurred.

Leeanna Susan Marie Warner
Missing 6/14/03, Chisholm, Minnesota
Age at Disappearance: 5 years
3', 30 lbs, brown hair, brown eyes

Leeanna Warner lived on the outskirts of Chisholm, Minnesota. She lived in an area called the "Iron Range," where it is a rural existence. On June 14, 2003, Leeanna walked down her road to visit a neighbor, but nobody was home. People had seen the girl going to the house and did not see anyone around the girl. Witnesses stated there were no vehicles in the area. After she went to the house, Leeanna disappeared.

Chisholm is 215 miles north of Minneapolis and has many lakes and creeks around the city. Five thousand people live in the city of Chisholm, and many more live on its rural roads surrounding the town.

Kaelin Whitaker, Leeanna's mother, was extensively interviewed by authorities. She stated that she and her daughter returned from a trip to a local lake, and she wanted Leeanna to take a nap. Leeanna didn't want to—she wanted to visit her friends. When Leeanna didn't return in the required thirty-minute time window, which was given to her to get to and from the neighbor's house, Kaelin went looking for her daughter. When she couldn't find Leeanna, she called the police.

The police responded in force for several days, using helicopters, bloodhounds, and ground teams, but they found no trace of the girl. Dogs did track the scent to the area of the roadway, the area that she would have walked when going to the neighbor's home. Authorities initially felt that Leeanna disappeared and died in the environment by getting lost. Police now believe that Leeanna may have been abducted somewhere in her journey to or from her neighbor's home.

Investigations continue, but there are still no concrete leads concerning what happened to Leeanna.

Kory Kelly
Missing 10/16/06, Red Lake Wilderness, Four Town, Minnesota
Age at Disappearance: 38 years

Jim Neprud and Kory Kelly were good friends. The buddies decided to go grouse hunting in northern Minnesota. Kelly made the trip from his home in Crookstown Minnesota to the Red Lake State Wildlife Management Area. Neprud joined him at the campsite mid-afternoon on October 16. The men started to set up their camp when Neprud realized they needed gas, which they had forgotten to get. Neprud stated that he would go into Four Town and make the purchase while Kory stayed behind with Neprud's dog. Neprud stated that he last saw Kory two hundred yards south of the camp with his shotgun, and he was headed out to shoot a grouse. Neprud left the campsite at 5:30 p.m. and returned at 7:00 p.m.

Neprud arrived back at the campsite to find evidence that Kory had been collecting firewood, but he couldn't find Kelly. It was getting late in the afternoon and close to dark, so he was starting to get nervous. He also realized that his own golden Labrador, "Sammy," was missing. He could see that Kory had taken his shotgun, so he felt he had probably left to kill a grouse. Late in the night it started to rain.

As darkness engulfed the campsite, Neprud honked his horn and flashed the truck lights in an effort to alert Kory of the location. It became late, and Neprud went to sleep hoping that Kory would return later, but he didn't. The next morning Neprud awoke at four o'clock and searched for his friend, but he could not locate him. He walked almost two miles from the campsite in an effort to find Kory and still could not locate any evidence of him. Neprud eventually flagged down two people passing by the campsite, explained that a camper was missing, and asked them to notify law enforcement.

Kory Kelly had been visiting this exact area of the Red Lakes Wilderness since he was a child; this was the first visit for Jim Neprud. They were a half-mile inside of Beltrami County, and the Beltrami sheriff, Keith Winger, took the lead on the organization of the search.

Searchers combed the area of the campsite and then with the use of ATVs started to expand their search into the wilderness. The terrain was difficult, with tall grasses, lots of water, swamps, and many bogs. For almost two weeks searchers found nothing. On Wednesday, October 25, two hunters nine miles from the Neprud and Kelly campsite found Neprud's Labrador, Sammy, wandering the woods. The dog was dehydrated and hungry but in generally good condition.

On Saturday, October 28, searchers found Kory Kelly's cigarette lighter and cigarettes. On October 29, trackers from the Minnesota Bureau of Criminal Apprehension found Kory's overalls, socks, and hooded sweatshirt fourteen miles from the original campsite.

On October 30, Beltrami County Emergency Management Coordinator Beryl Wernberg stated that weather had hindered the search and that they were terminating their efforts at this point. They stated that snow had started to fall, and there were two inches on the ground.

In mid-November, the search for Kory Kelly started again. The best search dogs in Minnesota were brought to the scene, and after thirteen more days were unable to locate Kory. On November 23, the search for Kory Kelly was terminated for the winter. Searchers had now conducted two different searches each lasting approximately two weeks. They had found clothing fourteen miles from the campsite and scoured that location for Kory. He was not found.

On April 28, the search for Kory Kelly resumed with the sheriff's department flying over the area where Kory's clothes and other personal belongings were found. North of the Rapid River walking bridge off of Rapid River Road near the Moose River Road and north of Four Town, the air team spotted a body among eight-foot tall reeds, fifteen feet off the trail. The body the air team spotted was Kory Kelly.

Jan Kelly, Kory Kelly's mother, was interviewed after the body was recovered and after the search team and the sheriff's department debriefed her. On October 31, 2006, Jan Kelly stated, "They [Sheriff's Department] can't believe he got fourteen miles from the campsite. He probably got there the first night. He must have been flying through the trees, the bushes. I can't believe he could have gotten that far."

I ordered the report on the incident from the Beltrami County Sheriff and a copy of the cause of death from the coroner's office. The death certificate stated that Kory died from hypothermia.

I am in total agreement with Jan Kelly. I can't believe that Kory Kelly could leave late in the afternoon and travel fourteen-plus miles through the swampy terrain to his final destination. It's seemingly impossible.

In the reports I did receive from the sheriff's department, there is one form that states that Neprud's dog was located. It was found in the general area that Kory went missing. Biological samples were taken from the dog and forwarded to a lab. The report states that the remains and samples were going to be checked for human remains or clothing. The samples were taken to the lab on October 26, 2006.

Case Summary:

I have personally studied the Kory Kelly case for two years; it has been a SAR incident that has disturbed me. Kory was not new to the area; he had been visiting this area of the Red Lake Management Area for over twenty-five years. He was an experienced hunter and camper and knew the dangers associated with hunting in November in Minnesota. Kory also knew not to hunt at night and that this specific area posed extreme dangers after dark because of the bogs and swamps.

Please refer to the statement that Kory's mother, Jan, made to the media regarding the location of Kory's body. The sheriff's department said that they could not believe that Kory got to a location fourteen miles away from the campsite in only one night. The sheriffs did not explain why they felt Kory died the first night but it is obvious to everyone that traveling that distance through that type of terrain does not make any sense. A person would have to be a super human to travel that distance in that time frame. Another part of this equation does not make sense—why were Kory's clothes off?

Many of the articles written about the Kory Kelly incident stated the possibility that Kory suffered from hypothermia and took his clothes off, as this is sometimes claimed to be a condition of hypothermia. If the sheriff's theory is correct, that Kory did die the first night, then no, hypothermia could not be the reason for taking off his clothes. Kory had a lighter and the ability to make fire. Why would he throw his lighter on the trail? He had his friend's dog with him. All hikers and campers know that if you snuggle with a dog, the dog will keep you warm through the night. Kory also knew that it takes many hours for hypothermia to set in when you are properly equipped, as Kory was. Kory also knew that his firearm was one of the main methods to attract attention or assistance. Why didn't SAR teams locate his firearm?

Kory Kelly was located in the middle of a very high patch of grass just fifteen feet from a main walking path. Think this through very clearly, why would anyone choose to stay in high grass versus a clear and defined walking path—no one would. If a person wanted to be found, he would stay in one place, not walk or run fourteen miles in one night.

There is no way in this world I believe Kory Kelly walked fourteen miles the first night he disappeared. If he was lost, I believe he would have found a cozy location among the trees, made a small shelter with branches, and started a fire to last the night with the cigarettes and lighter he possessed. Once the light of day came, Kory would have had better bearings and a much better chance to understand his location to walk out of the swamps and bogs. If the worst-case scenario had occurred, if he was injured, he could have used his firearm to alert others of his location.

Another oddity to this story is the condition of Sammy (Neprud's Labrador dog) that was found several days after Kory disappeared. Searchers stated that the dog had eaten deer meat to stay alive. How did the searchers know that the dog ate deer meat, through biological samples taken from his stomach? Where did the deer meat come from? Searchers also stated that Sammy was dehydrated. There is more fresh water in the Red Lakes area than most people could possibly imagine. How could Sammy be dehydrated unless the dog was somehow confined and restricted in its movements?

The last and most obvious indicator that something very, very odd happened to Kory is that his cell phone was never used. Yes, there was only intermittent cell reception in the Red Lakes area, but if a person were traveling fourteen to fifteen miles across a wide-open region, he or she would have had reception or the phone would have pinged a transponder/repeater of the phone's location. This did not happen.

The area that Kory disappeared is some of the most desolate, rural, and hard-to-walk locations in North America. I have no doubt there are thousands of acres in this area that have never been walked by a human, really. The water of the bogs and swamps offers complete isolation to the mammals and other animals that inhabit the wilderness area. It's a bit of a frightening scenario how many people have disappeared from Northern Minnesota, especially when most were alone and in that same rural environment.

I want everyone to understand that Kory left the campsite well prepared. He had the following items with him:

- Cell Phone
- Lighter
- Cigarettes
- Dog
- Coat
- Firearm
- Ammunition
- Warm winter clothing.

All of the above items were recovered except the firearm. One shell was recovered, but others were not. The dog was found several days after Kory disappeared. Kory's socks were found near other clothes, again, presumably discarded the first night. There is something very, very wrong with the scenario presented by the sheriff of Kory Kelly disappearing and eventually finding his body.

Counties and cities do not fall under the federal FOIA requirement. State, city, and county agencies do not have to supply the public with reports they have written. I did request reports from the Beltrami County Sheriff and did receive partial reports. It would be very revealing if the coroners report on the Kory Kelly's death were made public and we could understand the extent of his injuries and how much wear was apparent on the soles of his feet.

Wisconsin

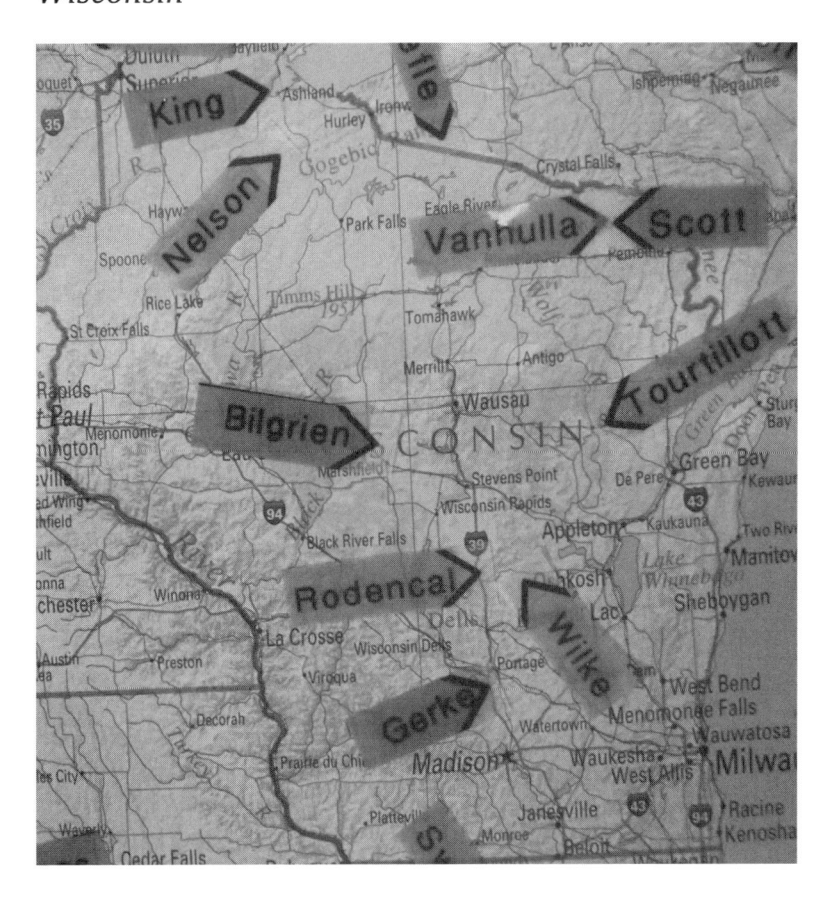

List of Missing by Date

Name	Date Missing•Age•Sex
Roy Bilgrien	10/21/1910•2•M
**Edward Gerke	06/11/18•NA•M
Thelma Ann Wilke	05/03/35•21MOS•F
Harold King	09/07/36•3•M
••Mrs. August Nelson	07/28/43•75•F
Judy Rodencal	10/30/56•15•F
Colleen Tourtillott	07/03/88•18MOS•F

**Details on the disappearance of Edward Gerke can be found in the chapter "Farmers."
••Details on the disappearance of Mrs. August Nelson can be found in the chapter "Berry Pickers."

Roy Bilgrien
Missing 10/21/1910, McMillan, Wisconsin
Age at Disappearance: 2 years

The Bilgriens lived in a rural area outside of McMillan, Wisconsin. On October 21, 1910, Mrs. Bilgrien placed little Roy in the front yard of their residence while she did household work. Several minutes after placing Roy in the yard, Mrs. Bilgrien returned to see a horrifying event unfold in front of her. An October 17 article in the *Daily News* describes what happened in the Bilgrien yard:

> Mrs. Herman Bilgrien was horrified on emerging from her home to see a huge black bear making for the woods with her child. Helpless from fright her hysterical cries attracted attention of a neighbor's daughter who was passing the Bilgrien residence and she immediately gave chase to the bear. Following the bear for about three blocks, on encountering a wire fence the bruin dropped his burden and disappeared in the forest.

The boy was found to be fine without injury. When I read this case, it struck me as a highly unusual event. Bears usually attack their prey on scene and do not run away with something alive in their mouths. It also seems quite late in the year for a bear to be out running in the snow. One would think it would be hibernating.

On October 26, 1910, the *Marshfield Times* had a different account of the Bilgrien event: "Mrs. Bilgrien coming out of the house suddenly to look after her child was horrified to see a large dark animal, which she thinks was a wolf, carrying her baby off to the woods."

I think it's fascinating that five days after the incident the Bilgrien story changed drastically from a bear to a large wolf—that is a significant change. If you read the woman's statement carefully, "see a large dark animal, which she thinks was a wolf." The woman sounds like she's is not sure what she observed but is trying to rationalize it away. I believe most of us know the difference between a wolf and a bear, especially if we followed it for over three blocks.

We will never know what attempted to kidnap Roy Bilgrien, but it is an aspect to the missing person scenario that we all need to understand if we are to fully comprehend the missing person phenomenon.

Thelma Ann Wilke
Missing 5/3/35, PM, Mauston, Wisconsin
Age at Disappearance: 21 months
**Blonde Hair

Mauston is thirty miles due west of Auroraville, which was the location where Judy Rodencal disappeared in 1956. Mauston sits just southwest of Castle Rock Lake and a number of reservoirs and streams.

Thelma wandered away from her rural residence when in the company of her invalid father. Thelma's mother was running an errand. Thelma's young brother followed the mother to the street, and when he returned to the residence, Thelma was gone.

There was a formal search started almost immediately after Thelma disappeared. The search lasted almost two full days. The search included the normal contingent of law enforcement personnel and volunteers. The search site was also hit by a severe snowstorm the day after Thelma went missing.

Almost two days exactly from the time Thelma disappeared, Albert McClellan a local farmer was walking in an extremely remote and rugged area not normally visited on his farm when he was under a large oak tree. As he walked around the tree he saw a small body on the ground. It looked like a dead body. He rolled the small bundle over and found it was Thelma Wilke, sleeping. The girl was missing one shoe, was groggy, but appeared to be healthy. Thelma's clothes were torn into shreds, but she was nicely sheltered from the snow by the tree. McClellan had found Thelma three and a half miles from her residence.

Thelma was transported to the hospital and found to have a temperature of 101 degrees, even though she had no chest congestion or pneumonia, per the articles reviewed. The doctors stated that they believed that the cause of the temperature might have been the slight case of exposure that she suffered. I find that exposure causing a temperature is a questionable diagnosis. From what I've read, exposure to the cold causes a drop in the body temperature.

Harold King
Missing 9/7/36, Washburn, Wisconsin
Age at Disappearance: 3 years

Washburn sits on Chequamegon Bay in Lake Superior in far northern Wisconsin. The town is just ten miles east of major forest land and is generally considered a farming region surrounded by many swamps.

His parents, who live at a nearby reservation, brought Harold to his grandparent's residence. While Harold was at the home, the boy somehow disappeared. The grandparents called law enforcement, and a search was initiated.

Searchers were restricted in their search by heavy rains that hit the area the day after Harold went missing. The local sheriff did bring in bloodhounds to search, but they could not pick up a scent, or they refused to search.

Late in the night on September 10, neighbors heard "wailing" coming from a swampy area three miles from where the boy disappeared. Neighbors worked their way into the swamp and found Harold.

A September 10, 1936 article in the *La Crosse Tribune* summarizes the incident: "Clad only in a pair of underpants, the rest of his clothing torn off by brush, the boy (Harold King) was suffering from exposure. At the hospital he was reported slightly delirious and doctors feared pneumonia might develop. The searchers found the child in a swamp three miles from the home of his grandparents, Mr. and Mrs. Alex King, from which he wandered Monday."

It's interesting how neighbors described the sounds coming from the swamp as "wailing," not crying, not screaming, "wailing." As we all know a three year old cannot yell or scream very loud. It's also interesting that every stitch of clothing had been removed from Harold, except his diaper. The clothing was never found. My question to the reporter who wrote that the "rest of the clothing [was] torn off by the brush," is how did he or she know that? The details of this story seem to mimic the facts of many stories in this book. I did not purposely look for stories that were similar; this is exactly what I found through a comprehensive search.

Judy Rodencal
Missing 10/30/56, Auroraville, Wisconsin
Age at Disappearance: 16 years

Auroraville sits ten miles west of Oshkosh and is considered a rural community with a large pond or lake (Mill Pond) and a river. Much of the area is swampy and flat.

On October 30, 1956, Judy Rodencal was walking to the bus stop for her ride to school. She never arrived at her high school and never returned home that afternoon. Her parents realized that something bad had happened when Judy's boyfriend arrived at the home that night for a date and Judy wasn't there.

This search was difficult because teams didn't understand where the girl might possibly be located. There were no leads until the following day when searchers were in a creek one mile north of Judy's residence. The creek is adjacent to a large swamp, and this is when they found a handkerchief and Judy's socks; her parents confirmed they were hers.

Bloodhounds were brought to search for the girl near the location of the found clothing; they couldn't pick up a scent. The search continued throughout Wednesday and Thursday without making any progress on locating the young lady.

At 7:50 p.m. Thursday night, farmer Edgar Timm made a very unusual find. A November 3, 1956 article in the *Stevens Point Daily* had the following:

> The girl of the nearby village of Auroraville was found unconscious Thursday night near the farm home of Edgar Timm, a mile north of the village. Judy had been missing nearly sixty hours and had been the object of a concentrated search by police and volunteers.

Another article on November 2, 1956 in the *Rhinelander Daily* had this: "Authorities were baffled as to how she [Judy] spent her time since she disappeared Tuesday. Sheriff Leon Murty of

Waushara County said, however, there were indications she hid alone in a shack on the farm where she was found." My question to sheriff Murty—hid from what?

Judy was transported to a local hospital where physicians were puzzled by her condition. They stated that she was suffering from shock and exposure. She is suffering from shock from what? Why would a Wisconsin girl take her shoes and socks off on a cold November morning in a creek and swamp land? Several articles stated that doctors believed that Judy had a "blackout," something we don't hear much about in the twenty-first century. Other articles confirm the girl was found barefoot but was otherwise fully clothed. It's interesting that almost all of the articles indicated that she was "fully clothed," as though someone somewhere was expecting her to be missing clothing. Judy was released from the hospital several days after she arrived.

I also think it's fascinating that many missing people are found in or near a creek or river bed as this is one of the few locations where footprints cannot be found if you are walking on rocks.

Colleen Tourtillott
Missing 7/3/88, 6:00 p.m., Menominee Indian Reservation, Wisconsin
Age at Disappearance: 18 months

Keshena, Wisconsin is approximately forty miles north of Oshkosh and ten miles south of the Menominee Indian Reservation. The area around the reservation and Keshena is wet and swampy. The majority of the farmland is south of Keshena, but the Keshena area has woodlands.

Colleen Tourtillott was reported missing at 6:00 p.m. by her parents (Janelle and Miles Tourtillott) from her home inside the reservation. Law enforcement officials immediately responded, and a search started soon after their arrival. By 10:00 p.m. on the evening of the disappearance many people were searching for Colleen.

Colleen still hadn't been found by 8:00 a.m. the following morning, yet there were hundreds of volunteers flocking to the area to look for the young girl.

Approximately one and a half miles from Colleen's residence, a deputy sheriff was directing traffic caused by volunteer searchers flocking to the area. The sheriff was taking a short break on his three-wheel ATV. He was driving down a lonely dirt road that had already been extensively searched when the deputy saw Colleen off to the side of the road. The girl was covered with scratches and had no clothing on. When she left her home, she was wearing a disposable diaper and a barrette—both were gone. The deputy took his shirt off to cover the girl and advised communications that he had found Colleen. The deputy advised that Colleen seemed very tired.

The night Colleen disappeared, temperatures had dropped into the forties, and law enforcement officials were shocked to see that she survived the night. Colleen was transported to a local hospital and then released the same day.

How did Colleen get one and one-half miles from her home in bare feet in less then twenty-four hours? What happened to Colleen's barrette and diaper? Why didn't Colleen suffer from exposure when she was essentially naked in the woods with temperatures in the low forties? These are all questions that will never be answered because Colleen hadn't learned to talk. You will find that many of the missing cannot speak or remember their incident and communicating about what happened while they were missing is impossible.

Michigan

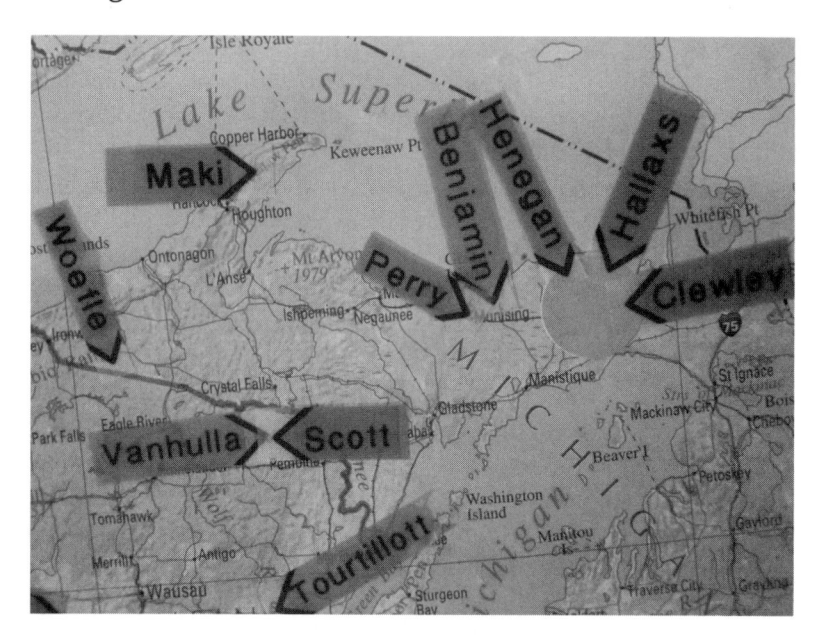

Missing People in Michigan by Date

Name	Date Missing•Age•Sex
Katie Flynn	June/1868•3•F
Raymond Maki	01/27/36•17•M
Edward Woelfle	10/06/46•15•M
Kenneth Scott	09/28/58•4•M
Carol Van Hulla	06/28/59•3•F
	**45-year gap
Christopher Hallaxs	03/17/04•30•M
Joe Clewley	07/13/08•73•M
Derrick Hennegan	08/04/08•35•M

Katie Flynn
Missing summer of 1868, Walhalla, Michigan
Age at Disappearance: 3 years

Henry Flynn ran a lumber camp in the forests just outside of Walhalla. During the summer months, his wife and daughter (Katie) would come from the city and stay with him.

Part of Flynn's job was to drive a team of horses carrying the lumber up the hill to the mill, drop the load, and then come back to get additional trees. During June of 1868, Henry would have Katie ride the horse on the way up the hill, and she would then dismount at the top and run back down the hill on an adjacent trail. On one of these trips back down the hill, Katie didn't make it. The mother thought she was with the father, and the father thought she made it back to the houses at the bottom of the hill. When Henry returned home at the end of the night and learned that Katie never returned, a search was immediately initiated.

Henry checked the path that Katie was taking and saw her tracks slowly merge with the path of a huge black bear. As luck would come Mr. Flynn's way, two hunters wandered into camp and offered to assist with the search for their daughter. The men scoured the area with the aid of torches made of wood shingles. The search for Katie went into early in the morning and was given up for that night.

Early the next morning, Mr. Flynn and a group of searchers went back out looking for Katie. At approximately 4:00 p.m. the men heard a "feeble cry" in dense underbrush. The men started to make their way through the brush and toward a river when they heard another faint cry. Just before the men reached the river, the article stated that the men saw a huge black bear jump into the river and disappear across the other side. Katie was found standing on a tree that was lying on the ground and crossing the water flow. The girl was picked up and taken back to camp. Katie had a badly scratched face and hands, but that was about the extent of her injuries.

When Katie got back to camp, Mrs. Flynn asked her why she didn't run away when she had the opportunity? This story was replicated in the April 24, 1932 *Ludington Daily*. Here is Katie's response: "Big dog came up to me, took me in his arms and walked away with me." Noting one of her shoes was missing the parents asked her where it was. "The big dog ate it," she replied.

The Katie Flynn story was again printed in the July 6, 1961 *Ludington Daily News*. In this copy of the story it had the following as to Katie's rendition of the events.

"In answer to questions, the child said that after her father had left, she had played a little while in the sand when a big black thing came along and played with her. Then it held out its paw and she caught hold of it and it had walked away with her. Just before dark it had left her for a while and when it came back its paw was full of winter green berries. The bear ate some of the berries and she ate some. Then it scraped a big pile of leaves close to her and lay down close to her and during the night had tried to cover her with its body."

The quote above needs to be reviewed at two different important points. I believe that Katie was trying to explain that she did not understand what had walked up to her by her first statement "big black thing." A person's first statement about an event is usually a very revealing and honest representation of a stressful event. It would appear from that first statement that Katie was having difficulty understanding what she was observing.

Katie's explanation about the mammal making a bedding area, covering her and keeping her warm is not indicative of bear heavier. Bears are not nurturing warm creatures that cuddle children.

As I have stated multiple times throughout the book, berries play a continual role in the disappearance of people, this story is another example of that as the mammal left and returned with berries for Katie to eat.

I do not know what took Katie but I do not believe it was a bear. Other articles indicate that a wolfe took her, also not a possible scenario. A wolf cannot pick berries, place them in its paw and carry them back in that paw.

This story is remarkably similar to an incident that occurred on July 7, 1868, in Ludington, Michigan, very close in dates and geography to the Walhalla incident. The name "Henry Flynn" is in both articles so we must think this is the same incident. We are including both renditions of the story so the reader can understand what might have occurred.

The other story that Katie's mimics is the disappearance of the two and a half year old daughter of Millard Davis who lived in Boiceville, New York. On or about May 9, 1888 Davis disappeared and was found twenty four hours and two miles from her residence in a deep rural valley. Davis told her family that she was taken by a "big bear" and slept with that bear through the night. This story was found in the May 15, 1888 edition of the *New York Times*.

Something took Katie against her will. Searchers saw something dark and hairy jump into the river as they approached. Most felt it was a bear, except the victim herself. Bears do not take little girls, coddle them all night, and carry them in their arms. Katie Flynn had something very unusual happen to her in the summer of 1868.

Raymond Maki
Missing 11/27/36, Keweenaw Woods, n/o Mohawk, Michigan
Age at Disappearance: 17 years

Raymond lived on the far northern peninsula of Michigan in Copper City. He knew the area very well and understood the associated dangers of being in the woods. On November 27, 1936, he was deer hunting from the Hibbard Hunting Camp near the Keweenaw Woods. Raymond was dressed for the winter weather, and his dog accompanied him. He and friends agreed to meet back at the camp later in the day. Raymond never returned to camp, which started a massive search of the peninsula.

Menominee County Sheriff's office took the lead on the search for Raymond and was assisted by the Houghton County Sheriff. Nearly six days into the search, deputies found Raymond's rifle lying on the ground. Several hundred yards from the rifle, and in a swamp, searchers found the interior liner of Raymond's mitten. As searchers returned to their SAR camp, Raymond's dog had also wandered in.

After two weeks of 150 men scouring the woods in Northern Michigan, deputies called off the search for Raymond Maki.

Several facets of this case trouble me greatly. If Raymond were alive, he would never give up his gloves or rifle, as they are a lifeline for survival. Searchers never found any blood in the snow or any other clothing articles. Bears in this region are hibernating during this time period, so they are not suspect. Searchers were completely puzzled about why their search dogs couldn't find a scent trail even though they found some of Raymond's clothing. Raymond knew never to walk into a swamp area, as this would be a life-threatening maneuver in late November, yet that is where searchers found his glove liner. I think it's interesting that Raymond's dog eventually made it back to camp several days after he went missing. The dog returning indicates to me that Raymond was long deceased.

Edward William Woelfle
Missing 10/6/46, 4 miles w/o Boulder Junction, Wisconsin
Age at Disappearance: 15 years
5'10", 150 lbs

Four newspaper articles were located that addressed the disappearance of Edward Woelfle.

Edward was an active fifteen-year-old who enjoyed the great outdoors. He specifically enjoyed hunting and trapping along the Wisconsin and Michigan border near Boulder Junction.

On October 5, 1946, Edward did not attend church and instead took his .22-caliber pistol, his shotgun, seven wolf traps, and a duffle bag that contained wolf bait. He also took a lunch and headed into the woods. Edward's parents felt that their son was going to an area near Whitney Lake in Wisconsin, as the boy knew this area very well. The area around Whitney Lake is quite lush, remote, and filled with dozens of lakes, creeks, and waterways.

When Edward did not return on Sunday night, Mr. and Mrs. William Woelfle contacted law enforcement.

Searchers methodically covered the area near Whitney Lake and did find six of Edward's seven wolf traps. It appeared to searchers that the seventh trap had been unlatched and could not be found. Searchers stated that there were no berries in the woods this time of year, but there was an ample supply of porcupines in the area that someone could shoot and eat.

On October 9, 1946, there was an article in the *Herald Times* about the search for Edward. The article was titled "Push Hunt for Missing Youth." The searchers stated that they were now using bloodhounds to aid in their search. Paragraph three of the article had an interesting notation: "Daniels (Dispatcher Trout Lake Ranger Station) said bloodhounds used the first two days were unable to uncover the youth's trail and that the dogs refused to follow footprints found in the woods."

There are two points of this paragraph that need to be evaluated. Did the writer mean to say "footprints" versus "boot marks"? It would be very odd if there were footprints in the middle of the woods in November. It would make more sense that there were tracks or boot prints. It doesn't make any sense that the dogs would not track boot impressions or even footprints in the woods.

On October 14, the sheriff involved in the search for William Woelfle decided to terminate all SAR operations. The sheriff stated that he felt that the youth had gone to Alaska. This was an amazing claim since the only personal items missing from the residence were hunting equipment and bait, not a suitcase or clothing.

A massive review of newspaper archives failed to show that William was ever found. The area where William disappeared is very similar to the topography of missing people throughout Minnesota and Michigan. The area around Whitney Lake could easily match areas of missing people throughout far northern regions of North America.

Kenneth Scott
Missing 9/28/58, 2:00 p.m., Norway Lake, Michigan
Age at Disappearance: 4 years

Norway Lake is located in the far northwest section of Michigan in a region surrounded by heavy forest and swamps.

Elmer Scott and his three sons had taken a short vacation at a hunting camp at Norway Lake near the Wisconsin Border on the upper peninsula of Michigan. In mid-afternoon on September 28, Kenneth was following his two older brothers through the woods back to camp, but he could not keep up. The older brothers arrived at the camp and realized that Kenneth had vanished. The brothers told their father of the missing brother, and a search party was organized.

The local police rallied every local person and organized nearly one thousand participants in the search for Kenneth. Helicopters, airplanes, horsemen, and ground troops worked through rain in their efforts to find the boy. The area they were searching had very thick woods with swamps, bears, and other wild animals roaming the area. Temperatures in the region dropped to forty-six degrees on some nights that Scott was missing.

Early on Thursday morning a helicopter crew was flying low over the trees and saw a small bundle on the ground. The crew led ground forces to the bundle and found it was Kenneth Scott. Kenneth was dead on a hillside quite a distance from the point where he disappeared. An October 3, 1958 article in the *Milwaukee Sentinel* had the following:

"The boy lay face up in a little clearing, his light jacket beside him. Searchers said he apparently wandered approximately fifteen miles through swamp and had come out onto higher ground before deciding to rest sometime Tuesday."

The coroner who examined the body stated that Kenneth had died sometime Tuesday of exposure.

Case Summary:

Searchers stated that Kenneth wandered fifteen miles in two days through swamps and up hills—unreal! According to the book *Lost Person Behavior*, page 135, children four to six years old are located more then 95 percent of the time in less then a 4.1-mile radius from the point last seen if traveling on flat ground. This distance doesn't include traveling across swamps, which means Kenneth is so far outside the search guidelines recommended by the experts that it's ludicrous. Kenneth traveled more than triple the distance of the maximum acknowledged in the search criteria of the book, and he was found on a hill.

Carol Van Hulla
Missing 6/28/59, 6:00 p.m., Dickinson County Picnic Ground, Michigan
Age at Disappearance: 3 years

Mr. and Mrs. Joseph Van Hulla and their four daughters traveled to the Dickinson County picnic grounds at Norway Lake for an afternoon outdoors. Around dinnertime the family realized that Carol had somehow vanished from the company of the other girls.

The family quickly searched for their daughter and then notified law enforcement.

A full-fledged search was started within one hour of her disappearance, which included five hundred searchers, helicopters, and bloodhounds. The first night of the search was not very eventful, and searchers had a difficult time finding any leads. Bloodhounds could not find the girl even though handlers stated that they had found her scent from time to time.

During the thirteenth hour that Carol was missing, searchers were working their way through a heavy swamp when they thought they heard a crying sound. The group broke through heavy brush and found Carol asleep on a small mound in the middle of water crying in her sleep. A June 30, 1959 article in the *Milwaukee Sentinel* had the following:

Although the spot where Carol was found is about one mile from the picnic grounds, authorities believed she had covered five miles in her wanderings. The search, begun an hour after Carol disappeared, involved the first major use of Michigan-Wisconsin Rescue Unit, organized to include men and equipment of various agencies, since Kenny Scott, 4, Kingsford, Michigan, vanished under similar circumstances last September. Kenny was found dead of exposure four days later, about 7 miles from where Carol was discovered.

A June 30, 1959 article in *The Sun* had this: "Following sounds of a child's crying, two 18-year-old youths wading through a swamp waist deep in water found Carol asleep on a mound virtually surrounded by water."

Carol was taken to the hospital for observation. It was found that she had numerous scratches and a slight case of exposure but was doing well.

Case Summary:

Two missing children from the same lake in nine months to the day is a highly unusual set of events. Both children disappeared in a four-hour window of each other, and both children supposedly traversed swamps on their own. The book *Lost Person Behavior* by Robert Koester states that a one- to three-year-old child will be found 95 percent of the time on flat ground in less than two miles from the point last seen. Carol had traveled over two and a half times that distance.

I'm afraid to say that I don't believe in coincidences, and I don't believe that two small children disappear from the same lake in a nine-month span without there being a connection. There were no children reported missing from the same lake in previous or subsequent years. The more disturbing question is how Carol got onto the mound surrounded by water? If the water was waist deep for adults, there is no way a three-year-old could walk through that to the mound. Plus, she would have to traverse thick bushes and bad terrain. The explanation doesn't make any sense. Remember, the newsmen covering this story thought the facts behind this case were so odd and unusual that they wrote about it.

Joe Clewley
Missing 7/13/08, Tahquamenon State Park, Paradise, Michigan
Age at Disappearance: 73 years
5'10", 150 lbs

Joe was born in 1934 in Lansing, Michigan. Joe served a term in the U.S. Navy on Guam. He married Loraine, and they had five children. Joe attended Lansing Community College where he studied electrical design, which led to the family moving to Roscommon, Michigan, 120 miles south of Tahquamenon State Park. Joe established an engineering services company, Industrial Control Design—a company he operated successfully for twenty-five years.

Joe and Loraine Clewley spent their winters in the mild climate of Panama City, FL. The retirees would go north for their summers into the Higgins Lake area on the lower-peninsula region of Michigan. It was a pleasant retreat they earned after a lifetime of hard work.

The Clewley family owned a small, two-room log cabin that they referred to as the "Chippewa Hunting Post." The cabin was built in the 1920s and was located southwest of Paradise near Whitefish Township. The cabin was built on the north bank of the Tahquamenon River. The view out the back window of the cabin would was reminiscent of a picture postcard—it was gorgeous. The cabin was rustic and did not have running water, electricity, or generators. A local spring furnished potable water for the residents near the Clewley cabin.

Joe truly enjoyed spending time at the Chippewa Hunting Post, but Loraine wasn't as attached. Joe would spend weeks at the cabin, and Loraine would come on the weekends. On Joe's last trip, he drove his silver, 1992, Oldsmobile Silhouette van and parked it on the north side of the Tahqua Trail in Tahquamenon Falls State Park. His nine-year-old black and white springer-chow mix dog, Chip, accompanied Joe. Chip had a nasty bark, but at forty-five pounds was not a real threat to anything living. Family members claim that Chip was very loyal to Joe and never left his side.

Joe parked his van at the trailhead, took Chip from the car, and made the one-mile walk to his cabin. The trail was well defined, easy to follow, and thick with surrounding vegetation. Joe's practice was to call Loraine every morning at 9:00 a.m. and every night at 9:00 p.m. as a way to keep in touch and to ensure all was good at both ends of the phone.

The story as to what happened to Joe takes a very unusual twist that law enforcement and the family cannot explain. It appears that Joe went on his usual hike with Chip. They arrived at the van and Joe may have gotten Chip water. At this point Joe and Chip disappear.

Law enforcement found Joe's keys in the van and the vehicle unlocked. According to the family, this is something Joe would never do. Joe's son, Joe, Jr. stated, "Something pulled him away, but what?" The search for Joe Clewley was the largest search in Michigan state history. The search included cadaver dogs, Michigan State Police, BIA officers, Border Patrol K-9 Units, Chippewa County Sheriff Search and Rescue, and a host of volunteers. The official search was suspended after the fourth day, but volunteers continued their efforts many weeks later. The search area was approximately ten thousand acres.

In another odd twist to this case, the family went back to the cabin on August 1, 2008 early in the morning. The family found Chip sitting at the front door, approximately 20 percent lighter but in generally good health. It did not appear as though the dog had been living in the wild for weeks. No ticks, bug bites, or other indicators were on the dog that showed it had been ravaged by forest-related hazards. In an even more interesting aspect to Chip's arrival, the dog did not bark for three days after its return. It had always barked when it was at the cabin.

Case Summary

Some factors about this case cause concern. Having search and rescue personnel terminate their search after four days is astonishing. After following hundreds of searches throughout North America, I know it is not uncommon for some jurisdictions to search for two weeks. There is no mention in any documents that I researched with any notation that an aerial FLIR unit was used, a key element in finding a large, warm body. The one aspect of the Clewley case that should be emphasized and publicized is that Joe was the second person in the last four years to disappear in the same region in Northern Michigan. I did an extensive search of missing people throughout the entire state of Michigan, and there are not two adults missing in the wild in such close proximity to each other as Clewley and Hallaxs. The fact that two individuals have disappeared without a trace in the same geographical region should have law enforcement concerned. I understand that the crime scene is large, but the impact to the families is even larger.

Christopher Hallaxs
Missing 3/17/04, Paradise, Michigan
Age at Disappearance: 30
6'1", 185 lbs

Christopher Charles Hallaxs was born in Battle Creek, Michigan. From the start of his young adult life Chris loved the outdoors. His family had a remote cabin located on the east bank of the Two Hearted River in Northern Michigan, one of his favorite locations to visit. Chris didn't stop at just visiting the family cabin; Chris once walked nineteen and one-half hours non-stop through the bush as a way to test his endurance and to make good time. He was the type of person that would rather make his own trail than travel a heavily traveled path.

One of Chris's favorite places to visit was a region inside of Lake Superior State Forest at Tahquamenon Falls State Park. This area is in pristine condition, and its 52,000-acre site was a nice location to disappear into.

Chris never got married and worked a variety of jobs over the years. He had worked at a brewery, a lodge, a public library, and had a job surveying—the list was quite diverse. For a very short time, he was a computer technician where he complained about sitting "on my butt and talking on the phone for ten hours a day, four days a week." This lifestyle obviously didn't suit Chris, and he eventually moved on.

Of the many people that go missing each year in the wilds of North America, Chris would not be one that you'd think would ever get lost. He had the ability to live off the land and make huts and shelters out of what was available. The only weapon that he was known to carry was a large bowie knife in a sheath on his right hip. He also carried the usual survivor accessories and knew the terrain he was traversing quite well.

On March 17, 2004, Chris stopped at a local BP convenience store. He purchased soda and snacks and told the clerk that he was "going out to his camp." Eventually, Chris was reported missing and the Chippewa County Sheriff and the Michigan State Police conducted an extensive search. A search and rescue (SAR) team found what they believed to be Chris's snowshoe tracks and were able to follow them for several miles. The tracks led to a very tangled and densely wooded swamp area. Darkness was starting to set, and the SAR team decided to call off the search. Many of Chris's family were initially not too concerned about his lack of contact because they knew his practices and his ability to live off the land. They knew that Chris actually stashed food and other supplies in various areas of the woods in case of an emergency.

During subsequent searches of the Mackinaw Wilderness and searches of specific areas they knew Chris had visited, teams found a variety of possible clues. There are several photos of what appears to be supplies that have been thrown around and displaced. A canteen on a belt was found lying on the ground. A very well-designed shelter was also located that seemed to be in very good condition. Buckets that contained shoes, cups, and plastic bags with various supplies were tossed on the ground and scattered. The scene was very discomforting.

A volunteer team that entered the region actually brought metal detectors in an effort to find evidence. The team did find an expended slug. It had not mushroomed significantly, but the find would concern anyone involved, as Chris was not known to carry firearms.

The search for Chris Hallaxs was similar to that familiar phrase of finding a needle in a haystack: nobody quite knew exactly where he would be. Chris isn't the only person missing in this region. Joe Clewley had also vanished nearby.

Derrick Henegan disappeared approximately fifteen miles from where Christopher vanished. The Tahquamenon State Forest and the Newberry State Forest are located between the locations where each person disappeared. The common element that crosses both locations is the Tahquamenon River, which is 89 miles long and flows west to east. There are no cities and few residences in this region of northern Michigan, it is quite remote.

Derrick Ray Henegan
Missing 8/4/08, Newberry, Michigan
Age at Disappearance: 35 years
6'1", 170 lbs

Henegan had friends who lived in a rural area of Newberry, Michigan. Henegan had made plans to meet his girlfriend at a deer blind in the woods, and at 4:30 p.m. was last seen walking across the street from his friend's home and into the woods. The girlfriend arrived at the hunting blind, but Henegan never did.

Derrick had two children who lived with his ex-wife, whom he called nightly. His girlfriend was pregnant with his child when he disappeared and she gave birth four months after his disappearance.

Law enforcement is handling this case as a simple missing persons case, yet Derrick's family believes there has been some crime committed.

Newberry has a population of 2,570 and according to the 2000 census has a median household income of $29,000. The area surrounding Newberry is remote with five large bodies of water on the perimeter of the city. State forests surround the city.

Iowa

Both missing people in Iowa are males.

Iowa Missing People by Date
Name	Date Missing•Age
Frank Floyd	01/07/1897•NA
••Leroy Williams	03/16/51•64

••Details on the disappearance of Leroy Williams can be found in the chapter on "Farmers."

Frank Floyd
Missing 1/7/1897, 15 miles north of Atlantic City, Iowa
Age at Disappearance: Unknown

I could find only one article on the disappearance of Frank Floyd, and this appeared January 8 in the *New York Times*. It stated the following:

Atlantic City, Iowa, Jan 7. Frank Floyd went hunting in the big timber fifteen miles north yesterday and not returning today, a party went in search of him. They tracked him through snow, and at last found his body literally torn to pieces. His gun was found near him, and a short distance away was an old sow lying dead with a broken leg and a bullet hole through her.

The article implies that the sow killed the hunter. I don't think so. Hogs don't move quickly with a broken leg, and Frank could have killed it with his rifle. I don't know what is in the Iowa plains in the middle of January that could tear a man to pieces. The article also states that it was known that there were many hogs in the area, and someone felt Frank was killed after he shot the sow.

Illinois
Illinois Missing People by Date

Name	Date Missing•Age•Sex
Helen Chenoweth	03/28/40•3•F
Susan Sweely	08/09/50•2•F
••John Sweet	10/26/53•NA•M
Lisa Schackelford	07/10/62•3•F
**45 Year Gap	
Hannah Klamecki	6/13/07•5•F

••Details on the disappearance of John Sweet can be found in the "Farmers" chapter.

Helen Chenoweth
Missing 3/28/40, 6:00 p.m., Breeds, Illinois
Age at Disappearance: 3 years
Blonde Hair

The Chenoweth family owned a farm on the outskirts of Breeds, eight miles east of Canton, Illinois. In the early evening of March 28, Helen Chenoweth (three years) was staying at the farm with William Long (seventeen years), a cousin, and her younger brother Howard, five years. At some point Helen disappeared. Parents were notified, and a search immediately ensued. The police questioned William and then took him into custody for further questioning.

While William Long was in custody, law enforcement continued to search the area up to two miles from the farm for the little girl. The night that she disappeared there was a rainstorm that lasted many hours and washed away any tracks that Helen may have made.

Forty-seven hours after Helen disappeared, Deputy Floyd Morse and Allen Clark were walking to an outer area to search when they were on an adjacent farm and climbing up a hill. The hill the deputies were climbing included a pig lot and mud. As they went up the hill they saw a small bulge in the mud but the bulge appeared to have clean clothing. The deputies walked to the bulge and found Helen Chenoweth unconscious but alive. The girl had clean hands and feet and her clothes were barely wrinkled. The more amazing fact was that

Helen's clothes were dry. The deputies picked the girl up and took her home and later to a hospital.

Helen Chenoweth was found three-fourths of a mile from her farm forty-seven hours after she disappeared. The area where she was found had been searched many times, and she was not there at those times.

An April 1 article in the *Pittsburgh Press* stated, "She couldn't tell the story of her adventures. Sheriff Ralph Cook said the child's clothes, face, and hands were clean and that she hardly could have survived two nights in the open under the unfavorable weather conditions." Deputy Sheriff Floyd Morse was interviewed by the *Telegraph Herald* on March 31 and stated the following:

Although the child was unharmed, Morse said he believed she had been held captive by someone who decided to release her Saturday because of fear of being detected. Her clothes were dry and did not appear as though they had been wet, despite the fact that a heavy rain drenched the district the night she disappeared.

The sheriff's department released William Long without any charges filed. It was obvious to all involved that he did not play any part in the disappearance of Helen.

This is just another in the long line of cases in which someone is missing, they are later found in an area that had been previously searched, and the children cannot or will not tell the story of what happened to them. It is blatantly obvious to all law enforcement involved in this case that Helen had been abducted and later released, as is the claim in many of the stories in the two books. It would appear that someone placed the girl in the pig lot just prior to her being found. She was too clean to have been walking the area during her disappearance. The real question is who was roaming near a remote farm and abducted the child?

Susan Sweely
Missing 8/9/50, 7:00 p.m., Pearl City, Illinois
Age at Disappearance: 2 years

Pearl City is in northwest Illinois, approximately ten miles from the Mississippi River and the Hanover Bluff Nature Preserve. It is also at the base of a mountain range that extends to the Mississippi River.

I could not find any articles describing the facts behind Susan's disappearance other than she was home with her mother when she realized Susan was missing at 7:00 p.m. The mother contacted the father, William Sweely, who was in town watching a free outdoor movie. The mother told William that his daughter and their three dogs were missing and asked assistance from the moviegoers. Almost five hundred people accompanied William back to his farm.

Mrs. Sweely called the sheriff's department, and they responded with twelve deputies. The deputies organized a search in which volunteers held hands and walked the high cornfields and waist-high wheat and hay fields looking for the girl. Searchers also checked local swamps and ravines in an attempt to find Susan.

At 2:00 a.m. on August 10, searchers were in a hay field approximately one mile from the Sweely farm and found Susan asleep surrounded by her three dogs. She was found in a field near marshlands, but she was generally dry and in perfect condition. Susan was later asked how she went missing. She couldn't explain it.

Lisa Schackelford
Missing 7/10/62, 11:00 a.m., Braceville, Illinois
Age at Disappearance: 3 years
Blonde Hair

Braceville, Illinois, is in the northeastern section of the state in a very swampy and wet area surrounded by game reserves, lakes, streams, and bogs.

In the late morning hours of July 10, 1962, Lisa Schackelford got into an argument with her two young sisters over a toy. Lisa became so upset she walked away (barefooted) from playing with the girls. As lunchtime approached, Lisa's mother called for her, but she didn't respond. Mrs. Inez Schackelford and Lisa's seventeen-year-old sister (Carolyn) traced Lisa's barefoot tracks through a cornfield and to a large oak tree where they found Lisa's pet kitten. The mother lost the tracks at this point because of a rainstorm. Mrs. Schackelford enlisted the help of her seven other children, and all started to search for the young girl. It was at this point that local law enforcement was called.

During two days of searching, over one thousand people combed the fields, bogs, swamps, and roadways looking for Lisa. At one point a canine team tracked her to a local major highway, and the canines stopped. The state police felt that Lisa crossed this major roadway and the canines lost the scent. There was some concern by state police that the girl may have been picked up by a vehicle and kidnapped.

Almost exactly forty-eight hours after Lisa disappeared, and outside the primary search area, Lisa was found wandering the railroad tracks five miles north of her farm in Coal City. This area was described in articles as very wild and with many coal tailings.

There was never a mention in any of the articles about the condition of Lisa's feet, just a general description that she was in satisfactory condition.

It's hard to imagine a three-year old girl traveling five miles alone anywhere let alone continuing to walk into the oblivion of a wild coal tailings area. It's equally hard to understand how cars would pass her as she crossed the interstate without people calling the state police or even stopping to render aid to a small and lost child.

In review, it's hard to believe that this event ever happened the way it is depicted. A young three-year-old girl cannot move that fast, thus making her a major target on an interstate. She was in bare feet, so she surely must have had injuries, again not noted in any article.

Hannah Klamecki
Missing 6/13/07, 7:00 p.m., Kankakee River, Momence, Illinois
Age at Disappearance: 5 years

Some of the greatest memories we have as children are the special times we spend with grandparents, and that's what Hannah Klamecki was doing on June 13, 2007. Hannah had left her home in Momence to go boating with her grandfather, David Klamecki, sixty-two years old. David and Hannah were riding the waves and enjoying the solitude offered by the remote locations along this stretch of the river. Momence is just west of the Lasalle Fish and Wildlife Area and the Wetlands Nature Preserve. There are areas along this stretch of the river that are very wild and lush and with few people.

Sometime in the late afternoon or early evening, David pulled their boat up to an island in the middle of the river. He roped the boat into position and jumped into the water. For some unknown reason, David disappeared under water, and Hannah lost sight of him. The girl was wearing arm floaters and apparently went into the river and came out on the sand of a nearby bank. Admittedly, this portion of the story is a little vague, and Hannah had not offered a lot of clarity.

Once Hannah and David didn't return from their trip, Hannah's parents contacted the sheriff, and a search ensued. For two days the sheriff's office felt that Hannah must have drowned. They were scraping the bottom of the river looking for a body, but didn't find it.

On June 15, the sheriff found the body of David Klamecki floating downstream approximately three-fourths of a mile from where he went in. The sheriff's team was on the sand recovering the body when unbelievably out of the bushes behind them walked a naked five-year-old girl eating a handful of wild mulberries. It was Hannah Klamecki.

Hannah had scratches over her entire body, had no clothes on, and seemed to be in fairly good health. The girl was taken to the hospital and found to be in good condition. Hannah's parents were shocked she was alive and equally shocked that she walked out of the lush vegetation and right up to the searchers, almost like she was delivered there, fed, and on time.

Chapter Conclusion

Four of the people listed in this chapter disappeared from a farm or ranch. The four children missing were females, all very close in age (two three year-olds, one two-year-old, and a five-year-old). Is this merely a coincidence?

Missouri

Name	Date Missing•Age•Sex
Joshua Childers	05/04/09•3•M

Joshua Childers
Missing 5/4/09, 11:45 a.m., Arcadia, Missouri

Age at Disappearance: 3 years
Blonde Hair

Sometimes it doesn't matter whether the doors are locked and you feel the house is secure. Children will still find a way to sneak out, and that's what happened in the disappearance of Joshua Childers.

Joshua's father worked a midnight shift and was sleeping in their home that borders the Mark Twain National Forest adjacent to the Ketcherside Mountain Conservation Area. Joshua's mother was in the kitchen thinking Joshua was playing in the home inside the confines of locked doors. Mrs. Childers went to look for the boy at 11:45 a.m. and found that he had unlocked the rear door and walked out into the forest. She woke her husband, and they both searched the immediate area. Then they called the sheriff.

The town of Arcadia sits in a small valley but is surrounded on all sides by large, rugged mountains that are thick with vegetation. Searchers who came to the Childers's residence had stated that they couldn't see twenty feet into the woods located behind the Childers home. It was a very slow search.

Approximately one mile from the home, and in the middle of the first day of searching, volunteers found one of Joshua's shoes. This was a big discovery and encouraged searchers to focus on that area.

By the second complete day of searching, several canines and specially trained bloodhounds joined the search. The SAR had people on horseback, ATVs, and in the sky. The first night that Joshua was missing a heavy rain hit the area and eliminated many of the tracks.

Approximately fifty hours after Joshua disappeared, a lone searcher was walking down a creek bed three miles from the residence and found a clump lying on the ground. It was Joshua Childers. The boy seemed groggy but responded when the searcher asked if he wanted to go home.

Joshua was found with only one shoe, his diaper had disappeared, and he was wearing only a T-shirt. The emergency room physician stated that Joshua was dehydrated but otherwise in good condition.

Joshua never explained how or why he left the residence.

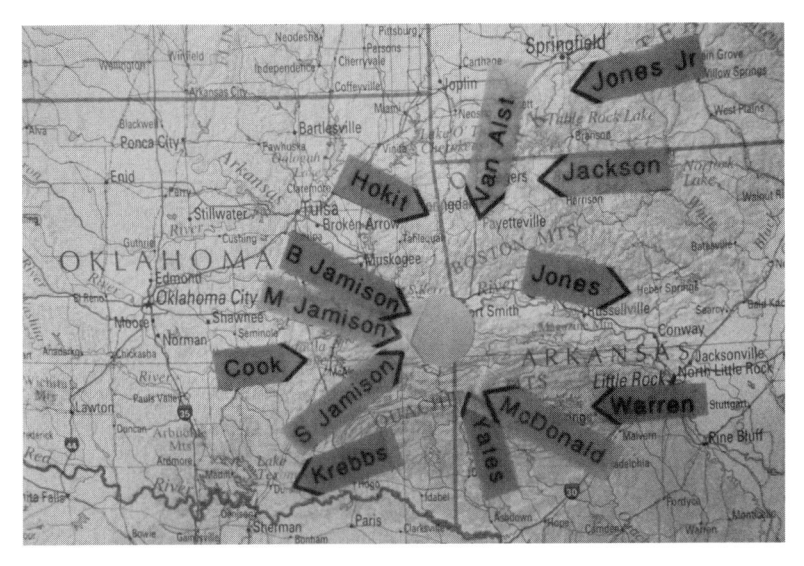

Oklahoma/ Arkansas

Missing people from Oklahoma and Arkansas are included on one list because of the proximity to the Oklahoma and Arkansas border, which represents the cluster. It does appear that the missing from this group was consistently young (two to nine years old), and then in 1999 the age profile of the missing changes, and it quickly gets older.

Missing People near the Oklahoma-Arkansas Border by Date

Name	Date Missing•Age•Sex
Charles Warren	12/20/36•2•M
Florence Jackson	09/06/37•4•F
Lloyd Hokit	10/21/45•9•M
Katherine Van Alst	06/16/46•8•F
Willard Eugene Jones Jr	01/17/59•3•M
**21-year time break	
Larry D. Krebbs	06/30/80•2•M
Ernest Matthew Cook	04/22/99•27•M
Gloria McDonald	01/26/01•68•F

Christopher L. Jones   04/05/06•37•M
Madyson Jamison   10/08/09•5•F
Sherilynn Jamison   10/08/09•40•F
Bobby Jamison   10/08/09•44•M

Charles Warren
Missing 12/20/35, PM, Hot Springs, Arkansas
Age at Disappearance: 2 years

Mr. and Mrs. Harold Warren lived in a rural area outside of Hot Springs, Arkansas. On December 20, 1935, Harold walked into the woods to cut a Christmas tree, and it is believed that Charles followed without anyone knowing. This was the third time in less than one year that Charles had disappeared in an unexplained manner. Once the family knew the boy wasn't in the home, they notified local authorities, and law enforcement asked the National Guard for assistance.

Almost exactly twenty-four hours after Charles went missing and after one hundred National Guardsman scoured the woods, he walked into a neighbor's farmhouse nearly four miles away. The boy had evaded over one hundred searchers and freezing temperatures to merely walk into the house of neighbor Mrs. Loy. He told the lady he wanted his father but refused to say what happened to him or how he became lost.

Charles was rushed to the local Army/Navy hospital where he was examined. A December 22, 1936 article in the Fayetteville Daily Democrat describes the doctor's feelings after the exam: "How the youngster endured the cold is nothing less than a miracle stated Major W.O. Prosser one of those that examined the boy."

Charles was given oatmeal at the hospital and then went promptly to sleep. The boy woke for his parents and then slept nonstop all the way back to his residence and through the following morning. He never said anything to his family about his disappearance.

Florence Jackson
Missing 9/6/37, Oak Grove, Arkansas
Age at Disappearance: 4 years

Mr. and Mrs. Arthur Jackson and their daughter Florence traveled from their home in Chelsea, Oklahoma, to visit relatives in Oak

Grove, Arkansas. On Monday afternoon, September 6, 1937, the parents went with Florence's grandfather to a wooded section outside the city while Florence and the grandfather took a walk to an abandoned saw mill. Approximately halfway to the mill, Florence stated that she wanted to go back to the car where her mother and father were located and turned and ran toward the auto. She never made it to the car. The grandfather got back to the auto and found Florence was not there and called authorities.

The area of Berryville and Oak Grove responded en masse as four hundred searchers attempted to find Florence. For four days the deputies and volunteers covered a vast area in an attempt to find the girl. They did find evidence. A September 9, 1937 article in the *Joplin Globe* had the following:

Shoes and stockings of the little girl were discovered late Tuesday afternoon by searchers within a half mile of where she was last seen. Tonight, however, no further trace of her had been found. The stockings were found on the side of a high ridge and were about fifteen yards apart, Morris (sheriff) said. Down the mountainside and high on another ridge a quarter mile away her shoes were found.

This finding stumped the searchers. Why would a little girl take stockings off at fifteen-yard intervals? It was almost as though someone was carrying her and stripping her clothing as he or she was running, but this was a four-year-old girl—not an easy feat.

Searchers were also stymied by heavy rain that hit the Oak Grove area after Florence disappeared. Reading further in the same *Joplin Globe* article was the following, "I believe she is alive Sheriff Morris said, but finding her will be like finding a needle in a hay stack. That country is the roughest you can imagine."

Late on September 10, a farmer's wife was outside her residence seven miles from where Florence disappeared and thought she heard someone calling her. Mrs. A. W. Godwin walked around her residence and down near Indian Creek and saw naked little Florence Jackson asking for help. All of her clothing was gone, her hair was full of burrs, and she was carrying one tomato and a handful of sheep sorrel. She told Mrs. Godwin that she didn't think she could cross the creek and could she come get her. The woman waded through the creek and grabbed Florence and brought her into her farmhouse. Authorities were quickly called. Florence told the Godwins that she had just eaten wild grapes, tomatoes, and lots of sheep sorrel. Mr. and Mrs. Jackson were escorted to the Godwin farm where they met with Florence. She was taken to a local hospital where she was found to have scratches over almost her entire body and a mild temperature but was otherwise fine.

Once Florence was at the hospital local law enforcement officers did meet and question her about her ordeal. The consensus of police was that there was a good likelihood that she was abducted, and they wanted to hear her complete story. The *Northwest Arkansas Times* ran a lengthy story about this incident on September 11, 1937. Here are a few excerpts:

Local officers listened closely to everything she said in view of the theory that she might have been temporarily abducted, but it was difficult to distinguish between actual experience and what she might have dreamed in fitful slumber in the forest.

Later, the same article states, "One night she said she slept on a log or inside a log. When darkness fell again she told of climbing a tree. Another night she recalled sleeping on a flat rock and I got a cold and called for mother to come." It was unclear whether she was calling for her mother or someone else in the area to come to her.

Later the article states, "Once she hid in the woods when she saw two strange men." It was unclear who these men were or what was strange about them.

One of the more fascinating parts of the story dealt with Florence's next statement,

She told of spending one of the nights in a house deep in the forest "after a black man and woman picked me up and took me there," she related that they "put me on a cot that night and then gave me breakfast and told me to get going on. I was mad and hit them with my hands," she said.

The writer of the story stated that he or she couldn't tell by her recollection what was true and what was false.

As someone who has interviewed hundreds of children after very stressful incidents, when they are not suspected of a crime, they are very truthful. I believe that something very, very strange happened to Florence, and she probably has subconsciously suppressed much of the story in an effort to block a very negative experience. She is probably trying to tell the truth the best she can without her mind going to a bad place.

Lloyd Neal Hokit
Missing 10/21/45, Found 10/23/45, Kiamichi Mountains, Oklahoma
Age at Disappearance: 9 years

On October 21, 1945 Lloyd "Sonny" Hokit joined his uncle (D. Richardson) and his uncle's hunting dogs for a day of squirrel hunting in the Kiamichi Mountains of eastern Oklahoma. The Kiamichi Mountains are known for their ruggedness and thick vegetation. The mountains sit directly on the border of Arkansas and act as a natural divider for the two states.

Sonny lived ten miles southeast of Talihina, Oklahoma, and made the trip to the mountains just east and then hiked into the rugged wilderness with his uncle. At one point during the trip, the uncle and the dogs stopped with Sonny to get a drink of water from the creek. As Sonny was getting a drink, Richardson's dogs chased a squirrel, and put it up a nearby tree. Richardson turned around and told nine-year-old Sonny to follow him. He looked back again and Sonny was following. Richardson went to the tree and was going to shoot the squirrel when he looked back again and he couldn't see the boy. Richardson felt that he would arrive quickly and waited a few minutes and then turned back to look for the boy. He couldn't find him. Richardson combed the area with his dogs for thirty minutes; he was yelling for Sonny, dogs were attempting to find a scent, nothing. In a matter of minutes Sonny had disappeared.

Richardson now returned to his vehicle and went to town to summon assistance. Just as night approached, the search parties were starting to get organized. Heavy rains hit the region, and the temperatures plummeted—not a good omen for finding Sonny.

The Oklahoma Highway Patrol was the lead law enforcement agency in the hunt for Sonny. Mrs. Claude Hokit, Sonny's mother, was one of the tireless searchers who worked day and night in the hunt for Sonny. Military personnel from Texas, Arkansas, and Oklahoma were sent to assist in the search for Sonny. In addition, Army soldiers from Camp Maxey and Camp Chaffee were sent to supplement the 150-plus people searching for the lost boy.

Two days after Sonny disappeared, Army Privates Herschell Kirkwood and Claude Busby from Camp Chaffee in Arkansas were searching a ridgeline high in the Kiamichi's approximately four miles from the spot where he was last seen when they found the boy lying on the ground unconscious. The soldiers stated that Sonny had a pulse when he was originally found but was unconscious. The soldiers had to carry the boy four miles back to a roadway where he was then taken to a hospital. He was pronounced dead at the hospital, where doctors stated he had died of exposure.

An article in the October 24, 1945 *Nevada State Journal* about the Sonny Hokit incident talked about the condition of his body when it was found:

The little farm lad's body was bruised badly and his lightweight clothing was almost torn from his body, giving evidence that he spent many terrified hours trying to keep warm in near freezing weather and find his way back home.

Case Summary:

There are several issues regarding Sonny Hokit's disappearance that do not make sense. Sonny's uncle specifically stated that he looked back and Sonny was following him to the location where the squirrel was chased by his dogs. A few minutes later he turned back and didn't see the boy. He walked backwards to look for the young lad and could not find him; he even yelled his name, and got no answer. In a matter of minutes I do not believe a boy, under his own power can get out of range of a grown man yelling. This portion of the story is of concern.

The idea that Sonny got four miles from the point he was last seen is also a confusing point. Sonny was on a creek when he was last seen. Someone with a nine-year-old intellect knows not to walk far from that creek because that creek is his salvation. To leave the safety of the creek and climb up a mountain to a ridgeline makes no sense.

The third and most disturbing part of the story is the condition that Sonny's body when discovered. The accounts indicate that the body had many bruises and his clothing "was almost torn from his body." I have personally been in the Kiamichis on several occasions. I have seen the hills and the forests. They are thick, but there is plenty of open space to hike. I do not believe that the answers about why Sonny had bruising and the clothes were torn from his body are because of the foliage. A nine-year-old boy has an intellect that would tell him to stay clear of certain elements that represent danger,and to stay in areas that would offer the least resistance to walking and hiking. Sonny would know to answer his uncle when he called. He didn't, and that is a major concern.

Katherine Van Alst
Missing 6/16/46, 2:30 p.m., Devil's Den State Park, Arkansas
Age at Disappearance: 8 years

The Van Alst family left their home in Kansas City and were vacationing in western Arkansas. They drove to Devil's Den State Park and rented a cabin for the five people in the family. After getting unpacked, John Van Alst (father) took Gene (thirteen), Bobby (eleven) and Katherine (eight) to Lee's Creek and an area where there was a small dam

Once the children arrived at the Devil's Den Dam, the children started to play in the water, and Katherine fell into a deep portion of the upper dam where an unknown woman supposedly pulled her out and told her not to play in the deep water. Katherine listened and went to the outflow of the creek below the dam. The outflow had several large boulders and rocks, and this was the last location that Katherine was seen at. It was 2:30 p.m. on June 16. The elevation of the dam is approximately 1000 feet, although peaks in the area go as high as 1600 feet.

After a short period of time Katherine's brothers realized they hadn't seen the girl and notified their father. In a very short time span many people were looking for Katherine. Once an initial search could not locate the Van Alst girl, the county sheriff and state park rangers were notified, and a formal search was organized.

On June 18, Washington County Sheriff Cap Gulley was in charge of the search and was focusing his efforts in a sixteen-foot deep pool of water beneath the dam under the belief that Katherine had drowned. The *Moberly Monitor* ran an article on June 18 stating the following: "Sheriff Cap Gulley said it was unlikely that the youngster had wandered into the wooded section of the park and that she had apparently drowned."

It was at approximately this time that newspapers reported that Katherine's father had a nervous breakdown and had to be placed under a doctor's care.

Sheriff Gulley managed to drain the pool below the dam and confirmed that Katherine did not drown, at least not at this location. While the sheriff and his assistants were focusing on the water, few resources were being put into searching the surrounding thick forests of the state park. Times were about to change.

The superintendent of the Arkansas State Parks System decided to respond to the search and eventually met with Sheriff Gulley. Arkansas Parks Director William B. Holman shared search duties with Sheriff Gulley and immediately started to put state police dogs, National Guard troops, and others into the mountains to look for the girl. Holman wasn't on the scene long when the *Arkansas Times* on June 22 ran the following statement: "There is a possibility Katherine was taken from the area by a passing motorist or other persons, Holman speculated."

When SAR leaders start to make claims about a possible abduction, it's an indicator that they are starting to believe that the victim may not be found.

On Saturday, June 22, at approximately 3:30 p.m., a group of searchers was seven air miles from where Katherine was last seen. The team was making its way up a mountainside through thick bushes calling Katherine's name. As the team neared the summit,

Katherine called out, "Here I am." University of Arkansas student Porter Chadwick was the first to find Katherine. She was wearing just a bathing suit, nothing else. She had scratches over her entire body and was also riddled with insect bites. The *Santa Fe New Mexican* ran a UP story on June 24 with the following statement: "She was found about seven miles as the crow flies from the vacationers' retreat where she set out, but, trail-wise mountaineers believed she had walked dozens of miles through the forests." She was found in an area downstream from the Devil's Den Dam.

Katherine was later interviewed by law enforcement sources and stated that she remembers sleeping in the warm grass the first night but doesn't remember the next few days or nights. She did state that she found a cave high up on a mountainside where she spent the last few nights before she was found. She stated that the cave had a pool of clean water and there were berries that she found in the area and eventually ate them.

Case Summary:

The recovery of Katherine Van Alst made worldwide news in 1946. The eight-year-old girl was missing for six days and nights without shoes, without pants, without a coat, yet managed to survive even though this was her first time ever in the woods. Rescuers claim that Katherine would have had to walk between twenty-four to thirty-six miles to get to the location where she was eventually found, yet she wore no shoes. The girl managed to make her way through thick and thorny bushes to reach the location of her cave near a mountaintop at nearly six hundred feet higher in elevation from where she was last seen. Katherine Van Alst defied every SAR profile regarding an eight-year-old girl who goes missing. Is this possible? She had never been in the woods but knew which berries she could safely eat? She just happened to find a cave on a mountaintop with fresh spring water inside?

Katherine was hospitalized for two days and released in excellent condition. The doctors stated that she was suffering from multiple cuts and bruises and a minor case of shock. There was never a mention of dehydration or her suffering from lack of food.

The exact location of Devil's Den Park is approximately sixty miles east of Eufala, Oklahoma, and sixty miles north of Mena, Arkansas.

Willard Eugene Jones, Jr.
Missing 1/17/59, Unknown Time, eight miles s/o Lebanon, Missouri
Age at Disappearance: 3 years
**This incident was placed with the Oklahoma and Arkansas cases because of its proximity to those cases.

Mr. and Mrs. Willard Jones, Sr. lived on a farm eight miles south of Lebanon Missouri. The location of their residence is near the Fuson Conservation area and is approximately twenty miles west of Fort Leonard Wood. The area of the farm is very wet and swampy. The farm is forty miles from the Oklahoma border

On a cold January day in 1959, Willard was with one of his eight brothers and sisters cutting firewood on the farm. At some point while Wilbert (fifteen) was cutting wood, he had to leave the woodpile to get fuel for the chain saw. Willard, at this point, wandered off. As Wilbert took a break from his chores, he went looking for Willard and couldn't find him. A notification went to other family members and a search of the farm started.

As the search for Willard escalated, up to five thousand soldiers, law enforcement officials, and volunteers scoured the farm and surrounding Ozark Mountains. Canines were brought to search, soldiers from Fort Leonard Wood were on scene for several days, and airplanes crossed the sky looking for the boy.

As searchers were looking for Willard, the weather turned very bad almost immediately after he disappeared. An icy rain hit the region, and everything froze. The weather greatly inhibited search efforts.

Eight days after Willard disappeared, two soldiers were in extremely dense woods two and one-fourth miles from the victim's residence when they found the boy lying on the ground, dead. The area where the boy was found was so dense and so far from a reasonable area that the boy would have wandered to, the soldiers had to call for instructions on how to get back to the command post, as they were lost.

The autopsy on Willard indicated the boy died of exposure probably twenty-four hours after he disappeared.

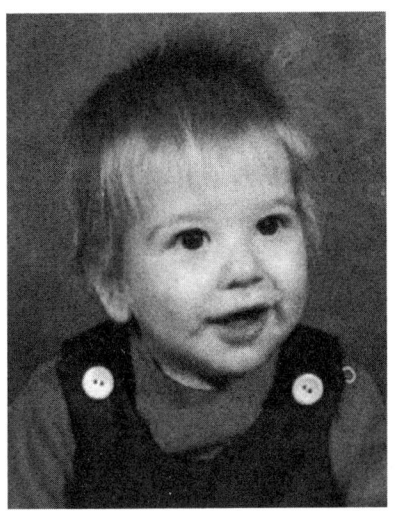

Larry Dewayne Krebbs
Missing 3/30/88, Lake Texoma, Oklahoma
Age at Disappearance: 2 years
2'4", 35 lbs

Larry Krebbs and his son were on the third day of a camping trip to Lake Texoma in southeastern Oklahoma. Larry and Dewayne were walking on the bank of a river that feeds the lake and were gathering firewood. The two were fifty feet from the river with the father walking in front by maybe eight paces and the son walking to the rear. A September 11 article in the *Daily Democrat* states how Larry recounts facts of the disappearance: "He says that he walked ahead of his son and when he turned around and looked, Dewayne was gone. He recalls never hearing a splash or any noise."

The article went on to report that investigators did follow a pair of small child's footprints that led to a small puddle and then didn't come out.

The disappearance of Larry Dewayne Krebbs occurred at the far northern end of Lake Texoma on the stretch of the lake where historic Fort Washita is located. This area has the Confederate Cemetary and some extremely remote and desolate areas. The area directly surrounding the river is lush with vegetation.

There was a massive search for the young boy, which did include the nearby river being dragged for a body, but nothing was found. Almost fifteen years after the incident, Larry's father contacted a psychic and asked for assistance in finding his son. The psychic stated that someone had abducted the boy, put his hand over his mouth, and took him away.

Case Summary:

This is another case in which I believe the father, but that facts almost defy belief. Child molesters and abductors go to great lengths to ensure their identity is hidden, and they are never seen. The idea that someone hid in the bushes, waited for the Krebbs to walk by (just eight paces behind his dad), jump out and then grab the boy and run off, is far-fetched and seems impossible. The person committing this crime would have to be extraordinarily fast, strong, stealthy, and know the area and a route to escape very well. Remember, the risk of an abductor being caught in the middle of nowhere trying to take a child could be very severe. How would the abductor know that the father wouldn't turn back and look at the precise minute that he or she was taking the child, unless this occurred with unusual speed and precision?

It appears that larry walked into a small puddle and was taken before he walked out, thus no tracks leaving the puddle. This is another of a long line of cases where children are taken while in very close proximity to their parents.

Larry Krebbs has never been found.

Ernest Matthew Cook
Missing April 22, 1999, Bache, Oklahoma
Age at Disappearance: 27 years
5'10", 180 lbs

Ernest Cook was living in a camper on property belonging to his grandfather in a rural area of Bache, Oklahoma. Cook was recently divorced and the father of two young girls. On the night of April 22, 1999 at 10:30 p.m. his father was driving Cook back to his camper. Ernest's father stated that his son got out of his truck, started to walk toward a wooded area that kept the camper, and he waved goodbye. That was the last time he was seen.

John Cook went back to the camper the next day to check on his son and found he was not in the camper. He did find his overnight bag in the camper; it was open with his shoes on top along with clean clothes and photos of his girls. John searched the immediate area and didn't see his son. Two days later John returned to the camp with his father and they both searched the area. Two hundred yards from the camper and out in the pasture they found Ernest's sleeping bag and pillow. The two continued to look, and further past the sleeping bag, they found a small road. In the middle of the dirt road, they found a barefoot track on the right side and a boot track on the right side. As they pushed down the road and toward a mud puddle, they again found another barefoot track and another boot track.

John Cook was later interviewed and stated he does not believe that his son left his camper voluntarily.

The location of this incident is in rural southeastern Oklahoma. It is located south of Eufala and south of Oknoname Reservoir. McAlester is just west of the city of Dow. This region of Oklahoma has thick underbrush and lots of water is in the vicinity. The specific location that Ernest disappeared is very remote.

Case Summary:

It appears as though something occurred to Ernest while he was sleeping in his camper. It would also appear that he was not wearing his shoes and was in his sleeping bag when his sleep was interrupted. The question is, was he grabbed and carried while in his sleeping bag, or was he forced to carry the bag and pillow? The idea of carrying the sleeping bag for warmth may make some sense, but the idea of carrying the pillow makes very little sense.

We don't know if Ernest made the barefoot marks in the mud or someone else did. We also don't know if the boot marks were previously there or if the person with Ernest made the marks. We also do not know whether Ernest had made the barefoot marks or whether they had been there several days. There are many aspects of this story that need further study and investigation.

This case is somewhat similar to the disappearance of Stephanie Stewart from a lookout tower in Alberta Canada. It appears that Stephanie disappeared in the middle of the night along with her sheets, blanket and pillow. Refer to Missing-411 Western United States for details on Stephanie's disappearance.

Gloria McDonald
Missing 1/26/01, Queen Wilhelmina State Park, Arkansas
Age at Disappearance: 68 years
5'6", 120 lbs
Red Hair

Daniel McDonald, his wife Gloria and their son Sean and his girlfriend Erin Jemmott decided to spend January 26, 2001 hiking a trail in the 460-acre Queen Wilhelmina State Park. The group started their day with breakfast at the McDonalds' restaurant in their hometown of Mena. Sean was in town from Florida visiting with his girlfriend. After breakfast, the group arrived at the park and walked to the trailhead. The ground in the area was very wet and there were a lot of trees and shrubs on the ground because of a recent storm

The group decided to hike a trail called "Lovers Leap." Everyone in the group enjoyed the outdoors except Gloria. She was a city person, but Gloria was a good sport and started to hike the muddy trail. It was an early Friday afternoon, and there was nobody on the trails, and the group didn't see anyone in the parking lot. Approximately 250 yards down the trail, the group encountered large trees blocking their path. It was at this point that Gloria decided she wanted nothing more to do with hiking. She told the group that she was going to hike back to the gift shop and would meet them there.

After Gloria left the group, Daniel, Sean, and Erin continued down the trail for another thirty minutes and then turned around and headed back. It was approximately 2:00 or 2:30 p.m. when the group finally reached the parking lot. They looked for Gloria in the gift shop and snack bar but didn't find her. They checked their car and found that her purse was inside just as she had left it. The McDonalds now notified park officials.

A massive search was started immediately. Gloria was a reporter for the *Mena Star* newspaper and was a very sharp and wise woman. It would have been hard not to spot Gloria, as she was wearing a bright yellow jacket and had red hair. Aerial searches, ground teams, and others scoured the park and the surrounding land for Gloria. She was never found.

For some reason law enforcement focused on Daniel as the primary suspect. This is an odd person to focus on since Gloria was last seen by three people leaving their presence simultaneously. Daniel stayed with the group. All three of the witnesses were interviewed separately, and still the focus was on Daniel. He became so frustrated with law enforcement that he demanded to take a polygraph test. They complied and he passed.

Case Summary:

This is a case in which it appears that law enforcement didn't place enough emphasis on the search and focused too heavily on the husband as a suspect. If three people all claim to have seen Gloria leave their presence, then Gloria left their presence on her own. Nobody in the park claims they ever saw Gloria except the group. It appears that Gloria was forcibly taken off the trail somewhere in the 250 yards between the parking lot and where the trees blocked the trail, and that's where law enforcement should have and hopefully did focus their search efforts. There is no mention in any documentation if SAR teams used canines but hopefully they did.

In an unrelated article to the disappearance of Gloria but related to the park, I did find an article about Queen Wilhelmina parks trails being closed. An article dated July 12, 2010 on *NWA* online states that all trails inside the park will be closed until further notice: "Due to increased wildlife activity." In all my years of researching activity in local, state, and national parks I have never seen that wording used. I can't ever remember a park or its trails being closed in the United States for any reason other than bear attacks in Yellowstone or Glacier National Park, and that wasn't the reason cited in this park release.

Case Comparison

The Gloria McDonald disappearance is very similar to the disappearance of Thelma Pauline Melton on September 25, 1981 from the Great Smoky Mountains National Park. Thelma was walking a trail with friends and started to walk faster than the others, who eventually lost sight of her. The group was heading toward the parking lot where their trailers and campers were located. When the group got back to the parking lot, Thelma hadn't arrived and was never seen again. A subsequent search for several days failed to find any evidence of what happened to Thelma.

Christopher L. Jones
Missing 4/5/06, Holland, Arkansas
Age at Disappearance: 37 years
6', 150 lbs

Holland, Arkansas, is located twenty miles north of Little Rock and twenty miles east of the Ozark and Quachita National Forests. Parts of the perimeter of the city can be quite remote. Chris Jones lived in one of those remote sections of the city in his house trailer. He had a white picket fence surrounding his property and a large creek running to the rear. Chris had just returned home prior to his disappearance. He was in the hospital with a severe case of gout that had struck both of his legs, making it almost impossible to walk. He was using two crutches to move around.

On April 5, friends and family went to visit Chris and found his front door closed, not locked. His crutches were leaning on his favorite chair. His vehicle was parked in his driveway, and nothing appeared to be moved or stolen. Shane Dickson is Chris's cousin and was interviewed during the investigation. Shane stated," It was obvious that he was probably carried out of there, but we don't know how, who, or why."

There were continuous ground and air searches of Cadron Creek and the property surrounding the trailer. Nothing of value was ever found. Chris had a daughter who was away at the time of his disappearance; she died in an auto accident three months after Chris disappeared. The family hoped that Chris would surface for the funeral, but he didn't. The family knew that if Chris didn't come to the funeral, this had to have a bad ending; he loved his daughter very much.

Law enforcement officials stated that Chris did not have a criminal record, was not under investigation for anything, and was working as an electrician prior to his onset of gout.

Case Summary:

I think it's obvious to all involved that Chris is probably deceased; he wouldn't have missed the funeral of his daughter. It's also obvious that Chris could not have walked out of the area of his home because of his disability, gout. The real question that puzzles everyone—who carried Chris Jones off his property and why?

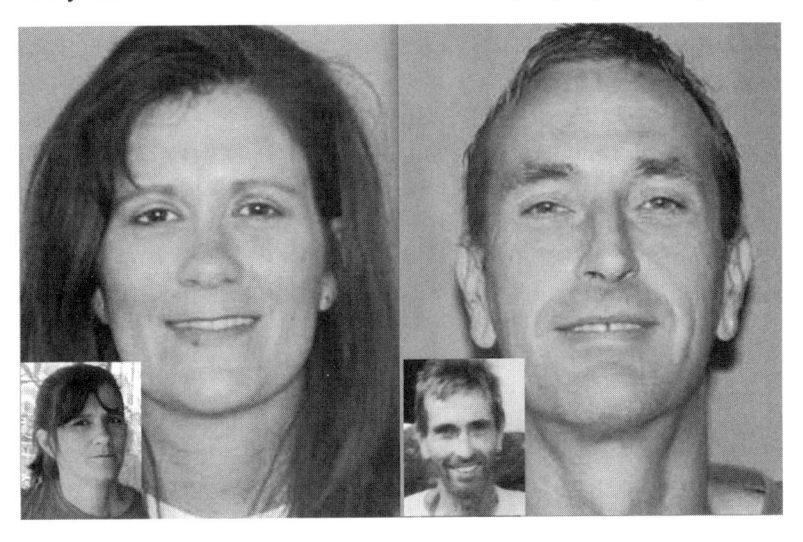

Madyson Jamison, Age at Disappearance: 5 years
Sherilynn Jamison, Age at Disappearance: 40 years, 5'7", 105 lbs
Bobby Jamison, Age at Disappearance: 44 years, 6'3", 180 lbs
Missing 10/07/09, 2:00 p.m.

One of the biggest and most unusual cases of missing people in the history of the state of Oklahoma is the case of the Jamison Family. Madyson, Sherilynn, and Bobby Jamison left their Eufala Lakeside residence and drove sixty miles to Panola Mountain in eastern Oklahoma. They were visiting a forty-acre plot of land that used to have a natural gas well on site. It has since been removed. The site is reached by way of taking a seven-mile-long dirt road.

The family met the owner of the land at the site, and he gave them a short tour. The family asked if they could stay behind and walk the property. The owner said that was fine. The owner indicated that he left the Jamisons and their truck on the site.

Several days after the Jamisons visited the well site, others in the area saw the Jamisons truck sitting on the dirt road just feet outside of the site they were visiting and called authorities. Latimer County Sheriff Deputies arrived at the location and found the Jamison truck with camper parked at the site with the Jamisons dog (Mazy) in the shell starving and dehydrated. Deputies removed the dog and searched the truck.

In a highly unusual find, deputies searched the Jamison's front driving area of the truck and found $32,000 in cash under the front seat, everyone's identification and wallets, and cell phones all in the car. They also found the family's overcoats.

Latimer County Sheriff initiated a massive search of the surrounding area. The search included a FLIR helicopter, FBI, and Oklahoma Bureau of Investigation (OBI) agents. The search lasted two weeks, and they essentially found nothing.

Immediately after searchers initiated their SAR, the sky opened up and a massive rainstorm hit the area and deeply impeded search efforts.

The FBI agreed to leave an agent on this case while OBI investigated the incident. OBI and sheriff deputies continued to interview neighbors of the family and friends. The family had been in a severe accident in their past and had a sizeable recovery. The investigation revealed that it was known that the family routinely traveled with significant amounts of money, so finding the cash in the truck wouldn't be unusual.

A short time after the initial search had been completed, the FBI, in a surprising move took this case and now has primary responsibility for follow-up.

Case Summary:

There have been several rumors about this family and the possible results of their disappearance. One of the rumors is that the family committed suicide, but I don't think so. The family took their dog and met with someone about purchasing property. If a family had decided to take their own lives, I think they would have gone directly to a remote location and done it. I also don't believe the family would have left the beloved family dog in the truck to suffer and possibly starve to death. It doesn't make sense. If the family had walked off to take their own lives, decomposition and and the associated odors would make finding the multiple bodies much easier.

I suppose it is possible that the family was followed to that location and stalked until the witness left and then was approached and abducted. The issue: it is very difficult to abduct three people without significant resources and personnel. If two people decide to fight one abductor, they have a good chance of winning the battle and disarming the culprit. There was no blood found at the scene, so there wasn't a struggle or battle.

The location where their truck was found is peculiar. The truck was located just off the dirt road, just feet outside the site they were visiting. It would appear that they started to leave and pulled over to stop. There was a camera found in the truck, and the sheriff developed the film. One photo shows the daughter standing against a backdrop at the site location with her arms crossed not looking at the camera, almost in a defiant pose.

The weather in the area during this time wasn't great. It was cold, and the idea that the family voluntarily left the area on a hike without their coats isn't a realistic scenario. They would take their coats.

If a crime did occur against this family, robbery wasn't the motive. The family's wallets, $32,000 in cash, and cell phones were all in the cab of the truck and undisturbed. There is no cell phone reception in the area, so if the family went for a hike, they would not have taken their phones.

The disappearance of the Jamisons is another of a long line of disappearances in the area of the Kiamichi Mountains that cannot be explained. In 2010, the FBI asked OBI if it could take over the investigation on the Jamison case. That agency was given the file. The FBI has not released new details on the Jamison disappearance in several years.

Chapter Summary

The missing people in the Oklahoma/Arkansas border area are in a fairly well-confined region that includes that Quachita and Ozark National Forests and Kiamichi Mountains. The missing in this region start in 1937 with the latest being in 2009, a seventy-two-year span. This is one of the few clusters where there is an escalation of people disappearing—eight people between 1999 and 2009.

SOUTHERN STATES

Alabama

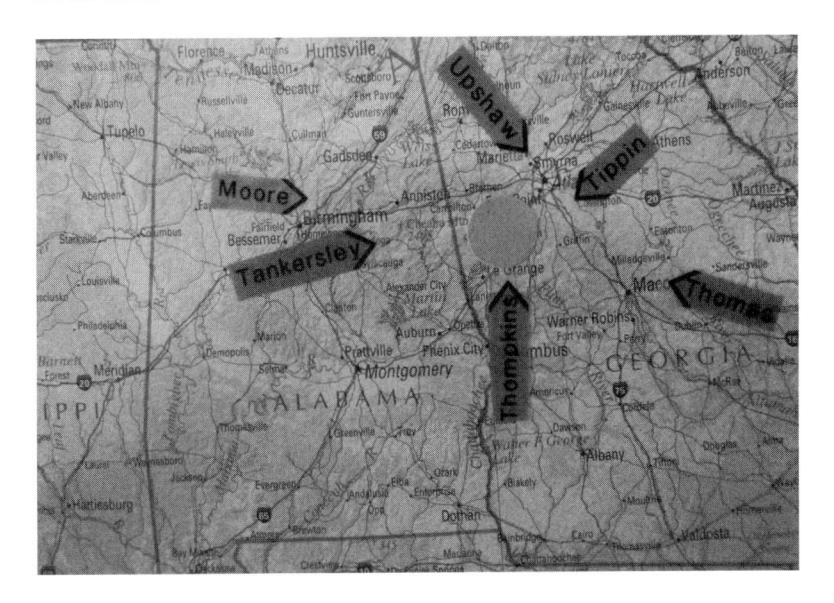

Name	Date Missing•Age•Sex
Rickey Tankersley	2/16/49•2•M
Nora Moore	7/18/55•78•F

Rickey Dunn Tankersley
Missing 2/16/49, 4:30 p.m., Sylacauga, Alabama
Age at Disappearance: 2 years

    L.C. Tankersley and his family lived in a rural area of Sylacauga, Alabama. On February 16, 1949 at approximately 4:30 p.m., Mrs. Tankersley realized that she couldn't find Rickey. She also realized that the family's two terrier dogs were missing. Mrs. Tankersley contacted her husband, who asked neighbors for assistance to search the area. The family and friends looked for the boy until 10:00 p.m. and then called law enforcement.

At the height of the search 750 professionals and volunteers were looking for little Rickey Tankersley. The search was separated into two specific areas, with each group working its confined region.

Searchers combed the woods for over sixteen hours until one lone volunteer found the boy in tall grass on the side of a mountain, four miles from his home. That lone searcher was Rickey's father. L. C. Tankersley had spoken to a psychic who had told him where to search for his son—it worked! When Rickey's father came upon the boy, he found him asleep and guarded by the two terriers. When he became semiconscious, Rickey mumbled something that was not understood. He was rushed to a hospital where it was reported that he was in satisfactory condition. Rickey continued to fade into and out of consciousness until he was hospitalized. The boy eventually fully recovered, but he could remember little of his journey.

Nora Moore
Missing 7/18/55, 4:00 p.m., Gardendale, Alabama
Age at Disappearance: 78 years

Approximately fifteen miles north of Birmingham Alabama is the small town of Gardendale. Mrs. Nora Moore was living in an elderly living facility in a rural area of Gardendale when she went outside for an afternoon of sun. At approximately 4:00 p.m. on July 18, Mrs. Moore had disappeared. Officials from the home searched the immediate area of the residence for the woman and could not find her. The people who managed the home were surprised they couldn't find Mrs. Moore because she had severe ankle and hip injuries that greatly inhibited her ability to walk.

The formal search for Mrs. Moore lasted six days. Searchers found nothing for the first five days, which had them greatly concerned. On the sixth day, a searcher was one-fourth of a mile from the home when the searcher found Mrs. Moore lying on her side near a creek in a semi-conscious condition. She was missing her shoes and her stockings, and she complained that someone was continually throwing water on her while she was out in the woods. She could never explain who was throwing the water.

Mrs. Moore was taken to the hospital and found to be in satisfactory condition considering six days in the woods. As searchers were carrying her from the forest, they found broomsage in the pockets of her sweater. The searchers asked her where she got the broomsage, and she could not explain it. When Mrs. Moore was later questioned about the six days in the woods, she couldn't remember what had happened to her or how she got to where she was found. She had briar scratches over her entire body, but she was in better condition than many searchers thought she should be.

How Mrs. Moore evaded airplanes, searchers, and others for nearly six days is a true question. Many believe she was placed in the location where she was eventually found, and she was some place else during the majority of the search. How and where she got the broomsage is another million-dollar question. Who was throwing water on the woman is another question that was never answered. The fact that she had briar scratches over her body indicates that she was probably carried through the patches, as it was nearly impossible for her to walk.

Broomsage is an eatable perennial shrub with a delightful fragrance that thrives in the southwestern portion of the United States. How the broomsage got to Alabama and into Nora Moore's pocket is a fascinating question.

Georgia Missing Persons

View the Alabama Map for Details on Georgia Missing

Every missing person on the Georgia list is a male.

Name	Date Missing•Age
Murray Upshaw, Jr.	11/08/40•2
	**62-year gap
Christopher Thompkins	01/25/02•20
David Tippin	08/01/04•4
Jeremy Thomas	02/16/07•22

Murray Upshaw, Jr.
Missing 11/8/40, Noon, 13 Miles North of Cartersville, Georgia
Age at Disappearance: 2 years

Betty and Murray Upshaw ran a farm thirteen miles north of Cartersville and four hundred yards off the Knoxville Highway. This was a rural location with few neighbors.

At noon on November 8, 1940, Betty looked out her back window and saw Murray, Jr. (two years) playing near the tractor in the back yard. There was a small lawn, and then thick forests started behind the tractor and barn. Betty looked into the backyard minutes later and Murray was gone. She ran into the backyard yelling Murray's name but did not receive an answer. She ran more quickly and covered more area and still couldn't find her son and then realized that their eight-month-old terrier puppy, Nickie, that was playing with Murray was also gone. She remembered that it had been only minutes since she last saw the boy and he couldn't have gone far being just two years old. When Betty couldn't find her son, she summoned neighbors and police to assist with the search.

Hours after Murray disappeared there were hundreds of volunteers and police combing the Upshaw ranch. The search was very organized, and people thought they were doing a thorough job. Hours after Murray left and in the middle of the search, heavy rains hit the area of the Upshaw farm, rains that didn't stop for over two days.

Within the first thirty-six hours of Murray's disappearance, Murray, Sr. told the press that he felt his son had been kidnapped. He didn't think that his son could get outside the search zone and not have been found at this point.

Three days into the search volunteers were looking two miles from the farm in a very rugged area and found "Nickie" walking. They picked the puppy up and brought it back to the Upshaw's. To the amazement of everyone, including the sheriff, Nickie was dry, clean, and well fed; she was not hungry even though she had been gone for over seventy hours. A November 12, 1940 article in the *Pittsburgh Times* stated the following:

In addition to being dry and clean (referring to Nickie), it had been fed so recently that it declined food, Sgt. Culbertson said. The dog had been missing for over 70 hours. Sullivan termed these circumstances 'peculiar' and 'suspicious' but added quickly that no clues to substantiate a kidnapping theory had been uncovered.

Further, the article states,

Everything else in that section is wet from the rain, said Major Len Sullivan, State Highway Patrol Chief. We can't explain how the dog came out of the woods without being wet unless somebody brought him there in the car.

On the fourth day of formal searching, Murray's body was found at the base of a pine tree on a rugged mountainside one and a half miles from his home. A November 13 article in the *St. Petersburg Times* described the boy's body: "Slight scratches appeared on the child's arms and legs, and his nose was bashed in." Later the same article states, "Searchers said that leaves and pine twigs near the body indicated the little dog had bedded down beside his master for at least part of the time since the child disappeared."

After Murray's body was discovered, Bartow County Sheriff George W. Gaddis went to the scene and then gave a press conference. A *San Jose Mercury News* article on November 12 stated, "George W. Gaddis called for an immediate inquest."

Several articles stated that Murray's body did not show any signs of violence even though one article did note the note scratches and bruises. The inquest concluded that Murray died from exhaustion and exposure, a typical conclusion when there is little evidence of anything else.

Case Summary:

As in many of the cases in which a two-year-old is missing from a rural setting, there are questions about the disappearance and the condition of the body. What really happened to Murray's nose? There is one mention in one paper about this condition. Nobody else wanted to mention it. Scratches and bruises about the body may be normal, but why was Murray on a rugged hillside? Children do not normally walk uphill when lost!

Several articles state that Nickie is believed to have been lying next to Murray because ground around him was pressed down and twigs were broken. An eight-month old terrier is a very small dog, how do they know it was Nickie? There was no mention of Nickie's hair found at the scene, so how did they come to their conclusions?

Several articles stated that Murray died seventy-plus hours after he disappeared, which means he died relatively soon after disappearing. Because they claim that Nickie was lying next to Murray, is the implication that the dog sat there the entire time? If the dog hadn't sat there, why wasn't the dog soaking wet and hungry? Nickie was found on the other side of the mountain more than a half-mile from Murray. Why wasn't he wet?

I think it's important to note the location of the farm in relationship to some geographical features of Georgia. The huge Allatoona Lake is less than two miles from the Upshaw property, and the Red Top Mountain State Park is less than three miles from the property.

In conclusion, the sheriff felt there was enough of a suspicion surrounding this entire event that he called for an inquest into the case. I believe there are many points about the disappearance of Murray that deserve a second look. I could not find another article that discussed the results of the inquest.

Christopher Thompkins
Missing 1/25/02, Ellerslie, Georgia
Age at Disappearance: 20 years
5'9", 130 lbs

Mrs. Ann McKenzie is the mother of Chris Thompkins. Ann was the babysitter for a man who owned a surveying company, and Ann's son (Chris) worked for him on his four-man team.

On January 25, 2002, Ann stated that Chris left the home at 8:10 a.m. and drove to the surveyor's office where he parked his car and rode to the work site with the business owner. Chris worked the morning hours with the three other men without any incident. Shortly after lunch, all of the workers were walking on the shoulder of Highway 85 between County Line Road and Warm Springs Road. The employees were approximately fifty feet apart walking the highway. When work associates last saw Chris, he was near the back of the group and near the side of the road. A minute more passed and the crew looked behind them and Chris was gone, completely disappeared.

There was a tall barbed wire fence between the shoulder of the road and the private property that borders the highway. When fellow employees went back to the area where Chris was last seen, they found one of Chris's boots lying near the fence and some coins lying near the boots on the grass. They also found tools that Chris had on him lying and scattered on the ground near the fence.

The owner of the surveying business did call Chris's mother and explained what had happened. They waited until 4:15 p.m. and tried to report him to the sheriff as a missing person, but the sheriff would not take a report until he was missing twenty-four hours. Well, the twenty-four hours passed, and an investigation started. Sheriffs found a piece of blue cloth on the barbed wire near where his boot was found, and it was fiber that matched the blue jeans he was wearing.

The area on the other side of the barbed wire fence was best described as heavily wooded with swamps, snakes, and very thick vegetation, a place most wouldn't want to go.

Almost a year after the disappearance of Christopher, the owner of the land where Chris would have had to cross once over the fence reported to the sheriff that he found Chris's other boot in the field. This piece of evidence was turned over to the sheriff.

Case Summary:

This disappearance is one of the most unusual I've ever read about. It's been over eight years since Chris disappeared, and nobody has heard from him. I believe that this shows that something very bad happened to Chris when he went over the barbed wire. I don't believe this was a voluntary disappearance.

Details from the scene make me believe that Chris was involved in a struggle—a struggle that ended up with Chris getting either knocked down or turned sideways so that coins and tools fell from his pocket.

There is no way anyone would walk the area on the other side of the barbed wire fence without boots or shoes. There is no logical reason someone would take his shoes off if he wanted to voluntarily leave the job site. It appears that Chris might have been dragged over the fence because cloth was found on the barbed wire. If someone is carried or turned sideways, tools, coins and personal items may fall from their pockets, as happened in this case.

Jeremy Thomas
Missing 2/16/07, 2:20 p.m., Tobesofkee Creek, Macon, Georgia
Age at Disappearance: 22 years
6', 235 lbs

On Thursday, February 15, Thomas left his home and went to Tobesofkee Creek to fish with his friend. Both men arrived late and spent the night. The next morning at 8:00 a.m. Thomas called his fiancée and told her they were putting the boat in the water to fish. This was the last time the outside world spoke to Jeremy.

Both friends fished until 2:00 p.m. when Jeremy's friend stated that he was tired and cold and called his girlfriend. The girlfriend picked the friend up and left Jeremy alone in the boat. Jeremy never came home and was reported missing.

On February 17, the Bibb County sheriffs found Jeremy's boat with his personal belongings still inside. The items were shown to Jeremy's family, and they confirmed that they belonged to their son.

The sheriff conducted a search with fifty professional and volunteer searchers and could not find any evidence of what happened to Jeremy.

David Tippin
Missing 8/1/04, AM Hours, Stockbridge, Georgia
Age at Disappearance: 4 years
Red Hair/ Disabled

Sometime early in the morning on August 1, 2004, little David Tippin woke before his parents, unlocked the rear door of his rural home, and disappeared into the wild countryside south of Atlanta.

Stacey and Robert, David's parents, awoke to attend Sunday morning church. Robert went to David's room and found that he was gone and the rear door was open. He went into the rear yard, called for David, and did not receive a response. A call to emergency services brought an immediate response from law enforcement. The Tippins told law enforcement that their son was mildly autistic. The call for searchers brought off duty firemen, local residents, and many on-duty law enforcement personnel.

Sunday afternoon brought a response of several canine teams to search for David. The dog teams reportedly took the searchers to a number of neighbors' homes, and for two days they could not find the boy.

On Tuesday morning, a mile from the Tippin residence, Bobby Hinton (seventy years old) noticed floodlights on at his rental house on his property. The home was used predominantly for storage, and he knew that the front floodlight should not be on unless someone had activated the motion sensor. Bobby walked to the home and found the rear door unlocked and partially opened. Bobby looked inside and saw a small lump on the floor in front of the refrigerator. He walked toward it and found David Tippin unconscious and on the floor in front of the refrigerator. Bobby picked the boy up and brought him back to his main home where he met with his wife, Martha. Martha woke the boy and fed him cookies and milk as Bobby called the police. The boy was quickly taken back to his residence.

Robert Tippin stated that David suffered scratches, bug bites, and was moderately dehydrated. An August 3, 2004 article in the *Elizabethon Star* stated the following: "The house where David was found had been searched Sunday." This same item appeared the following day in the Albany Herald, confirming the Hinton home had been searched.

According to an article dated August 4, 2004 in the *Atlanta Constitution*: "The boy (when found) was barefoot and wearing a *Finding Nemo* T-shirt."

Case Summary:

What would have caused David to leave the comfort of his home and wander in the woods? Where was David when the Hinton home was searched and nothing was found inside? Did David wander the woods shoeless for three days, and, if so, why weren't there any notations about cuts and bruises to his feet, just a notation of scratches on his body and face. Why didn't the canines find David if they were on his scent?

The area in which David disappeared is less then one-quarter mile from the Clayton County Reservoir and four other small lakes in that immediate area. Readers should start to make note that many of the disappearances occur in close proximity to wilderness areas, lakes rivers, streams, forest preserves and parks.

Chapter Conclusion

I think it's interesting that there are two distinct groups of missing people in Georgia. Two males very young in age and two adults near twenty in age. The two age groupings are not seen anywhere else in North America. Only males are missing in Georgia.

APPALACHIANS

Great Smoky Mountains National Park and region

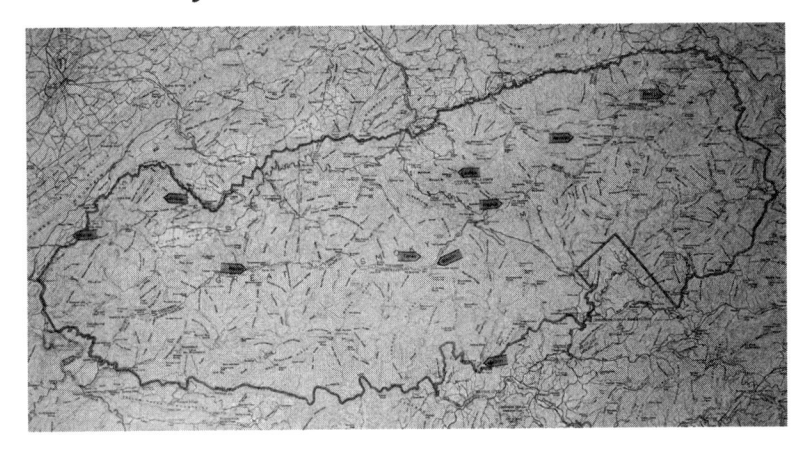

The Great Smoky Mountains National Park straddles North Carolina and Tennessee. The mountains have had a very long and rich human history from prehistoric Paleo Indians to settlements by the Europeans and later by loggers harvesting trees. Arrowheads found inside the park have been dated as nine thousand years old.

The park has 521,085 acres with 276,343 in North Carolina and 244,741 in Tennessee. There were nine million visitors in 2008, and the park had the highest number of visitors of any of the fifty-eight National Parks (Yosemite was number three with 3.4 million visitors). Ten campgrounds with 1000 sites accommodate 350,000 campers annually. There are 2,115 miles of streams and rivers, 384 miles of roads, of which 238 are paved. Clingman's Dome at 6,643' is the high point in the park with Abrams Creek at 875' as the lowest elevation. There are 800 miles of back-country trails that 400,00 hikers use every year at some level or distance. Seventy miles of the Appalachian Trail go through the park.

Great Smoky Mountains National Park has an annual budget of $18.2 million. The park employs 250 permanent employees and 100 seasonal workers.

**The Great Smoky Mountains (GSM) National Park website claims that the park generates $718 million a year for the surrounding communities.

Several of the people on this list disappeared inside Great Smoky Mountains National Park but others went missing in the outlying region.

Alphabetical list of missing people in the Great Smoky Mountains National Park Region

Name	Date Missing•Age•Sex
Auberry, Michael	03/17/07•12•M
Davenport, Larry	07/17/83•20•M
Edwards, Bonnie Lee	01/09/65•9•F
Gibson, Trenny Lynn	10/08/76•16•F
Hague, Geoffrey	02/07/70•16•M
Hanson, Mark	03/07/75•21•M
Haun, Minnie	10/08/57•3•F
Hearon, Michael Edwin	08/23/08•51•M
Lavies, Brad	03/28/93•13•M
Lindsey, Eloise	11/04/89•22•F
Lorimer, Evangeline	06/08/51•21•F
Martin, Dennis Lloyd	06/14/64•7•M
Melton, Thelma Pauline	09/25/81•58•F
Ramsay, Abe Carroll	03/11/19•3•M
Reel, Michael	07/02/83•8•M
Toney, Jay Charles	05/25/82•17•M

GSM Missing People by Dates

A few issues with the list below need to be highlighted. As with most lists in both books, there are consistencies, you just need to look. In the GSM list by dates, you will notice that two to three males go missing and then two females go missing. The pattern is consistent. If the list stays consistent as it has in the past, either one more male will go missing followed by two females or it will directly go to two females. Starting in 1951 there is almost a consistent five to seven years between groups of missing.

Name	Date Missing•Age•Sex
Ramsay, Abe Carroll	03/11/19•3•M
Lorimer, Evangeline	06/08/51•21•F
Haun, Minnie	10/08/57•3•F
Martin, Dennis Lloyd	06/14/64•7•M
Edwards, Bonnie Lee	01/09/65•9•F
Hague, Geoffrey	02/07/70•16•M
Hanson, Mark	03/07/75•21•M
Gibson, Trenny Lynn	10/08/76•16•F
Melton, Thelma Pauline	09/25/81•58•F
Toney, Jay Charles	05/25/82•17•M
Reel, Michael	07/02/83•8•M
Davenport, Larry	07/17/83•20•M
Lindsey, Eloise	11/04/89•22•F
Lavies, Brad	03/28/93•13•M
Auberry, Michael	03/17/07•12•M
Hearon, Michael Edwin	08/23/08•51•M

16 Cases
10 Males
6 Females

4 Cases in March (All Males)
2 Cases in June
2 Cases July—Both in the same year.
2 Cases October

Gibson and Melton (females) disappeared on a Friday
4 Males disappeared on a Saturday
3 Males disappeared on a Sunday

Michael Auberry
Missing 3/17/07, 1:00 p.m., Doughton Park, North Carolina
Age at Disappearance: 12 years
Last seen wearing red coat, pants

Doughton Park is a rural seven thousand-acre heavily wooded area near McGrady, North Carolina. The park contains many of the old settlements from pioneers and is known for its trout fishing and many miles of hiking trails. Doughton Park is a state park approximately one hundred miles northeast from the Great Smoky Mountains National Park but in the same mountain range.

In mid-March 2007, Michael Auberry went camping with his Boy Scout troop into the wilds of Doughton Park. On Saturday, March 17, Michael had slept late and found himself in camp with another leader. Michael stayed in camp and ate lunch when the other scouts returned. At approximately 1:00 p.m. the other boys realized that Michael was missing and notified the adults. A cursory search of the area around the campsite was completed, but the boy wasn't located. Authorities were notified.

Late in the first night that Michael was missing, searchers found the boy's mess kit less than a mile from camp. Searchers thought they were converging on the boy and felt positive. National Park Service, State Park Service, and county and state personnel all assisted in the search for Michael. Searchers were compromised at an early point when rain hit the search area and hindered the SAR process. During the first few days of the search, SAR commanders brought in a FLIR-equipped helicopter that combed the area where the boy was missing, but, unfortunately, they didn't find anything useful.

When Monday morning arrived and Michael was still not found, searchers became alarmed and felt that foul play may be involved, as they couldn't find a reason why they hadn't found the boy. In a very strange turn of events, the FBI arrived at the SAR center and stated that they were monitoring the search for Michael. The FBI does not participate on searches for missing people, ever. They are only involved when a crime has occurred, and that crime must usually cross state lines for their jurisdiction to be activated. They will become involved in some crimes at the request of the local jurisdiction. I find it highly unusual that an FBI agent would be monitoring this case at this early stage unless they knew something that the press hadn't been told. But, we must remember there are a few children missing under highly unusual conditions from the Great Smoky Mountains National Park just one hundred miles south. Perhaps the FBI is quietly monitoring this area.

Three days after Michael disappeared, searchers were approximately one mile from where he was last seen and saw the boy near a creek. A March 21, 2007 article in the *Washington Post* said that searchers found the boy disoriented but able to talk with searchers. A March 21 *Fox News* story stated the following: "Auberry (Father) said Michael still hasn't been able to tell them the whole story of what happened to him. He's not aware of how many days he was out there."

After Michael was found, the press was notified that local law enforcement had issued an area-wide missing person alert as a precaution should the boy have gotten outside the search area. Wow, I know that this isn't usually done. When children are lost in the woods, they are usually really lost. The idea that local law enforcement got the FBI involved and then made an area-wide alert tells me that someone somewhere had concerns that weren't expressed to the press.

This is one of the few times in which an SAR in the Great Smoky Mountains area was successful in finding a young person alive. This is another case in which Michael should be politely but intensely interviewed to understand all of the facets behind his disappearance. An understanding of what happened to Michael may help searchers in this area the next time a person goes missing. To completely understand what happened to Michael, he may need to go through hypnosis.

Bonnie Lee Edwards
Missing 01/09/65, 4:30 p.m., Pilot Mountain, North Carolina
Age at Disappearance: 9 years

The Edwards and their eight children lived on a tenant farm 1.5 miles outside of Pilot Mountain, North Carolina. The farm is approximately one hundred miles northeast of the Great Smoky Mountain National Park but is included in this chapter due to its relative proximity. The area of the Edwards' residence has many farms surrounded by thick woods.

On January 9, 1965, Bonnie was playing with neighbor children in an area that was in sight of the girl's farm. Bonnie always stayed close to home because of a disability that gave her the age of a six-year-old. As she was playing with the children, she told them she was getting tired and heading home. She was last seen walking directly toward her farmhouse. When Bonnie never arrived home, her parents called law enforcement. It was approximately 4:30 p.m.

The Surry County Sheriff was placed in charge of the SAR and within hours he had over one thousand local volunteers, firemen, police officers, and National Guard on scene looking for Bonnie. The National Guard brought a helicopter and supplies to aid in the search.

On January 10 at approximately 4:00 p.m., a local farmer who was assisting in the search found Bonnie curled up in a brush pile within view of her residence. The girl was dead. According to a January 11, 1965 article in the *Florence Morning News*, doctors had the following statement: "Dr. Henry Newsome, Pilot County physician examined the body at the request of the coroner, a dentist. Dr. Newsome said the child died of exposure early Sunday morning."

Wow, the coroner was a dentist? It appears that there was not a medical examiner to check the condition of Bonnie. That was unfortunate.

The night that Bonnie disappeared temperatures dropped to thirty-nine degrees. There were hundreds of searchers everywhere around the Edwards' residence. The specific area where Bonnie was located had been searched three more times throughout the night without finding her. It makes no sense that Bonnie wouldn't have seen and heard searchers if she had died early Sunday morning—impossible!

Since Surry County did not have a medical examiner, no autopsy was made so a thorough exam of Bonnie's body was never completed, so it was merely a presumption she died of exposure. We will never truly know what happened to Bonnie Lee Edwards.

Trenny Lynn Gibson
Missing 10/8/76, 3:00 p.m., Great Smoky Mountains National Park
Age at Disappearance: 16 years
5'3", 115 lbs

Details regarding the disappearance of Trenny Gibson were obtained through a FOIA request and through review of numerous newspaper articles. The NPS sent a box full of reports that outlined the search and subsequent investigation into Trenny Gibson's disappearance. The official NPS case number is 762590.

On October 8, 1976, Bearden High School in Knoxville took a group of students for a hike at the Great Smoky Mountains National Park. The school was taking forty children to hike the Appalachian Trail from Andrews Bald to Clingman's Dome. Wayne Dunlap was the school official escorting the students. This hike would be made on the North Carolina side of the park; Trenny Gibson was part of the group of students taking the hike.

During the course of the trek, Trenny had bounced from group to group and had hiked with different people throughout the day. At approximately 3:00 p.m. Trenny was with a group that was three-fourths to one-half mile from the Clingman's Dome parking area. It was at this time that something catastrophic went wrong on the Appalachian Trail—Trenny disappeared.

The area where Trenny was last seen has a very defined trail and is in an area where people probably would not want to leave the established route. I personally went to the area where Trenny walked off the trail and can guarantee that it is not a spot where anyone would want to leave. I can understand maybe stepping off to look at something close by but never stepping off to take another direction in the hike. It is much too steep and rugged. Nothing is on the other side of that trail except miles and miles of rough forests without defined trails. It's hazardous.

The NPS conducted interviews of students who were with Trenny when she vanished. Here is a summary of each person's interview and his or her account of what happened, per the NPS file.

Official *NPS report* regarding its initial response on the night of October 8, 1976: "Weather at this time was strong winds and heavy rain with temperatures in the low 30s. 2115 hours, moderate to heavy rains."

The NPS determined that a full-scale search would start the next morning at 7:00 a.m., but the weather was too detrimental to continue the search at this point.

"A summary of witness statements describe Trenny as studious, athletic, sarcastic but not the type to panic."

"Counselor Dunlap didn't think that Trenny was the runaway type."

Miss Coghill was approximately two hundred feet from Trenny when she made the following observation. "Witness, Miss Coghill states that Trenny bent over on the trail as if looking at something near a flat rock and then disappeared to the right of the trail."

Robert Simpson—He was overheard to say that he had stayed behind the group to track a bear when Trenny went toward the parking area with the group.

10/9 at 2015 hours—Interview with Anita Bounds who was with Trenny when she was last seen. The main group in which Anita was a part stopped to rest and Trenny continued on. "She was on the trail when I last saw her, I looked away and when I looked back Trenny was nowhere in sight. I should have been able to see her if she went up the trail. I checked the area where Trenny was last seen, no trail leading off, very rough, small stream, brush and trees, yelled but no answer."

10/9 at 2044 hours—Phone interview with Bobby Coghill who was in the group with Anita Bounds. "She was up the trail and it looked like Trenny stopped and bent over, then made a right turn off the trail. I checked the spot where

Trenny was last seen. I do not believe that she could have went [sic] off trail at that spot, too rough, rocks, bushes and trees."

10/11 at 9:26 a.m. hours—Commander John Maddox of the Swain County Civil Air Patrol called search headquarters to complain. He had forty men, two doctors, fourteen pilots, and five planes all standing by to assist with the search for Trenny. Due to the lack of cooperation from the park service he took all the people off the search.

**This was a sad side note to the search for Trenny. A large contingent of searchers was available to respond and assist, and the NPS ignored them.

10/13—The FBI officially entered the investigation. The Knoxville division states they are only looking for violations of federal law, and they have found no evidence of a crime so far. The FBI had sent two agents to monitor the case.

10/13 at 0932 hours—A psychic called search headquarters and said he or she "Saw Trenny sitting in a hollow in what might be a bear den or something—rocky area—not a lot of undergrowth—several very large trees, lots of acorns on the ground."

Several reports from specialized searchers outlined what they had done. One specific report from the Swain county rescue squad canine unit had interesting information: "Dog #1 picks up scent at Andrews Bald and heads toward the Forney Creek Trail. Two dogs had hit on this same area."

The official search for Trenny Gibson continued from October 8–22. Ranger John Linahan wrote in his NPS report, "Trails and drainages were walked out as far as Elkmont, in TN, a distance of 15 miles and Fontana Lake in North Carolina, a distance of 13–14 miles."

Three hundred people had participated in the search for Trenny. The search included trackers, dogs, rescue squads, helicopters, airplanes, two additional Army helicopters, deputies, bloodhounds, and German shepherds.

On April 7, 1977, Trenny's father, Robert Gibson had requested the NPS assistance for another extensive search of the location where Trenny was last seen. The community was still quite interested in understanding what happened to the young girl, and hundreds of searchers would have responded. Park Superintendent Bob Gibson wrote that he would allow only twenty-five searchers because he wanted to avoid, "back country use, and, again, to minimize any chance of a circus atmosphere." I can only imagine how frustrated Trenny's parents were at Bob Gibson's response. I can only guess that Bob Gibson felt that damage to the backcountry was more important than finding a missing girl.

There are many inquiries in the Gibson file from law enforcement agencies across North America when they have found a body and are requesting dental charts on Trenny to see if there is a match. There has been no match to date.

The NPS and other law enforcement agencies followed up on almost every conceivable angle of Trenny's life. No suspects were ever arrested, and no confirmed sightings of the sixteen-year-old are in the file.

Case Summary:
Trenny disappeared within sight of a group of fellow students. Multiple student witnesses confirmed that Trenny left the trail approximately one-half mile from the Clingman's Dome parking lot. Witnesses saw her leave at this point, but they couldn't believe she could leave at that location. Another witness even states that she was looking down at something at this same location, and per Anita Bounds, Trenny left the trail near a small creek bed. You will notice that many missing children are found in and around creek beds. I find that Trenny left the trail in a creek bed discomforting.

Prior to Trenny disappearing, Robert Simpson is overheard stating that he was tracking a bear near the area. Understand, a bear did not take Trenny. There would have been screams, blood, and a macabre scene at the point she left the trail. I do find it interesting that Robert Simpson claims to have been tracking a bear at the approximate time Trenny vanishes.

I believe that the key to Trenny's disappearance is what she was looking at just off the trail before she disappeared. Either someone or something pulled her off the trail, or she voluntarily left the trail to investigate it. There is no possible way that a sixteen-year-old girl left the trail voluntarily at that point to hike cross-country—no way!

It's also quite coincidental that heavy rains hit the area of Trenny's disappearance in the same manner that they hit the region of Dennis Martin's disappearance.

I do believe there are many similarities in the Martin and Gibson disappearances that have never been publicly spoken.

Similarities
- Both disappeared within view of friends and family.
- No trace of either person was ever found (clothes, body, etc.).
- Both disappeared in close proximity to the TN/SC state line that divides the park.
- Heavy rains hit the exact area of the disappearance the night that each went missing.
- The incidents occurred in an area where there were many people.
- Other children were in the immediate area of the disappearance.
- The NPS and the FBI refuse to admit abduction had taken place.
- The FBI has refused to release files on either case.
- Both incidents occurred on or very near the Appalachian Trail.

Geoffrey Burns Hague
Missing 2/8/70, 3:20 p.m., Great Smoky Mountains National Park
Age at Disappearance: 16 years
5'11", 130 lbs

It was a cool February morning when Geoffrey Hague left his Morristown home with Boy Scout Troop #95, led by Scoutmaster Eugene Smith. There were three scouts and four adults going to the Great Smoky Mountains National Park to hike the Appalachian Trail. The hike was going to start at Icewater Springs and complete at Newfound Gap. Most of the hiking was at the 5000' elevation, and there was approximately six inches of snow already on the ground. Geoff had three years of scouting and was very familiar with camping and the outdoors. The first night the boys and the head scoutmaster camped at Icewater Springs, and the other two adults returned home.

The scouting group made a fire and ate their dinner in the presence of their head scoutmaster.

On Sunday, February 8, the group collected their belongings and started their hike along the Appalachian Trail. This trail is very well marked with large signs and a very distinct path. At 9:30 a.m. the group had reached the intersection of the Appalachian Trail and the Boulevard Trail, and this is where they took their first rest stop. It was also at this time that the group realized that Geoffrey was lagging behind, not sure why but he was traveling slowly. At 9:30 a.m. the group started westward on the trail for the Newfound Gap parking lot. Geoffrey stated he was going to wait for another scout that was a senior scout and the last person in the line, and they would walk out together.

Scoutmaster Eugene Smith reached the parking lot of Newfound Gap just as snow flurries were starting. The remaining scouts arrived without Geoffrey. The scoutmaster reminded the group that Geoff was going to wait for the last scout, but he had arrived; everyone agreed that they hadn't seen Geoffrey. It was at this point that the three hikers walked the entire route back to Icewater and found no sign of Geoffrey. The group then hiked back to the Boulevard trail intersection and then walked down that trail a distance and didn't see any evidence of Geoffrey. All of the hikers now went straight for the car at Newfound Gap and drove to park headquarters to report Geoffrey as missing. It was now after 3:00 p.m., and there was a heavier snowfall. The scoutmaster and the scouts were puzzled at Geoffrey's disappearance because the trails and signs clearly showed the direction he was supposed to travel.

The park service immediately sent search teams to three different trailheads that were in the area where Geoffrey disappeared. The trails were quickly searched, and Geoff was not found on any of the clearly marked and obvious trails. The group was concerned, but they also knew that Geoffrey was carrying warm clothes, a sleeping bag, food, and had matches.

On Monday, February 9, search teams met at the chief ranger's office. Six inches of snow had fallen during the night, and conditions were dictating a full winter search. Search dogs, the civil air patrol, county sheriffs, and other emergency personnel were contacted and started to converge on the park. Ground searchers again covered the trails in the area where Geoffrey was last seen, but recent snows had obliterated any new tracks that he would have made.

By the end of the first full day of searching Geoffrey had not been found. Geoff's parents had been contacted, and they were traveling to the park. The snow flurries in the park were getting lighter, but the temperature was dropping, and the wind was intensifying.

The following week saw hundreds of searchers join the effort, covering thousands of acres of the park; nothing of value was found until February 16.

At noon on February 16, searchers found Geoffrey's pack. It was located downstream from the Boulevard Trail toward Newfound Gap. The pack had a few items of clothing and equipment lying on a rock in the middle of Walker Camp Prong, approximately one mile downstream from the Boulevard Trail. This point was clarified when I personally met with retired NPS Ranger and a participant on this search, Dwight McCarter. He told me that the pack was on a large rock in the absolute middle of the river. He said that the boy would have had to be in the river to place the pack in this location. Articles inside the pack were lying on the rock or the pack as though someone was taking inventory.

The pack was taken to his parents who identified it as Geoffrey's. Concern for Geoffrey was now peaking, as it was obvious Geoffrey did not have his needed supplies to survive the winter weather. The sleeping bag, food, matches, and other equipment were with the bag on the rock and not with Geoffrey—where was he?

On February 17 the Army used a canine search team that followed a scent trail, and they came to the conclusion that Geoffrey was out of the park. They followed the scent downstream until it eventually met U.S. 441, where the scent supposedly ended. The results were given to the parents, and they believed that the Army had made the correct conclusion (They probably were wishing this was the correct hypothesis).

On February 18, the search teams (now consisting of only thirty searchers) decided to focus on Walker Camp Prong. A Green Beret Team had entered the search and focused on an adjacent ridgeline and an avalanche team from Seattle, Washington, took the creek basin.

At 10:17 a.m. an encrypted message was relayed to park headquarters that Geoffrey's body had been found. He was dead.

Dwight McCarter's book *Lost!* has a very detailed account of what occurred and what was seen by the rangers when they observed Geoffrey's body. I am going to place the paragraph from Dwight's book below:

Geoff has been found 1000 yards below the Boulevard Trail, about a mile from the point he was last seen. He is in the Walker Camp Prong drainage about 1000 yards upstream from the location where his sleeping bag and pack were found 2 days ago. Geoff is at the base of a tree; half sitting, half slumped into a fetal position and is still covered in deep snow except for parts of his right arm and part of his right leg where the snow has melted off him. He has no socks on and one boot is lying 6 feet away. The other is unlaced and half on his right foot. His orange toboggan cap is off, his mittens are off, his coat is open and partially off. His left arm is pulled up inside the sleeve. His shirt is on but his pants are unzipped and partially removed.

Geoffrey is airlifted to a local airport and later examined by a state medical examiner, Dr. John Hickey. The body had minor scratches and bruises, but no broken bones. The doctors believed that Geoffrey died of exhaustion and exposure late the first night he went missing or early on the second day.

Dwight McCarter asked the perfect question in his book on page 59:

What happened to Geoffrey Hague? How could he have disappeared so quickly without a trace and how and why did he wind up deep in the drainage of Walker Camp Prong, half undressed and without his pack and sleeping bag which could have saved his life?

I could not have said it any better—how did all of this occur?

You may hear some SAR people state that Geoffrey just froze to death. I don't think so—it's much more complicated. Geoffrey didn't have broken bones, and he could walk. His pack, sleeping bag (warmth), and supplies were not that far away. He could have recovered them if he was free to do this. Geoffrey had Boy Scout training, he had just spent a night in the cold, and he knew how to start a fire. When Geoffrey disappeared, the trails were very clearly marked. There could be no mistake about this. There would be no reason for Geoffrey to voluntarily leave a trail and travel a thousand yards down into a drainage—none!

Geoffrey knew he was getting cold—we all know when we are getting cold. The natural reaction to getting cold is to find the comfort in a warm coat or sleeping bag. Geoffrey had this at his disposal up the creek, and he didn't get it. When the body starts to get very cold, people start to shiver, they can't sleep, and it's very uncomfortable. Only after many hours in this very uncomfortable condition things start to change and go numb. This process doesn't happen quickly. Geoffrey suffered for quite some time until his body started to shut down. He had to have gone through extreme anxiety knowing that the comfort of his sleeping bag was just up the creek. There is no logic to explain why Geoffrey didn't get his pack—if he was free to do so.

No articles or reports mention Geoffrey's pants. Were they frozen stiff from being in the river? Were the pants even wet or frozen? Remember, Geoffrey was a trained Boy Scout and had survival training. There is no logical reason for him to enter a freezing river during heavy snow—*none*.

I now refer readers to the case of Charles McCuller at Crater Lake National Park (see the Crater Lake section in Missing-411 Western United States). Charles disappeared at lakeside on October 14, 1976. Charles's skeleton was found years later and investigated by the FBI and the National Park Service. I personally interviewed the ranger who was first on the scene for the NPS. He explained that it was one of the oddest sites he had ever observed. Charles McCuller's bones were scattered over a wide area. There were no large bones except the skull and jaw. It had appeared as though Charles had melted into his pants, yet there was only one smaller broken bone in the pants. At the bottom of the pants were socks with toe bones inside. But what concerned the rangers and prompted them to call the FBI for a full investigation was that the blue jeans that Charles was wearing were *unbuckled*. The belt buckle Charles was wearing was *unbuckled*, and his boots were missing. The rangers on the scene couldn't develop a logical reason why the pants and belt were in this condition or how his boots disappeared. The location of the skeleton was in the middle of a wilderness area, and Charles had disappeared in the middle of winter where there were twenty-foot snowdrifts. The entire staff of the NPS at Crater Lake could develop no rational way that Charles could have traveled from lakeside to the scene of his skeleton in the middle of winter—none.

The interesting facts of these two cases are that two bodies are found in *drainages* in national parks thousands of miles apart, both males, one sixteen, one nineteen. Both have their pants opened—one is confirmed pulled down. One boot is off of Geoffrey. McCuller's boots were never found. Survival for Geoffrey is with his backpack just upstream, but it isn't retrieved. McCuller's coat that he was wearing was never found.

If it weren't for the absolute candor and concern by rangers investigating these incidents, people would never hear about them. It's only because I've been researching cases across North America that I've found a consistency that is unsettling. Some administrators will try to state these incidents are examples of what happens when a mind becomes confused and a person is near death. I state that there have been hundreds who have frozen to death on Mt. Everest, and many have been found. I've never heard of any climber who has frozen to death who was found with his or her pants partially on. There is something about the deaths of McCuller and Hague that needs a special law enforcement team to take a second look—not a National Park team. It seems very odd that a Green Beret team enters the search for Geoffrey and, as in the case of Martin, are unable to find the boy. The Army canine units didn't even believe Geoffrey was in the park and believed he exited via a highway.

Geoffrey was found next to a creek, deceased. His backpack is found in the middle of a creek, a creek that no reasonable man would ever enter during a winter storm, yet a creek someone entered and placed Geoffrey's belongings on a rock. The person that set Geoffrey's pack on the rock will never be identified because there are no tracks that can be recovered in a creek bed! Missing people are repeatedly found in or near creek beds. Think about the reasons why this may be occurring.

Mark Hanson
Missing 3/7/75, Great Smoky Mountains National Park
Age at Disappearance: 21 years

There is no greater bonding experience than a group of friends taking a hike into the woods. The adventure and solitude of the event brings lifetime memories and the bond of trust that endures forever. The following story is an event that none of these young men will ever forget.

Mark Hanson was from Newport, Kentucky, and he joined fellow Eastern Kentucky University students Ben Fish and John Chidester for a hike on the Appalachian Trail. The guys were going to enjoy their spring break by hiking the historic trail and challenging their stamina through a tough hike in difficult weather.

The guys probably didn't know the extent of the bad weather that was hitting the park upon their arrival. A tornado had touched down in the park earlier in the day, and this was just a prelude of what was going to happen throughout the area.

The guys started their hike in Big Creek near Mt. Sterling at the 1700' elevation on the eastern edge of the park. They had planned to hike west and spend their first night at the Tricorner Shelter. The first day of hiking was not going to be easy. It was an uphill walk of almost sixteen miles. The men were hiking directly into the wind, rain, and eventually snow flurries—it was getting brutal. As the group approached Low Gap, John Chidester complained that he was getting wet and cold and didn't think he could or wanted to go on. He told his two friends that he was turning around and going back to their car. One mile after Chidester turned back, the remaining two men passed the shelter and possible life-saving warmth at Cosby Knob.

Hanson and Fish continue to hike, with Fish doing the better of the two. Fish seemed to be able to handle the weather and pack much better than Hanson. As they are hiking, Hanson yelled to Fish that he was dropping his pack and leaving it on the trail. He stated that he didn't think he could make it carrying the weight. Fish was shocked at Hanson's proclamation but stayed calm and tried to convince him that he needed the pack, as that could be a life-saving decision. Hanson countered that they can make it to Tricorner, and they will find shelter and warmth there. At approximately 7:00 p.m., the guys reached Mt. Guyot. The weather was now getting worse. The wind was blowing, and the temperature was dropping. Fish was still leading the pair and encouraging Hanson to continue the pace.

At 8:30 p.m., in total darkness and with snow falling hard and the temperature plummeting, Hanson yelled to Fish that he was quitting. He lay down in the middle of the trail and appeared to almost pass out. Fish tried to prompt his friend to get up and keep moving. He refused or couldn't respond. Fish got back up and started down the trail two hundred yards. He now decided he couldn't go any farther, and he lay down in his sleeping bag. Ben Fish did not realize that he was two hundred yards from the protection of the shelter at Tricorner.

During the night, Ben Fish either heard or had a dream that he heard Hanson calling for help. Ben was so tired he couldn't delineate between a dream he may have had and the reality of his friend calling for help.

At 7:00 a.m. the following morning, Ben Fish woke up and quickly looked for Hanson, but he can't be found. Several inches of snow were on the ground, and tracks could not be seen. He turned around and headed for Tricorner, where he was able to meet other hikers that could assist him in calling for help. Late in the afternoon on March 10, Ben Fish contacted NPS personnel and officially reported Mark Hanson missing.

Early in the morning on March 11, NPS personnel with Ben Fish assisting found Hanson's backpack exactly where he left it in the middle of the Appalachian Trail. Nothing appeared to be disturbed or removed in the pack. Searchers combed the area where Fish last saw Hanson and could not find any evidence of his being in the area.

March 12 had an escalation of the number of searchers involved. Ranger Dwight McCarter searched Mt. Chapman on the Tennessee side of the park. McCarter found a cave on the side of the mountain that appeared to have had a large mammal living in it. He found several bones on the floor of the cave, but nothing was inside.

The search for Mark Hanson continued to escalate over the following several days. By March 14, four inches of rain had fallen in the previous three days. Heavy rain and high creeks had now washed away the heavy snow that had fallen earlier in the search. Grid searches continued over the following three days using helicopters, dogs, and ground teams.

At 2:00 p.m. on March 17, the ninth day of the search, Mark Hanson's body was found. Mark was located two miles down Buck Fork Creek from the Appalachian Trail. Searchers found Mark leaning against a tree, his parka open, and his gloves and boots lying nearby in the snow. Mark was carried to a helo site where he was airlifted out of the park.

An autopsy concluded that Mark died twenty-four to thirty-six hours after Ben Fish last saw him.

This is another of the cases from Great Smoky Mountains National Park that does not make sense. Mark Hanson was lying on a very well-worn Appalachian Trail. There could be no mistake where this trail was located, even in darkness. Mark's fatal route took him downhill almost three miles. There is no way that Mark didn't know that he had left the trail and was walking into oblivion. He and Fish knew the route to Tricorner, and it wasn't downhill into Buck Fork Creek. It's a very uncomfortable feeling to know that Geoffrey Hague was also found downhill from his location in a creek bed, under full cover and nearly impossible to see from the air, same as Mark Hanson.

Again, the manner in which Mark's body was found, without gloves or boots on, is troubling. If he did die twenty-four to thirty-six hours after Ben Fish saw him, this means that much transpired in that short period of time. It's also a concern that Ben Fish may have heard Mark calling for help. Mark could have crawled up the trail to stay on the path. If he was fit enough to walk two miles to his final destination, then he would have been fit enough to crawl the trail, but, remember, he was too weak to hike on and collapsed on the trail. But how in the heck was he able to hike three miles in the middle of the night when he had just passed out on the trail of exhaustion. This makes no sense. The key to understanding what happened to Mark Hanson is to know why he was screaming for help in the middle of the night. There are too many similarities in the Hanson and Hague disappearances to ignore.

Minnie Haun
Missing 10/08/57, 1:00 p.m., Well Springs, TN (Ten Miles E/O Lafollette)
Age at Disappearance: 3 years

Mr. and Mrs. Frank Haun lived in a very rural area ten miles east of Lafollette. On October 8, 1957 at approximately 1:00 p.m., Mrs. Haun took Minnie and her sisters on a walnut collecting expedition in the area behind their home. Mrs. Haun left Minnie briefly with her four-year-old sister while Mrs. Haun walked a distance away with the other girls. Minnie was given instructions to wait at that location until they came back. Several minutes after leaving the girls alone, Mrs. Haun returned and found Minnie was gone. Mrs. Haun asked the four-year-old where Minnie went; the girl stated that she had decided to walk toward home. Mrs. Haun searched the area, couldn't find her daughter, and called the sheriff.

Within hours of Minnie's disappearance, there were dozens of sheriff's deputies, state police, neighbors, and friends all searching for the three-year-old. In the first twenty-four hours that Minnie was gone, the search parties swelled to over two thousand scouring the hillsides. Shortly into the second day of the search the sheriff called the FBI for assistance. Mr. and Mrs. Haun could not believe that Minnie had disappeared so quickly and told reporters this, explaining their astonishment of her disappearance.

Those first few nights that Minnie was missing, temperatures dropped into the forties. Searchers asked for assistance from the Air Force radar station in Briceville, and sixty men responded. SAR teams had the mountains covered with people looking and yelling for the young girl. After a mere fifty-two hours of searching, the sheriff called off searchers, an astounding decision after a short period of time. Mr. Haun vowed to keep looking for his daughter as long as it took to find her.

Six days after Minnie went missing, volunteer searchers continued and were over six miles from the Haun residence when they started to find pieces of Minnie's clothing. They first found one shoe containing a sock. A short distance from an old saw mill, men found Minnie's cap. The team climbed to the top of a ridgeline and through "a mile and a half of rough underbrush and wooded mountain land from the saw mill where her tracks were located" (*Daily Middleboro News*, 10/15/57), and they found her body. Some reports indicated that Minnie was located at the base of a cliff, but this was not true. She was found on a ridgeline, without shoes, without her hat, and wearing only a very light dress. Coroners indicated that Minnie had been dead for three to four days.

An article in the *Kingsport Times* dated October 15, 1957 had the following description of finding the child, "The searchers, led by Campbell County Sheriff Willie Chapman, said the child had climbed to the top of one of the many cliffs that dot the Cumberlands in this area."

I find this statement very hard to believe. A three-year-old girl whose parents cannot believe that she disappeared as quickly as she did tells her sister she is walking home and then climbs a cliff—why? This same girl supposedly strips her clothing off, yet succumbs to exposure?

FBI agents were on this case when the body was found and one article indicated that they closed the case once Minnie was found deceased. I did file a FOIA with the FBI regarding this case. On September 28, 2011, I received a letter from Section Chief of the FBI, David M. Hardy. Agent Hardy stated, "Records which may be responsive to your FOIA request were destroyed February 1, 1999. Since this material could not be reviewed, it is not known if it was responsive to your request."

The points of concern in the Minnie Haun case reflect my concern on many of these cases. The girl climbed a cliff, yet took her shoes off before she accomplished this feat, but why? She lost her hat—how? She was wearing only a very light dress when found. Where was the rest of her clothing? Mr. and Mrs. Haun expressed concern that they felt their daughter may have been abducted—yes, abducted in the middle of the woods, but by whom? How many times do we need to hear this concern by parents before law enforcement starts to react to their concerns? This is another of the many cases cited in both books in which the FBI is concerned enough to be on the scene of a very unusual case. If I've put these cases together and made the connection about the unusual nature that's linked them all, don't you think federal law enforcement would have a clue about what is occurring? FBI Special Agent Jim Rike is the individual whom the FBI sent to all of the cases in the Smoky Mountains where children disappeared. I think he had a very good grasp of the complexity of the issue, but the FBI won't release its documents.

I know that many of you may believe that the idea of an abduction in the middle of a wilderness is ridiculous, understood. Also understand that the FBI is a very conservative, intelligent and methodical group that does not send special agents to missing person cases unless there is the possibility of criminal activity. The only criminal activity relevant to a missing person in the woods is abduction.

Michael Edwin Hearon
Missing 8/23/08, Happy Valley, TN
Age at Disappearance: 51 years
5'10", 185 lbs

Michael was a contractor, with his primary residence in Maryville, TN. He had a weekend residence at the end of Bell Branch Road in Happy Valley; his parents lived on an adjacent property.

Michael had two sons, Matt, twenty-five, and Andy, twenty-seven. Michael's parents Verl and Sue Hearon liked living on the northern fringe of the Smoky Mountains National Park. Their son would make the trip from his residence to the country to mow his parents' lawn, as was his intention on this trip. He had taken his truck and trailered mower to his house and parked it at the beginning of his driveway near his residence, as he normally did.

After Michael arrived at the family property, 6728 Bell Branch Road, Michael entered his residence and placed his wallet, keys, cell phone, money clip, credit cards, and gun on the counter. He took one of his ATVs from his garage and drove it back up his street. The property had a large meadow, an adjacent lake, and a large river less then one-fourth of a mile south. Chilhowee Lake, a very large lake, is less than three miles southwest of Michael's residence. The elevation in the area of Michael's house is approximately 1500'.

After Michael did not arrive to mow his parents' property, they went to his residence. They found his truck in the driveway, mower on the trailer, and his personal property on the counter in the residence. Nothing was disturbed. The parents waited another day, hoping Michael would return. When he didn't, they called Michael's two sons. They responded to the property and eventually contacted law enforcement.

Sheriff's deputies determined that Michael was operating his Yamaha Wolverine yellow ATV. The deputies found Michael's ATV approximately one mile from his residence in an area near Adams Creek. The ATV was sitting idle with the ignition switch turned on; it had been turned off using the kill switch, something his children stated that he would never normally do. The vehicle was parked on a steep hill in high gear, undamaged. This location is less then one-fourth of a mile from the Great Smoky Mountain National Park's northern border.

The local sheriff's department searched the area of Michael's ATV with helicopters, horses, canines, and ground teams and had assistance from the National Park Service. Nothing was found. As in many cases in this book, search teams have been compromised during their efforts by heavy rains that were inundating the Happy Valley area while the search for Mike was occurring. The rains that hit this area were very heavy and could have washed away a major portion of the scent trail used by the bloodhounds.

The Blount County Sheriff has stated that there does not appear to be any foul play in Michael's disappearance, and they further stated that they did not believe that Michael was involved in any illicit activity.

Follow-up

In August 2011, I took a trip to Michael Hearon's weekend residence. Another investigator and I found the home abandoned and decided to take a nearby road and contact a neighbor. We were quite fortunate to meet Ken and Irma Blythe. They were an older couple who were very hospitable and welcomed us into their rural home. I explained we were there to learn more about Michael's disappearance, and they were happy to inform us about what they knew.

Irma explained that she was Michael's aunt and had always been close to him. She and Ken had lived in their home for the last nineteen years. She said that she routinely saw Michael come to his house to do weekend maintenance and the additional maintenance on other family homes in the area. She said that Michael liked to hike and knew the area very well.

I asked Irma if she could explain what happened the day that Michael disappeared. She gladly offered to show us the exact location where his ATV was found parked. It was quite different than what news articles had explained.

Michael had left his residence on Bell Branch Road and waved at residents as he drove toward Happy Valley Road. He made it to Happy Valley, turned east, went five hundred feet, and then turned north on Happy Valley Loop Road. This is a gorgeous rural road with lush surroundings. Michael drove approximately one thousand feet, and the road made a right turn and headed east again. He was expected to travel another four hundred feet to a location where he was going to check on another residence he was watching for friends. For some unknown reason, Michael made an almost immediate left turn and headed up a rural road (well maintained) that led slightly uphill to a very nice home located one-eighth of a mile up the road on the west side. Michael turned his ATV into the driveway of the residence and disappeared. The only notable geographical landmark in the area is a creek just east of this location.

Irma and Ken showed us the locations and explained how the family and Michael's children were still devastated about the disappearance. They stated they appreciated our interest and quickly left the area. They made it clear that it made them nervous being in this area.

The other researcher and I spent time in the area of the disappearance going over the possible options of what happened to Michael. We came to the conclusion that Michael was driving up Happy Valley Road, made the right turn, and surprised someone doing something. The turn in the road is quick, and a driver could surprise someone on the roadway. Irma and Ken stated that if Michael had seen something unusual, he would have gone to investigate. He probably did. He drove up the road and turned into the residence where something unexpected and overwhelming happened.

The Abrams Creek entrance to the Great Smoky Mountains National Park is just two thousand feet southeast of where Michael disappeared. The park participated in the search along with deputy sheriffs and SAR teams, but they didn't find anything.

Case Summary:

There are a few details about Michael Hearon's disappearance that seem unusual. If Michael knew beforehand that he was going to meet someone up Loop Road he would have taken his truck. The truck would offer additional protection and safety from the elements and any possible confrontation, but Michael obviously wasn't going to a meeting like this. What if Michael saw something unusual as he was driving up Loop Road near his friend's residence? The condition of the ATV almost indicates that he was accelerating up the hill when he came off it, somehow. The ATV was still in high gear and was only stopped by the kill switch. What took him off the ATV is the key question. Michael was not a small man. Whatever took him was strong, quick, and determined. There are 500,000 acres in the National Park that Michael could be wandering, or worse.

**Another very strange coincidence occurred when we went to Michael's aunt's home. Just prior to meeting with the Blythes, we met with William Martin at his residence about the disappearance of his son, Dennis. The Martins had a very unusual doorknocker, very colorful and designed so you would pull a string downward and the woodpecker's nose would bang on the wall. When we went to the front door of the Blythe's residence, they had the exact same doorknocker. We were floored.

Brad Lavies
Missing 03/28/93, Great Smoky Mountains National Park, TN
Age at Disappearance: 13 years

Brad Lavies was taking a day hike with his family and friends on the trail to Rainbow Falls on the Mt. Leconte Trail inside the Great Smoky Mountains National Park. The waterfall is located at approximately the 3200-foot elevation on the 6,593-foot tall Mt. Leconte. Sometime in the late afternoon while walking up to the waterfall, Brad became lost and separated from his family and friends. This was an unusual disappearance because the trail is clearly marked.

Parents Randy and Nancy Lavies realized that their son was not with them, stopped their hike, and returned down the mountain to notify authorities.

NPS officials contacted Fort Campbell Kentucky for the assistance of armed forces and got it. Five helicopters with infrared sensors were used in the six-day search, along with 150 backcountry experts. An April 2, 1993 article in the *Times Daily* identified the search area: "The primary search area is only about a half-mile wide and 2.5 miles long. The search has been underway since shortly after Brad's disappearance on Sunday." This explained a very defined corridor in which NPS was looking for Brad, not a lot of area to be covered.

Brad disappeared at approximately the three thousand-foot elevation on Mt. Leconte. On the sixth day of the search Brad's body was found. He was found in a steep and rugged area one-half mile off the Rainbow Falls Trail. The *Times Daily* on April 4 ran the following description of where Brad was located: "Cave (NPS Official) said the boy's body was found by a park volunteer and a coworker of Randy Lavies at the base of an unnamed eighty to one hundred-foot waterfall on a tributary of Leconte Creek about two thousand feet off the Rainbow Falls Trail."

Later the article added the following:

Cave said searchers were surprised at how far and how high the boy had traveled. He was found at the upper limits that we searched at about 4800 feet. The area is so steep and so thicketed that the possibility of him going that far was something that surprised everyone.

Remember, the NPS is claiming that Brad climbed an additional 1600 feet after he was lost; he essentially climbed to his death, their claim.

The NPS has publicly stated that they were surprised where they found Brad; his family was probably very surprised. The *Times Daily* story on April 4 also had this: "Park officials were conducting an investigation at the scene late Saturday afternoon, and the body had not been moved, Cave said." This tells me that whatever the park service found at the bottom of the waterfall was perplexing. The NPS stated that the parents chose not to travel to the scene because of the difficulty of the trip. Park officials stated that the boy died of head trauma.

Imagine you were the investigator on Brad's case. You find the boy in an area that defies common sense. It appears that the boy travels out onto a ledge in icy conditions and supposedly slips and falls almost one hundred feet to his death. When you get to the body, something at the scene concerns you, and an investigation is conducted—sounds fairly thorough at this point. A copyrighted Associated Press article on April 4 had the following:

The boy died from a massive head injury and multiple traumas, said Lisa McNeal, spokeswoman for University of Tennessee Medical Center. No autopsy was performed. McNeal said a visual inspection was declared satisfactory by doctors to pronounce the cause of death.

> *I had to read this last statement three different times*—no autopsy? An attended death is when a physician can sign a death certificate when the victim is directly under the doctor's care. In an unattended death, someone dies not under the care of a physician, and an autopsy is automatically conducted to ensure there is no foul play. Brad died without any witnesses under very odd circumstances; I cannot believe an autopsy was not conducted. Knowing what I

know about the region where Brad disappeared, knowing how many children have disappeared and not been found, I cannot believe that the NPS didn't demand an autopsy— unless they didn't want this information disseminated and publicly available..

Eloise Lindsay
Missing 11/4/89, Table Rock State Park, SC
Age at Disappearance: 22 years

This is definitely one of the strangest stories in this book. This was included in the Great Smoky Mountains section because the event started less than fifty miles from the park border.

Twenty-two-year-old Eloise Lindsay planned a detailed 43.3-mile hike along the Appalachian Trail starting at Table Rock State Park in far northwestern South Carolina on November 4, 1989. She was going the first seven days alone and then meeting a friend to refresh supplies and get companionship. The third day into her hike, Eloise stated that she knew she was being followed by a group of men that meant her harm. A November 21 article in the *Syracuse Journal* quoted Lindsay's feelings about the hike: "I was terrorized the whole time."

After several days of being chased, Eloise says that she ditched her backpack and much of her supplies and left the trail in an attempt to lose the men. She stated that she never saw the men, but she did hear them regularly.

Eloise missed meeting her friend at the seven-day interval and that friend called law enforcement. For the next nine days after authorities were notified, Eloise says she was in complete fear of being caught by the men. She stated that many nights she didn't sleep and did everything possible to avoid them. On the sixteenth day after being declared missing, Eloise was found by a hunter five miles off the trail and deep in the woods but still inside Table Rock State Park. She was escorted back to law enforcement where she gave a complete statement.

One of the best interviews of Eloise was written in "*The Item*" on November 21, 1989. Eloise stated that she doesn't have any evidence that she was chased, but "I just know I was terrorized for two weeks." Later in the article Eloise clarified: "On Tuesday (November

7) I felt like I was being chased through the woods by a group of men. Up until this morning I felt like I was being chased." She was found the morning of the interview.

During Eloise's chase through the woods, she stated that she did find two pieces of pound cake and stale doughnuts hidden in the trunk of a tree. How Eloise found the food in the trunk of a tree wasn't explained.

There were people in law enforcement that didn't believe all the details of her story, but in reading the various articles, her story stayed consistent.

In the last article quoted, reporters also interviewed Eloise's mother. Gayle Lindsay stated, "I'm not sure what she saw." This statement from Eloise's mother implies that Eloise did see something even though she claims she didn't see the men. My question for Eloise and her mother is what did the girl see? Her mother indicates she saw something and what she saw is something that she obviously does not want to make public, for whatever reason.

Case Summary:

I am inclined to believe what Eloise states. Nobody ditches their backpack so they can run faster unless they are in serious fear. When a hiker leaves her backpack, she also may be leaving her life behind. She didn't have her sleeping bag, food, water purification, or personal hygiene material.

A November 23 article in the *Aiken Standard* had an interview with law enforcement personnel about Eloise: "I think she became extremely paranoid for whatever reason, said Tim Morgan, Assistant Sheriff of Pickens County." The article later stated, "Although there was no clear indication the mysterious men meant harm, Miss Lindsay said: 'I could tell there was no good intent involved.' Eloise stated that when she was found by the hunter, 'I was kind of delirious.'"

The state of being delirious or semiconscious is a recurring fact among people who are found after being lost in the woods. There is something about this physical state that needs to be examined more carefully.

I would like every reader to refer to the Dennis Martin story in this chapter, specifically, the statements made by retired NPS Ranger

Dwight McCarter about "wild men" in the Smoky Mountains. While law enforcement seemed to doubt Eloise's story, McCarter seems to confirm that this event probably occurred. McCarter claims there are wild men living in the mountains surrounding the park who have done illegal things in the past. McCarter specifically told us about an NPS ranger who was brutally attacked by one of these wild men who was never apprehended. You may be asking yourself why the NPS and local law enforcement do not acknowledge the existence of the wild men? If the NPS and sheriff deputies admit that the men exist, they must also admit that they cannot be controlled, monitored, or apprehended, as McCarter explained when we met with him.

Evangeline Lorimer
Missing 6/08/51, Unknown Time, Great Smoky Mountains National Park
Age at Disappearance: 21 years

Evangeline Lorimer was taking a summer vacation with her father in the Great Smoky Mountains National Park. Evangeline was a student nurse at Cincinnati's Jewish Hospital. Mr. Lorimer had traveled to the park from his home in Seattle.

On June 8, Evangeline told her father that she was going to take a hike from their camp in the area of Cades Cove. Evangeline was wearing a coat, low profile shoes, and pants and walked into the forest. When Evangeline didn't return to camp, Mr. Lorimer called authorities and a search was initiated.

In the days after Evangeline disappeared, canines were used as well as a plethora of law enforcement agents, local state and regional personnel. As the canines were coming in, rainstorms were hammering the park for several days. The canines were not having any luck finding Evangeline.

The search continued for twelve days. In the middle of the search, officials found Evangeline's coat hanging from a tree limb five miles from where she disappeared.

On the thirteenth day Evangeline was missing, the park supervisor's son found Evangeline walking down a trail on Chilhowell Mountain. The girl had swollen ankles and insect bites but was in relatively good condition. When she was interviewed, she stated that she drank water from brooks and ate huckleberries.

When Evangeline came out of the woods, Great Smoky Mountains rangers had an opportunity to interview her. A June 22, 1951 article in the *Tuscaloosa News* stated, "They [rangers] stated, 'The girl was "vague" and seemed confused.'" There were some people who believed that Evangeline may not have been lost but it was a staged event. From the interview with the ranger it would appear that her confusion is consistent with people missing in this area of the U.S. As you read on in this book, you will find that many people who are found after being missing for several days are confused or are delirious, a recurring theme.

Dennis Lloyd Martin
Missing 6/14/69, 4:30 p.m., Spence Field, Great Smoky Mountains National Park
Age at Disappearance: 6 years
Last Seen Wearing Red Shirt, Pants

The facts behind Dennis's story come directly from newspaper accounts, NPS documents obtained through an FOIA that I initiated, and from a personal interview I conducted with Mr. Martin at his residence and Dwight McCarter (Retired NPS Ranger) also at his residence. Another investigator and I have also spent many days in the area where Dennis disappeared, attempting to understand the terrain and the associated possibilities of what really occurred.

Dennis Martin was vacationing at the Great Smoky Mountains National Park with his father William Martin, grandfather Clyde Martin, and his older brother Douglas, nine years old. They had spent the night of June 13 at a cabin at the Russell Field Shelter, two miles west of Spence Field. On June 14, they hiked to Spence Field and spent the day playing in the meadow.

Spence Field sits on the divide of Tennessee and North Carolina and is part of the Appalachian Trail. The field is grassy and runs in an east to west direction, with the north drainage going into Tennessee and south going into North Carolina.

As William and Clyde Martin were sitting on the grass with Dennis and Doug (two brothers), another family met them in the meadow and asked whether they could join their boys in playtime. In one of the more coincidental parts of this case, this other family was also named "Martin."

As both Martin clans were sitting on a grassy spot just to the southwest of the Anthony Creek Trailhead, the William Martin boys and the two other young Martin boys were playing in the field and sneaking up to the adults. It was a great atmosphere for the children to enjoy a national park setting. At one point, the boys decided to split up and play hide and seek. Dennis was last seen on the Tennessee side of the field, fifty feet from where Clyde and William were sitting. After three to five minutes of not seeing Dennis, Mr. Martin became concerned and began calling out loud for his boy, but there was no answer. Clyde Martin saw his son's concern and got up and started to join the search. It was approximately 3:30 p.m., and William Martin's life was about to change forever. During the next several hours, the Martins, rangers, volunteer searchers, and various other volunteers covered every trail in the immediate area. They searched behind every plant and tree on the field. Dennis Martin had vanished.

According to a July 21, 1969 article in the *Knoxville News Sentinel*, the Harold Key family was visiting a region five to seven miles from where Dennis Martin disappeared the same day sometime between 4:30 and 5:30 p.m. The Key family was in the area downhill from where Dennis disappeared in a region known as Sea Branch Creek near Rowans Creek in Cades Cove (Sea Branch Creek flows into Rowans Creek near the valley). The Keys had asked park rangers where they could go to see a bear and were directed to that location. The family exited their car and walked one-half to three-fourths of a mile uphill when they heard an "enormous, sickening scream." The group walked two hundred additional yards, and Mr. Key's son had just told Mr. Key that he had heard a bear somewhere in front of them. In an article on the same date in the *Maryville Alcoa Times*, Mr. Key states, "But it wasn't a bear. It was a man hiding in some bushes. He was definitely trying to hide from us." Mr. Key stated at the time that he didn't realize a boy was missing. Mr. Key read about the disappearance of Dennis Martin and then called the FBI two days later.

At approximately 8:30 p.m. heavy rainstorms had moved into the national park and were greatly hampering search efforts. There was an estimated 2.5 inches of rain before midnight, rain that continued almost nonstop for two weeks.

The Great Smoky Mountains National Park was starting to initiate one of the largest searches in the history of the NPS, and they were starting to call for major reinforcements.

June 15, Sunday

NPS personnel searched all major drainages in the area of Spence Field. Thirty Boy Scouts on an outing were used as searchers along with fifty-one ranger students who were on a field trip in the area. Special approval was requested from Tony Stark, the regional chief of Visitor Protection to hire a helicopter to transport equipment and establish a base camp at Spence Field. This was approved. Various North Carolina rescue squads were contacted and started their response. Two Huey helicopters from the Air Force were requested and dispatched. Forty Special Forces (Green Berets) from the Third Army Headquarters in Fort Benning, Georgia, were requested and dispatched. Remember that this was all in process less than twenty-four hours after Dennis disappeared. Forty additional Green Berets would arrive later in the week.

After reviewing dozens of NPS missing persons cases, I never found one that came close to the immediate massive response for searchers as was requested in the Dennis Martin case. I applaud the effort and the response, but it was almost as though someone knew that this case was going to be different. It was going to be one of the most difficult in the history of NPS. In researching hundreds of missing people, I have never seen this level of response for someone missing less than twenty-four hours. The fact that Green Berets were dispatched almost makes it seem as though they were up against something very unusual, and someone knew it. It is a very rare event in missing person cases when Special Forces are dispatched.

June 16, Monday

A grid search of Spence Field was conducted. Rescue squads were being organized and given assignments. The Tennessee Air National Guard sent seventeen men to Cades Cove. Many of the military personnel were calling for assistance without any prompt from search personnel. A heliport was established at Cades Cove to accommodate the air traffic supporting the SAR. Total force for June 16 was three hundred NPS, rescue squads, National Guard, volunteers, and student foresters.

The next four days showed more intensive searching and a huge interest in assisting by the public and the military. The number of searchers swelled to almost eight hundred on June 20. On June 21, the searchers numbered 1400. The area around Spence field was saturated. Drainages were searched inch by inch. Armed Special Forces personnel were looking for tracks, broken twigs, anything leading toward evidence of where the boy may be. It was at this point that the chief ranger contacted the media to advise the public that no more searchers were needed; they were reaching a saturation and support point, which they could not accommodate. It was from this date forward that the number of searchers started to diminish.

On June 24, the NPS had a meeting with FBI Special Agent Jim Rike. The circumstances of the disappearance of Dennis Martin were explained to the agent. It was unclear per the NPS reports why the FBI agent arrived or who called the agency for assistance. There were no reports in the FOIA documents stating what was discussed in this meeting or any documents outlining why the FBI was on site. Almost everything about the FBI's involvement was absent from NPS reports.

On June 27, Mr. Ed Crabtree, one of William Martin's neighbors in Knoxville telephoned Tennessee Senator Howard Baker and asked for three hundred additional federal troops to search for Dennis. The Coast Guard had committed two boats to Fontana Lake to search for any possible evidence, even though the lake was outside the park boundary and was miles away.

On June 29 at 5:00 p.m., a meeting was held with the Martins, NPS personnel, and the FBI, with the NPS posing the question which way the search would go from here. The FBI stated that absent any evidence of a kidnapping, the FBI could not launch a full-scale investigation, but they would continue one agent on site to monitor activity, that one agent was Jim Rike. The NPS told the Martins that they were willing to continue the search for thirty to sixty or ninety days, with three of the best park services men. Dwight McCarter was one of the personnel they committed. At 6:00 p.m., the SAR operation on Spence Field was officially closed down. A total of 13,240 man-hours were expended on the search for Dennis and 200 helicopter air hours.

Mr. Martin was a draftsman for an architectural company and took weeks off of work to assist with the search for his son. He was a man possessed by finding the boy. The amount of guilt that poor man must have felt would bring tears to anyone's eyes. He gave several interviews during and after the formal search. He was convinced that Dennis was abducted, but he couldn't convince the FBI, or the local FBI had orders not to be involved. It was unclear what path the FBI was taking or the motivation or reason for its interest in this case.

The NPS and the FBI did conduct interviews on many peripheral issues associated with the disappearance of Dennis. One of the more interesting and unusual interviews was with Harold Key of Carthage, TN. One of the fascinating parts of this interview is that Mr. Key had volunteered to come to the park and meet with investigators. This did not happen. FBI agent Jim Rike intercepted Mr. Key and met him away from the park to have the debriefing. Mr. Key later told the press that he was near Rowans Creek in the Sea Branch area with his family when they heard, "an enormous, sickening scream." The newspaper stated that a few minutes later he saw a "rough looking man stealthily in the woods near where he had heard the scream." Key did not know the boy was missing until the next day and at that point he contacted authorities. Park officials discounted the likelihood that this sighting was involved in the disappearance because they felt it was too far from the point Dennis disappeared. They wouldn't even go to the area and investigate. One interesting side note to this observation is that Mr. Key's son had stated to another newspaper that he had heard or seen a bear in this same area just as they saw someone or something darting between the trees. This seems a bit too coincidental.

Dwight McCarter was an NPS ranger at the time and participated in the search. Many years later McCarter did give an interview about the event and specifically addressed the scream and sighting near Rowans Creek. McCarter stated that Sea Branch is downhill from the location that Dennis disappeared and it was his opinion that a physically fit man could carry a small boy between the two points. Nobody ever did address the huge scream that was heard. I did meet and interview McCarter on this point and will address this issue later.

On July 17, 1969 the NPS received a letter from the *ESP Research Associates* in Little Rock, Arkansas. Harold Sherman, the president of the organization, authored the letter. Mr. Sherman had some notoriety at the time for authoring several books and being accurate on his premonitions. The following letter was in the pages of documents sent from the FOIA request.

Mr. Sherman wrote an extensive letter that defined an area where Dennis may be located. The last three paragraphs of the letter are very discomforting:

I am impelled to ask you if you know whether or not there have been, or are, any questionable characters in this region. Camping out in the wild in this area? Like hermits, squatters? Such an individual may not be connected with the boy's disappearance at all, but I feel that a sex maniac, so called, does exist in the vicinity and could have trailed the boy.

I hesitate to write anymore as my conscious mind is trying to reject such a feeling. I see something red and something being carried or dragged. Are there any caves in the vicinity? A stream may even run through it, or part of it.

I am always tormented when impressions come to my conscious mind trying to tell me that they couldn't possibly be true, but I get a feeling of sudden panic on the part of Dennis. What happened to him occurred suddenly, unexpectedly, and he could not, or did not cry out. He seems to be struck down by something...the area is rugged.

As a reminder, Dennis was wearing a red shirt, and there are mines in the area where Harold Key and his family made their observation.

On July 21, 1969 the *Knoxville Journal* ran an article titled "Foul Play Suggested in Martin Boy Mystery." The paper had a formal interview with Harold Key; the article had many more details than were available through the NPS reports. Mr. Harold Key is a highway engineer, and his cousin is Baxter Key, who was the attorney general for the district. It was his cousin who convinced him to make his information public.

Key stated that his family went to Cades Cove, an area below the region where Dennis Martin disappeared. They were there the afternoon the boy disappeared. Key stated that the family went looking for bears. The family parked their car and started to hike. Key stated,

My wife and daughter did not go far with us. We had gone a half-mile or so when we heard an awful scream that sounded like someone in trouble. There was a stream there. As we were going up to it, one of my boys said, "Look daddy there's a bear." I looked. It wasn't a bear. It was a man. I didn't get a good look at him because he seemed to be trying to stay hidden behind bushes.

Later in the article Key again explains the scream they heard: "He described the sound they heard as 'One long, loud, painful scream.'" As a former twenty-year law-enforcement veteran, I'd like to know what transpired when the FBI interviewed Mr. Key away from the park, but it appears we will never know. The FBI has refused my FOIA request on this case and the NPS either never wrote a report or failed to supply the report to my FOIA in regards to the interview with Mr. Key. What was it about the appearance of the subject that the Keys observed that caused their son to believe they were witnessing a bear? I find it nearly impossible that NPS investigators never wrote a report about the interview with Mr. Key. This was probably one of the most important developments in the disappearance of Dennis, and the NPS is claiming that they never documented this interview—unbelievable! The idea that a witness would mistake a hairy bear for a human doesn't make allot of sense unless the human was very hairy or they were wearing a shaggy large coat.

In an NPS document titled Appendix F under "Suggestions," there is the following paragraph: "On June 26, Carson Brewer of the *Knoxville News Sentinel* called and forwarded a suggestion received from a lady telling searchers to start looking in trees and tree tops and stop looking on the ground." There was no other explanation. You will read about a missing girl later in this book that disappeared and was found high in a tree—a coincidence?

There were several letters in the NPS file about the observation made by the Key family. Mr. Martin was quite upset at one point because the NPS went public with the Key family observation and hadn't informed him of the finding or of the FBI interview away from the park. Mr. Martin met with Mr. Key and heard firsthand the story and felt that the FBI and the NPS had misinformed the press of the actual facts of the observation. That letter is in the file. Mr. Martin also felt that the FBI and NPS were purposely trying to keep the Key family observation from him.

In the summer of 2011, I made a special trip to Tennessee to visit the Great Smoky Mountains National Park, to observe locations of this event where people have disappeared, and to interview people who were witnesses.

On a Sunday morning in August 2011, I went to the Martin residence in Knoxville. This was the same residence that was listed in wanted posters in 1969. The Martins had never moved and never changed their phone number.

Another investigator and I knocked on the front door, and I immediately recognized Mr. Martin as he came to the door. The man was still in exceptional physical condition and very recognizable.

Mr. Martin answered the door, and I explained I was a researcher/investigator and writer working on his son's case for the last three years and wanted to ask him a few brief questions. I also stated that I deeply admired him for his refusal to give up the search for Dennis. It was a great effort on his part. Mr. Martin very politely stated that his family has lived with the disappearance for a lifetime and has tried not to talk about it. I explained I had traveled from California and only wanted to ask a very few questions. Mr. Martin now closed the front door and stepped onto the porch.

I asked Mr. Martin how far he was from his son on Spence Field when he disappeared? He stated that he could have thrown a rock and hit Dennis where he was hiding; he was no more than fifty feet away behind a few bushes. He reminded me that Dennis was wearing a bright red shirt, a shirt that was never found. I asked if Dennis's brother, Doug, had seen or heard anything strange while he was hiding. Mr. Martin stated that he had not.

I told Mr. Martin that I was familiar with the statements made by Mr. Harold Key and his sighting in the area of Sea Branch and Rowans Creek. Mr. Martin stated that he eventually got to speak with Mr. Key and was told things that you won't read in a newspaper. He stated that he was so concerned that he and a National Park Service Fire Prevention Officer hiked from Spence Field to the area of the Key sighting in ninety minutes. They didn't find anything, but they did prove that the hike could be made in the time frame of when Dennis disappeared and the Key family sighting.

I asked Mr. Martin what Mr. Key had told him that was not in the papers. Mr. Martin stated that the Keys had thought they saw a dark figured man running along a ridgeline carrying something on his shoulder. I again asked Mr. Martin to explain what he just stated. I was in shock. Mr. Martin again stated that the Keys had seen (the paper originally stated that the son thought they heard or saw a bear) and later reported the sighting as a dark-figured man running along a ridge carrying something on his shoulder. I asked Mr. Martin why the news and the park service had never reported this information. Mr. Martin stated he didn't know. I asked Mr. Martin if he felt that the park service was withholding information from him. He paused at this point. Mr. Martin stated that the head of the park service was a mere figurehead, and there were times information flowed smoothly, and other times it did not. It appeared that Mr. Martin was contemplating saying something additional so I again asked if there was something else I should know? Mr. Martin hesitated several seconds, was looking at the ground and slowly raised his head to look at me and stated, "Do you know Jim Rike?" I stated yes, he was the lead FBI agent on several of the missing children cases in the mountains around the time Dennis disappeared. Mr. Martin stated, "Do you know he committed suicide?" I was speechless for several seconds. I asked him if he felt that the suicide had something to do with the cases of missing children, he stated he didn't know.

Many weeks after meeting with Mr. Martin, I read what I had written and reviewed my notes of the interview with Mr. Martin. It was my opinion and the opinion of the second researcher who was present that Mr. Martin's statement that the head of the Great Smoky Mountains National Park was a "mere figurehead" was important. It appeared that he was implying that another administrator somewhere else in the NPS system was dictating the orders, and the superintendent was barking them out. The real question is why the NPS and the FBI were not being open and honest with Mr. Martin—why be evasive? What was it about Dennis's disappearance that caused the federal government to withhold information from the Martin's? It would appear that the FBI and the NPS did not want the information from the Key family made public, specifically the part about see something being carried on the individuals shoulder. This information is not in any official documents that were forwarded to me.

One of the last two items I asked William Martin was what he believed happened to his son and were there any other strange events in conjunction with this case that were never reported? Mr. Martin stated that he believes that someone took his son off the mountain. He says that there was no way his son could have gotten away as fast as he did without people finding him.

In my years of interviewing people under a multitude of circumstances, that was one of the hardest face-to-face meetings I have ever had. Mr. Martin's eyes were watery. I had tears in mine. I shook his hand and told him he did everything possible to find his son. I knew it, and his son would have been proud of his father's effort. I thanked William Martin for his time. I walked to our car shaking and teary-eyed.

If you were Dennis Martin, you would have been very proud of the intensity and effort William Martin placed in getting him back. The man hiked valleys and stayed with the search long after everyone else gave up. He was a man consumed with finding his boy. It appeared to me that he had a very good handle on the politics of the search and efforts made by certain groups. William Martin should forever be commended for the effort he made in finding Dennis. He should be admired.

The more I dug into this case, the more questions seemed to pop up. In October of 2011, I had developed more questions than answers and decided to again return to the park and attempt to interview Dwight McCarter, retired NPS Ranger and author of *Lost!: A Ranger's Journal of Search and Rescue.*

Dwight's book was about his work recovering missing people in and around the Great Smoky Mountains National Park. It was also about his failure in finding some of those missing. Dwight McCarter retired from the NPS as one of the premier trackers ever to walk the park. His knowledge is vast, and his tracking skills probably one of the best in North America.

Another researcher and I found Dwight at his residence just outside the park boundaries. He was working on a car for his son when we walked up to his garage. We introduced ourselves as researching a book on missing people and asked if he wouldn't mind answering a few questions about his years of tracking. Dwight stated, "Sure."

I started our conversation with Dwight explaining that we had interviewed Dennis Martin's father and that he had given us specific insight that was not found in any other public documents. I told Dwight that I was specifically interested in the Key family observation in Rowans Creek where they saw someone darting between trees carrying something over his shoulder. Dwight started his response by explaining that he felt that it was very possible that a man could carry a boy between the point that Dennis disappeared and the Rowans Creek location in the time frame of the disappearance and the observation made by the Keys. I asked why the FBI and the NPS downplayed the sighting. Dwight stated that it was the FBI that told the public and the NPS that this wasn't feasible and to discount the event. He stated that the FBI knows nothing about people moving through the woods and time frames of possibilities, yet they told everyone involved that the Key family sighting was not relevant. Dwight went into an explanation of how he has made the walk from Spence Field to the area of Rowan's Creek and knows for a fact this can be accomplished in the time allotment that was made from when Dennis went missing until the Keys made their observation.

I asked Dwight what he thought had made the sickening scream heard by the Keys. He stated it might have been Dennis. I advised Dwight that the description of the scream by the Keys appears to be too loud for a small boy to have made. There was no response.

I asked Dwight if he and other rangers were armed when the Dennis Martin disappearance occurred. He stated, "No." The vast majority of NPS rangers were not armed until the 1970s. I then asked whether he thought it was odd that the Green Berets came into the park, set up their own communications and went out into the woods armed. Dwight stated that he did think it was a little strange, but he also stated that it was the military. Then he hesitated and stated that when the National Guard has assisted in the past, they were not armed. He stated that the Green Berets really acted on their own and didn't interact with the NPS.

I asked Dwight why one of the children of the Keys would first state that he observed a bear and then his father stated they saw a man? Dwight hesitated for several minutes and then said that in and around the park there are "wild men." He stated that there is more than one. They are hairy, dirty, and one even had an old bearskin that he wore. Dwight was careful with his words but did state that these men lived in the wild and were essentially living off the land in and around the park. I asked if he thought Dennis was taken by a "wild man." He stated that at the time he really gave it little thought. The only wild man he knew in the park at the time lived at the other end near the Cataloochee Valley and didn't venture into the area where Dennis disappeared or the area of Cades Cove at the bottom of Rowans Creek.

Dwight McCarter made it clear that the "wild men" he was speaking about were humans who decided to live in the wild. They had little contact with humanity and they appeared as the name implied, wild and unkempt. This was the first, last, and only time I have ever heard anyone mention "wild men" inside of the Great Smoky Mountains National Park.

Case Summary:

Dennis Martin avoided the efforts of over fifty county SAR teams that converged on the park to find him. The U.S. Green Beret Special Forces had almost eighty personnel at the park for ten days searching for the seven-year-old boy. They couldn't find him. Canine units from across America responded with bloodhounds and German shepherds. They couldn't sniff him out. The list of emergency personnel responding and assisting on this event ran three pages, single-spaced, on an NPS document. The response was phenomenal.

The Dennis Martin incident should be a case study every SAR commander reviews. Many elements of this event—the initial response, the inhibition of the search by rain, the organization of search resources, federal law enforcement's response, the organization of the law enforcement investigation, the decision to

$5000.00 REWARD
For information leading to the safe return of

DENNIS LLOYD MARTIN

Disappeared on June 14, 1969 at Spence Field, in the Great Smoky Mountains National Park. After extensive search efforts, no trace has been found.

Age .... 7 (Born June 20, 1962)
Height .... Approximately 4 feet
Weight .... Approximately 55 pounds
Hair .... Dark brown and wavy
Eyes .... Dark brown with long eyelashes

Family names: Father, Bill Clyde
Mother, Violet
Brothers, Douglas and Michael
Sister, Sarah

Dennis has a German Shepherd dog called 'Lady.'

Anyone having information regarding the whereabouts of this youngster, please contact your local law enforcement agency or:

William C. Martin

terminate the search, and the subsequent long-term investigation—should be analyzed and understood for their effectiveness (or lack of effectiveness).

I do not believe that more resources and more searchers would have changed the outcome of this event. There was something different about this search. If SAR leaders would open their minds, understand that they don't have all the answers, and allow new ideas and strategies to enter their minds, a different method for addressing search and rescue could take place. The best method for changing a paradigm is through brainstorming sessions with enlightened leaders—leaders not involved in daily issues related to SAR, but rather people who can see the issue from a different perspective. Decisions about searching, how people could move through the woods, distances people could travel, etc, those opinions should be rendered by people living and working the parks, not by the FBI. It appeared from Mr. Martin's statements that some type of behind-the-scenes politics was taking place and that the park superintendent wasn't really in charge.

In all of the SARs I've read, it's a rare event when Special Forces are used to find a child outside of the Great Smoky Mountains. The NPS literally turned much of the SAR for Dennis over to Special Forces, as is described in a June 20, 1969, article in the *Rock Hill Herald*: "The search can be compared to a military operation complete with a headquarters, a commanding general, squad leaders, and a mass of privates." This was truly a unique search—it used resources never before used to look for a small boy. What is more amazing is that the Green Berets entered the park, armed themselves, and then conducted a search without coordinating efforts with NPS trackers. They had their own communications system and their own camp, and they seemed to want to work independently and away from others. Very unusual.

Park officials seem to have used every available resource to find Dennis, yet the efforts failed to find one single clue of his whereabouts. This fact should tell us something. In one of the more surprising twists to the SAR, it was discovered that the park service closed Cades Cove Loop Road for three days, without explanation. The area was closed just after the Key family had made their observations near Sea Branch and Rowans Creek in Cades Cove. There is nothing in the documents I received explaining why the cove was closed.

I believe that one change in strategy could have altered the course of events in this SAR. Once leaders understood that the Harold Key family had a viable sighting, SAR commanders should have immediately expanded the perimeter ten miles into Cades Cove and searched outside-in, starting at the farthest point out from where Dennis was last seen and searching toward where he was seen by the Key family. I actually believe this happened, and that's why Cades Cove was closed. The real question is, why wouldn't SAR commanders admit to having expanded the perimeter and to including Rowans Creek and Sea Branch in the search area? I believe that the Green Berets were given this task, and this is why *they had special communications that did not interact with NPS radios and* why their helicopters were landing at the cove. Everything the Green Berets did, what they saw and how they proceeded was veiled in secrecy because of the lack of communication between their group and NPS.

I am very interested in what transpired in the meeting between FBI Agent Rike and Harold Key away from the park—was his story buffered in some way? Mr. Key's son stated that he had heard and observed a bear, which was later changed to his father saying that he saw a human. A bear normally walks on four feet, not two. What was the difference in the sighting that changed the description? Why wasn't the fact that the Keys saw someone carrying something over his shoulder in any NPS document, any newspaper article, or in any government documents ever released? Dwight McCarter confirmed he knew of this fact and didn't know why it was never made public. It almost sounds as if Special Agent Jim Rike knew the Keys had an unusual event happen to them, so unusual that he didn't want them coming to the park. He met them twenty miles away. It's obvious that the FBI and park officials never wanted this information made public, but why? The FBI still does not want this information released, and I believe this is why they refused my FOIA request for documents on the Martin case. Even if Dennis was abducted, wasn't it in the best interest of the park and the FBI to conduct a full-fledged investigation and advise the public of the threat that existed? The park and nearby communities generate over $700 million for the state and nearby cities; therefore, maybe the NPS and local communities didn't want specific information released.

A major concern that I've developed over the years I've investigated this case is what is in the FBI file, and why won't they release it? What did FBI Agent Jim Rike document that could be so damning fifty years after the event that our government cannot tell the public? The information that agent Rike accumulated through his investigations of child disappearances in the Great Smoky Mountain area are part of a very large file of hundreds of cases that the FBI has accumulated over the years that have no doubt made their way to the profiling unit and now sit in a large filing cabinet.

Imagine you read a storyline like this:

- Little boy disappears in meadow at National Park within fifty feet of parents.
- Searchers scour park for weeks with no results.
- Eighty Armed Green Beret Special Forces brought into park to search.
- Strange screams reported by a family in park.
- Something similar to a dark-figured man is seen running through the forest in park carrying something over shoulder.
- Psychic tells of seeing boy in cave-like setting.
- Another psychic tells of seeing a boy possibly in a tree.
- No trace of the boy ever found.
- Eleven people have disappeared under unusual circumstances at or near this park.
- The lead FBI agent on this case commits suicide.

Doesn't this sound like something someone would make up for a movie? Unfortunately, all of the elements listed above are fact.

Most of the people involved in this case have retired or passed away. Mr. Key died in 2010. I would like to know why there is not one mention in any park service document about the interview with Mr. Key or why there is no mention of someone carrying something over his shoulder in the woods. Does this seem like some type of censorship? It almost sounds as though the FBI and NPS was trying to manage Mr. Key's statement before it was heard by the media and Mr. Martin. I did file a second FOIA request asking for a review of the file to ensure that Key's interview and statement weren't missed in their original search. The park service responded stating that they did not have any such document.

I would gladly assist any congressional investigation into the NPS and its censorship of documents and its failure to meet FOIA requirements.

Let's pray that the Martin family has happiness and peace in their lives.

Thelma Pauline Melton, AKA "Polly"
Missing 9/25/81, 4:15 p.m., Great Smoky Mountains National Park
Age at Disappearance: 58 years
5'11", 180 lbs

The information regarding this case was gleaned from NPS documents retrieved via an FOIA request, review of archived newspaper articles and interviews with potential witnesses and participants in the search.

Thelma and Robert Melton were married and lived in Jacksonville, Florida. Every summer since 1958 the Meltons would pull their Airstream trailer to the private park and spend several weeks camping in the Deep Creek Campground in Swain County, North Carolina. There were usually several other older couples that also camped in the same area enjoying the summers in the National park sitting adjacent to their parking lot. The couples had a social gathering that included cookouts, card playing, and general socializing that goes with a group setting.

The people camping in the Deep Creek Campground came to the area because they loved the outdoors. Pauline Melton and her friends regularly walked the trails in the area and knew the park in that region quite well.

September 25 started like every other day in the Deep Creek Campground for the older sect vacationing in the area. At 10:45 a.m. Pauline and Jack Cannon arrived at camp and started to arrange their housing area. At 11:15 a.m. Pauline Melton helped Pauline Cannon cut up apples for drying. At noon, Pauline Melton had lunch with her husband and then napped in their trailer.

At 3:15p.m. Pauline Melton, Trula Gudger, and Pauline Cannon started on a hike from their trailers onto the Deep Creek Trail. The trail parallels Deep Creek and is a smooth gravel road for the majority and then has a gate that limits vehicular travel. Once inside the National Park (this area was located on the fringe of the park), the road becomes essentially a trail, and vehicles cannot enter—just pedestrians. The women took a leisurely hike, talking and enjoying the beauty that exists in the Great Smoky Mountains Park. The group saw a few horseback riders when they first started and a few people wading in the creek. As the group reached a spring near Jenkins Place, Pauline Melton commented to the group that she was thirsty but didn't want to leave the trail to get a drink. The other women asked Pauline if she wanted to turn around, but she politely said, "No." The group made it to the turnaround point when Pauline started to accelerate her pace and pulled away from the other women. Pauline Cannon stated to Pauline Melton, "I wouldn't want to be in a foot race with you, Polly." Ms. Melton turned and laughed but kept her pace, walking straight ahead down the trail.

At this point in the group's hike back to their trailers, Pauline "Polly" Melton was approximately seventy-five yards ahead of the group and approaching a slight rise in the trail. The group was .2 miles above Hammer Branch; this was the last time Pauline Melton was ever seen.

The two women arrived back at their trailers and notified Robert Melton that they had not seen Polly on their return. Robert stated that she hadn't come back down the trail. It was at this point that the group set up their own search parties to look in the obvious places that Polly would go. After an extensive search of the campground and trail, the group went to the ranger station at 6:30 p.m. and reported Polly missing.

The NPS committed fifteen men the first day to the search for Pauline Melton. The following five days saw four different canine search teams from a variety of agencies (including the FBI) comb the area around where Pauline was last seen, but nothing was found. Dennis Barnett was the NPS supervisor in charge of the search for Pauline. On October 2, Mr. Barnett made the following statement: "If she had been in the park, dogs would have found her." I find this is a very bold statement considering the history of canines finding lost people in the Great Smoky Mountains National Park; it hasn't been an overwhelming success. Maybe Polly wasn't in that exact area they had been searching, but to say that she wasn't in the park is bold, very bold. Maybe Mr. Barnett should have read the case file on Dennis Martin that occurred twelve years earlier than the Melton incident. Canines never found Dennis. In fact, canines never found a majority of the people listed in this chapter.

Case Summary:
This is another case in which a person goes missing inside the Great Smoky Mountains National Park, almost in the presence of others and is never found. Not only is Pauline never found, nothing belonging to her, shoes, scarf, jewelry, nothing is ever found. The campground where the group was staying is located in North Carolina near the far eastern end of Fontana Lake and just west of the Oconaluftee Indian Village. Deep Creek is the first valley west of Indian Creek at an elevation of 2200'. Pauline disappeared on a trail directly next to Deep Creek.

Robert Melton had a heart condition, and once he realized that Polly was missing and wasn't quickly being found, he had to be hospitalized.

Abraham Lincoln Ramsay
Missing 3/11/19, 3:15 p.m., Dunn Creek, Tennessee
Age at Disappearance: 3 years

Only three sources I could find described the events regarding the disappearance of Abe Ramsay. I used these sources, and they essentially told quite similar stories. Both of the books are excellent, and I encourage anyone who has an interest in the topic to read them. They mimic each other as far as the story. I have also used special sections of each book in the detail I have chronicled on several other missing people in the Great Smoky Mountains National Park area. The third source is an article in the *Atlanta Constitution*, dated March 20, 1919: "3-Year old Boy Vanishes in Smoky Mountains; Posses Vainly Search." The article states that Abe was attempting to follow his sisters to a local country store when he was turned back. The boy took a mountain path back to the house and not the road. Hundreds looked for Abe for days. They did find his footprints many miles from the location he was last seen, and this confused searchers. "The mysterious disappearance has aroused the entire mountain section," per the article. The article states that searchers did find the boy's footprints, but they "end so abruptly as to mystify the experienced mountaineers who are leading searchers."

Lost!: A Ranger's Journal of Search and Rescue, authored by Dwight McCarter and Ronald Schmidt, is one source I used for this disappearance. McCarter spent twenty-five years as a backcountry ranger and participated in many of the SARs that occurred in the Great Smoky Mountains National Park. Dwight's book is an excellent account of many cases in which people have disappeared into the mountains.

Unsolved Disappearances in the Great Smoky Mountains by Juanitta Baldwin and Ester Grubb is another book I have used as a source. The two women have chronicled many of the disappearances in the Smoky Mountains and have authored a very good book. The following is the general account that mimics facts presented in the two books:

Abe Ramsay was a healthy and happy three-year-old who was living with his family in the Cosby section of the Great Smoky Mountains. The family lived on the boundary of Sevier and Cocke Counties where forty-one-year old John Ramsay had established a small ten-acre farm that barely kept the family in vegetables in a good year. There were seven children in the family, with the oldest living at home being fourteen or fifteen.

The morning of March 11 was a nice day. John Ramsay left the home and went to work at his still (John was a moonshiner), and his school-age children started the walk to the schoolhouse. The family owned a "giant rawboned hound" (*Unsolved Disappearances*, p. 115), Motley, that stayed at the family home and acted as protection. On the morning of March 11, Motley suddenly took off across the porch and ran into the woods. Motley ran off just as a number of dogs started barking up the hillside. Just as this was happening, there was an "explosion of muffled barks" up the hillside (*Unsolved Disappearances*, p. 117).

At approximately 3:00 p.m. Abe put his coat on and ran around the yard and then down toward Dunn Creek in an effort to find Motley, who had still not returned. Abe's mother was now calling for Abe to come back as she walked onto the porch and looked under the house. As she looked under the house, she was surprised to see Motley, frozen in a whimpering stance and not moving. She looked at the dog with a firm stare and could see that it had been in some type of fight.

An hour after Abe disappeared, the family's other children started to arrive home from school. They were sent out to look for Abe.

During the following four days every inch of every piece of land in a three-mile radius of the Ramsay farm was searched by concerned neighbors and friends. There was only one unusual report that was forwarded to the Ramsays. There was a footprint of a barefoot child that was found in the dirt roadway quite a distance from their house, but it was never known whether it was Abe or anything related to his disappearance. In 1919 there were no formal search and rescue teams. There were no official responses to such a loss, and John Ramsay was probably concerned that if law enforcement did start to look around, they might find some stills. John did love Abe a lot. He talked to almost everyone about his son's disappearance, and it was obvious that the disappearance haunted him for decades.

There were many stories and theories about what happened to Abe, but nothing was solid, and there was no evidence supporting any specific theory.

Case Summary:

I do find one aspect of this disappearance as being unusual and not consistent with the normal behavior of a family guard dog, and that was the behavior of Motley. I also find it unusual that the behavior of the dog and the other dogs barking coincided with Abe's disappearance. Big family dogs are not afraid of bears. Bears are afraid of dogs. This wasn't a bear that took on a group of dogs and caused Motley to run and hide under the house. Whatever caused Motley's injuries and the disruption of the other dogs on the mountain was probably somehow related to the disappearance of Abe.

Michael Eugene Reel
Missing 7/2/83, 9:30 a.m., Roan Mountain State Park, TN
Age at Disappearance: 8 years
3'10", 65 lbs
Blonde Hair

**The disappearance of Michael Reel and Larry Davenport both occurred in Roan Mountain State Park. Reel disappeared from a campsite on July 2, 1983, and Davenport disappeared from a campsite on July 17, 1983. Yes, it is peculiar that both males vanished in the same park within fifteen days of each other. Once you read the specifics of each case you will understand why there is much more to these two stories than just the disappearance. There is no doubt that these two incidents have a viable connection. Roan Mountain State Park is located just north of the Great Smoky Mountains National Park.

Michael was at a campsite with his mother and one sister. He told his mother that he was going to retrieve water for the site and took a bucket and started to walk up the road. That was the last time his mother saw him for seven days. Once Michael did not immediately return, his mother started to search and then called law enforcement authorities.

In the day after Michael disappeared, the weather turned to rain, which hampered search efforts. From the beginning of this search, law enforcement was frustrated with the lack of any viable clues as to where the boy may be.

On July 5, 1983, Michael's mother made a statement to the press about his disappearance, and this was documented in the *Daily Herald* on July 5, 1983: "The boy's mother said she feared he had been kidnapped." Later in the same article was the following: "Carter County Sheriff Bill Crumley said there was no reason to suspect foul play, but Bob Carey, Toecane District Ranger for Pisgah National Forest said, 'I've been on a lot of searches; things seem a little fishy.'"

The search continued not to produce results, and it was at this point that thirty paratroopers from Fort Bragg came into the park aboard four Army helicopters. These troops scoured the park in a very defined way to find the boy. An article in the July 8, 1983 edition of the *Star News* said that Michael's father told the press that he felt his son had been abducted. Temperatures in the park at night were now in the low twenties and our Army still could not find Michael.

One hundred and forty Green Beret troops arrived at the park and divided into two-man teams. They searched specific areas of the park and used their special skills and night vision equipment to attempt to find Michael. Bloodhounds and canines were brought into the park daily to supplement the search, and nothing seemed to be working. The Green Berets knew these mountains well, they spent two weeks searching 20 miles south for Dennis Martin. On July 10, 1983 the *Hutchinson News* had a story indicating that Michael had been found exactly one week to the day and hour from when he disappeared. The article stated, "Bailey said that rescuers found the child two and a half miles from the campsite where he disappeared last Saturday." The article stated that Michael made a few interesting statements: "Taylor Bailey, one of the men who found the boy, said Michael indicated he spent part of the week in a deserted cabin that was not searched by the Army trackers or Green Berets and hundreds of others who joined the hunt. But park superintendent Glen Hatfield said he found it hard to believe any cabin was missed in the exhaustive week-long hunt." Rescuers stated that they had found the boy in an area searched many times before, as he was in a blackberry thicket.

Other articles stated that Michael described events to rescuers that seemed incredible:
Rescue squad members said the boy talked of having spent time watching television with his grandfather, but they believed he had hallucinated. Doctors said he was alert and oriented by the time he reached the hospital, but because of the boy's confusion, authorities hadn't been able to learn how he spent the past seven to eight days.

In later interviews with Michael's mother, she stated that she found Michael's stories amazing, especially since he had no recollection of ever meeting either grandfather, as both were deceased.

Michael's mother did say that Michael explained to her that he had spent time on the mountain with someone on Friday night, but he was unable or refused to say who or what. On July 11, 1983 the *Tuscaloosa News* ran a story with the following regarding Michael's story:

The boy also said he had seen his mother Thursday near the campsite and called to her so he "wouldn't get lost again." Michael said he had seen "an old man getting drunk on Budweiser beer and a gallon of bourbon." He said he didn't seek the man's help because he doesn't talk to strangers. Michael also said he'd eaten bacon and eggs with his grandfather Saturday morning. But a relative said both his grandfathers are dead, and the boy remembers neither of them.

Several of the articles I reviewed for this story indicated that when Michael was found, he appeared well kept and his hair seemed to be combed and or clean. His clothes were dirty and torn, and he did have many scratches around the ankles. Doctors who examined Michael were amazed at his condition, given the number of days he was missing.

Case Summary:
Parents usually know their children and associated behavior. When both of Michael's parents stated that they felt their boy had been abducted, maybe law enforcement should have taken them seriously. One forest ranger did make a statement about the incident being "fishy."

It seems highly unusual that Michael was gone over seven days in temperatures that got quite cold at night and did rain, yet he was found in a fairly neat and clean state.

Some of the doctors and searchers claimed that Michael was hallucinating about meals with his relatives, seeing family members, etc. Why would a healthy young boy in good shape be hallucinating (especially hallucinating about people he'd never met)? He had made statements that he had eaten fruit, berries, etc. and then later made a statement about having a full breakfast.

I find it incredible that the best soldiers we have in our military could not find Michael on Roan Mountain, yet that is exactly where the boy was located at the end of seven days. There are many stories in this book that document searchers looking in a specific area for a lost individual and then that person appears exactly in the area previously searched.

I believe that the family was very fortunate to get Michael back alive. The huge response from military and locals was the catalyst for a healthy recovery of the boy.

Larry Davenport
Missing 7/17/83, Evening hours, Roan Mountain State Park, North Carolina
Age at Disappearance: 20 years

Larry was camping with friends on the Western Peak on the North Carolina side of the Roan Mountain State Park. Just like the Great Smoky Mountains National Park, Roan Mountain straddles both North Carolina and Tennessee. The Roan Mountain cases are included in this section because they are just north of the Great Smoky Mountains National Park and are located in the same continuous mountain range.

On July 17, 1983, Larry was sitting at a wooden table with friends when he got up and headed to the woods. Nobody at the table thought much about Larry leaving. Some thought he was going to empty his bladder. When Larry didn't return, friends obtained assistance from the Forest Service and park rangers, and a search ensued.

The three-day effort to find Larry was very uneventful, and searchers found little evidence of where he might be located. It was near the end of the third day that searchers got a call to respond eight miles from Larry's campsite near an abandoned home where witnesses saw a man wandering. Search teams went to the area and found Larry naked except for a curtain wrapped around his shoulders. Larry had scratches covering his entire body, and he seemed to be incoherent. He would ramble and make statements that made little sense. He didn't know where his clothing was but did state he found the curtains in an old cabin.

Bloodhounds and hundreds of trained searchers had failed to find Larry—the same as what happened with Michael Reel. Larry was transported to an area hospital where he was treated for "acute brain syndrome" and held. The hospital stated that Mr. Davenport was confused when he arrived, and the facility did admit him.

Case Summary:

In both the Davenport and Reel cases, the males walked away from a campsite setting to immediately go missing. Both males were found confused, hallucinating, and making little sense. Davenport was found naked, which follows many cases cited in this book where people shed clothing when they are lost. I do not believe that these are both random occurrences with random males. Two missing people exhibiting similar physical and mental traits all disappearing at the same park in a two-week time span—there has to be a connection.

Jay Charles Toney
Missing 05/25/82, 1:30 p.m., Clingman's Dome, Great Smoky Mountains National Park
Age at Disappearance: 17 years
6'1", 175 lbs
Diabetic

Jay Toney and four friends took a short vacation and went to the World's Fair in Knoxville, TN. Once the group was done with the fair, they headed for the Great Smoky Mountains National Park and Clingman's Dome. The Dome is the highest point in the park at 6,643 feet. The men parked the car and took the one-mile hike to the summit and then headed back down. On the way down the paved trail, Jay told the group that he was going to take a shortcut through the woods and would meet them at their car. He never arrived.

The group was very concerned for Jay because he was a diabetic and needed insulin. They immediately contacted the National Park Service and a search was initiated. It was approximately 1:30 p.m. when they last saw Jay.

The first night that Jay was missing a torrential rainstorm hit the park and the surrounding area, and that was followed by very thick fog. This is a familiar theme: people disappear and a storm immediately hits the area of the disappearance. The storm completely cleaned much of the scent from the air and also removed any footprints that were in the dirt. The first day of the search didn't produce significant results, and searchers felt frustrated. This scenario at this point was almost identical to the disappearance of Trenny Gibson.

The second day of the search the park service brought in six different canine teams and spread throughout the area. At 2:30 p.m. one search team was over eight miles from the last location at which Jay was observed, and they were searching a creek bed when they saw a body lying on the ground near the creek. Searchers walked up to Jay Toney and found him unconscious. Rescuers stated that

Jay had an ashen-colored face, and when he was shaken, he stated, "I want out of the Smokies." An article in the *Milwaukee Journal* dated May 28, 1982 stated the following:

A team of tracking dogs combing a remote section of the 518,000-acre park found Jay Toney, 17, of Mounds, Oklahoma, along a stream Thursday afternoon. Rescuers stated Toney was wearing only one shoe and a tank top shirt when found. He slipped into unconsciousness in the four hours it took to ferry him by helicopter from a rugged section of the park to University of Tennessee Hospital in Knoxville, 35 miles northwest.

Jay was placed in intensive care and did survive.

Several articles made note of the "mysterious" disappearances of several people in the Great Smoky Mountains National Park and named names.

Case Summary:

The obvious question comes to mind in the Jay Toney case—what happened to his clothes? There was never any notation that his clothes were found. There were many notes in several articles about two torrential rainstorms that hit the area since Jay disappeared and a thick fog that appeared. Jay was found eight miles from where he was last seen. That seems like an extraordinary distance for him to travel in one-plus day. The fact that Jay was found unconscious, lying in a creek bed and missing clothing is bothersome, as these circumstances mimic those of prior incidents cited in both books.

Chapter Conclusions

I want readers to bookmark the first page of this chapter that lists the missing people. I want you to look at the times listed for the missing people. It is extremely significant that six people disappeared in or directly near the park and that they all disappeared in a time span between 3:00 p.m.–4:30 p.m., ninety minutes. The odds that six people would disappear over a ninety-year time span and that they all disappeared within a ninety-minute window are astronomical. What is it about this time window?

Another very odd fact is that all three women disappeared on a Friday. The closest two disappearances by date were Trenny Gibson and Mark Hanson, seventeen months apart. The disappearances of Gibson, Hague, Hanson, and Martin were immediately followed by extremely bad weather. SAR teams made note of the weather in every report and indicated that the weather played a major role in the search.

Each of the rank-and-file searchers in these incidents should be commended for their personal sacrifice and extreme effort to find the missing. The top administrators at each park are ultimately responsible for all operations occurring inside their system. I can tell you from personal knowledge that rangers are similar to police officers. They do their job because they like serving the public, and they will make great sacrifices in an effort to save a life. We are blessed to have people of this character working in public service.

Ohio

Missing People in Ohio by Date
Seven of eight people on this Ohio list are males. The missing fitting the criteria in this book in Ohio is confined to a fifty eight-year span between 1902 and 1960. It seems a bit unusual that there are four consecutive cases in Ohio where all went missing in the first half of August.

Name	Date Missing•Age•Sex
Riley Amsbaugh	07/25/1902•55•M
E.C. Jones	11/12/1903•NA•M
Johnnie Lembke	08/12/1910•15•M
William Pitsenbarger	08/07/31•61•M
Carolyn Peterson	08/20/47•20MOS•F
Jerry Lee Huffman	08/05/48•3•M
Randy Moy	01/08/60•3•M

Details regarding Lembke can be found under the "Berry Pickers" chapter. All others except Peterson and Hoffman can be found in the "Farmers" section.

Carolyn Peterson
Missing 08/20/47, 11:00 a.m., ten miles s/o Marion, Ohio
Age at Disappearance: 20 Months

The location of the Peterson residence was ten miles south of Marion and adjacent to the Delaware Wilderness Area and Delaware Lake. It was a rural location with few homes or cars in the area.

On August 20, 1947, Carolyn was placed in her yard by her mother and told she could play. A short time after Carolyn was placed in the yard, Mrs. Peterson went out to check on her, but couldn't find her. A search was made of the surrounding farm area, but the girl could not be located. The Petersons contacted law enforcement and neighbors who soon arrived and started a formal search.

The Marion County Sheriff's Office was the primary law enforcement agency leading the search, and Sheriff Leroy Reterer was the person on scene heading the effort.

Soon after Carolyn disappeared, the Marion area was inundated with two severe thunderstorms that dropped several inches of rain. Searchers were temporarily impeded in their efforts by the rain but did complete dragging of Ququa Creek, mowing fields, and probing old wells, all without finding Carolyn. At the height of the search, the sheriff stated that over one thousand people were combing the area looking for the little girl.

After a short forty-eight hours of searching, Sheriff Reterer terminated the search claiming that he felt the girl had been kidnapped. The sheriff did not believe the girl could be in the area due to the extensive searching and her inability to move a long distance because of her age. An article in the *Telegraph Herald* dated August 22, 1947 had the following: "Her father, Charles Peterson, and Sheriff Leroy Reterer believed that the tot was kidnapped, possibly by a childless couple who were attracted by her beauty."

On Saturday, August, 23, 1947, a local farmer, Samuel Almendinger (seventy-five years of age) was walking a perimeter path of his farm and heard a faint voice in a briar patch. The farmer couldn't believe someone would be in the patch, but he struggled his way through the thickets and found Carolyn Peterson, alive. The girl had blackberry stains on her hands, but when found she was sitting on the ground with her hands through a wire fence, and it appeared she had been playing. He picked the girl up and took her back to the Peterson farm.

Carolyn was taken to the hospital for an examination. She was found to have dozens of small scratches throughout her body. She was in remarkably good condition. Doctors couldn't explain how the girl had been missing over four days and hadn't suffered sunburn.

Jerry Lee Huffman
Missing 8/5/48, 6:00 p.m., Philo, Ohio
Age at Disappearance: 3 years

Philo, Ohio, is ten miles southeast of Zanesville and approximately sixty miles west of the Pennsylvania border. The town sits on the Muckingam River and has a population just shy of eight hundred.

On August 5, 1948, Jerry Lee Huffman was playing with his pet collie "Laddie" in the yard of his family's farm on the outskirts of

Philo. At 6:00 p.m., Jerry's father, Dan Huffman, went to look for the boy and could not locate him or the family dog. Mr. Huffman searched the perimeter area of the farm and did find the child's clothes at the far end of his property. Mr. Huffman was very concerned for Jerry's safety and called authorities for assistance.

The local sheriff and state police responded to the Huffman residence and started to formalize the search process. Over two hundred neighbors responded to look for the boy and immediately set out into the fields of corn looking and yelling for Jerry Lee. The search for the boy continued through the night nonstop.

At 6:00 a.m. the morning after Jerry Lee disappeared, the family Collie, "Laddie," walked up to the family residence. Mr. Huffman calmed the dog and then asked it to take them to Jerry Lee. Mr. Huffman and a neighbor followed the dog for a mile and a half across an adjacent cornfield to a wire fence. At the wire fence the men found Jerry Lee with his foot caught in the fence and a wild grapevine wrapped around his neck. The boy was semiconscious and turning blue. The temperature outside was fifty-five degrees and Jerry Lee was naked.

Jerry Lee was transported to Bethesda Hospital where he was found to be in satisfactory condition. Jerry Lee never explained why he left or what he did during his night in the fields—or why he removed his clothes.

Randy Moy
Missing 01/08/60, 3:30 p.m., Vernon Township, Ohio
Age at Disappearance: 3 years

Randy and his family lived in a rural community just outside of Vernon, Ohio. On January 8, 1960 at approximately 3:30 p.m., Randy was outside with his two dogs when, for an inexplicable reason, the dogs went running straight into the woods. Randy followed. When Randy's mother came out onto the porch, other children told her what Randy had done, and she started the search for the boy.

Four hundred people responded to the request for searchers for Randy Moy. Law enforcement obtained the assistance of helicopters, bloodhounds, civil defense workers, and off-duty foremen in the search for Randy. Seventeen hours after the boy disappeared, two searchers were one and a half miles from his residence and found the boy in a briar patch near a stream.

Police officers were called to the area where Randy was found and were asked to transport him immediately to the hospital. The *Gazette Mail* ran a story describing the trip on January 10, 1960: "He (Randy) was gasping and his eyes rolled back into his head." The boy made it to the hospital and was listed in satisfactory condition with shock and exposure. The boy was admitted to the hospital "groggy and sleepy" and was released two days later.

Two days after being found, Sheriff Wayne Mumma stated that he tried to question Randy about his journey, but he refused to talk. Randy's father John Moy described it as a miracle that Randy survived. One of Randy's dogs was found in the general region in which searchers found the boy.

Randy's condition when found is very similar to many children when they are located. Several children have been found deceased in fields, and it may be assumed that Randy would have died without being found when he was.

Pennsylvania Region

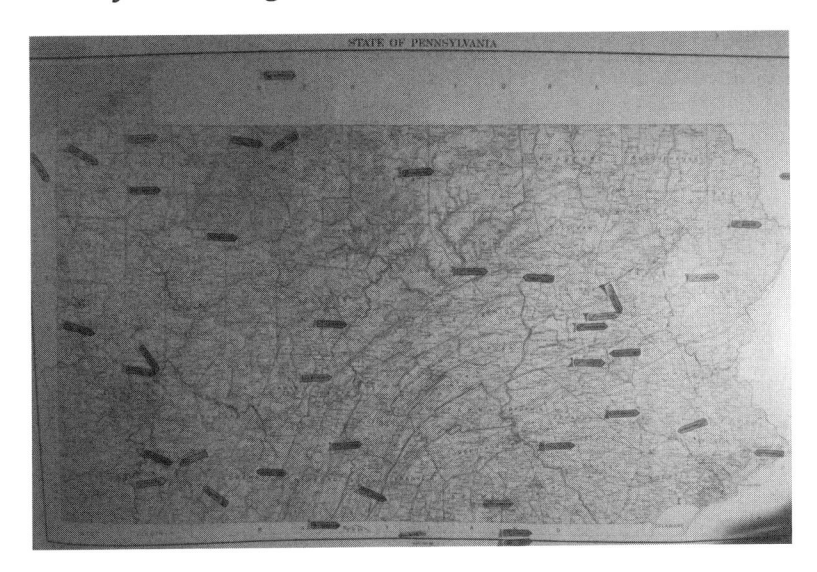

P ennsylvania offers a wide diversity in missing person cases.

The reader should be aware that Pennsylvania had more children disappear from 1934–1957 than any other state. The factors behind each disappearance were quite similar, and the geographic proximity to each other should not be ignored. Pennsylvania has had more children under the age of ten disappear (twenty-eight) than any other state or province; no other location is even close.

With eight two-year-olds, ten three-year-olds, and five four-year-olds missing, everyone should take a deep breath while reading this chapter. Some cases occurred just over the state lines but are in close geographical proximity to the cases within the state; thus, they are included in this chapter. Something very peculiar was happening in Pennsylvania in the early to mid-1900s. You will see the similarity in cases. Some seem like cookie-cutter cases, almost identical to each other. I did not look for cases that mimicked each other—they presented themselves.

In 1968 the profile of people who went missing in Pennsylvania changed—they got older. It's also noteworthy that the last seven cases in this state were all men. The profile of people who went missing changed, but there was also an eleven-year gap of people reported missing prior to that change taking place. The big question is why there was an eleven-year gap in people who went missing in Pennsylvania.

Missing People in Pennsylvania by Date

Name	Date Missing•Age•Sex
Stephen Ford••	08/05/1880•9•M
Wolfe	07/08/1882•10•M
Bachman	06/10/1883•4MOS•M
Davis	05/09/1888•30MOS•F
Mary Sholtas	04/21/1897•3•F
Augustus Staneker	04/21/1897•4•M
Simpson	05/27/1901•3•F
James Glass	05/12/15•4•M
Geraldine Markline	10/26/29•2•F
Else Flothmeier	02/24/32•22•F
Rita Lent	11/22/34•2•F
Marjorie West	05/08/38•4•F
Donald Farrington	09/11/38•3•M
Emma Steffy	07/18/39•75•F
Ronald Rumbaugh	09/15/40•2•M
Rudy Kunchick	10/21/40•4•M
Eldridge Albright	05/21/41•3•M
Betty Bossier	06/25/41•3•F
Joseph Prato	10/25/41•19MOS•M
Alvan Diggan	05/30/42•3•M
Eugene Shue	10/20/46•3•M
Jimmy Sensor	04/06/47•4•M
Ronald Collier	07/02/48•23MOS•M
Billy Abbott	02/18/49•3•M
Billy Clever	04/26/49•3•M
Otis T. Mason	10/11/49•6•M
Anna Thorpe	05/05/50•6•F
Jackie Copeland	05/14/50•2•F
Emma Bowers	07/22/53•5•F

Fred Holmes   05/25/55•23MOS•M
Candida Streeter   10/03/57•2•F
                    **Eleven-Year Gap
Karen Cooney   07/08/68•15•F
Harold Mott   03/02/76•12•M
Duane Scott   07/27/78•31•M
Jon Dabkowski   01/14/82•11•M
Greg Minarcin   01/14/82•10•M
Emerson Carbaugh   11/11/85•64•M
Michael Malinoski   10/24/96•37•M
Charles Beltz   06/07/05•56•M
Total Cases= 39
Females= 14
Males= 25

••Refer to "Berry Pickers" Chapter for information about the Stephen Ford disappearance.

Largest group of missing by age:
2-Year Olds = 8
3-Year Olds =10
4-Year Olds = 5

Pennsylvania Missing by Month

Month	Total Missing
January	2
February	2
March	1
April	4
May	9
June	3
July	6
August	1
September	2
October	7
November	2
December	0
Total	39

I've put many hours of thought into why more people go missing in May than any other month, and I can't develop a rational reason. It is one of the first months that people can get into the outdoors after a long winter, but that should not account for such a large number.

Years with the most missing: 1941 & 1949, with three missing.

Unknown First Name, Wolfe
Missing 7/8/1882, Girard Manor, Pottsville, Pennsylvania
Age at Disappearance: 10 years
*Deaf-Mute

A massive periodical search through multiple databases allowed me to locate a July 19, 1882 article in the *New York Times* outlining what happened to the ten-year-old boy. The article describes the boy as the ten-year-old son of a wealthy farmer named George Wolfe. The family's residence had a high fence surrounding their home and yard. The family lived in a rural area described as being three miles east of Girard Manor in the Catawissa Valley of Pennsylvania.

At some point in the late afternoon, the door in the yard fence was open and their son somehow left. The family didn't recognize the boy's disappearance for several hours.

The family immediately gained the assistance of local neighbors and twenty-five people combed the woods near the house. The search continued for six days and included 250 searchers by the sixth and final day. Searchers had to walk through swamps filled with snakes, forests, fields, and many other obstacles.

On the sixth day of searching, George Wolfe found his son sitting on a rock five miles from his farm. The boy was in horrible condition, per news article. The article states that he had snake and insect bites and numerous scratches and bruises.

The last line in the article states, "His clothing consisted of a night shirt only."

Unknown first name, last name Bachman
Missing 6/10/1883, PM, e/o Pottsville, Pennsylvania
Age at Disappearance: 4 months

John Bachman, his wife, and their two children took an afternoon walk to their favorite spot. The Bachmans had left their four-month-old son (unknown name) in a crib inside their unlocked home. The house was in a very rural area in the Tumbling Run Valley of eastern Pennsylvania, four miles east of Pottsville. The home was left protected by the family guard dog.

The family was gone just a matter of minutes when they heard their dog howling in a way that made the family very uncomfortable. The Bachmans rushed back to their home and found their baby missing, but all of their valuables in the home were left untouched. The family searched into the night and could not find the child.

The day after the disappearance the family went into Pottsville and asked for the assistance of the sheriff and local residents. Another search was initiated, and the baby was still not found.

The disappearance of the "Wolfe" boy was in close proximity to the disappearance of Bachman. I never found another article indicating the child was found.

Unknown First Name-Davis
Missing 5/9/1888, Boiceville, New York
Age at Disappearance: 30 months

There was one article about the disappearance of Millard Davis's daughter from the family's residence in Boiceville, New York, in the Catskill Mountains. The article was in the *New York Times*, May 15, 1888.

Millard's daughter disappeared, and a search went through the night looking for the girl. The day after she disappeared, a trout fisherman two miles from the family's residence was in a deep ravine and spotted the girl standing in the middle of the brook. The fisherman took the girl to the parents where she was questioned about her ordeal.

The little girl was never known to tell stories and in fact is too young and innocent to practice deceit. When her father asked her where she had slept all night the little one answered, "In the woods with a big bear, papa." She was closely questioned but the child adhered to her story that she had slept with a bear in the woods, and people in Boiceville believe that the little girl did really meet with a bear and not knowing what it was, went up to it, and for some reason the beast refrained from hurting the wanderer.

This story is very similar to other stories in this book of children claiming to be abducted by a bear. Sometimes they sleep with the bear, and sometimes they are merely carried away. In all of the instances that are cited, the victim is never seriously injured.

I find this and other stories about bear taking children highly suspicious. I believe that the children believe what they are saying; I question whether it was really a bear.

I have placed the Davis incident in the Pennsylvania section because it occurred just thirty miles east of the eastern border of the state, and it matches other cases that have occurred in this chapter.

Readers need to take note of where the Davis girl was found, standing in the middle of a creek, a location where no tracks of footprints will be found.

Mary Sholtas, 3 years
Augustus Staneker, 4 years
Missing 04/21/1897, Hazleton, Pennsylvania

Mary Sholtas and Augustus Staneker were living in a small village called Hazle Brook, two miles west of Hazleton. On April 21, the two children were playing behind their home and apparently wandered away and into the woods. The parents of the children soon realized that the kids were gone and started to search. The local community had only a dozen homes in the area. The residents all assisted in the search.

The area where the children lived was very swampy with a small mountain just to the northwest. The search lasted several days and combed the small mountain that was near the residence. The children were not found after the search, and it was felt by the community that the children must have been abducted. In the following months, families of the children went as far as New York in search of possible information and sightings of their children, but nothing ever panned out.

On July 6, 1897 a berry picker was on the mountain behind the residences in Hazle Brook and found the bodies of the two children. The bodies were in an advanced state of decomposition, but they were identified. One article stated that volunteers had heavily searched the area that the children were found.

Two miles southwest of Hazle Brook is Sheppton. In 1940 Rudy Kunchick disappeared from watching his father work with coal. He was found after a fifty-one-hour search.

I find it almost unreal that two children disappear at the same time and then are found deceased in the same area. It is rare that people disappear and die together especially when the climate isn't severe, such as in April. A cause of death was never established, but this is another case in which berries play into the location of the missing and the missing were found in an area that was previously searched.

Unbknown First Name, Simpson
Missing 5/27/1901, Cresco, Stroudsburg, Pennsylvania
Age at Disappearance: 3 years

This is another case in which the article did not give the first name of the missing child. The May 28, 1901 *New York Times* article merely stated that missing girl was the daughter of Frank Simpson.

The article states that the girl was playing with family members when she walked into the woods for some unknown reason. The children tried to lure her out, but she disappeared. The family summoned neighbors and friends to search the woods but could not find the girl.

I could not find any other articles about this incident, but there was one sentence in the article I found that was disturbing: "Is believed to have been carried off by a bear in the woods near here." There is no explanation why the family believes the child was taken by a bear.

James Glass
Missing 5/12/1915, Greeley, Pennsylvania
Age at Disappearance: 4 years

Mr. and Mrs. Charles Glass and their son Jimmie left their residence in New Jersey and headed for a summer cottage just outside Greeley, Pennsylvania. Mr. Glass was an auditor for the Erie Railroad and enjoyed his summer weather with a jaunt to Pennsylvania.

One day on vacation, Jimmie accompanied his mother to the Greeley Post Office. The post office was three hundred feet from their summer home and was an easy walk. Mr. Glass watched as Jimmie and his wife made the short walk, and Jimmie disappeared behind a tree enroute to do the mailing. Mrs. Glass deposited their letters turned behind her and realized that Jimmie had disappeared. She immediately searched the area and then ran back to get her husband. Before too long, the entire neighborhood was looking for Jimmie. It wasn't long before the police were involved in the search for the boy, but no leads could be found.

In the weeks that followed the disappearance of Jimmie Glass, his father made several statements that he felt his son had been abducted. He stated that he didn't think the boy could disappear that quickly without someone taking him (This same language repeats itself throughout both books on several cases).

During the next few years the search for Jimmie Glass went across the United States. The Glasses traveled near and far on reports that their son had been found or someone looking like their son was found.

Eight years after Jimmie Glass disappeared, a hunter was in the wilds of Pike County, Pennsylvania, and found a small skeleton in the middle of a swamp among a thorn thicket. One shoe was found next to the body, and that was identified as Jimmie's. Mr. Glass adamantly stated that his son did not wander off and die, as many law enforcement officers stated but that his boy had to have been abducted to get to the location where his body was found. There was no way Jimmie could have walked to that location in the swamp. The location in the swamp was approximately two miles from the farmhouse that the Glasses were staying in when Jimmie disappeared. There was only a small buckle, a few bones, and the shoe found at the location where Jimmie was discovered.

What happened to Jimmie Glass? Well, someone or something took him to the thorn thicket. A December 6, 1923 article in the *Toledo Blade* had the following: "The father reiterated his belief that the boy did not wander away and die of starvation, as Pennsylvania authorities believe. Jimmy was either murdered by kidnappers or died of exposure, and his body was thrown into the swamp."

Put a marker on this page, as the facts surrounding where this boy was found will appear several times in this book.

Geraldine Markline
Missing 10/26/29, 3½ Miles northeast of Hanover, Pennsylvania
Age at Disappearance: 2 years

Hanover is located approximately fifteen miles southwest of York and is located in the southeastern portion of Pennsylvania. The city is surrounded by several large and small bodies of water with significant open space. Approximately three miles northeast from Hanover is the Pigeon Mountains. The mountains rise from the valley floor at an elevation of 600 feet and rise to the summit at 1200 feet. The hills are still covered with lush vegetation and are surrounded by farms. At the northeast corner of the hills is Lake Pahagasco. The Markline farm was located approximately halfway between Hanover and the Pigeon Hills and twenty miles north of the Maryland border.

On October 26, 1929, Mrs. Markline needed to travel to Hanover on business and decided to put her oldest boy (Luther) in charge of the children while she was gone. After Mrs. Markline left, Luther took the children into the backyard, and they started to collect leaves for the barn. He put Geraldine in a sitting position in the backyard at the bottom of a large tree and told her to stay put while he ran into the house to get food. After a very short time, Luther returned and found Geraldine was missing. The children and Luther searched for their sister but could not find her. When Mrs. Markline returned from her excursion, Luther told her Geraldine was missing, and she contacted authorities.

There were dozens of searchers scouring the wooded trails and hillsides near the Markline farm before it became dark on October 26. Many searchers were yelling for Geraldine and couldn't find any evidence of her whereabouts. The searchers quickly became very concerned because the Markline farm was in a very rural area and near the heavy woods of the Pigeon Mountains 1.5 miles to the northeast.

Searchers started the second day with the assistance of Hanover police and were baffled by where a two-year-old girl could go without being detected. On October 28, 1929, the *Pittsburgh Post*

Gazette ran the following article: "While some feared that an abandoned waterfield quarry near her home held her body and her father thinks the child kidnapped, thousands of persons last night scoured the Pigeon Hills in a hope of finding a trace of Geraldine Markline, 2, missing since Saturday." Imagine thousands of searchers scouring a very confined area for a missing two-year-old child, a child who can't run, can barely walk, and the searchers are finding nothing. This is another case in which the parents know their child, they know how far she can travel, and they start to believe that searchers are not finding her in an area where she should be located, so they conclude that she must have been kidnapped.

On Monday, October 28, searchers were working the area in the Pigeon Mountains and up in elevation from the Markline Farm and found Geraldine. The girl was missing her coat, hat, one set of leggings, and one shoe. None of the clothes was ever found. Geraldine had numerous scratches over her body but was in very good condition.

Geraldine was unable to explain what happened or where she was during the search.

There are other disappearances of people in close proximity and just south of Hanover. Geraldine's disappearance was really the modern-day start to disappearances of children and young adults in Pennsylvania that continued from 1929 until 1957 and then inexplicably stopped.

Else Flothmeier
Missing 2/24/32, PM, Near Burholme Park, Fox Chase, Pennsylvania
Age at Disappearance: 22 years

Reverend Frederick Flothmeier had taken his daughter (Else) to a parishioner's home for a visit. When the reverend went inside, Else stated that she was going to take a walk in the park across the street. After a short visit, the reverend entered the park and couldn't find his daughter. After a short search of a small area near Burholme Park, the police were called.

The police determined that Else had made her way to near Fox Chase and an area of heavy undergrowth near a river that flows to the Delaware River. A February 25 article in the *Meriden Record* quoted a witness near the area where Else was eventually found:

Mrs. Helen Soltes, whose home is about 200 yards from where the body was found told police about 7 o'clock last night (February 24) she heard a woman scream and then another sound that might have been a man's voice. It seemed to come from the direction of the field; she said it was so dark she decided not to investigate.

Approximately twenty-four hours after Else disappeared, two men searching with the assistance of the police found Else's nude body inside a clump of blackberry bushes. She was found face down, her head resting on her right arm, and her fist clenched. The police searched the area and found her clothes hanging on a blackberry bush two hundred yards from her body.

The police made an initial statement that they found scratches on Else's face, back, and legs, which indicated to them that she had been dragged on the frozen ground. The police changed their story a day later when Else's father asked whether she was attacked. They stated, "No, she died of natural causes."

An autopsy was conducted on Else's body, and the cause of death was listed as "exposure." In an interesting note, the doctor stated that Else was suffering from a small temperature at the time of her death.

Case Summary:

Police went to great lengths to develop an explanation for Else's death. A *Reading Eagle* article dated February 26, 1932 quoted Dr. Thaddeus Bolton, a psychologist from Temple University who stated that Else died of "Moon Madness." He stated she was driven insane by the rays of the full moon. Yes, really, the doctor stated "Moon Madness."

Else was a college student, bright, attractive, and energetic. The night she disappeared was a brutally cold winter night in Pennsylvania. Something happened to Else, highlighted by the scream and "other noise" heard by Mrs. Soltes. I'm not sure how the police ignored Mrs. Soltes's statement or how they retracted their statement about Else being dragged.

Read each of the Pennsylvania cases and make your own decision—are there similarities?

When humans have temperatures that are above normal, it makes us hot, and we sometimes shed clothing. There are a few cases in which physicians made statements to the press that the missing person was found with a slight fever. A majority of cases in this book indicate that the victims never saw a doctor after they were found, or they saw the doctor long after they were recovered and maybe didn't exhibit a fever. In conversations with other researchers, we started to question whether many of the missing in this book that shed clothing may have somehow developed a high temperature, shed their clothing, and for some unexplained reason the temperature started to subside near the time they were located, or, they never took their own clothing off. The temperature is a theory based on a very small number of the missing in which the doctor told the press about a minor temperature.

Rita Margaret Lent
Missing 11/22/34, Noon, North Richmond Township, Ohio
Age at Disappearance: 3 years
Blonde Hair
**This case is from Ohio but it happened less than five miles from the Pennsylvania border, thus will be included with Pennsylvania.

On November 22, 1934, Rita was playing in her yard in a rural area of northern Richmond Township. The area is spotted with small and large farms and wet and marshy areas. It was near lunchtime and Rita's mother looked out the window of her home and saw Rita playing with her German shepherd police dog (Buddy). The mother checked again fifteen minutes later and didn't see Rita or Buddy and went into the yard to search for them.

Mrs. Oliva Lent (thirty-four years) walked out to her farm and could not locate Rita or the dog. She called the child's name several times and did not get a response. Rita immediately summoned neighbors and law enforcement for assistance. Within hours after Oliva discovered Rita missing, dozens of searchers were combing the grounds of the farm and the surrounding areas.

Oliva was legally separated from her husband, Rita's father, Darrell. The father lived outside of Richmond in Conneault but spent considerable time around the farm looking for his daughter. Seven days of searching did not produce one lead in Rita's disappearance.

It was at this point that Oliva stated that she felt her daughter had been kidnapped. She stated that the area had been extensively searched and didn't believe that she could have walked further.

During the search for Rita, one very odd occurrence did happen—Buddy returned. It had rained the night that Rita disappeared, and Buddy returned home late that night, but Buddy was completely dry, something that promoted the idea that a kidnapping may have occurred.

During the initial investigation, police were convinced that something unusual happened to Rita. They called Oliva and her ranch hand into the police station and questioned her for hours. It was obvious that the police felt that Oliva knew more than what she was saying, and they were trying a tactic to get her to say something incriminating. The only thing Oliva said was that the police held her for an unreasonable amount of time, they wouldn't let her leave, and she fell asleep exhausted while being questioned.

Nothing happened on the Rita Lent disappearance for almost three months. On February 16, 1935, a farm hand two miles from the lent farm was walking through a cow pasture and saw something bulky on the ground in a large mud puddle. He walked to the puddle and found the body of Rita Lent. The body was moderately decomposed and it was missing a shoe, but it was Rita. The body was found three hundred feet from a barn in a very muddy area near the edge of a ditch.

The finding of Rita's body caused even more concerns to law enforcement. The farmer and ranch hand that found the body made statements indicating that the body may have been there for months, but they doubted it. They stated it was an area where they would normally pass, and they didn't think they had ever seen the body before.

A February 18, 1935 article in the *San Antonio Express* stated the following: "Coroner Watson said he does not believe the child's body had lain in the mud hole in which it was discovered since last November. Its good state of preservation indicates to me that it had been in a cool place, either a cellar or basement and only recently placed in the mud hole where it was discovered, Watson stated. There are several mysterious circumstances surrounding this case, stated Sheriff Benson." The article didn't list one other possibility of where the body may have been located, a cave.

A February 16, 1935 article in the *St. Joseph Press* stated. "Deputy Sheriff R. M. Blancha, who led the search, said he believed Rita had been kidnapped."

A February 16, 1935 article in the *St. Petersburg Times* stated the following:

The mother was brought to Jefferson for questioning. She alternately wept and discussed the case in an analytical manner. "The child was kidnapped," stated Mrs. Lent. "There is no doubt that Rita was kidnapped and placed there. How could the little thing have walked that far? Why, she would have had to have walked four miles and crossed a creek to get to the place where she was found."

I believe that Mrs. Lent was talking about the route that Rita must have walked, four miles; the location where she was found was two air miles from the Lent front yard.

Rita's body was sent to a training hospital where the coroner requested that all internal organs be analyzed for poisons. They even kept Mrs. Lent in custody while the testing was completed. No poisons were found in Rita's body.

The final death report indicated that Rita's body did not show any inflicted violence, and it was felt that she died of natural causes.

Case Summary:

This is probably one of the best-documented cases I have ever read in newspaper articles. There was a massive search by two hundred people; many felt the area where Rita was eventually found had been thoroughly searched. Months went by without Rita being found. The girl was eventually found on a nearby farm. Coroners believe that she had been moved to the location where she was found; she didn't die in the muddy ditch.

Many questions arise from the police and coroner's investigation. If Rita's body was placed in the cow field, it was placed there to be discovered, but why? The coroner stated that the body had been kept in a cool place. Could that have been in one of thousands of caves throughout Pennsylvania and Ohio? If the coroner determined that Rita died of natural causes, why would someone have concealed the body for months?

The last major question deals with Buddy, the family dog. The canine was a trained police dog, yet it left Rita alone and came home, why?

I do agree with Sheriff Benson that there are several issues with this case that are very mysterious, but,many of the facts surrounding this disappearance can be found in disappearances of other children in Pennsylvania. It would almost appear as though Rita's body fell out of the sky.

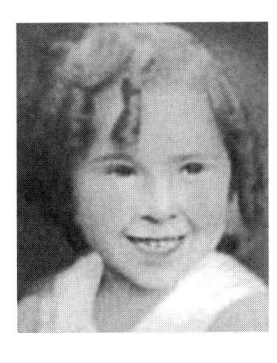

Marjorie West
Missing 5/8/38, Marshburg, McKean County, Pennsylvania
Age at Disappearance: 4 years

Mother's Day in 1938 started with a religious service for the West family. They attended church in their hometown of Bradford. The parents decided to take a forty-minute drive into a region called "White Gravel" where they would have a picnic, fish, and pick wildflowers.

As the family arrived, Marjorie and her eleven-year-old sister, Dorothea, walked off to look for flowers while her father stood nearby fishing in a creek. The mother stayed in the family car and enjoyed the gorgeous scenery. The girls were warned to stay away from several large boulders, as their father was concerned about rattlesnakes.

At 3:00 p.m., Dorothea left Marjorie momentarily to go to the vehicle and speak with her mother. As Dorothea returned, she couldn't find Marjorie. After an initial search, the mother left to call police while the father stayed at the scene frantically searching for Marjorie.

Bloodhounds responded to the site and started to track. They went around the boulder where Marjorie was last seen, and they stopped near a dirt roadway. That's where the trail ended.

The two weeks following Marjorie's disappearance had the state of Pennsylvania in turmoil. Hundreds of Native Americans assisted in the search of the remote areas near the location Marjorie was last seen. There were dozens of isolated hunting and fishing cabins, all checked without finding any evidence of the young girl. Several hundred volunteers, the CCC, law enforcement, and firefighters participated in the search for Marjorie, but she was never found. The governor of Pennsylvania sent a group of one hundred state policemen to search for Marjorie. A local mayor made a passionate plea for one thousand able-bodied men to walk the brush for ten miles in every direction from where Marjorie was last seen. It was an unprecedented search.

There were rumors that Marjorie was abducted and transported across the state, but these were never confirmed.

The Wests were in a fairly remote area of the Allegheny National Forest without significant vehicular or pedestrian traffic. The idea that a predator was lurking behind boulders is quite scary. The intense search that was conducted essentially eliminated the idea that Marjorie was lost in the wild. If an abduction did take place, the suspect had to be fast and strong so that the parents and Dorothea never heard Marjorie's screams.

There is a consistency among some of the missing person cases cited in both books. It seems that large boulders play some role when a person disappears. When there are boulders in the area, the person is rarely ever found.

Donald Farrington
Missing 9/11/38, 8:00 a.m., Holland, New York
Age at Disappearance: 3 years

This case is being included in the Pennsylvania section because of its proximity to many of the northeast cases. In one of the articles I found on Donald Farrington, law enforcement officials stated that many of the facts surrounding Donald's disappearance matched the circumstances in the Marjorie West disappearance, including the fact he disappeared forty-five miles north of Marjorie.

Holland, New York, is about forty miles north of the Pennsylvania border near the northwest section of the state. On September 11, 1938, Donald was walking around the side of his home headed toward the barn the last time that his father, Emmett Farrington, saw him. When Emmett hadn't seen the boy for several minutes, he started to look for the lad. After several minutes of searching, Emmett called for more assistance.

Within an hour of Donald's disappearance, there were police, volunteers, and other farmers combing the Farrington farm looking for Donald. Searchers worked through the night looking for the boy and found nothing.

Early in the morning of the first full day that Donald was missing, searcher Ray Becker was in a gully with a small creek two miles from the Farrington farm. Next to the creek was a berry patch from which Ray thought he heard a noise. The searcher walked toward the bush and found little Donald Farrington sitting deep under the briar bush. Rain had been falling hard since Donald had disappeared, and the bush and the area around the boy were very wet.

Donald was found "badly scratched by thorns" and suffering from exposure but was otherwise in good shape. In total, over three hundred people had searched for the boy since the time he disappeared.

Ronald Rumbaugh
Missing 9/15/40, 2:00 p.m., Scottdale–Dawson Rd, Scottdale, Pennsylvania
Age at Disappearance: 2 years

Before going into the specifics of the Rumbaugh disappearance, I want to put a window frame around this region. Ronald Rumbaugh's disappearance occurred within a ten-mile radius of three others:

Name	Date Missing•Age
Stephen Ford	08/05/1880•9
Anna Thorpe	05/05/1950•2
Emma Bowers	07/22/1953•5

Stephen Ford disappeared sixty years before Ronald Rumbaugh did, but the two disappearances occurred within two miles of each other. Considering that Pennsylvania has 44,816 square miles and that the state's dimensions are approximately 280 miles wide by

160 miles long, the statistical odds of two children disappearing in essentially the same place is mind-boggling.

Ronald was outside his rural home located on the road between Scottdale and Dawson, Pennsylvania. On September 15, 1940, Rumbaugh's father walked to a nearby baseball game and left his five children in the yard. It is theorized that Ronald must have tried to follow his father to the game and became lost. The father returned from the event after a short period of time and, when he couldn't find Ronald, he called the Pennsylvania State Police.

The area where Ronald disappeared is a region that was starting to become a hub for child disappearances in the ensuing thirteen years. The state police officers responded to the incident and did the normal search-and-rescue functions that were commonplace in 1940. They had equestrians, hikers, police officers, sheriffs, and state police officers combing the area. There were cornfields that needed to be searched, and Jacobs Creek needed to be swept. Near the third day, the police gathered hundreds of volunteers, and they searched the fields row by row to ensure they didn't miss the young lad. In total, 1700 people searched for Ronald Rumbaugh for three days, and they didn't find one trace of him.

State police officials stated publicly that they didn't feel that a two-year-old could survive the elements for three days, and they were going to terminate the search efforts.

Just as the state police were terminating the search, local pilot and volunteer David Patterson and spotter Paul Vrholla were flying over a cornfield almost three miles from the Rumbaugh residence. As they flew over the center of the corn, they spotted a boy lying on stalks. He was not moving. After a second fly-over at low altitude, the boy started to move and sit up. Patterson knew he had just spotted Ronald, and he lowered the plane and did a slow flyover the Rumsbaugh property while Vrholla yelled at the family below where their boy was located. In a scene reminiscent of an Alfred Hitchcock movie, the Rumsbaughs and state police officers raced to the cornfield, ran through hundreds of rows of corn, and found Ronald alive and groggy. The boy was transported to Connellsville

General Hospital, where he was found to have various scratches and bruises but was generally in excellent health.

Headlines in the *Evening Independent* newspaper on September 19, 1940 said, "Lost Baby Found, Officers Still Believe He Was Kidnapped."

Officers stated that the cornfield where the boy was located was searched row by row the day before he was found. They did not believe there was any way that they could have missed him in the location where he was found. The same article stated

The boy showed no ill effects expected if he had wandered through woods and fields coatless since vanishing from his home Sunday afternoon. Johnson [police officer] said the boy's light jumper suit was not soiled much or torn, and a new pair of white shoes he wore for the first time Sunday did not show the wear and tear of an outdoor tramp. The sergeant said he believed that someone had snatched the child, then, frightened by the hue and cry aroused, had left him in a safe place, the cornfield, where he would soon be found.

The local police stationed an officer at Ronald's room for the two days he was hospitalized for observation. The officer reported that he tried to question the boy several times about the disappearance, but it was nearly impossibly to get a coherent answer to any question.

Mr. and Mrs. Rumbaugh were questioned about the kidnapping theory, and they agreed that someone grabbed Ronald and sheltered him during the days he was missing. In a *Gettysburgh Times* interview published September 19, 1940, the boy's father stated that his son "could not have walked that far and stayed almost three full days and lived."

A police sergeant (Johnson) investigating the case made one last pointed remark: "Whoever brought him back knew the terrain and was careful to leave him where he would be found."

Case Summary:

This is another incident where quality investigators and police officers saw the subtle signs of kidnapping versus someone being lost. I am extremely confident that a vast majority of the cases in Pennsylvania have the same factors in them as was apparent in Ronald's event—law enforcement just didn't recognize the indicators.

I realize that it's difficult to understand how two disappearances sixty years apart can be related, but the disappearance of Stephen Ford and Ronald Rumbaugh have too many similarities in geography alone not to be considered somehow related. I am in no way blaming anyone in law enforcement for not connecting the dots on these cases in Pennsylvania—there are decades between cases and simply too many missing people. Without scanning technology, the Internet, and newspaper archive sources, these incidents and the clusters would never have been identified.

Rudy Kunchick
Missing 10/21/40, Sheppton, Pennsylvania
Age at Disappearance: 4 years

Rudy Kunchick disappeared from his home in Sheppton on October 21, 1940. The residence was in a rural area, and nobody saw the boy wander away. Rudy was watching his father screen coal when he disappeared.

After a fifty-one-hour search by police officers and forestry officials, searchers found the four-year old boy lying under a rock overhang. Rudy heard people calling his name and was able to call out. Searchers found Rudy's arms and legs very swollen, supposedly from extensive exposure. A doctor who examined Rudy called his condition "miraculous" considering the length of time the boy spent in the woods.

The area in which Rudy was found was described as heavily wooded. It was nearly two miles from where he was last seen. Several canines were used to search for Rudy, but none could pick up his scent.

Eldridge Albright
Missing 5/21/41, 2:00 p.m., Woodstock, Maryland**
Age at Disappearance: 3 years
(**Note: This case was placed with Pennsylvania because of its close proximity to other cases.)

Mrs. Albright was staying with her son, Eldridge, at their grandmother's house in rural Woodstock. It was approximately 2:00 p.m. when Eldridge was playing in a creek bed 300 yards behind the home. The boy was with two family dogs while his mother took a nap. The grandmother, Cynthia Miller, was on the back porch when she heard the distinctive scream for help coming from Eldridge in the creek bed. She started to move toward the creek when she heard a second scream for help coming from further down the creek and even farther away from her. Seconds after the second scream, she heard a muffled third scream coming from still further away.

Miller ran into the creek bed and looked for the boy, but she didn't hear or see anything. She ran a little further and found one dog in a nearby meadow looking further down the creek. She called for the dog, but the dog didn't flinch. It stood, rock-solid, staring down the creek. There was no sign of the other two dogs that were with Eldridge.

Cynthia ran back to the home and woke Eldridge's mother. They again ran to the creek and searched, but they found nothing. Cynthia called the police. When they arrived, she told them she believed that Eldridge was abducted because he was continually calling for help and the calls kept getting further and further away until he vanished.

Soon after Eldridge disappeared, many people volunteered to help search for the young boy. State police came up with only one theory that made any sense: a tramp from nearby railroad tracks must have taken the boy, but they had no proof. Bloodhounds were brought to the farm, but they too were unable to find the boy.

Searchers did find some tracks for Eldridge, but as a May 22, 1941, article in the *Telegraph Herald* states police said tracks of the child were found in the sand by a stream for about fifty yards and "then mysteriously disappeared."

Searchers scoured the area around the farm, and for the first twenty-four hours they didn't find anything. Another search team had been working since 4:00 a.m. and was slowly edging toward a swampy area four miles from the residence. The team was making a lot of noise when they thought they heard a slight whimper coming from under a rock ledge near a swampy growth of weeds. They approached and found Eldridge. He was groggy and appeared to be trying to wake up, although it was now about 3:00 p.m. The boy was lying on a bed of leaves, protected from the elements by the rock ledge.

Eldridge was found without shoes, and his clothes were torn badly. When searchers and family members asked Eldridge what happened and how he got to the rock ledge, he wouldn't or couldn't explain anything. When his parents asked what he had seen, he said only one thing, "twains," which everyone interpreted as "trains," from the nearby railroad tracks. That was all the boy said.

Many missing people are found in or very near creek beds, Eldridge disappeared in a creek bed. Creekbeds and swamps are two locations in the wild where, if you are walking directly in the middle of the creek or in swampy water, you will rarely leave a track.

Betty Bossier
Missing 6/24/41, 10:30 a.m., Altoona, Pennsylvania
Age at Disappearance: 3 years
Blonde Hair

Betty and her parents had traveled to their summer home three miles north of Altoona, Pennsylvania. The family was spending a holiday there, and Betty went to an adjacent farm to play with local children. At some point while Betty was playing with the children, she wandered off. Nobody saw her leave.

Volunteers and local law enforcement searched for Betty for over twenty-four hours without finding the girl. State police organized the search effort and were assisted by local citizens and regional sheriffs.

Twenty-eight hours after Betty disappeared, she was found sitting on a rock in dense brush in the woods surrounding the farm. Canines had failed to find the girl; it was an intensive ground search that eventually located the young lady. She was taken to a local doctor, who deemed her to be in satisfactory condition.

Why can't canines seem to track the missing people that are written about in these books?

Joseph Prato
Missing 10/25/41, 12:30 p.m., Bald Eagle Mountain, Williamsport, Pennsylvania
Age at Disappearance: 19 months
Blond Hair

At 2008 feet, Bald Eagle Mountain is the highest peak in the area of Williamsport. The residence where Joseph Prato lived was near the base of the mountain. On October 25, 1941, Joseph wandered from his residence at 12:30 p.m. and disappeared in the area of the mountain. There was concern from the searchers that Joseph could wander into water from the many sources that are near the residence.

Many people did not believe that a nineteen-month-old boy could wander far from a house, and thus many thought he was kidnapped. Searchers did scour the bottom of the mountain and the hillsides, without finding anything the first night. Searchers were hindered because the area of the mountain near the Prato home had thick vegetation.

At approximately noon the first day that Joseph was missing, his brother Pete and other searchers were searching the base of the mountain approximately two miles from the family residence; they found Joseph lying on the ground not moving. The searchers ran to the boy and found him asleep, yes, asleep at noon. The boy had his pants, shoes, and socks removed even though the temperature had dropped to below fifty degrees the prior night.

Joseph Prato couldn't explain what happened to him because he was only nineteen months old. It is not understood how the boy traveled over two miles, stripped his clothes off, and still survived an overnight ordeal.

Case Summary:

Readers should look at the Rudy Kunchick case in this chapter for similarities. The disappearance of Joseph Prato occurred one year almost to the date from the disappearance of Rudy Kunchick. The disappearance of Alvan Diggan in May of 1942 occurred in very close proximity to the Prato disappearance.

Alvan Diggan
Missing 5/30/42, Montgomery, Pennsylvania
Age at Disappearance: 3 years
Blonde Hair

Montgomery Pennsylvania is approximately eight miles east of Bald Eagle Mountain, the location where Joseph Prato disappeared in October of 1941. The locations are on the same side of the Susquehanna River, which flows through the region.

On May 30, 1942, Alvan was with relatives who were working a wild strawberry patch approximately one mile from a farm where they were employed. Alvan had gone along and somehow became lost while his parents were picking. Not long after the boy disappeared, the civil air patrol, local police, and sheriffs were all searching for the young boy. Bloodhounds from the local penitentiary responded to the search but were unable to pick up the boy's scent or refused to track—we don't know which.

Many of the articles stated that there were many poisonous snakes in this region, and most of the searchers were wearing snake boots. The state police stated that they killed two copperheads as they were conducting the search. A total of 150 searchers participated in looking for Alvan.

After two days of not finding the small boy, Montgomery residents two miles from where Alvan was last seen, heard someone sobbing in a small pine grove. Mrs. June Reed walked into the grove and found Alvan sitting on the ground sobbing. Alvan was naked and lying on the ground.

Mrs. Reed transported Alvan to Muncy Valley hospital where his condition was listed as satisfactory. Alvan had been cut by briars from head to toe but was otherwise fine. There was very little information on Alvan after he was located. The boy's clothes were never found.

Eugene Shue
Missing 10/20/46, 2:00 p.m., Manheim, Pennsylvania
Age at Disappearance: 3 years

Eugene Shue lived in rural Lancaster County with his mother, Mrs. Martha Shue and his grandparents. The family lived north of Manheim in a rural location surrounded by swamps, forests, and a very rural environment.

On October 20, 1946 at approximately noon, Martha fed her son a sandwich and sent him into the yard with the family dog, Whitey. Mrs. Shue had to leave the residence for a short time. When she returned, Eugene and Whitey were both gone. She searched the yard and the bordering woods but found no trace of either.

By late in the afternoon on October 20, searchers were scouting the woods near Eugene's residence and could not find one trace of the boy or the dog. Teams were looking at two creeks near the property. They were shallow and did not reveal any clues. Teams were more concerned about adjacent swamps.

The second day of searching had crews moving further and further from the residence. One team was four miles from the point Eugene was last seen and were at the top of Cornell Lookout. This location is the highest point in the region and is approximately six hundred feet up from the Shues' residence elevation. At the bottom of the lookout, searchers found Eugene. The team made special note that they were shocked to see that the boy didn't have any scratches, even though he had wandered through thick woods for four miles to reach his present location. They were also surprised to see Eugene on top of the highest mountain in the area, quite a feat for a three-year-old. In a very odd twist, Whitey was never found.

**There are twelve disappearances in the 1940s of children ages two to six in Pennsylvania, an astronomical number compared to any other state.

Jimmy Senser
Missing 04/06/47, Loch Lomond Rd, Philipsburg, Pennsylvania
Age at Disappearance: 4 years

William Senser and his family lived in an extremely rural location outside of Philipsburg, Pennsylvania. On Easter Sunday in 1947, Jimmy (four years) was playing outside with his brother Sylvester (seven years) and his sister Leona May (five years). Jimmy's mother and father were working in the house preparing a traditional Easter dinner.

At approximately 5:00 p.m., Jimmy's mother came outside and told the children that dinner was ready, and they should come inside and get clean. It was at this point that the family realized that Jimmy had disappeared.

During the next seven days, over one thousand people arrived at the Senser house to assist in the search for Jimmy. Aircraft were called in; trucks with loudspeakers were used along with sheriffs, firemen, and volunteers.

Many of the articles describe searchers finding Jimmy's red sweater five hundred yards from the home, lying on railroad tracks in an area having small barefoot tracks. Searchers also found a watering hole that had barefoot tracks around one side. Bloodhounds were eventually used but were unsuccessful at pulling up a scent and tracking. The inability for canines to track even with the presence of barefoot tracks seems very odd.

Articles in various papers described the area in which Jimmy disappeared as "Exceptionally treacherous as it is partly stripped from coal mining operations and is pitted with abandoned coalholes" (*Lewiston Evening Journal*, 4/8/47).

On the last day of the formal search, searchers combed the banks of Moshannon Creek and failed to find any trace of the boy.

Ronald Collier
Missing 7/2/48, p.m. hours, Somerset, Pennsylvania
Age at Disappearance: 23 months

Mr. and Mrs. Lloyd Collier decided to take a short vacation. Lloyd was a coal miner and enjoyed time in the woods away from his job. The family went to vacation cabins just one mile north of Kooser Lake on the perimeter of Kooser State Park, which is located approximately eight miles northwest of Somerset. Lush forests and state parks surround the entire area.

On July 2, 1948, Mrs. Collier was outside with Ronald, sat for a short time, and then realized it was time for his afternoon bottle. She briefly left the boy to enter the cabin to retrieve the bottle and thought that her husband was close by. When she returned from the cabin, the boy had vanished. A call was made to law enforcement and almost immediately search teams formed in the area. Hundreds of police officers, firefighters, rangers, game wardens, and volunteers swarmed the region looking for young Ronald.

On July 5, Sheriff Karl Hare stated, "The boy can not be within ½ mile of this cabin, we thoroughly searched shoulder to shoulder with more than 100 men through thick brush, he isn't here."

This search had strange undertones as I read articles that continued to describe activity. At one point the sheriff asked the parents to take lie detector tests about the incident. It was apparent that the sheriff was frustrated that he couldn't find the boy, and he felt that his parents knew more than what they were saying. The parents passed the polygraph test and were not under any further suspicion.

An article in the July 9, 1948 *Pittsburgh Gazette* stated the following:

The possibility that a bear had attacked 23-month old Ronald Collier was discounted Thursday by District Attorney Thomas Lansberry. "I have talked to forest rangers and game wardens and they all agree that there are no bears in the vicinity where the boy disappeared."

Police stated numerous times that they could find any evidence of a kidnapping and no motive. Mr. Collier did not have significant resources, and there was never a demand for cash.

Ronald was never found.

Billy Abbott
Missing 2/18/49, 4:40 p.m., Laureldale, Pennsylvania
Age at Disappearance: 3 years

The Abbotts lived at 3525 Oak Street in Laureldale. The home was at the base of Mt. Laurel, the tallest mountain in the area at one thousand feet in elevation. The mountain used to have a small ski resort, and that's where Billy and neighborhood friends went to play in February of 1949. Somehow Billy became separated from his friends, and when they came home, they told his mother that he was missing. Billy's mother promptly contacted local authorities, and a massive search was conducted.

The first night of the search firemen from four local communities directed bright spotlights onto the mountain where Billy was last seen. They used bullhorns to call his name, and hundreds searched the forest area on the mountain. The searchers were unsuccessful in finding Billy that first night.

It was after the first night that the parents of Billy Abbott adamantly told authorities that their son would never walk off and not come directly home. They stated that he was a very good boy, somewhat timid, but knew that he should be home. The parents strongly believed their son had been abducted.

The first morning Billy was missing search parties formed and searched Mt. Laurel. They combed every inch of it meticulously. At 1:00 p.m. the searchers reorganized and again started to comb the woods. Approximately five blocks from Billy's home, in a thick wooded area rich with deep leaves, a searcher saw something red lying in the trees. The searcher walked to the red object and saw Billy lying on the ground sleeping; it was approximately 1:30 p.m. The searcher screamed for assistance, which woke Billy. The searcher tried to carry the boy, but he stated that he'd rather walk.

When the searchers and Billy got back to their home, police officers at the residence made a note that the ground and the area of the search was quite wet, yet Billy's boots were almost dry. They also noted that Billy was not hungry, seemed in very good spirits, and his clothing wasn't dirty, as you would expect from a young boy in the woods the entire night.

Detectives tried to question Billy about his experience but were confused over his answers. He did state that he followed a neighbor's dog into the woods, but wouldn't state anymore after that. He later saw one of the lawmen with a lighter and stated that he had played with one of those last night. The detectives asked him where he played with the lighter. Billy stated, "At the house where I slept." Billy didn't elaborate on where he stayed and, in fact, almost stopped making statements at that point.

Case Summary:

The specifics of this incident that everyone should consider are listed below.

Billy was with his neighbor's dog walking toward the woods at approximately 4:00 p.m. when he disappeared. A massive search with spotlights and loudspeakers didn't locate him. With all of the noise and lights, why wouldn't Billy have responded? Billy stated that he stayed at a "house." What did that mean? Billy stated that he played with a lighter. Where did this occur? The lawmen were so perplexed by his answers that they couldn't tell whether he was kidnapped, fabricating a story, or was merely lost. There are too many consistencies with Billy's disappearance and the disappearance of other youngsters in this book to ignore what the boy is saying. He was obviously in a location that was covered from the weather and appeared to be similar to a home. It could also be deducted that Billy was at a location far enough from the search, noise, and lights that he didn't hear searchers calling for him.

Billy Clever
Missing 4/26/49, p.m. hours, Mercersburg, Pennsylvania
Age at Disappearance: 3 years

Mrs. Harry Clever took her son to the outskirts of Mercersburg on a hunt for mushrooms. The couple was near Cross Mountain when they started their journey. At some point during their search, Mrs. Clever lost sight of her son. The mother immediately went home and retrieved the other fifteen children, and they all started to search the mountain area for Billy.

Local police officials were notified of the missing child, and they responded with bloodhounds. The dogs were unable to pick up any scent for the boy. At the height of the search, three hundred area residents and law enforcement officers searched for the boy.

At 9:00 a.m. the first morning that Billy was missing, a searcher found the boy three miles from where he disappeared. The boy's clothing was torn to shreds, but he was otherwise in fine shape.

When a rescue worker walked up toward Billy, he turned and ran from the man. The searcher easily overtook the boy and took him back to his mother. Billy was taken to the hospital and found to be in good condition.

Otis T. Mason
Missing 10/11/49, 5:00 p.m., Colesville, Maryland
Age at Disappearance: 6 years
Blonde Hair

Otis Mason was last seen by his mother playing in a sand pile in the front of his house with the family's three dogs. Otis had five brothers and sisters, but they were not in the yard with him when he and the dogs inexplicably disappeared. At 5:00 p.m. Otis's mother had called him for dinner, and when he didn't answer, she went into the yard to look for the boy. Once the mother couldn't find the boy, she called authorities.

The Mason family had lived in their large home for eleven months, and the children knew the area well. They also knew the rules about not leaving the immediate area of the home. Several hours after Otis disappeared, two of his dogs returned to his home. The third dog was still missing.

After Otis had been gone twenty-four hours, searchers near a vacant home two miles from the Mason residence thought they heard a strange, muffled sound from an underground area. Searchers pulled the lid off an empty septic tank and found the dog inside. Searchers couldn't explain how the dog managed to enter the tank, especially since the lid was on it.

Searchers scoured the woods behind the Mason home. The woods were a conglomeration of heavy timber, swamps, and thickets. The search extended almost two miles and couldn't find any evidence of the boy. Nearing the end of the second day of searching, a police officer working a creek that had been searched several times before looked under a bank and found the boy's body. People were shocked. The specific area where the boy was found had been searched several times without finding anything. The creek was very shallow except for the one four-foot-deep hole where the body was found.

There was an autopsy on Otis's body, and officials ruled that the cause of death was drowning.

The fact that Otis knew never to leave the yard and that he left with two of his dogs makes this case mimic others from this same area. It would be easy to discount this case and state it was merely a drowning, but I don't know. The fact that his dog was found confined in an empty septic tank makes it seem as though something unusual happened. Dogs don't enter septic tanks and close the lids behind them.

Anna Pearl Thorpe
Missing 5/5/50, Dunbar, Pennsylvania
Age at Disappearance: 2 years

Anna Thorpe was playing at the edge of the woods near her home on Friday, May 5. Anna's mother was inside the home when she heard a sharp scream from the direction of Anna. Mrs. Thorpe ran into the backyard and could not find the girl. She yelled the child's name and immediately searched the area but could not find her daughter. Anna's two brothers assisted in the search but could not locate her. It was at this early point that the Thorpes called local police for assistance.

Hundreds of searchers converged on the Thorpe property by early the next morning. SAR teams scattered over the snake-infested woodlands looking for the young girl. Searchers were covering the area inside of one mile from her house, as they didn't believe she could get much further. One group decided to search much further away from the residence. Approximately twenty-four hours after she disappeared, Anna was found a phenomenal three miles from her home, tucked under a blackberry bush. The girl was naked except for one shoe. Her sweater and dress were lying on the ground near her.

Anna was taken to a nearby physician who stated that she had not been molested and only had minor scrapes and bruises. She was in almost perfect condition considering the amount of terrain she covered in twenty-four hours.

A May 7 article in the *Los Angeles Times* had the following paragraph: "State police took the child's clothes for further investigation. There is some mystery as to how she got over 10 picket, barbed wire, and stone fences that separate the wooded area from the field in which she was found."

Case Summary:

I want readers to go to their computers and pull up Google Maps. Look at "Kooser Lake," Pennsylvania and compare that to Dunbar, Pennsylvania. My estimate is that the distance between the two locations is approximately ten miles. Ten miles and twenty-six months is the difference between the disappearances of Donald Collier and Anna Pearl Thorpe. There are many similarities between the two cases. The time frames are much too close to be ignored.

In between the two locations where the children disappeared are Indian Creek Valley and two large state parks with massive open areas. There are no large cities between the two spots where the children disappeared.

I believe the state police took Thorpe's clothing because they knew she had been abducted. There is no way a two-year-old girl is going to travel three miles and over ten barbed wire fences in twenty-four hours—no way! There would be no reason for police to take the clothing if this was merely a missing person case. I could never locate a follow-up article explaining the police theory of what might have happened. There is the possibility that police found something on the girls clothing that caused them concern.

Jackie Copeland
Missing 5/14/50, 1:00 p.m., Pleasantville, Pennsylvania
Age at Disappearance: 2 years
Blonde Hair

Jackie, his three sisters, and parents went to a picnic at an oil company's property outside of Pleasantville. The family was socializing with others when Jackie's seven-year-old sister told their father that Jackie was gone. At 1:00 p.m. the family started to look for the boy and could not locate him. It was at this point that everyone at the picnic started to participate in the search for Jackie Copeland.

In a very short period of time, the state police had arrived, and they called for a team of bloodhounds. The oil company called for additional volunteer searchers until there were hundreds of people looking for the boy. It was evident by late in the evening that the bloodhounds could not pick up a scent (or refused to search) and ground searchers were not having luck finding the boy.

At 8:00 a.m. the morning following Jackie's disappearance, a man named Bevier was searching outside of the main area in a location where an oil repressuring plant was located. The area is completely surrounded by what many newspaper articles called "impassable swamps." As Mr. Bevier and a crew of searchers were walking through the swamps, he accidentally saw Jackie looking around the side of a tree, almost peering. Bevier called his name and Jackie answered. Jackie was found over two miles from the picnic and across swamps that were deemed impassable by search coordinators.

Jackie was transported to the hospital where he was met by his family. After being examined by doctors, they stated that the boy had a number of scratches but that he was in generally good health.

An article in the *Logansport Press* dated May 17, 1950 had an interview with the Copelands and heard Jackie's rendition of what occurred during his night in the woods. The press wanted to hear how the boy got to his location in the swamp, what he had to drink or eat, and how he kept warm. Jackie first was asked why he left the picnic and here is his quote: "He saw something peering at him from behind a big tree. When he approached, the creature scampered into the brush." Jackie didn't explain anything more about leaving the picnic at that point. The article later explained more of what Jackie stated: "[He] recounted in child talk his adventure in an awful blackness, peopled by a great throbbing giant and a tall friendly tree and wild animals howling in the distance and the unfamiliar shouts of strangers prowling nearby."

Jackie Copeland's explanation of what occurred to him could be a very sobering narrative of what might possibly be occurring with the plethora of missing children outlined in this book from the Pennsylvania area. Jackie had gone through a very frightening experience. In the safety of his parents' presence, he was able to recount certain elements of what happened. He did say that he believed he slept through the entire night in the woods. How Jackie was able to sleep under conditions he described is a true mystery, yet many young children are found by searchers in a groggy and semiconscious state.

The question I pose to each and every reader: what was the "creature" peering at him from behind a tree? I think it's ironic that Jackie mimicked the behavior of the creature when he was approached by a searcher. How could a two-year-old boy traverse impassable swamps without the aid of some type of mammal?

I know that many people will discount Jackie's explanation and say that it was a fantasy. The location where Jackie was found was not fantasy. The description Jackie gave of his incident is something that we should all ponder and attempt to understand.

Emma Bowers
Missing 7/22/53, Noon, Mill Run, Pennsylvania
Age at Disappearance: 5 years
**Deaf Mute (Per newspaper article)

The Bowers lived in a region that had very few homes and was in a rural setting. At noon on July 23, 1953, Emma was playing with three other children while two went to a nearby spring; she lagged behind and was lost. Mrs. Bowers realized that her deaf-mute daughter was missing from her residence and started to scream for help. She called law enforcement officers, who responded en masse. Mrs. Bowers described her daughter as "frail" and small for her age.

Two trucks that had very powerful floodlights came to the area of the residence and scoured the region for the girl. Searchers stated that they were baffled that the girl wasn't in the immediate area because they had searched every conceivable place she would normally be. In two days searchers had covered nine square miles without finding the frail girl. Mr. Bowers stated that he didn't believe that his small daughter would go far in the thickets that surrounded the home.

Bloodhounds were brought to the search site and could not pick up a scent or refused to search. Rain fell for eight straight hours shortly after Emma disappeared and this hampered search efforts.

Sixty hours after Emma disappeared searchers found the girl sitting and eating wild berries on a ledge near the Baltimore and Ohio Railroad tracks over two miles from where she was last seen. The girl had "thousands" of scratches over her body, and her feet were described as "raw," but she was otherwise in very good condition. In a July 25 article in the *Reading Eagle*, Private Anthony Sywinski of the Pennsylvania State Police stated, "She was only two miles from home, but how she got that far in these terrible forests, I'll never know." The girl was found naked.

Case Summary:

When I initially reviewed this case, Emma's age seemed slightly older than other children who went missing in Pennsylvania. It wasn't until I read that Emma was a "deaf mute," couldn't talk or hear, and she was described as frail did her profile match others. Many of the children missing in this chapter couldn't speak (they were too young) and couldn't walk well because of their age, facts also attributed to Emma. The children really couldn't explain what happened to them, and they couldn't exactly sprint for safety because of their age. The statement from the state police officer is very revealing.

Fred "Tookie" Holmes
Missing 5/25/55, 9:00 a.m., Grahamsville, New York
Age at Disappearance: 23 months
**Blonde Hair

This case is placed with Pennsylvania based on its proximity to the state's border.

The Holmes lived in a rural home on the border of the Catskill Mountains in Grahamsville, New York. On May 25, 1955, Tookie was home at their farm with his mother while his five other brothers and sisters were at school. At approximately 9:00 a.m., Mrs. Roderick Holmes was out in her yard tending the garden, and Tookie was somewhere in the yard playing. Mrs. Holmes stated she lost sight of the boy for ten to fifteen minutes, and he disappeared. Mrs. Holmes called neighbors and the police for help, and they responded.

Searchers believed the blonde-haired, twenty-three-month-old Tookie would be found quickly and close to the farm. They were in for a shock. Within two days, there were three hundred people searching for Tookie in the remote mountains of Grahamsville. Searchers were very frustrated because there were no clues about where the boy may be.

On May 27, 1955, an article in the *Oneonta Star* stated the following: "State Police ordered the search continued (for Tookie Holmes) until the boy is found dead or alive." Police ordered an Army helicopter from Chicopee Falls, Massachusetts to aid in the search.

The first day after the boy disappeared the weather turned bad and heavy rain fell in the area. Bloodhounds were brought in to search, and they couldn't pick up a scent, or refused to search.

The area where Tookie disappeared was one mile from Rondout Reservoir, one mile from Neversink Reservoir, and three miles from the Ashokan Indian Reservation. The family lived on Denman Mountain with an elevation of 2900 feet.

Police were convinced that something very strange happened with the disappearance of Tookie and asked Gertrude and Roderick

Holmes (Tookie's parents) to take polygraph tests. They did and they passed.

After two weeks of formal and informal search efforts, Tookie was never found. There have been many articles written about this disappearance, and it is still puzzling over fifty years later.

Candida "Candy" Streeter
Missing 10/3/57 at 5:30 p.m., Pottstown, Pennsylvania
Age at Disappearance: 2 years

Candy was playing in the front yard of her residence with her seven-year-old brother Middy. Middy came into the house and told his mother that Candy wasn't outside. Mrs. Streeter went into the yard and could not find the young girl.

Mrs. Streeter called her husband, John, at his place of employment at Fels Planetarium, and he came home. Local and state police officers responded to the residence and combed the woods surrounding their farm's two hundred-acre property.

Searchers scoured the property owned by the Streeters and also checked brooks and creeks in the area. Bloodhounds were supplied by the state police. The dogs supposedly entered the woods and were unable to find a scent on the young girl, or refused to track.

The following morning at 8:00 a.m., a sixteen-year-old girl getting ready for school at a nearby farm saw something by their chicken coup. The girl walked out to the coup and found Candy Streeter wet and cold standing by the chickens. State Police would not identify the farm where Streeter was found but did state it was in the general area of the Streeter residence.

The police were called and Candy was reunited with her family.

Case Summary:

There are many questions about this case that will never be adequately answered—mainly, why didn't Candy walk to a farmhouse where she saw light? Why would she stay by a dirty chicken coup instead of going to a farmhouse to seek warmth and assistance? What caused the girl to leave her property, property that was two hundred large acres? Why couldn't or wouldn't the canines track the girl down?

Karen Cooney
Missing 7/8/68, Corry, Pennsylvania
Age at Disappearance: 15 years

The Cooney family lived in a rural setting adjacent to a small county highway approximately twenty miles west of the Allegheny National Forest. On the morning of July 8, 1968, Karen was asked by her mother to go to the rear yard and hang clean clothes. The girl happily did the chore and was in the backyard for a few minutes when her mother and her brother heard her scream. The two family members ran to the backyard and found that Karen had vanished.

The Cooney family quickly searched the yard and then called the sheriff and state highway patrol. Within hours of the first call for assistance, bloodhounds and scores of searchers were working the farm area looking for Karen. The local sheriff told several news teams that he felt Karen had been kidnapped and that the FBI had been requested to assist. The Pennsylvania State Police was the lead agency for the investigation, and they used their helicopter, canines, horses, and many volunteers.

Twenty-seven hours after Karen disappeared, a state police helicopter was patrolling the sky three miles from the Cooney residence when they saw Karen walking along the banks of Leisure Lake. The helicopter called for ground teams to converge in the area and Karen was picked up. The girl was described as "dazed" when she was met by searchers.

Karen was taken to a hospital for observation and later questioned about her ordeal by her parents. In a July 10, 1968 article in the *Titusville Herald* Mrs. Cooney explains what her daughter told her: "Mrs. Cooney said her daughter was still hazy about what happened, but she remembered being chased from the house by a big man with a knife. He chased her for a long ways through the woods until she said she fell asleep."

Case Summary:

Remember, the police were absolutely adamant at the start of this investigation that Karen had been kidnapped—maybe she was. It does seem unusual that someone would be so bold to enter her backyard and take the woman near her own home. The description that Karen used was "big man"—he must have been very big if he was going to force a fifteen-year-old girl into his custody in the middle of the woods.

It's interesting that she stated that she was chased until she fell asleep and then was later found as being "dazed." This would seem to be a consistent condition for many missing people when they are located.

The disappearance of Karen Cooney matches the circumstances of many young children in this book. The difference in this case is that the girl can partially explain what happened.

This case is not the only case in which strange looking men are described in the woods associated with a disappearance. Eloise Lindsay describes being chased for many days in Table Rock State Park (Great Smoky Mountains Chapter) by men that she cannot describe, or won't and a witness in the Dennis Martin disappearance describes a sickening scream and seeing a stealthy looking man in the woods (Great Smoky Mountains Chapter). It's an odd coincidence that both Eloise Lindsay and Karen Cooney describe being chase by men and they don't or won't supply descriptions, why?

Karen Cooney went missing just forty-five miles west of where Marjorie West disappeared and was never found. Karen's residence is just forty miles west of where Harold Mott disappeared.

Harold Mott
Missing 3/2/76, 5:00 p.m., Corydon Township, Pennsylvania
Age at Disappearance: 12 years
**Special Education student

On Tuesday March 2, 1976, twelve-year-old Harold Mott arrived at his rural residence after school and decided to look for the family dog, Snowball, which had been missing several days. Harold, his brother, and a neighbor went to a hill behind the Mott residence and decided to split up and look for the family dog. This was when Harold disappeared.

Once the boys realized that they couldn't find Harold, they went to Harold's parents and explained the circumstances, and everyone started to look for the boy—it was now 5:00 p.m. In a strange and odd twist to the story, as the family was searching for Harold and it started to get dark, Snowball arrived back at the house. One missing party is found and another goes missing. Soon the family realized they couldn't find the boy, and they called the state police.

Corydon Township is located just four miles from the New York State line in far northern Pennsylvania. The town is just two miles from the Allegheny Reservoir and sits adjacent to Willow Creek. The woods around the town are very lush and thick with almost the consistency of a wooded area that had never been logged, with few home sites and almost no land that's been cleared.

Harold vanished just five miles west of the location where Marjorie West disappeared while on an outing with her family on May 8, 1938. Marjorie was never found.

The state police committed significant resources to the effort to find Harold. Local sheriffs and other law enforcement officers came to the area along with other farmers and families that volunteered in the search effort. There were equestrians, helicopters, all-terrain vehicles, and even psychics assisted in the effort.

On Wednesday and Thursday violent thunderstorms rocked the region around Corydon, dropping several inches of rain. Canines were unable to pick up Harold's scent and couldn't locate the boy.

On Friday afternoon at 12:30 p.m., two searchers were nine miles from the Mott property, walking a rarely used trail when they looked up and saw Harold. A March 6, 1976 article in the *Bradford Era* had the following statement from the searcher, Monty Edel, who found Harold,: "He (Harold) just came out of nowhere." Harold was walking with a walking stick and seemed to be in very good health. Harold immediately asked if Snowball had been found and then continued walking with the searchers back toward their vehicles.

Harold was taken to Bradford Hospital by a state police officer. The hospital stated that Harold had a slight fever, was groggy, and tired and would be kept the night for observation.

Case Summary:

This case is fascinating because two family members were missing at the same time under two separate incidents. Snowball had been missing for several days when Harold disappears looking for the dog. The dog appears the same night that Harold goes missing—quite a coincidence.

The fact that Harold disappeared in such close proximity to the disappearance of Marjorie West is something that can't be overlooked.

This is another case in which a missing person is located in good health but has a slight fever. Why did Harold have a fever? The disappearance of Harold five miles from where Marjorie disappeared cannot be ignored and should be a clue to this disappearance.

Duane Scott
Missing 7/27/78, Camp Tree Farm, Fombell, Pennsylvania
Age at Disappearance: 31 years
5'7", 140 lbs

Duane Scott was a moderately disabled man who needed medication to control his physical disability and his ability to walk. He was described by relatives as frail and weak.

On July 27, 1978 Duane attended a dance at the Camp Tree Farm just outside of Fombell. The camp was operated at the time by the Allegheny County Chapter of the Pennsylvania Association of Retarded People. The camp had operated since 1970 and had over 12,000 disabled people attend its events and the camp never experienced any type of incident, until now.

It is confirmed that Duane was at the dance, and when people arrived to pick him up, nobody could find him. Camp docents attempted to locate Duane and eventually knew they needed additional resources and called the state police. The Pennsylvania State Police called local law enforcement for assistance, and with the added assistance of camp counselors and volunteers, hundreds were scouring the rolling hills and forests that surrounded the camp. The state police used helicopters, canines, equestrians, and hikers to call the man's name and search the countryside.

Camp Tree Farm was located approximately twenty miles north of Pittsburgh, and it was in a very rural setting.

The search for Duane continued for almost two weeks until eventually state police admitted they couldn't find the man.

Ninety-four days after Duane Scott went missing, two hunters were two miles from Camp Tree Farm when they discovered a decomposing body on a hillside. It was Duane. The coroner confirmed that Duane did not have any broken bones, and it was a puzzle why he had died. The biggest question in the disappearance is how Duane got to the location where he was found.

Searchers had confirmed that they had scoured the lower elevations where Duane was found but were turned back by the steepness and the thorny brush that was shredding their clothes. Duane's parents had apprised searchers that Duane was a frail and weak man and couldn't climb any hillside that was steep. This hillside was quite steep. A November 1, 1978 article in the *Pittsburgh Press* had an interview with Mrs. Scott: "The place where they found him was almost impossible to get to," she said. "I'll never, ever believe he went in there by himself." Duane's sister, Karen, also assisted in the search effort and made this statement about the location of the body: "But they couldn't have made it to where he was without having their skin torn off."

For Duane to get to the location where he was found, some searchers believed he had to hike three and a half miles, a near impossibility for the man. Robert Neikin was the director of the association running the camp. Neikin stated that the man either walked the miles to get there, "Or he got there some other way."

A November 2, 1978 article in the *Tyrone Daily Herald* had one last interview with Mrs. Ina Scott, Duane's mother. The article states, "Mrs. Ina Scott said she did not think her son (thirty-one-year-old Duane Scott) could ever have made his way into the nearly impenetrable brush where his body was found, 'The place they found him was almost impossible to get into.'"

The coroner didn't find any obvious cause of death and no serious cuts or bruises, making it more confusing how the man got into the location.

Case Summary:

This case is yet another example in which family members believe there is foul play involved in the disappearance and subsequent death of their loved one. A family knows the abilities of its children. If Mrs. Scott states that her son could not have made it into that position, I believe her. A common-sense question is why would anyone voluntarily enter an area so rough and thorny?

The coroner stated that he could not determine a cause of death, another common element when missing people's bodies are eventually found. If Duane didn't have cuts and bruises on his body, how did he manage to get into the thorny bushes where he was found? Many people who go missing are eventually found in thickets and berry bushes—why?

Jon Dabkowski
Missing 1/14/82, Tarentum, Pennsylvania
Age at Disappearance: 11 years
4'10", 72 lbs

Jon and his friend Gabriel Minarcin were residents of Tarentum. On January 14, 1982, Gabriel had dinner at Jon's house. At 5:30 p.m. the boys finished dinner and walked outside to make the trip three houses down the street to Gabriel's residence. They were never seen again.

The homes border the Allegheny River, and there was some belief that the boys fell in. There were tracks in the area, but no indication that there was an ice break. An extensive search of the river could not find either boy. Dabkowski had been counseled by his parents to stay away from the river and his friends state that he obeyed that rule.

Both boys are still considered missing, and the Tarentum Police still have an open case file. The city is surrounded by thick woods.

Gabriel Minarcin
Missing 1/14/82, Tarentum, Pennsylvania
Age at Disappearance: 10 years
4', 60 lbs

See the Dabkowski case above for details on this incident.

Emerson Carbaugh
Missing 11/11/85, Robertsdale, Pennsylvania
Age at Disappearance: 64 years
5'9", 190 lbs

Emerson and his longtime hunting partner Ralph Isett, his brother-in-law, went turkey hunting. On November 11, 1985, the two men drove state route 913 approximately two miles south of Robertsdale. They started their day late, 3:00 p.m., and immediately split up. Emerson was carrying a Remington 870 shotgun. The men had agreed on a meeting location and time, but Emerson never arrived. Isett did happen to meet an off-duty firefighter who was also hunting, and they both searched for Emerson. As they were searching, a cold rain started to fall, and that rain lasted through the night. They never found Mr. Carbaugh

Emerson was hunting on New Grenada Mountain, also known as Robertsdale Mountain, adjacent to the state lands designated area just off the highway. A long ridgeline rising five hundred feet runs the entire length of the state game area. The ridge has a road that runs its entire length, north to south, and either side is dotted with dozens of farms.

State police participated in a massive search for Emerson without finding him or any of his property.

It does not make any sense that Emerson became lost. He knew that he could walk on either side of the ridge to find a farm. If he walked west, he hit a road. Something happened to Emerson that took him from this area. Emerson's family made the following statement: "I think he was taken out of the woods. I don't think he is alive." Ida Carbaugh, Emerson's wife, was at the search site for an entire week as locals, firefighters, and law enforcement participated in the search.

Ida waited the required seven years and then had Emerson declared legally dead by a local court. The Pennsylvania State Police still have a missing persons file on Emerson.

Michael Joe Malinoski
Missing 10/24/96, Gaines, Pennsylvania
Age at Disappearance: 37 years

West Chester, Pennsylvania, sits very near Pennsylvania's Grand Canyon, otherwise known as Pine Creek Gorge. No, it doesn't look like the Grand Canyon in Arizona, but it is a deep gorge with great views. West Chester hosted a psychology conference the week of October 21, 1996 that attracted the attendance of Michael Malinoski.

Malinoski was a divorced father of one. He was a clinical psychologist whose ex-wife and son lived in San Francisco. He was a very caring father who communicated regularly with his son.

Malinoski attended the conference on men's issues and then traveled to the Pine Tree Lodge near Gaines, Pennsylvania. Malinoski had stayed at the lodge in the past and knew the area. The lodge was built in the 1930s and was surrounded by thousands of acres of state and federal land and sits in the middle of Pennsylvania's wild country. Every cabin has a covered porch, and the lodge advertises that it is known for fishing, hunting, festivals, photography, and general leisure activity.

Malinoski checked into the lodge, turned on the heater, and apparently spent the night. He called his roommate that night and advised him that he was safely in the room and said good night. Malinoski was scheduled to spend an additional night and never showed back at the lodge after that first night. The lodge worker cleaning his room saw that his bed was not made and that he had left items in the room. He called the police after he didn't show up the second morning.

On November 2, 1996, a Pennsylvania forestry worker found Malinoski's 1995 Nissan Sentra parked at a trail access point at Barbour Rock Overlook of the Pine Creek Gorge. There was a pair of hiking boots lying on the floor of the car along with a box of half eaten snacks and water. Malinoski's cell phone was in a backpack on the seat, and there was a classical tape in the stereo.

Malinoski's disappearance was immediately acted upon by Tioga County law enforcement. The county searched with helicopters, canines, volunteers, and trained SAR teams. They found nothing. SAR supervisors felt sure they would find his body below the overlook; they didn't find any evidence that Malinoski was outside his car.

The commander of the Tioga County SAR team stated that this is the first time in their history the team didn't find the missing. He stated that they always find at least the body.

Law enforcement people were interviewed for several articles I reviewed. It was a fifty-fifty split on whether Malinoski was still alive or dead in the woods. Some people felt that Michael went to San Francisco to start his life again. Others felt he took a walk and never came back. The last idea on what happened to Michael is that he was the victim of a violent crime. He was a very meticulous person, and some things about his room and car didn't match with his personality. Others say this isn't so. I don't think Michael took a hike, as his boots were found in his vehicle.

The search for Michael Malinoski is registered as the biggest and most expensive search in the history of Tioga County. Michael's credit cards and social security number have not shown any activity, and his son has not heard from his dad.

Case Summary:
The disappearance of Malinoski is very similar to the disappearance of Nita Mayo on August 8, 2005 in an overlook turnout outside Sonora, California (Missing 411 – Western United States). The woman stopped and appeared to be taking photos and vanished. Her car was found locked in the parking lot of the turnout. Nita Mayo was never found.

Charles Beltz
Missing 6/7/05, Clear Creek State Park, Pennsylvania
Age at Disappearance: 56 years
5'10", 220 lbs

There are varying stories as to the last location that Charles was seen. The most credible information indicates that Charles was in Spring Creek Township at a campsite at Clear Creek State Park, the location where his 1992 Plymouth Caravan was located. Clear Creek Park is located in the north central portion of the state in the Allegheny National Forest. Dubois is the largest and closest city, approximately ten miles south of the park.

Once it was determined that Charles was missing, law enforcement officials claim that they searched for two weeks in a 200-mile radius of the park without finding Charles. Charles is from Pitcairn, approximately 150 miles southwest of the park.

Beltz disappeared approximately forty miles south of Mott and West.

There are no other details on this case.

Chapter Summary
Pennsylvania is the only state in North America where there are large numbers of missing juveniles, twenty-eight of thirty-nine missing people in the state are under ten years old. From 1880 through 1968, eighty-eight years, there are thirty-two missing people; twenty-eight of these people are juveniles ten years old or

younger, an amazing statistic and coincidence! No juvenile (under ten) who fits the criteria in this book had been reported missing in Pennsylvania since 1957, why?

It would appear that something drastically changed on July 8, 1968 when Karen Cooney disappeared. This was the turning point when young people no longer went missing in the Keystone State. It would also seem odd that immediately after Ms. Cooney disappeared, there was not another missing person in the state for eight years.

It's important that you read all of the cases in this book like you are the investigator trying to solve a major crime. Many of the disappearances in this chapter have law enforcement alluding to a possible kidnapping. Some directly state they believe the person was kidnapped/abducted. How can so many supposed kidnappers be lurking in woods and rural settings?

The disappearances of Anna Thorpe in May of 1950 (two years), Ronald Rumbaugh in September of 1940 (two years), Ronald Collier in July of 1948 (twenty-three months), Emma Bowers in July of 1953 (five years) and lastly berry-picker, Stephen Ford in August of 1880 (nine years) all occurred in a seventy-mile radius. Read these cases carefully and then look at a Google Map of the region. Bowers, Thorp, and Collier all disappeared in a five-year time span while Ford happened in the 1880s. As I've stated throughout this book, missing people is not a new issue. It has been happening for hundreds of years. Whatever paradigm you have about missing people will probably start to change.

West Virginia

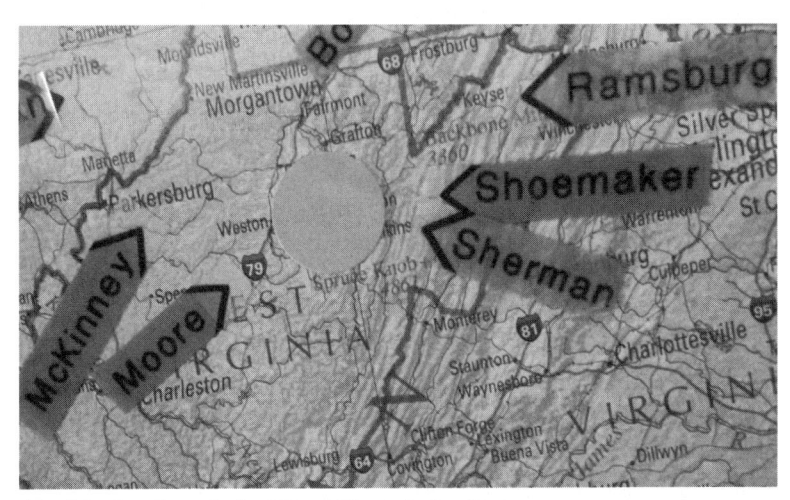

Missing People in West Virginia by Date
Each case in West Virginia is a male except for Shirley Ramsburg and Shirley Sherman.

Name	Date Missing•Age
Shirley Sherman	04/18/54•3
Shirley Ann Ramsburg	12/27/57•3
Johnny McKinney	03/17/58•5
*38 Year Gap	
Victor Shoemaker	05/01/94•4
Joseph Moore	03/11/00•22

Shirley Sherman
Missing 04/18/54, 1:00 p.m., 29 miles n/o Franklin, West Virginia
Age at Disappearance: 3 years

Shirley Sherman was with her parents visiting her grandparents in a rural area outside of Franklin, West Virginia. It was Easter afternoon when Shirley wandered away from the residence without anyone immediately realizing. An article in the April 21 edition of the *Daily News* described the initial event: "Her absence was detected when the family set off to look for ramps, a pungent onion-like plant that grows wild in the area." This is an interesting aspect of the case. Many children go missing when berries become ripe in an area of their residence; Shirley went missing when ramps came into season.

A substantial search for Shirley included local law enforcement, neighbors, friends, canines, and SAR personnel. Canines did attempt to track Shirley but could not locate her. Four hundred people participated in the SAR for Shirley. Forty-eight hours after Shirley went missing, and one and a half miles from her grandparent's residence, Shirley was found lying in Will Run Creek, adjacent to an apple orchard. Doctors evaluated Shirley and found she had numerous cuts and bruises but was in good condition.

Shirley was found in an area previously searched, and law enforcement officers wanted to understand what happened with her. Shirley stated that she never heard any searchers and made no other statement.

Time after time, SAR personnel find missing people in or near creeks in a sleepy or groggy state.

Shirley Ann Ramsburg
Missing 12/27/57, 5:00 p.m., Charles Town, West Virginia
Age at Disappearance: 3 years

Mr. and Mrs. Robert Ramsburg lived in a rural area of Charles Town. On the afternoon of December 26, 1957, the winter weather was cold. Little Shirley Ann was playing in the family's yard with her mongrel dog "Brownie." Shirley had been in the yard for approximately one hour when her father went to check on her. Robert couldn't find the girl but did see Brownie running down the mountainside behind the family home. Brownie was alone, and Shirley was not in sight.

Robert ran down the street to the nearest neighbor, and the two men searched the nearby hillside. The Ramsburgs and nearby neighbors did not have a phone; thus, authorities were not notified as the two men did not want to stop searching. The men searched through the night with torches and still could not find Shirley. It was at this point that the neighbor drove into town and got assistance from law enforcement officers.

Within hours after police were notified, over one hundred searchers were combing the hillside for Shirley. Searchers brought in bloodhounds that tracked the girl from her home yard to the Shenandoah River, indicating to searchers that she must have drowned. The searchers used another bloodhound and that dog also tracked to the same spot in the river and then walked several feet into the river and stopped, again, indicating the girl went into the river, one way or another.

Almost two days to the hour after Shirley disappeared, searchers were walking a path over two miles from the family residence when they found Shirley lying next to a tree. The girl was missing her shoes, coat, and socks, even though the temperature outside was very cold. The girl had scratches on her face and arms and was quiet. Shirley was transported to the hospital where doctors stated she was suffering from exposure. SAR coordinators told the press that Shirley was found at a location where searchers had passed many times during the last two days.

An article in the *Dispatch* dated December 30 stated, "By late last night she hadn't said a word, just cried and cried."

During my years of reading SAR and missing person reports there have been many that indicated a canine tracked a scent to a river and stopped. Many of the handlers have taken the dogs reaction to mean that the missing drowned: I think this action by the canine could be misinterpreted. Another logical explanation is that the missing person went to the river and crossed, somehow to the other side. There have been too many instances where dogs tracked to a river or creek and the missing was found days later alive.

Case Summary:

It would appear from the behavior of two different bloodhounds that Shirley Ann had traveled to the Shenandoah River and had either crossed or entered it. The noses of two bloodhounds, especially two tracking to the same location do not lie. How Shirley got into and across the river has only one answer: she was carried. Creeks and rivers seem to be a location that repeatedly is a center point for many missing people.

It would also appear from the path that Brownie was seen taking home (down a mountain behind the house) that Shirley left walking up a hillside, a rare event for a young child.

John Wayne McKinney
Nickname "Johnny"
Missing 03/17/58, 3:00 p.m., Gallipolis Ferry, West Virginia
Age at Disappearance: 5 years

Paul and Elizabeth McKinney lived on a dairy farm adjacent to the Ohio River in far northern West Virginia near the Ohio Border. The farm had 1300 acres, hundreds of cattle, and beautiful pastures. The farm was just four miles north of the Crown City Wildlife Area.

On March 17, 1958 in the afternoon hours, Johnny McKinney went outside to play with his two dogs. The family had only one dog up until just ten days before the disappearance when a Collie appeared on the farm. The family described the dog as "fearless," and nobody knew where it came from. Johnny loved playing with his canine friends and would often wander the nearby pastures to have fun. At 3:00 p.m. a family member went outside to look for Johnny, and he couldn't be found. The inability to find Johnny set in motion a six-day search that would rival any in West Virginia to that date.

Immediately after Johnny went missing, both dogs also disappeared, a strange coincidence. The collie returned after dark the day of the disappearance, but the smaller dog, Spitz, didn't come home until 4:00 a.m. the following morning. The first day that Johnny was missing, several hundred searchers combed the farm and adjacent woods for the boy. During that first day of searching, over three inches of snow fell, hampering the search effort. By the fourth day of the search, there were over 1200 searchers and 300 cars parked at the farm. Every inch of the area was being combed, but nothing was found.

The sixth day that Johnny was missing, a farmer three miles from the McKinney property was walking in a remote area of his farm with his daughter. They were making their way slowly through a region they rarely walked when they came upon a small body clothed in a T-shirt, overalls, and shirt. The body did not have shoes, and the shoes were never found. Johnny McKinney had been found, found in an area that was not previously searched because the search teams never thought he could have made it that far and over that many fences. The coroner ruled that Johnny died from exposure probably the first night he was missing.

In the middle of the search for Johnny McKinney, several theories were floated by law enforcement. One of the most prominent thoughts was that Johnny was kidnapped. Maybe he was, and the kidnapper kept the shoes as a trophy. The farm pastures in this area were huge, and anyone would understand that being in the woods would be disorienting, yet to find the way home, a person would just cross the field. Johnny never did.

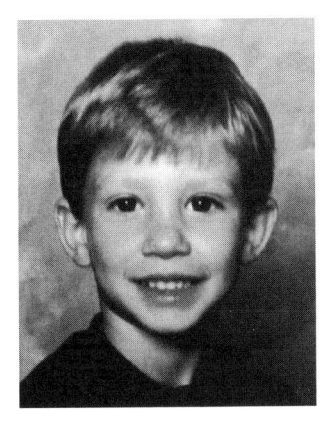

Victor Dewight Shoemaker, Jr.
Nickname J. R.
Missing 5/1/94, Augusta, West Virginia
Age at Disappearance: 5 years
4', 40 lbs **Blonde Hair
Wearing Red Shirt

The case of J. R. Shoemaker ranks in my top ten as one of the most strange and unusual disappearances I have ever researched.

Augusta, West Virginia, is an unincorporated community located in the northeast corner of the state. It is a very small and isolated community approximately forty miles west of Martinsburg, Virginia and thirty miles east of the Hampshire county seat of Romney. According to the 2000 census, Augusta had a population of 4,728 with 8 churches, the Hampshire County Fairgrounds, Augusta Motor Speedway, and the Short Mountain Wildlife Management Area just south of the main portion of the city.

On May 1, 1994, Victor and Nettie Shoemaker, along with their sole child, J. R., were at their grandfather's house south of Augusta near the Short Mountain Wildlife Area. Four times a year the family gets together so that the cousins can play and the families can reconnect. It was a Sunday when J. R. and his two cousins headed into the forest to play as they had dozens of times before. They would play a hunting game and walk the woods looking for wildlife. After a few hours they would get tired, and the three boys would make their way back to grandpa's house and eat. This day was going to be different.

J. R. and his family made the drive from Leesburg, Virginia, while his two cousins were coming from Pennsylvania. The entire family was eager to see grandpa, Oscar Wolford. He had lived on the property near the base of Short Mountain for many years and had accumulated a lot of old cars, construction material, old smaller homes, and a variety of stuff that littered the property. There was one neighbor in the area, but the long, winding, and steep road leading to the Wolford house kept outsiders away and the family isolated.

On Sunday May 1, 1994, J. R. and his cousins made their way into the forest and toward Short Mountain. This was a state wildlife area and known for turkey hunting. It was a Sunday morning, and no hunting is allowed on Sundays in West Virginia, but that didn't matter to the cousins because they were just "play" hunting.

After a few hours in the woods, J. R. blurted out that he was hungry and headed back toward his grandpa's house. The other boys didn't think much about it and didn't follow him. After approximately an hour, the other boys decided to go back and eat. When the boys arrived at grandpa's house, J. R. was not there. He never arrived. J. R.'s father immediately went outside and asked the boys to show him where they last saw J. R. After an initial search, a call was made to the police. Inside of two hours there were dozens of people searching for the five-year-old.

In an unfortunate turn of events, a freezing rainstorm moved into the area of Augusta just hours after J. R. disappeared. The temperature dropped to near freezing the night of the disappearance. The county sheriff and state police were on the scene interviewing the cousins, parents, and relatives during that first night.

The search for J. R. formally continued for five days. Up to 350 people searched a two and a half-mile radius from the Wolford home, finding no evidence of J. R. Searchers used a heat-sensing FLIR-equipped helicopter, the Appalachian Search and Rescue Team, local and regional law enforcement, and every volunteer they could muster. Nobody found any evidence of J. R.

On May 4, 1994 the *Free Lance Star Newspaper* had the following account of what searchers found on May 3: "About 7:00 p.m. they found a spot where they believe the boy may have slept, said his adult cousin, Valeria Cooper. Three rocks were arranged in a triangle, with a stick in the middle, three logs on the sides and dirt freshly disturbed, Cooper said." It's interesting that police and SAR workers didn't state the find to the news but that a cousin told the papers about the rock formation and stick. The article didn't state where the rock formation and stick were found other than it was in a search location. I find it also interesting that the stick and rock formation was even mentioned. Could it have possibly been an arrow indicating where the boy may have been?

The region of Short Mountain and the wildlife area would remind you of a pencil lying on the landscape if you looked at it from the air. The land around the mountain has an elevation of 2000 feet, while the top of the long and thin mountain rises to 2400 feet. The area is very thick with heavy timber, and there is ample fresh water throughout the area.

Five days after J. R. disappeared a number of news crews were at the Wolford residence and attempted to interview family members. The reports indicated that the family looked exhausted and depressed. Law enforcement had stated that the two cousins were interviewed several times, and they did not believe any foul play occurred. In a very odd twist to the law enforcement statement, one news reporter asked one of the cousins what he believed happened to J. R. The cousin stated, "Somebody hiding behind a tree got up and grabbed him." Wow, if there is one ounce of truth to that statement how could law enforcement say there was no foul play involved? A more volatile question is why did law enforcement officers terminate a search after only five days if they didn't believe foul play was involved, and why was the search area set at only a two and a half-mile radius?

As someone who has read thousands of accounts of search and rescues, a five-day search for a little boy lost in the woods isn't a very long search. Again, maybe law enforcement officers knew more than they were releasing to the public—we don't know. Remember, the Wolford property is deep in the woods, isolated, and with thick vegetation surrounding the property. Who would be prowling the woods in the hopes that a young child would wander by? It doesn't sound plausible. The statement that someone was hiding behind a tree and grabbed J. R. is still rattling around in my head.

After the initial law enforcement search was terminated, West Virginia State Trooper C.J. Ellyson stated that he did not believe that J. R. was the victim of a hunting accident, a question that had lingered at search headquarters.

The disappearance of J. R. got worldwide attention and press. The informal search for the boy continued for weeks through volunteer assistance.

On November 22, 1994, Investigator Robert Cooper of the West Virginia State Bureau of Criminal Identification (BCI) made a statement to the press saying that there was no sign of foul play in the disappearance of J. R., but the state did ask the FBI to enter the investigation for assistance. As I have stated before, the FBI has a formal policy that they do not assist on missing persons cases. They have made this statement repeatedly to the press on many other cases. Why join the J. R. case six months after the event? What was it about this case that triggered their interest?

On May 3, 1996, Sgt. David Burkhart of the West Virginia BCI was again interviewed and asked to comment on the J. R. disappearance. The sergeant stated, "It's something that's constantly on my mind."

Let's recount what law enforcement has stated: this isn't a hunting related accident where the hunter may have buried the body. Police do not feel that foul play is involved, so there hasn't been an abduction, kidnapping, or murder. I then go back to one of my original questions for law enforcement officers—why is the FBI involved? It would appear from all of the law enforcement statements, the lone conclusion is that J. R. was still roaming the landscape when they called off the search, a horrible scenario. Looking at an aerial view of the region where J. R. disappeared, he wouldn't have had to walk an exorbitant distance to eventually walk into a road. If he'd been on the mountain, the visual would have given him ample opportunity to pick a location, farmhouse, or ranch and walk to it.

The idea that J. R. got lost and died in the environment is not plausible to me; there were too many roads and homes in proximity to where he was playing. He had been to grandpa's house many times, walked the woods with his cousins many times, and knew the landscape. It's hard to fathom that a perpetrator was watching the boys, waiting for an opportunity, and took J. R., but I believe that this is what happened, per his cousin's statement. The portion of the statement "He got up" is particularly intriguing because it's hard to imagine someone sitting or kneeling behind a tree. The words "he got up" indicate he was on the ground or kneeling, an odd visual but something the cousin said that still resonates with me.

To drag or carry a boy a long distance, keep him quiet, or to carry him that same distance requires significant strength and endurance, yet that is what this perpetrator must have done. I would hope that law enforcement contacted and searched every residence in a five-mile radius, not an improbable task when you look at the openness of the area.

There is one other case with vague similarities to Victor's cousin's description of someone hiding behind a tree. The disappearance of Jackie Copeland (5/14/50) in Pleasantville, Pennsylvania, and Jackie's description of the incident does have similarities. When Jackie was found he stated that he saw someone peer at him from behind a tree and follow him into the woods. He described a "Great Throbbing Giant." Refer to the Pennsylvania chapter for details on the Copeland case.

J. R. is one of a number of boys who have disappeared wearing a red shirt.

J. R.'s father made a statement to the press just as the last day of the formal search was concluding: "I just don't understand why or how."

I couldn't agree more, Mr. Shoemaker!

Joseph Allen Moore
Missing 3/11/00, Charleston, West Virginia
Age at Disappearance: 22 years
5'8", 174 lbs

Moore was last seen approximately eight miles northeast of Charleston in an isolated area near 360 Mill Creek Road, about one mile south of State Highway 79. The location of this disappearance is also just one thousand yards from the Elk River. This location is in the middle of heavy woods and is fairly desolate.

The Kanawha County Sheriff is the lead investigative agency on the Moore case and has released few details.

Chapter Summary

The disappearances of Shirley Ramsburg (12/27/57 at 5:00 p.m.) and Johnny McKinney (3/17/58 at 3:00 p.m.) occurred three months apart and within two hours of each other. Geographically there is approximately 150 miles between disappearances. The Monongahela National Forest sits almost in the middle of the two locations. This is another one of the cases that repeatedly happens in this book where time and space of the disappearances cannot be ignored. Is there a common thread here? It would appear that many of the children in this book disappear in close proximity to parks, rural habitat and lonely places with few people, an ideal location for a predator to lurk.

Kentucky

Debbie Greenhill is the only female missing from Kentucky meeting the criteria in this book. It's unusual that everyone missing from Kentucky who fits the criteria of this book is between the ages of two and four. Ronnie Weitkamp disappeared in Indiana but is included in this chapter because the location of his disappearance is in close proximity to Kentucky.

Debbie Greenhill disappeared on August 9, 1958 in Stamping Ground, Kentucky. Frank Downey disappeared August 16, 1999 in Olive Hill, Kentucky, approximately fifty miles east of Stamping Ground. Considering that the state of Kentucky is huge, having the last two children missing in the state disappear within fifty miles of each other, both in the month of August, is an odd coincidence. It's even more unusual that three of the four missing people in this chapter disappeared in August.

Name	Date Missing•Age
Eddie Prigley	08/22/1874•3
Ronnie WeitKamp	10/11/55•3
Debbie Ann Greenhill	08/09/58•2
**41-year gap	
Frank Downey	08/16/99•4

Eddie Prigley
Missing 08/22/1874, 6:00 p.m., Crothersville, Indiana
Age at Disappearance: 3 years

On August 22, 1874 at approximately 6:00 p.m., Eddie Prigley was left inside his residence adjacent to the family cornfield. Mrs. Prigley entered the field for a few minutes and then returned to find Eddie was missing. An immediate call went into the area for volunteers to search for the boy.

During the first night that Eddie was missing a severe storm hit the area that caused the river adjacent to the farm (Muscattatack) to rise several feet, flooding the adjacent fields. When Eddie could not be found the next day, Mrs. Prigley attempted to commit suicide by drowning herself in the river. A neighbor saved her life. Mrs. Prigley was extremely depressed over her son disappearing.

Seventy-six hours after Eddie disappeared, a boy named Isaac Warner was on the opposite side of the river from the Prigley farm, hauling stones. The boy was four miles from the Prigley's home when he heard a moaning sound and walked toward it to find Eddie lying on his back. An August 30, 1874 article in the *New York Times* had the following: "Its face was turned up and presented a pale and ghastly appearance. Warner went up to the poor little thing and took it in its arms. It moaned piteously and it was nearly dead from fatigue, hunger, and exposure." When Eddie was found, the river had gone back into its banks and was able to be crossed. Eddie eventually recovered from his poor health.

The last few paragraphs in the *Times* article have the following:" It appears also that the search for the child was made on the side of the river on which the Prigleys' house is located, no one dreaming that the boy had crossed over in the bottoms on the other side of the river." No, I do not believe that little Eddie had the ability to cross the river, even if the water was low. It was a river, not a creek. Eddie also was too young to navigate in a boat—that idea would be ridiculous. We will probably never know how Eddie crossed the river or how he survived three days.

As I've stated in previous cases, when children disappear they often cross a creek or river, somehow and probably with the aid of someone.

Ronnie Weitkamp
Missing 10/11/55, Noon, Crane Depot, Indiana
Age at Disappearance: 3 years

The Weitkamp case is included in Kentucky because he went missing on nearly the same longitudinal line as Greenhill and Downey. The disappearances occurred approximately one hundred miles from each other.

Mr. and Mrs. Lawrence Weitkamp lived on the Crane Naval Depot in Crane, Indiana. Lawrence was a civilian inspector at the depot, and they had lived in a three-bedroom home on the base for eight years. The family had three children. Crane is surrounded by heavy woods and swamps and sits within one mile of Greenwood Lake.

On October 11, 1955 three-year-old Ronnie was playing in the yard of a neighbor across the street from his residence. At approximately noon Ronnie wandered into the thickets behind the home without saying anything. Ronnie's four-year-old friend (Debbie Gallagher) told her mother of Ronnie leaving the yard, and a search was started immediately.

Because Ronnie and his family lived on Navy property, the Navy had the right to do many things that could never happen in a normal city. The Navy locked down the entire base, and it gathered thousands to assist in the search. Airplanes, helicopters, and masses of military personnel all assisted in the search for Ronnie. The search went on for weeks without searchers finding any clue of where the boy may be.

On October 14, 1955 after three days of a massive search, the *Herald Examiner* ran a story that stated the following: "Police are convinced now that brown-eyed Ronnie Weitkamp was abducted at play." Later the article adds: "Commander Richard Turner, Depot Executive Officer said: 'We are convinced the boy didn't move away under his own power. He must have had some assistance, and that of course is kidnapping.'"

An October 15 article in the *Spokesman Review* stated that the commander had ordered four hundred homes on the base searched and to leave no stone unturned. This could never happen in a city, but because the Navy owned the homes and the land, every home on the base was searched. Nothing was found.

Searchers encompassed many problems during the weeks of searching. The grounds around the base are swampy and wet. Greenwood Lake is located one mile north of the depot. In total, a ten-square-mile area was covered multiple times by searchers without the boy being found. The statement by the commander believing that Ronnie was abducted was partially attributed to the extremely rough thickets that Ronnie would have to travel to get out of the area. Nobody believed he could have removed himself from the area.

Fifty-four days after Ronnie disappeared, three boys playing in the weeds one-half mile off of the base and one and a half miles from Ronnie's residence found the boy's body. Ronnie's body was severely decomposed and one strikingly strange twist.

Ronnie's overalls were removed from his body and sat six feet away. This despite the fact he disappeared on a cold October afternoon.

The coroner investigated the incident and examined Ronnie's body. It was reported that Ronnie had scratches on his legs, meaning he had walked or was carried through the thickets without his overalls. The coroner made a determination that Ronnie died of exposure.

Case Summary:

You will find no other case in this book where there were more searchers, more organization, and more controlled containment than the Ronnie Weitkamp case.

Remember, the base commander and police officials were absolutely adamant that Ronnie could not have made his way outside the search perimeter without aid. Officials stated to the press that they were sure that the boy was kidnapped. The FBI was brought into this case near the beginning. The newspaper articles stated that officials believed that Ronnie took his own overalls off. Why would a boy who, according to the coroner died of exposure, take his overalls off? If the officials were correct that Ronnie was abducted, who did it? If Ronnie had taken the overalls off, this meant he walked through the thickets carrying the overalls and getting his legs cut and scratched and then laid the pants next to him and laid down and died. This scenario defies logic.

This is another in a long line of cases where the FBI has the data and has probably a far better understanding of the phenomenon then anyone, and they don't share.

Debbie Ann Greenhill
Missing 8/9/58, 8:00 p.m., Olive Hill, Kentucky
Age at Disappearance: 2 years

Saturday August 9, 1958 was a huge day in the life of the family of Mr. and Mrs. Earl Greenhill. The family was moving into its new residence one thousand feet from a beautiful fifty-four-acre reservoir on the outskirts of Olive Hill, Kentucky. The home sat two miles down a rut-filled dirt road and in the mountains alongside the city's water supply for Olive Hill.

The family had a long Saturday moving into its new rural home. Another family was already living in the home, and that family would stay in the home with them a few days during the transition. While the move was taking place, Debbie Ann was playing on the side of the house alone. Mrs. Greenhill left Debbie Ann alone at 7:45 p.m. for twenty minutes. When she returned, she could not find her daughter. A search of the area was made by everyone in the house, and they could not find the girl. Residents were screaming for little Debbie Ann, but they did not receive a response. One member of the house called the local police who also called the sheriff's department, who in turn called the state police.

After the full second day of searching, law enforcement officials felt that Debbie Ann must have been kidnapped because she wasn't inside the confines of the search area that was covered. Searchers didn't have an easy task; there were two violent rainstorms immediately after Debbie Ann disappeared. The storms greatly hampered searchers' efforts.

The area of the search was composed of rugged mountains with very thick berry bushes, trees, and brush. The home sits in a small valley two miles outside of town and surrounded by rolling hills. The hills and the surrounding area were dotted with an occasional home, but the population in that area was sparse.

On the third day of the search, local law enforcement was adamant that Debbie Ann had been kidnapped. They were convinced that the girl was not in the hills near her home. Local law enforcement called the FBI for assistance. On August 12, 1958, the *Tri City Herald* had the following paragraph: "Special Agent Charles Weeks said in Louisville that FBI Agents have no evidence that Debbie was kidnapped. But he said four agents would offer FBI facilities to help in the search." This was an interesting aspect to the search. The FBI doesn't get involved with searches for missing people, yet they are somewhat assisting. It was an interesting twist. Other articles confirmed that the FBI had four agents on the scene the entire time of the search, a very large number considering the agency wasn't investigating the situation.

During this point in the search, the local reservoir was dragged, but searchers found nothing. Bloodhounds were brought in from Lexington, and they failed to pick up the scent.

On August 13, one day after the majority of searchers had left, a National Guard searcher working approximately three-fourths of a mile from Debbie's residence heard a small girl crying. The searchers followed the sounds and found Debbie Ann Greenhill crying. She was found 150 feet up from the reservoir with a berry-stained face sitting on the ground. She was carried down to the water and taken by boat to a waiting ambulance.

Debbie Ann was examined by a pediatrician who gave the following statement to the *Park City News* on August 13, 1958: "Dr. William Schnitzker, Ashland Pediatrician said she [Debbie Ann] must have lived on berries, which grow thick and wild in the area. There was little evidence of malnutrition, although Debbie was very hungry." Debbie Ann had been missing for ninety hours, without food or water, and the doctor stated she was in remarkable condition—how? The doctor also stated that Debbie had lots of cuts and abrasions. An article in the August 14, 1958 *Charleston Gazette* stated, "The child was naked, her blonde curls matted and body scratched, bruised and insect bitten but she was declared in remarkably good condition."

Debbie had moved into her new residence the day she disappeared, how did she know the berries were eatable?

Case Summary:

The Debbie Ann Greenhill case is like many, many others in this book. Law enforcement officials strongly believe the victim is kidnapped, yet he or she is later found in an area that had been previously searched. Is law enforcement so incompetent that their assumptions are that wrong? I don't want to think so. There are so many consistencies in the stories that they cannot be ignored. As with many other children who go missing and are later found, Debbie Ann was found missing clothing and had scratches over her body. Berries seem to be involved in many of these missing person cases.

Frank Downey
Missing 8/16/99, 8:30 p.m., Stamping Ground, Scott County, Kentucky
Age at Disappearance: 4 years

The Downeys lived in an extremely rural section of Scott County, Kentucky, north of the small town of Stamping Ground. It's an area of rolling hills, very thick woods, and few people or residences.

It was approximately 8:30 p.m. on August 16, 1999 when Mrs. Frank Downey was home with her four-year-old blonde-haired son, Frank. Near 8:30 p.m., somehow, Frank got the door open, and he and his two German shephard dogs wandered outside. It was a highly unusual act for the little boy, especially since it was nearly dark. Mrs. Downey immediately started to search for the boy and then called her husband who was at work. The husband came home, and law enforcement was called.

Scott County Fire Chief Billy Willhoite responded and was one of the authorities in charge of the search. A *Lexington Herald* article dated August 18, 1999 stated the following: "Rescuers chose the one-mile radius distance, Willhoite said, because that's how far a boy Frank's age should be able to travel." Searchers focused their efforts inside the one-mile perimeter.

At approximately 8:30 a.m. the morning following Frank's disappearance, there was a major break in the case. A farmer was tending his grape vines when he thought he heard a boy's voice. The farmer walked a few hundred yards and found Frank Downey and his two dogs. An August 19, 1999 article in the *Harlan Daily* stated, "Strong [farmer] said he had never seen the boy before. Strong's farm is about six miles from the boy's home by road, or about three miles if going straight through the woods, Scott County Sheriff Bobby Hammons said."

How did Frank Downey get at least three miles from his home and three times the distance that search professionals believed he could travel?

Frank was checked by a doctor and found to have severe scratches. He was not wearing shoes when found, and his feet were scratched.

It's an interesting coincidence that Debbie Ann Greenhill disappeared August 9, and Frank went missing August 16, if you believe in coincidences. It just so happens to be the approximate date that berries become ripe in this area of the country.

New England Missing People

For purposes of this book, New England includes the states of New Hampshire, New York, Delaware, Maine, Massachusetts, and Connecticut. Missing people in these areas fall into specific clusters that are easily identified, thus the grouping.

There are two distinct groups of missing people in Maine. There is a group in the northwest section of the state and another group in the south. The northern group includes a case along the same latitudinal lines of Halifax, Nova Scotia. I have also included two cases just across the western border of Maine and into Quebec. The point of including cases in Canada is to show that the issues surrounding missing people do not stop at our border. The facts surrounding all of the cases are quite similar.

The group in southern Maine also includes Patric McCarthy, who disappeared from a location close to Maine in New Hampshire.

Look at the dates of the missing people closely and you will notice that there are clusters. First, there is March, 1934–July, 1934 then October, 1947–June, 1950 and July, 1956 followed by June, 1971, September, 1975 then July, 1983, and July–August 1986. I don't believe these groupings are random occurrences as they appear at other locations across North America.

The northeast sector of the United States has more missing children under very similar circumstances than any other location in the continent. Read carefully the sections on Bobby Connor and Claire Benson. They went missing eighty miles and nine days apart. Both children were exactly twenty-one months old when they disappeared. Common sense and my law enforcement background indicate these cases have to be related. I don't believe in coincidence.

New England Missing People by Date

Name	Date Missing•Age•Sex
Horace Marvin, Jr.	5/4/1907•4•M
Elsie M. Davis	07/30/11•24•F
Edward Gately	10/27/17•2•M
David Brown	11/18/22•51•M

Mertley Johnson	11/18/22•24•M
Kenneth Swanson	08/24/30•2•M
••Clarence Clark	10/17/32*62•M
Alden Johnson	03/27/34•4•M
Bobby Connor	07/13/34•21MOS•M
Claire Bensen	07/24/34•21MOS•F
Louis Dunton	10/07/47•3•M
Michael Fontaine	05/30/49•6•M
Nicole Renaud	06/03/50•3•F
••Gary Bailey	07/17/54•3•M
Diane Abbott	07/06/56•2•F
Brenda Jean Doud	07/06/58•5•F
Douglas C. Chapman	06/02/71•3•M
Douglass Legg	07/10/71•8•M
Kurt R. Newton	09/01/75•4•M
Andrew Warburton	07/01/86•9•M
Patric McCarthy	10/13/03•10•M

••Details on the following disappearances can be found in the chapters next to the individual's names.
Clarence Clark: Farmers
Gary Bailey: Berry Pickers

Horace Marvin, Jr.
Missing 3/4/1907, Kittshammock, Delaware
Age at Disappearance: 4 years

    This is probably one of the highest profile missing persons cases ever in the United States in the early 1900s. Dr. Marvin had recently moved his family from Iowa to Delaware. Shortly after they arrived, little Horace Marvin disappeared from the yard at the farm. There were few initial details on the case, and many thoughts of kidnapping and other bizarre theories proliferated at the beginning of the investigation. From the first day the boy went missing, the search instantly became massive. There were searchers carrying torches on the property every night for over one week. It was a twenty-four-hour effort.

Dr. Marvin was raising wheat on his farm. After days of searching for Horace without having success, a decision was made to burn the fields in an attempt to locate the boy. When the search was two weeks old, local authorities became frustrated and wanted to terminate search operations. Dr. Marvin got the governor and local federal authorities to intervene. The U.S. Secret Service actually got involved in the case along with other law enforcement jurisdictions. Authorities were so convinced that Horace Marvin was taken against his will, there were headlines stating the boy *was* kidnapped. The doctor stopped working for months and concentrated exclusively on search efforts. Every inch of the farm was examined in minute detail, with no evidence found.

Dr. Marvin hired Pinkerton Detectives to interview ranch hands, locals, and even law enforcement personnel. No leads developed. Local law enforcement officers sent detectives to Iowa to research the family history to ensure the kidnapping wasn't a family issue—it wasn't.

Exactly two months after Horace Marvin, Jr. disappeared, a local hunter was crossing the Marvin farm and was walking through a bog when he saw a small bulge. The hunter went to the bundle on the ground and found the decomposing body of Horace Marvin, Jr. It would be fair to say that everyone involved in the search was shocked at the discovery. The exact area that the body was found had been searched and the area combed dozens of times, with searchers never finding the body. The coroner had an inquest.

There were no broken bones on the boy, but the coroner also stated that the body showed over forty hours of privation. This meant that the boy was alive for at least forty hours after he went missing, but this doesn't make sense. It also didn't make sense to searchers that Horace would lie down to die in that spot. An article in *The Telegraph* on May 6, 1907 stated the following:

To have reached the spot where the body was found the boy must have walked across frozen and snow-covered fields in the face of a driving wind and then climbed two high embankments besides crawling through a barbed wire fence.

The official cause of death for Horace Marvin, Jr. was listed as "exhaustion." There was no uniform acceptance of any theory about what happened in this incident. It doesn't make sense that Horace would leave the confines of his farmyard and head into atrocious winter weather and die in the bogs. It also makes no sense that the body wasn't located when searchers were scouring the area, yet it appears months later.

Elsie M. Davis
Missing 7/30/1911, Noon, Howe Hill, Maine
Age at Disappearance: 24 years
5'6", 135lbs

Elsie was a beautiful, young organist at the church in Bethel, Maine. On Sunday July 30, 1911, Elsie attended and played at services and then went to her home in Howe Hill. Sometime around noon Elsie vanished. Elsie's parents looked for the young woman and couldn't find a trace. It was generally felt that she must have wandered off into the woods behind her house. Because of the parents' concern that Elsie may be lost, a search was initiated.

A volunteer group found Elsie's comb and several footprints in the hills behind her home. Over eight hundred people volunteered in the search for Elsie, but no significant progress was being made after the initial find. At the end of the third day of searching, a Portland, Maine, clairvoyant hand wrote a note indicating where Elsie was going to be found. She stated that she would be in a tree, deep in the woods, and that searchers needed to look up to find her.

Late in the afternoon on the fifth day of the search, volunteers combed an area almost three miles into very rugged and thick woods. The group found a number of Elsie's personal items (hosiery, coat and shoes) scattered on the ground. The search continued further into the woods until they heard a stick break. The searchers continued deeper into the woods and under a large pine tree they thought they heard something above them. Twenty feet up into the tree searchers saw a scantily clothed Elsie Davis.

Searchers called to Elsie, but she did not answer. Searchers made their way into the tree and found the woman unable to speak and seemed to be quite confused. They were able to bring the woman to the ground, and her father eventually made it to a point where they understood each other. She didn't say anything to her father but did lay her head on his shoulder.

An article in the August 2, 1911 *Lewiston Daily* explained what happened when Elsie got to her home:

At her home tonight where she had been put to bed immediately after she arrived, Miss Davis was questioned briefly regarding her movements. She seemed able to recall only a little. In fact her memory appeared to have lapsed shortly after she reached the woods Sunday until she was discovered in the tree today. Miss Davis said she remembered leaving the church Sunday morning.

The *Syracuse Morning Herald* ran a story on August 6, 1911 explaining the condition that Elsie was found in by doctors: "Miss Elsie Davis will probably recover, although slowly from the remarkable fever and delirium of which she has been a victim." Again, a missing person is found with a fever and various other symptoms that match many others. In an interesting twist, this same article describes searchers finding "the bed of opine boughs." How would Elsie have known to comfort herself in that manner?

Through all of the questioning, investigators were never able to determine how Miss Davis lived for the five days in the woods.

Case Summary:

Many of the children you will read about in this book are found after being reported missing and are too young to speak or have a disability and are unable to speak. Some children who are found are reported to be in a state of confusion or choose not to speak. The Davis case exemplifies the condition that is found in very small children when they are missing. The people seem to lose their memory at the point they go missing and then recover once in the presence of people. It's almost as though the missing are under some type of spell that eliminates memory and the ability to speak. If searchers had not specifically been looking up in the tree, it would appear that Elsie would not have been able to call to them because she could not speak. Elsie's case has every element that we have seen in many other cases: loss of clothing, inability to remember what happened to them, disappearance from a rural area, knowledge of the area in which they disappeared, fever, and found in a state of confusion about what had just happened.

Psychics in the past have offered assistance to searchers and specifically have told them to look in trees for lost children. See the Great Smoky Mountains section.

Edward Gately
Missing 10/27/17, 10:30 a.m., Brighton, Massachusetts
Age at Disappearance: 2 years

On October 17, 1917 there were two children that comprised the Gately family. Edward was two years old, and the family had a new baby who was still not walking. At 10:30 a.m., Mrs. Gately put Edward in the backyard with his apple and told him to stay on the step while she took care of the younger one in the house. Edward was wearing a large overcoat, diaper gators, pants, and shoes that were tightly tied on his feet.

Mrs. Gately checked on Edward just minutes after she put him in her rural backyard and found that he had somehow disappeared. She immediately started to yell for the boy, but received no answer. She called the police, and a search soon started.

The Gately residence was within four blocks of Brighton High School and large quarry that contained water. There was also a large abandoned and vacant lot near their home that was thoroughly searched early in the SAR process. The article in the *Boston Globe* stated that the area around the quarry and vacant lot could look like a wilderness area in a child's mind.

As the night and search proceeded on, a thunderstorm hit the area at approximately midnight, wiping out all tracks of the child. The search was getting desperate, and more police were brought to the residence in the early morning hours. At 6:30 a.m., Sergeant M. J. Muldoon was looking through the outskirts of the vacant lot near the quarry and found the child calling, "mama." The October 29 article in the *Boston Globe* stated,

Sergeant Muldoon hastened to a clump upon the form of Teddy (Edward) stark naked and blue from exposure to the elements. Close by the little form was a pile of baby clothing–overcoat, hat, undershirt, underwear and drawers, pair of overalls, shoes, and stockings drenched from the heavy thunderstorm shower which broke shortly before midnight.

The article also stated that the child was delirious and taken to the hospital for a two-day stay.

Edward (a.k.a. Teddy) and his clothes were taken to his parents. The parents saw the pile of clothes and adamantly stated that there was no way that he could dress himself or remove his clothing. The mother found the T-shirt inside out and the shoes pulled off the feet.

The Gatelys demanded an investigation of the incident because they felt that Edward had been forcibly abducted. The lot where he was found was thoroughly searched the night before he was found, and then he was found exactly where searchers had already been looking.

It's apparent from this case that someone took Teddy, moved him, stripped him of his clothes, and then gently placed him under the cover of bushes. There was never a mention of molestation, so the question is why were his clothes removed?

David Brown, Age at Disappearance: 51 years
Mertley Johnson, Age at Disappearance: 24 years
Missing: 11/18/22, Big Bog Dam, Maine

One of the most dangerous jobs in any law enforcement classification is that of a game warden. Wardens are commonly confronting people with legally loaded firearms in the middle of nowhere, and many times the law enforcement officer is alone.

There are numerous incidents in which wardens are confronting people who legally cannot possess firearms because they are convicted criminals yet don't believe they will ever see someone in the middle of the woods. Other times people are illegally taking game and never believe a law enforcement officer will catch them. In almost any instance in which a warden confronts an individual, the warden does not have back up for tens of miles in any direction, and sometimes the next law enforcement officer is over an hour away.

The biggest news in the northeastern United States in 1922–1923 was the case of two Maine wardens who disappeared on November 18, 1922. The wardens (Brown and Johnson) had been briefed about an ongoing case of beavers disappearing. Commissioner Willis Parsons of the Maine wildlife department felt that Canadians were illegally crossing the border and taking the beaver, and he wanted the violations to stop. It is unclear from all articles I've read why Parsons felt Canadians were doing this, but it is clear that beavers were disappearing.

Parsons sent two of the best wardens in the state of Maine to camp in an area near Big Bog Dam sixty miles north of Kineo Station. David Brown and Mertley Johnson were hand picked by the Chief Game Warden from Maine to work the beaver incident. Both men were known to be extremely tough, very safe and dependable, and knew the outdoors. Several people stated that the men knew never to walk on ice when it was melting. They would never unnecessarily risk or put themselves in a dangerous situation. They were true professionals.

The plan was to put several wardens into the area of Big Bog Dam during the winter months on a surveillance assignment to catch the culprits. Brown and Johnson went into the area November 13 and were last seen at Desroches Half-Way Camp on November 14; both were to be out by November 18. When the wardens didn't appear back at the office, law enforcement teams went into the area to search.

Commissioner Parsons made several statements to the press that he felt that both wardens had met with death at the hands of Canadian poachers. He enlisted the assistance from detectives in Quebec and their own warden force. Parsons also stationed six teams of three wardens each into the Big Bog Dam area in the middle of winter to help search for the bodies and to catch poachers.

Wardens investigating the disappearance of Brown and Johnson were able to find and interview people who stated that they saw the wardens enter the area of the supposed poaching. After the wardens entered, witnesses stated they heard several shots in rapid succession. The failure of the wardens to arrive back at the location of their meeting on November 18, coupled with the witness's statements of hearing several shots, bolstered Parsons's belief that the wardens were shot and killed by poachers.

The six teams that Parsons placed at the dam searched daily for Johnson and Brown. They did not find the bodies, and they never saw any poachers.

After the spring thaw, on May 2, 1923, wardens were patrolling the area of Big Bog Dam and were advised by witnesses that they thought they observed a body stuck in the spillway. Wardens investigated the reported sighting and found the body of Mertley Johnson. Johnson was transported to Moosehead Lake and later to state medical examiners. A May 4, 1923 article in the *Biddeford Journal* stated, "Commissioner Parsons advised that it [the body] was in an excellent state of preservation. No comment was made on the cause of death." The very next day another report was forwarded to wardens that someone thought they saw a body on the west branch of the Kennebec River. Wardens responded and found the body of David Brown, approximately one mile below the Big Bog Dam location where Johnson's body was found. The initial examination of both bodies did not disclose any sign of bullet wounds.

Both wardens' bodies were transported to the Somerset County Medical Examiners office where doctors Sawyer and Stinchfield conducted their exams. A May 5, 1923 article in the *Boston Daily Globe* stated:

It seems likely that both wardens were drowned in Aboconet Bog last November when proceeding north to the Canadian Boundary country to search for Canadian beaver poachers. The bodies will be brought to Greenville tomorrow for burial.

A joint decision made by two medical examiners determined that both wardens died from drowning. This decision caught many of their peers completely off guard and quite surprised. Brown was one of the most cautious and experienced lawmen in Maine and knew the dangers of icy water; the idea that he died by falling into the river or lake had few believers.

No poachers were ever found or prosecuted in relation to this incident.

Case Summary:

The wording in the paragraph above is very telling. "It seems likely" aren't the most affirming words a physician can use to describe the cause of death of two seasoned wardens. I read articles that specifically stated that these two men were very safety conscious and would never walk on thin ice; they would not risk themselves unnecessarily. Many questions have never been answered in relation to the death of these two fine lawmen.

What did Johnson and Brown confront when they went into the woods that caused them to fire their weapons in rapid succession? If they were alive immediately after that event, why wouldn't they have asked for more assistance and called for backup? I can almost guarantee that if lawmen had confronted something that caused both to fire in rapid succession, they would have left, reported the incident, and asked for assistance.

Both bodies were found within a mile and almost inside of twenty-four hours of each other. Whatever happened to each man probably happened simultaneously. I believe that it's telling that eighteen wardens entered the Big Bog area looking for poachers and for six months nothing was found and nothing was seen. Why didn't the wardens find the bodies of Johnson and Brown while they were in that specific area looking for the bodies and for poachers? While it's possible that both bodies were preserved because of the freezing river conditions, it doesn't seem probable that others wouldn't find the bodies until May, considering the number of wardens blanketing the area, or at least finding the canoe they were supposedly in. This case mimics many others in this book. Searchers are in the area where people disappear yet cannot find the victim. Months, days, or hours after the incident, the victim is found in the exact area they originally disappeared.

All of the articles specifically stated how knowledgeable Brown and Johnson were and they were known for their professionalism. The articles also stated that these two men were hand chosen for their knowledge and their abilities. I don't believe that Johnson and Brown died accidentally. Something happened in the woods to both of these fine men. The shooting of bullets in rapid succession is proof that these two wardens confronted a very dangerous predator and lost. There were never any statements about the condition of their firearms or the number of bullets they were found carrying.

I believe another factor needs to come into play, the missing beavers. Who or what was taking the beavers? It's hard to imagine that eighteen wardens in a small, confined area could not catch a predator taking beavers. The area where the wardens disappeared is very desolate in winter months. I believe there is probably some link between the missing beavers and the wardens' deaths, and the predator may be one and the same.

Kenneth Swanson
Missing 8/24/30, Noon, Colebrook, Connecticut
Age at Disappearance: 2 years

Kenneth Swanson and his mother went to visit their grandparents in rural Colebrook, Connecticut. Kenneth was playing in the yard with his pet collie, Prince. When dinnertime came along, Kenneth's mother called him for dinner, and he did not answer. A search of the yard found that the collie and Kenneth were missing. The police were quickly called, and a search was initiated. Kenneth's father was at their house in Barre, Vermont, and he drove to the grandparents' home.

Two days of searching produced no evidence of where little Kenneth might be. One witness did arrive at the house—Prince, the collie, walked into the yard without Kenneth. The dog appeared at midnight, tired and hungry and unable to offer any clues about where Kenneth might be.

George Swanson, Kenneth's father, assisted in the search for his son through the swamp and woods of the grandfather's property. Many theories were floated about where the boy might be, and one of the most prominent dealt with an abduction scenario. Searchers continued to scour the region and found no evidence of where the boy could be. Bloodhounds thoroughly searched the area where Kenneth was last seen, but they could not pick up the scent, or refused to track.

Two months after Kenneth Swanson vanished, a hunter was in the woods in mid-October and found a crumpled bundle on the ground approximately two miles from the grandparents' farm. There were very few details about the condition of the body at the time of the discovery other than it was decomposed. The coroner did an autopsy and confirmed the bundle was the body of Kenneth Swanson. The coroner also found there were no broken bones or other signs of violence. Many searchers felt the boy could not have wandered that far and died of exhaustion or exposure. To law enforcement it did not make any sense. The area where the body was found was thoroughly searched, and nothing of evidentiary value was located.

Kenneth Swanson's grandparents were so distraught about the boy's death they abandoned the farm and never returned.

Alden Johnson
Missing 3/27/34, 3:30 p.m., North Rehoboth, Massachusetts
Age at Disappearance: 4 years
**Blonde Hair

Alden lived with his family in a rural area of northern Rehoboth. The area around the residence was filled with swamps, lakes, and small creeks, with significant ground cover.

On March 27, 1934 Alden was playing in the side yard of his residence with his sister, Jeanne, (five years) and another friend. At 3:30 p.m. a large thunderstorm hit the area, and Alden's mother called the children inside. Alden didn't come in. Alden's mother, Mrs. Lee Johnson, went into the yard and searched for ten minutes and then called neighbors for assistance. In a matter of a few hours, the local and state police were on the scene, and soon hundreds of searchers were scouring the forests and swamps looking for Alden.

For the twenty-four hours after Alden disappeared, there had been continuous search efforts by hundreds of volunteers. The state police had placed an airplane in the sky and had sent two bloodhounds to search. They never did find a scent.

Twenty-six hours after Alden disappeared and more than two miles from his residence, searchers were adjacent to a turkey farm and found the boy in a swamp. A March 28, 1934 article in the *Boston Globe* had the following statement from the searcher: "I was walking along and came to the swamp. It was very deep in the center and it was decided that we would sweep in both sides. I was on the left. I came into the clearing and saw the boy. He seemed to be in a daze." Alden was carried to his residence and placed in his mother's arms.

Alden was home only minutes when his mother exclaimed, "He is dying." Alden had become unconscious, and a doctor was summoned. The doctor ordered the boy to the hospital where he stayed for two days.

When Alden was found, all of the bodies of water in the area had a light freeze, and it was quite cold. Searchers stated that Alden had scratches on his face and arms and was wet from the waist down, yet no mention was ever made that he was cold or freezing.

Case Summary:

Alden made statements to the searchers that he had not slept during the night and he had not seen any lights. The search party had built a giant bonfire that would have been visible tens of miles away, so, searchers believed that Alden had slept. It is also a mystery why Alden was not freezing when found since he was wet and it was late in the afternoon (5:30 p.m.).

One of the major questions was how Alden got into the location in the swamp where he was found. Searchers and his parents tried to question Alden about his experience, but he couldn't answer what was posed. He was found in a "daze," and he did become unconscious after he was at his home. Doctors did not know why this condition occurred.

Bobby Connor
Missing 7/13/34, 6:00 p.m., Hartsdale Manor, Greenburgh, New York
Age at Disappearance: 21 months
**Blonde Hair

The Connors lived in a suburban neighborhood of Greenburgh, New York, called Hartsdale Manor. Mr. and Mrs. Connor had four children. Hartsdale Manor was considered an upper-end area of nice homes and fairly wealthy people. The neighborhood was on the edge of a forest with lots of water and heavy timber.

On July 13, 1934 Bobby Connor was with an older neighborhood friend playing at their residence. At 5:00 p.m. Bobby's mother called the friend's home and stated that it was time for Bobby to return. While enroute home, Bobby stopped at a sand pile adjacent to an abandoned automobile and started to play. The older playmate told Bobby that he had to go home, but Bobby refused. The older playmate went to Bobby's home and notified the mother that she would have to come out and get Bobby. When Mrs. Connor arrived at the sand pile, Bobby had vanished.

Family and neighbors searched for Bobby until dark and then notified local and state police. Police brought in bloodhounds and volunteer searchers. Searchers combed the area around the home for a one-mile radius, but they found nothing. The bloodhounds couldn't find a scent.

At the end of the first eighteen hours of searching, police made several public statements about the lack of clues and lack of evidence about where the boy may be. Law enforcement felt that Bobby might have been abducted. Police actually scoured the neighborhood for leads and did arrest a suspicious peddler for the disappearance and held him in custody.

Searchers continued to look in the woods for Bobby but couldn't find tracks or other evidence that he was in the forest behind the house. As the search days went from the third, fourth, and onto the fifth day of searching, police started to believe that Bobby could not survive in the cold rain hitting the area and continued to privately think the boy was kidnapped.

On the fifth day at 2:45 p.m., searchers were going over an area that had been covered many times in the past. They came to a wall in a bramble thicket where the grass appeared to be trampled down. Lying on his back under the brambles was the small body of Bobby Connor. The searchers picked up the groggy boy and did find him alive, nearly three-fourths of a mile from his residence. Bobby was taken to his residence and then to the hospital. In a July 17, 1934 article in the *Milwaukee Sentinel*, police described their thoughts on Bobby being found:

Baby Bobby Connor found scratched but smiling in a nearby woods after he had been missing for five days lay seriously ill of exposure and starvation tonight while police expressed the belief he had been abducted and then freed. "I am forced to the conclusion it was a kidnapping," said Captain Philip J. Mcquillan, head of the Greenburg Police. "I feel the baby was placed in the woods (which had been searched frequently) in the last twenty-four hours. I don't think he could have crawled or walked that far back into the woods."

Bobby was transported to a hospital where it was found that he had severe cuts on his face and was suffering a *low-grade fever*. An article in the *Meriden Record*, dated July 19, 1934, titled "Mysterious Angles in the Connor Case Puzzle Police," states, "Dr. Charles L. Suttles pointed out an absence of mosquito bites and sunburn." Both of these items are important and go to the police department's opinion that Bobby was harbored somewhere where he would not get sun, and mosquitoes would not bother him.

As is a current theme of many of these cases, Bobby was found without his shoes and socks. One shoe was found high on a bush, thirty feet from where he was found. Officers couldn't explain how the shoe got to a point so high off the ground. Grapevines a short distance from where Bobby was found concealed the second shoe.

Case Summary:

This is a special case, probably the most investigated case from a law enforcement perspective in this region during this time in history. The local police actually had the FBI involved because of their belief of a kidnapping. Even after Bobby was found, law enforcement still believed that he was kidnapped based on the location where he was found and the lack of sunburn or mosquitoes bites.

I want all readers to pay close attention to the case that follows this one, Claire Benson. Claire disappeared just eleven days after Bobby and eighty miles north of his location. Claire was also twenty-one months old and disappeared under circumstances very similar to Bobby's. As I've stated before, I don't believe in coincidence. There is more here that we need to comprehend.

Claire Bensen
Missing 7/24/34, Cromwell, Connecticut
Age at Disappearance: 21 months

Mr. and Mrs. G. M. Bensen lived in a rural area of Cromwell, Connecticut. Mrs. Bensen allowed Claire to sit and play in their backyard while she ran into the home to do a few errands. She came back to check on Claire and found her missing and notified neighbors and police.

Mrs. Bensen called police, who then summoned bloodhounds to conduct a search. Within hours of the disappearance, dozens of people were searching the area, yelling the girl's name, but not getting a response.

Approximately twenty-four hours after Claire disappeared, a bloodhound took his trainer to within twenty feet of the girl, but Claire wasn't discovered then, or she wasn't there. The handler was a long distance from the girl's home and in an area of a massive swamp. The handler initially did not believe the girl could get to this area and then survive because of the swamp and the vast amount of water in the area. Hours later, another young searcher went back to the same area and found the young girl sitting naked on moss in the swamp. The girl did not have on the sunsuit she was wearing when she disappeared.

Searchers later stated that Claire was found over two miles from her home, and they never explained how she got into the swampy location. The sunsuit was never found.

Case Summary:

The similarities in the Connor and Bensen cases are striking. Both children are twenty-one months old (the age fact is odd by itself). Both children live in a rural area near swamps. Both were found in areas where searchers cannot understand how they got there. Both children were missing clothing. Both were found in areas that were previously searched.

Louis Dunton
Missing 10/7/47, 6:00 p.m., Fitzwilliam, New Hampshire
Age at Disappearance: 3 years

The city of Fitzwilliam, New Hampshire, is in a rural area approximately three miles north of the Massachusetts border and ten miles east of the Green Mountain National Forest. Dozens of lakes are in the immediate area of the Denton residence, and the region would be described as very swampy and wet. There are five state forests within eight miles of the victim's residence.

On October 7, 1947, Mrs. Arthur Dunton was getting her twelve children seated for dinner when the family realized that Louis wasn't in the house. The family checked the backyard where he was last playing and could not locate the boy. A call soon went out to the Cheshire County Sheriff for assistance. Law enforcement from the entire region responded in force, including the state police and local law enforcement. There were nearly one hundred searchers looking for Louis by 10:00 p.m. People were walking with torches and yelling throughout the countryside for the boy, but there was no response.

At approximately 1:00 a.m., County Sheriff Arthur Jennison responded to the Denton home with his newly acquired and recently trained bloodhound, Queenie. The sheriff allowed Queenie to sniff an old pair of Louis's shoes and off the bloodhound ran. The path the dog took wasn't easy; it was directly through a nearby swamp, for two straight miles. It was an arduous trip that took almost an hour for the sheriff, the dog's trainer, and a news cameraman who went along for the story.

At almost 2:00 a.m., Queenie found a small game trail, walked a few feet out of the swamp, and stopped next to a large group of bushes. A short distance off the trail, the sheriff shined his light into the area and saw little Louis Dunton sitting naked under the brush. At the exact moment that Louis was found, the newsman snapped a photo of the boy sitting in the leaves. This photo actually won an award in 1947 for one of the best news action photos.

The photo of Louis Denton is worth discussing. There is absolutely no doubt the boy is completely naked. There were several news reports that stated he was found partially clothed, missing some clothes, etc., but, no, the boy was completely naked. Another interesting comment about the picture is that Louis's legs are buried in the leaves to just below the left knee and half buried on the right leg, almost as though the leaves were keeping his feet warm as insulation.

In the newspaper the *Evening Independent* (October 9, 1947) there was the following comment on this story: "Still somewhat of a mystery however was why he [Louis] removed his clothes. The only theory I have, says Sheriff Jennison, is that when it got dark he thought it was time to go to bed so he took his clothes off."

This statement makes zero sense since his clothes were never found and the temperature in the area was plummeting. A *Times* article also dated October 9, 1947 had the following regarding the missing clothing: "Still somewhat of a mystery, however was why he [Louis] removed his clothes. Little Louis just smiles when they attempt to pry the information out of him. To him it seems a big joke." The only statement that any article attributes to Louis is that he made a statement about collecting blueberries while he was missing (*Youngstown Vindicator*, 10/8/47).

The greatest question to me, and one that was never asked or answered in any article, was how Louis got through two miles of swamps in the eight hours he was missing. Many articles did state that the boy had cuts and bruises and the photo shows that the boy appears dry, but it doesn't answer the question about how he managed to get through the swamps.

Michael Fontaine
Missing 5/30/49, Eastman, Quebec, Canada
Age at Disappearance: 6 years

The Fontaine case is placed in this chapter because Eastman, Quebec, is only twenty-five to thirty miles from Chain of Ponds, Maine, and the location where Kurt Newton disappeared and was never found.

Michael Fontaine was on his family's farm pasture when he disappeared. Police Chief Edmond Rioux was leading the search for Michael and had the assistance of almost one thousand volunteers. For one week they found nothing. A June 7 article in the *Ottawa Citizen* had the following: "Small footprints were found in the bush late yesterday. They appeared relatively fresh said the chief and it is not believed other children could have been in the area." This was the only lead searchers had for many days.

The *Ottawa Citizen* on June 11 ran an article stating that rumors were running wild throughout the farmland about the disappearance of the boy. The rumors were never explained in the paper, and I have no idea what they may have been. Chief Rioux did make a statement on June 11, a statement I wish I heard more SAR commanders make: "The search is strictly local now but it will continue until the boy's body is found."

On June 15 the *Saskatoon Star* had the following update regarding Fontaine:

The emaciated body of little Michael Fontaine was found Tuesday in a swamp two miles from his father's farmhouse. Provincial police came upon the body partly buried in damp, spongy ground that is thick with tall reeds and bulrushes.

Michael's body was recovered and given to a pathologist for examination. The verdict was that Fontaine died of exposure and exhaustion, possibly the first night. The same *Saskatoon Star* article stated, "To reach the pond the boy apparently was walking away from the house. He must have passed through pasture land and across a bridge before entering small bush." Law enforcement officers estimated that Fontaine walked in excess of two miles before he "fell in the swamp."

Case Summary:

I'm not gullible, and I don't believe the vast majority of the public is either. I don't understand how a six-year-old boy living on a farm, knowing the landscape, knowing his home pasture can get completely turned around, lost, and then purposely walk into a swamp and die. Yes, he had to purposely walk toward the swamp because tall reeds surrounded the swamp. I could not find any reports on the details of the body other than the article stating he was "partly buried in the damp, spongy ground." A six-year-old child knows when he enters tall reeds and grasses that he's not heading home. A six-year-old knows what pasture land looks like versus a swamp.

During the research for this book, I have read too many stories in which children and adults are found in a swamp, and the explanation given for their death is "exhaustion or exposure." Like I've stated before, I don't think physicians use "exhaustion" as a cause of death nowadays.

Articles I reviewed for this story had searchers looking as far as five miles away from the farm. In fact one searcher got lost. Michael was found two miles from his father's pastureland and in a swamp. Imagine your child at six years old; could he or she have walked two miles, over a bridge he or she has never traveled, into high reeds, past a farmhouse that had its lights on? Yes, there was a farmhouse with its lights on within site of the location where Fontaine's body was found. Why wouldn't Michael have gone to the farmhouse if he had the ability to do it? If he died from exposure, as the doctors state, he must had been in a very serious and severe state and, thus, his passing the safety and warmth of a farmhouse to continue into reeds does not make any logical sense. We are led to believe that the boy bypassed safety to walk into the one location anywhere near the farm that was concealed and the most dangerous.

Nicole Renaud
Missing 6/3/50, Bourg-La-Reine, Quebec
Age at Disappearance: 3 years

Nicole and her mother were staying at their summer home in Bour-La-Reine. The home backs up to open space and heavy forests. Nicole's parents had explained to her the dangers of the woods, and she absolutely knew never to go into the forest alone.

On July 3, 1950, Nicole was visiting the home of a friend and playing in the backyard. At some point, for an unexplained reason, Nicole walked into the woods. Nicole's friend ran into their house and screamed at the mother, "Mommy, Nicole has gone into the woods!" The mother ran into the backyard and immediately ran into the woods looking for Nicole, but she could not find her. The mother now ran to Nicole's home and got her mother to help in the search. The two women searched for almost an hour and then called authorities for assistance.

Almost one thousand people searched the woods behind the Renaud's neighbor's home for three days. The only thing of value that was found were alleged bear tracks 1500 feet back into the woods. Searchers never saw a bear, and there were no tracks anywhere near the homes. Regardless of this fact, a June 6, 1950 article in the *Edmonton Sun* stated the following: "Police definitely decided that little Nicole Renaud was devoured by bears and are abandoning the search for the 3 year old child." Residents stated that bears had been seen in the past but none recently. The police questioned about the history of bear attacks in the greater Quebec area stated, "There have been no bear attacks in recent memory in the Quebec area."

On June 8, 1950 in the *Saskatoon Star*, Phoenix, Nicole's mother made the following statement: "Mrs. Lorenzo Renaud stated that she believes her daughter was kidnapped."

Case Summary:

When researching this case I was deeply saddened for the Renaud family. The police in Quebec made several catastrophic mistakes in the investigation of the disappearance. The first major mistake was to assume that bears ate Nicole. The police had no evidence that she was eaten. They did not find any blood, tissue, or clothing of Nicole's in the woods or recent bear scat. There were no bear tracks anywhere near the homes, and neighbors had not seen bears in months. The police force made a public statement that they hadn't even had a bear attack in anyone's memory in the Quebec area. The police also stated that they had black bear only in the area around Quebec. Black bear are not known as fearsome creatures that regularly attack people; in fact, it's a rare occasion when someone is attacked by a black bear.

Mistake number two by the police was calling off the search for Nicole Renaud after three days. Even with all the manpower that they could absolutely muster, three days is too short of a period to call off a search for a three-year-old girl. It is confirmed that two thousand searchers scoured the woods for Nicole in addition to low-flying airplanes and support teams.

A June 6, 1950 article in the *Schenectady Gazette* stated that search crews found a small piece of cloth that they believed came from Nicole's dress. All other articles that I researched stated that searchers did not find any evidence in the woods.

I believe that the greater question that police needed to understand is why Nicole Renaud went into the woods and why Nicole's mother felt she was abducted. Not finding any viable evidence in the woods, not finding any evidence of bears in the woods, and knowing that parents were in the woods searching and calling for her minutes after she walked into the woods, makes it very difficult to understand how a bear could have grabbed her when she walked into the forest. There is no way Nicole could have walked 1500 feet in the time it took parents to get into the woods. She would have had to have been walking and heard the calls if the bear option was still viable.

In the many articles I reviewed for this case, there was never one mention of the police utilizing hounds to track down the supposed bear. If there was a bear involved in the disappearance, hounds would find the closest bear, police never tried this tactic, probably because they knew a bear was never involved.

I believe Nicole saw something, something that didn't scare her but something that intrigued her, but something that eventually took her life.

Diane Abbott
Missing 7/6/56, Hebron, Maine
Age at Disappearance: 2 years

At 2:00 p.m. on July 6, Helen Abbott heard her daughter Diane crying in the backyard. She couldn't go to her immediate aide, as she was assisting another child in the house. Once done with the child in the house, Helen went outside and couldn't find Diane. The other Abbott children were asked to look for Diane, but they couldn't immediately find her. Once it was determined that Diane wasn't on the property, the sheriff was called.

The Abbotts lived in an extremely remote area. They lived on the Karle Pulkinen farm, located at the end of a dead-end road and more than one mile from the nearest neighbor and more than three miles from any development. Anyone approaching the farm would be seen, and nobody was observed driving the road. Swamps, heavy brush, and forests surround the residence.

Within the first twenty-four hours, one thousand people were searching the Maine woods for Diane Abbott. The searchers could not believe that the girl hadn't already been found because of the huge response from volunteers. In the lengthy archive search I performed, I could never find any information that Diane was found.

Brenda Jean Doud
Missing 07/06/58, Eagle Pond, New York
Age at Disappearance: 5 years

Readers should first take note that Brenda disappeared exactly two years after Diane Abbott vanished from Hebron, Maine, almost exactly one hundred miles directly east of Diane's location in Maine.

Eagle Pond is located in far northern New York, approximately sixteen miles south of Malone, just outside the Titusville Mountain

State Forest. This is a very rural and rugged area with many lakes, creeks, and rivers.

Eagle Pond is approximately 1500 feet long and 750 feet wide. Mr. and Mrs. Robert Doud took their daughter Brenda with them to the pond to build a small camp for vacation purposes. Sometime on July 6 Brenda disappeared, and her parents called local law enforcement officers.

The day after Brenda disappeared the area was hit by heavy rains, which caused searchers additional problems. Bloodhounds, two hundred volunteers, two helicopters, and two Army National Guard Units searched two days without finding the young girl. At the fiftieth hour of the search, and two miles from Brenda's camp, searchers were covering a swampy region with numerous downed trees and thought they saw something odd. The men approached the object and found Brenda. The girl was missing her shirt, shoes, socks, and pants and was wearing just panties. She was in good condition.

Searchers were attempting to understand how Brenda disappeared for such a long period of time and how she managed to eat and drink. Brenda was very quiet about her experience except to explain what she observed. A July 11, 1958 article in *Stars and Stripes* had the following: "Scott said Brenda enjoyed telling of her experience. She even had seen three bears, two asleep and one awake, he said." I've hiked hundreds of miles in the woods and have never walked up on a sleeping bear. What did Brenda really see in the woods? What happened to her clothes that were never found? How did this young girl eat and drink when she was missing?

Douglas Chapman
Missing 6/2/71, Alfred, Maine
Age at Disappearance: 3 years
3', 35 lbs

It was 10:00 a.m. on June 2, 1971 when Carole Chapman looked out onto her front yard and saw her son, Douglas Chapman, playing in a sand pile. Carole never knew this would be the last time she saw her son.

At 10:30 a.m. Carole Chapman looked outside and couldn't see Douglas. She went to the yard and started to call out for the boy—no answer. Carole walked the perimeter of her property and couldn't find any sign of Douglas. Carole now started to get quite worried and called police.

At the peak point in the search for Douglas, over one thousand law enforcement officers, game wardens, volunteers, and family scoured the swamps, forests, and farms for Douglas. Searchers didn't even find a footprint.

Police brought tracking dogs into the search and they did pickup a scent that they traced through a field, past an apple orchard, onto a farm, and then down a driveway. People in those areas were interviewed and did not see any strange people or vehicles.

This case was reopened by law enforcement in 1993; there has been no resolution, and there are no known suspects. This is one of three cases in the southern Maine/New Hampshire area in which children have vanished.

Douglass Legg
Missing 07/10/71, Newcomb, New York
Age at disappearance: 8 years

This case is an example that even the wealthiest families can be victims of horrific incidents as in the disappearance of Douglass Legg. His family was vacationing at the 13,000-acre estate of relative and Syracuse banker Crandell Melvin. The property sat just north of the small hamlet of Newcomb in a very tranquil and remote setting next to a Newcomb lake. This was a very private setting with a large lodge to house the owner and all of his guests. The location was not open to the public—family members only.

William Legg told law enforcement officers and the press that Douglass was going hiking with his uncle (Myron Melvin, Jr.) and arrived on the trail wearing a T-shirt, shorts, and tennis shoes. Myron told him that he would catch poison oak if he wore those clothes and told him to head back to the lodge to change. As they were just at the entrance to an overgrown logging trail, Douglass started back to the lodge. A July 17, 1971 article in the *Gadsden Times* described the event as the boy left the trail:

Legg said the boy was walking back along a ridge near the properties Newcomb Lake when he saw some other children on the beach below. The others shouted to Doug to join them, and he said that he would take a short cut to meet them going down the other side of the ridge. That was the last time he was seen.

    Douglass's family spared no expense or effort in the search for the young boy. The family flew out specially trained SAR dogs from Washington State and a twenty-man SAR team from California. This was a methodical search using ropes to mark quadrants and to ensure not one inch of ground was missed.

    The bloodhounds and canines in this search appeared to find Douglass's scent and started tracking even though what they were doing seemed unbelievable to SAR team members. The dogs tracked the scent north into an area of the Adirondack Mountains called "High Peaks." The "Peaks" is an area with mountains reaching to 5000 feet in elevation with hundreds of small lakes and streams in a very rugged and remote setting. The canines tracked through the peaks and then went around the city of Lake Placid, a huge journey for a man, let alone an eight-year-old boy. A July 21, 1971 article in the *Wellsville Daily* had this comment on the canines' search: "If the missing boy had indeed walked through the outskirts of Lake Placid, officials said, he would have had to have traveled at least 30 miles." The path that the canines took was directly through the roughest and most difficult terrain anywhere in the region and then back around the periphery of a city environment.

    Fourteen days after Douglass disappeared, the search was again given a spark by the addition of a detachment of Green Berets from Fort Devens, Massachusetts. I couldn't find any information on who requested the team or why a special-forces group would be used on this search. Why a special detachment of highly trained Green Berets would be utilized instead of normal National Guardsmen unit is a major question in my mind.

    The military continued to add support to this SAR as the Plattsburgh Air Force Base contributed airplanes with infrared equipment to spot heat signatures on the ground, while others brought helicopters and ground support.

    The search for Douglass captured the heart and soul of nearly every county resident. One local man searched for the boy for thirty-eight days and found just one track in the moss near a shallow creek miles from the lodge. Eventually people had to go back to their families and work, and the SAR was terminated. Articles were written about this event decades later and described a number of hunters and hikers who have disappeared in the Adirondacks under very perplexing circumstances, Douglass Legg being the most unusual.

Case Summary:
The idea that Douglass walked north into higher elevation through the rugged "Peaks" and then back down into Lake Placid, circling the city seems unrealistic. I do not doubt that the canines were tracking his scent; too many dogs were involved for it to be mistaken identity. The real question is, why was the scent in those locations? Who called the Green Berets and what was their role in the search? This case is very reminiscent of the Dennis Martin Search.

Kurt Ronald Newton
Missing 8/31/75, Chain of Ponds, Maine
Age at Disappearance: 4 years
3'8", 45 lbs

It was Labor Day weekend in 1975 when Jill and Ronald Newton took their six-year-old daughter and four-year old son Kurt to the Natanis Point Campground in Chain of Ponds, Maine, for a weekend getaway. The Newton's had made the drive from their home in Manchester.

The campground is located at the far western end of two large ponds and is located less than one mile from the Canadian border. There isn't much in this area, and there are no large towns for many miles. The entire area around the campgrounds and the lakes is heavily wooded.

On Sunday, August 31 in the morning hours, Kurt was riding his tricycle in a loop around the campground when his parents theorized that he became confused and lost. An article in the May 30, 1985 *Lewiston Daily* states: "A girl who passed him on a narrow road near the campsite asked him if his parents knew where he was. When he did not respond, she kept walking. The boy was never seen again." Kurt's tricycle was found on an adjacent dirt road near the campground. The game wardens and state police used every available search option for Kurt Newton. Eglin Air Force Base in Florida actually sent a plane with an infrared sensor to Maine to fly the skies and find heat-producing entities on the ground. Two hundred volunteers and law enforcement personnel combed the countryside for six days with no success.

The night the search for Kurt started it was immediately compromised because heavy rains hit the region and obliterated many tracks and took the scent off the ground that canines would have followed. Heavy rains again hit the area on Tuesday that brought a halt to the search. Area lumber mills closed operations on Tuesday of that week to allow its workers to assist in the search. At the peak of the SAR nearly one thousand people participated in looking for Kurt Newton. Searchers concentrated on an eight-square-mile area near the campsite during their search. The SAR for the boy culminated the week of September 8 without finding any evidence of his location.

In May of 1976 the search for Kurt was put into gear again. A one-day SAR that covered ground previously searched was searched again. Warden Inspector Duane Lewis headed the effort and stated in the *Lewiston Daily* of May 12, 1976: "We are convinced that Kurt Newton is not here."

Case Summary:

I would agree with inspector Lewis. Kurt was probably not inside of that eight-square-mile area where they were concentrating their efforts. If Kurt were abducted, he would have been many miles from that location. If Kurt had simply gotten lost and walked away, a cadaver dog should have been used on the 1976 search. No notes show that this occurred.

The remote location of the Natanis Point Campground makes the idea of a serial abductor driving along a lonely dirt road looking for a victim seem ludicrous. There aren't that many people camping at this location in September to make abduction a feasible option for a roadway predator. Witnesses in the area would see someone driving, lurking, who hadn't been camping. If an abductor was driving through the area and had been seen taking Kurt, the ability to apprehend him would be much easier than in an urban setting. There is only one road to the location, Highway 27. You either leave the campground and drive southeast to leave or go northwest. Both are easy paths to put roadblocks up to stop a kidnapper. I don't think that the predator would go northeast; the Canadian Border checkpoint is just down the road, and that left one escape path, southeast. Kidnappers don't like locations where there is only one path to escape. This leaves only the forest as a location to look for Kurt.

Andrew Warburton
Missing 7/1/86, Beaver Bank, Tucker Lake, Halifax, Nova Scotia
Age at Disappearance: 9 years

This case is submitted in this section because of its proximity to Maine.

Canadians spend their summers traveling and visiting friends in the same manner as people in the States vacation. The summers for most Canadians are a little shorter of warmer weather than in the States, and because of that they spend a great deal of time outdoors when the weather is warm.

Tom and Doreen Warburton took their nine-year-old son Andrew with them when they went to spend a few days with relatives in Beaver Band ten miles outside of Halifax, Nova Scotia. This location would be approximately seventy-five miles from the Maine border.

The family was staying with relatives who lived near Tucker Lake, a body of water approximately one-fourth of a mile long and a thousand yards wide. This location has hundreds of small lakes with homes now scattered around many of them. In 1986 there was less development than today, but there was still scattered housing among the very flat land.

The Warburtons were visiting friends when their children stated they were going to swim in the nearby lake. Andrew asked if he could go, and the parents obliged. The main group of children left before Andrew was ready, but the path was very clear, and it was a short distance to the lake. Andrew was wearing tennis shoes and a swimming suit when he left following the other boys by just a short distance.

After swimming and getting cold, the boys headed back to the house and realized that they had never met up with Andrew. Parents were notified, and a search was immediately started. Inside of one hour, law enforcement officials were notified, and RCMP officers were in the vicinity of Tucker Lake. Within hours over one hundred people were scouring the woods near the path to Tucker Lake for Andrew Warburton. They were calling his name and searching the marshy area for the boy.

Within twenty-four hours almost one thousand searchers were completely combing the Tucker Lake area, almost bumping into each other looking for the boy. An article on July 5, 1986 (Saturday) in the *Winnepeg Free Press* had a very strange statement made by a spokesperson for the RCMP: "He is spooking; he is just running around like a little animal." The article states that two searchers believed that they saw the boy, but he ran so fast through the bush that they couldn't keep up with him. Remember, almost one thousand people were searching a very confined area, and helicopters and canines were assisting in the search. Is the RCMP implying that canines couldn't keep up with someone running from them? Searchers were also hampered by inclement weather that hit the Beaver Bank area. On Wednesday it started to rain and the temperature plummeted to forty-nine degrees.

It appears that RCMP and searchers started to become frustrated that they couldn't find the boy and requested the assistance of the military. On Sunday the Canadian Armed Forces deployed troops in the marsh area and started a systematic SAR. On Tuesday, July 7, near midday, military personnel found two tennis shoes near Tucker Lake. The shoes were shown to the parents, and they confirmed that they did belong to Andrew. A more intensive effort concentrating two hundred yards outside the primary search area found Andrew's body at 5:30 p.m. A July 8 article in the *Ottawa Citizen* stated the following: "The body was found in an alder thicket in a gully of marshy ground three kilometers from the Beaver Bank home of relatives the Warburton family was visiting." Andrew was deceased, and the body was transported to Nova Scotia's Chief Medical Examiners Office for an autopsy. Dr. Roland Perry stated on July 10 in the *Lethbridge Herald*, "The youngster probably died sometime between Friday and Sunday." This means that Andrew was alive for three days with searchers standing almost shoulder to shoulder searching for him?

Case Summary:

There are many facets about this disappearance that are worth review and analysis.

Andrew disappeared on a Tuesday and a search was immediately started. His parents were yelling his name, yet the boy never answered. Inside of twenty-four hours hundreds of people were searching, and Andrew still was not found. One group of two searchers felt they saw the boy, but he ran so fast they couldn't keep up. The question is, did they actually see Andrew? If the boy was missing and inclement weather hit the area and he was cold, it seems reasonable to believe that he would have come out if he could. Searchers had canines with them—why weren't the canines used to track the person who was running from the searchers?

How could one thousand searchers miss tennis shoes that were found by military personnel seven days into the search? It almost seems as though the tennis shoes may have not originally been at the location where found. If it were cold, as is quoted in the articles, why would Andrew take his shoes off? How could searchers claim to have seen Andrew "running like an animal" on Saturday and the medical examiner state he was deceased between Friday and Sunday? If Andrew wasn't the one running, who was eluding searchers? If Andrew was the one running, how did he manage to run through alders and thickets without shoes so fast to elude adults?

It is a fact that the weather turned bad immediately after Andrew disappeared. If he were alive in the time frame from Tuesday–Friday (at a minimum) why would he lie in a gully of marshy ground? If it was cold, if he was cold, I don't think the boy would purposely lie in wet marshy ground when dry ground was nearby.

It's amazing when I review statements of searchers and facts concerning cases that law enforcement officers purposely refuse to address areas of concern. Tom and Doreen Warburton were very concerned about the facts surrounding this case and asked for a legal magistrate associated with the Canadian government to open an inquiry into the death of their son. Four months after Andrew was found, the request was denied. The magistrate stated that "this was merely a case of a boy getting lost in the woods." I don't think so. I don't think Canadian armed forces are brought into a routine case of a missing boy; something unusual was at play in this incident and that's why the military was requested.

Patric McCarthy
Missing 10/13/03, White Mountains, New Hampshire
Age at Disappearance: 10 years
4'10", 85 lbs

Steve McCarthy and his family were vacationing near the Loon Mountain Ski Resort in the White Mountains of New Hampshire on October of 2003. The family was staying at their condominium in the Clear Brook development.

On the afternoon of October 13, Patric was playing with his stepbrothers, Gabe and Noah Fritz. The boys were approximately four hundred yards from the condo when Patric challenged them to a race back to their residence. The boys agreed to the challenge and started to run through the woods back toward the condo. Patric took what he thought was a shortcut.

Noah and Gabe made it back to the condo, but Patric never arrived. The boys notified Steve that Patric was missing, and a search was started almost immediately. Simultaneous to Patric disappearing, wind and rain started to hit the area of the search, and it seemed that this was one of the first major obstacles to finding Patric.

Five hundred people participated in the search for the boy. Eventually, on day four of the search, Patric was found on the back side of White Mountain, dead, over two miles from the condo. As I've stated many times, children who are lost usually walk downhill. Patric seemingly walked 1400 feet uphill.

The medical examiner checked the body and determined that Patric died of hypothermia, as the temperatures in the area got down to the thirties and forties at night.

Patric's parents doubted the medical examiner's opinion from the onset. They couldn't understand how Patric got so far from the condominium or how he got so high in elevation. There were also rumors that a witness came forward and claimed that Patric was murdered. Steve McCarthy went to the FBI and asked them to investigate the case. Patric's body was found on federal land, but the state has jurisdiction.

There are people not related to the McCarthy family who believe Patric was murdered. As of this point it does not appear that federal authorities are going to override the decision of the state investigators, and Patric's death is still classified as an accident, hypothermia.

Case Summary:

I agree with Steve McCarthy. This case needs to be reexamined, and new faces need to look at the evidence. I don't believe that Patric would have walked 1400 feet higher than he was in an effort to find his condominium. Something pulled Patric from his path, and that something needs to be identified.

Chapter Summary

There are twenty-four people listed as missing in this chapter. The largest group of missing is twelve boys under ten years of age.

The most unusual occurrence on the missing list for New England is the following:

M – Bobby Connor (21mos) 07/13/34, 6:00 p.m.
F – Claire Bensen (21 mos) 07/24/34, p.m.

Bobby and Claire were exactly twenty-one months old and disappeared just eleven days apart. They are the only people listed in New England who are exactly twenty-one months old and who both went missing in a very short time period.

The reader should now be getting a clear understanding the number of times a child has gone missing, the parents believe there was an abduction and the FBI was called. It is a guarantee that the FBI has a very large and aged file on missing children under very suspicious circumstances, a file we will never see.

Vermont Missing People

The cases listed below all occurred in the far southwest corner of the state. In the years of research on this project, I have never seen such a condensed and consistent grouping of missing people as has occurred in the Bennington area. Many of the incidents occurred on Glastenbury Mountain, and many items I've read have stated that Native Americans consider this area a forbidden zone where they will not travel. I can't confirm this is true as I've never spoken with Native American Elders from the area; however, it does appear there is something very uncomfortable about the Bennington area during the time frames outlined below.

It's an amazing fact that six of the seven missing people went missing in the months of October to December, months in Vermont when people rarely spend extensive time in the outdoors.

Name	Date Missing•Age•Sex
Alfred J. Bishop	11/03/26•Unk•M
Alice Baker	08/16/37•20 mos•F
Carl Herrick	11/26/43•37•M
Middie Rivers	11/12/45•75•M
Paula Welden	12/01/46•18•F
Paul Jepson	10/12/50•8•M
Freida Langer	10/28/50•53•F

Alfred J. Bishop
Missing 11/03/26, Reading, Vermont
Age at Disappearance: Unknown

Alfred Bishop and his friend Morris Gallagher left their residence in Felchville and traveled a short distance to their hunting area in a region near Reading, Vermont. The men arrived early in the day and decided to split up and meet back at their cars at an agreed-upon time. Alfred never came back. Once Morris realized his friend wasn't going to arrive, he searched the immediate area of their cars and then headed to Springfield to get additional assistance.

Approximately twenty-four hours after Alfred disappeared, searchers found his body under very, very strange circumstances. On November 4, the *Lewiston Daily* ran the following description of the scene:

> *Bishop's body was found beside an abandoned road in the woods near the summer camp of Attorney General John G. Sargent. There were evidences [sic]of a terrific struggle in the snow, which was beaten down for a distance of 60 paces about the body. Strewn about in different directions were Bishop's rifle, coat, and gloves.*

The article also stated, "The state's attorney said he was puzzled by the lack of blood stains in the snow. A preliminary examination disclosed no wounds on Bishop's body."

Alfred's body was sent for autopsy. The *Bridgeport Telegram* had an article on November 6 that described the autopsy result: "An autopsy was performed today on the body of Alfred Bishop of Felchville and failed to dispel the mystery of the young man's death during a hunting trip Wednesday. No external marks of violence were disclosed on the autopsy." Later in the same article it had this describing the area where Alfred was found: "The snow had been trampled over a considerable area and there was every evidence of a terrific struggle."

Thirty-five miles southeast of Reading is West Townshend, a location where an equally baffling death occurred with some parallel elements, the case of Carl Herrick, identified later in this chapter.

Alice Lorraine Baker
Missing 08/16/37, Bald Mountain, Bennington, Vermont
Age at Disappearance: 20 months

Mr. and Mrs. Kimball Baker were from Hudson Falls, New York, when they chose to spend a summer vacation at a Bald Mountain cabin five miles north of Bennington, Vermont. The Bakers had three children, Alice being the youngest at twenty months. The vacation cabin was located on an isolated side road approximately one mile from Highway 7, which links Bennington and Rutland.

Late in the afternoon on August 16, Mrs. Baker needed to go to a neighbor's house and left Alice alone at the cabin. She returned ten minutes later to find Alice missing. She quickly searched the area around the cabin, yelled her name several times, and did not get a response. Mrs. Baker went back to the neighbor's house and requested additional assistance and asked that law enforcement be notified.

After two intensive days of searching for the twenty-month-old girl, law enforcement officials made several interesting statements. On August 18, 1937 the *Telegraph* ran a story carrying a series of quotes. The first statement is from the local constable in the area, Ralph Young: "Maybe Alice didn't wander away alone into the woods. I'm afraid something else happened to her." County Sheriff Clyde Peck stated in the same article that he felt Alice Baker had been kidnapped.

Weather in the area during the search had turned quite cold at night with occasional showers. On August 19, 1937 The *Meriden Daily* ran a quote from Sheriff Peck: "The child could not possibly have survived the cold and exposure of the past two nights." He went on to say that searchers are continuing to look for Alice and have found nothing. The same article stated, "Searchers continued to tramp the woods about the Baker's summer home today, but they were not hopeful after failure of three bloodhounds to find a scent yesterday."

The search for Alice was going to be terminated on August 20 when something drastic happened. Volunteers searching a seldom used logging road thought they heard moaning. The searchers broke through thick undergrowth and found Alice sitting under a spruce tree. The girl was naked sitting on her one-piece blue sun suit. Doctors later examined the girl and and stated that she would be up and playing in a few days. There was no statement about dehydration or her appetite.

This case has many similarities to the disappearance of Kevin Ayotte in Sugar Bush, Minnesota. Both kids were close in age. Both disappeared while their parents were outside their vacation home. Both vacation homes were in very remote areas.

Case Summary:

Wow! I wish I had been a criminal investigator in Bennington in the late 1930s to early 1940s. Again, high strangeness strikes the Bennington area. The disappearance of Alice has left many unanswered questions, and I'm surprised the sheriff didn't make additional statements after she was found.

It's obvious from the articles and quotations that law enforcement felt that something abnormal occurred to Alice. It's also obvious from the quotations that nobody thought she would be found alive. Remember the rationale behind people's belief the girl would not be found alive—cold weather and her age. She was found naked. Does this sound like a person who was supposed to die from exposure?

Sheriff Peck made a statement that he felt Alice had been kidnapped. He made that statement because she was nowhere near the cabin, and she was only twenty months old. The sheriff knew the girl could not have gone far because of her size and age; she also didn't have the ability to withstand in the wilds alone. How did Alice survive if she didn't have assistance?

The last item of interest on this case is the lack of success by the bloodhounds. In almost every case in which small children disappear, and are found at a distance from their original location where law enforcement officers don't feel they could have gotten on their own, canines can't seem to find a scent, or won't track. This is an issue that SAR officials wouldn't understand unless they have researched hundreds of cases with similar canine behavior.

Carl Herrick
Missing 11/23/43, West Townshend, Vermont
Age at Disappearance: 37 years

West Townshend is approximately ten miles northeast of Bennington. It's a rural area with thick woods surrounding the community. The town is on the east side of Glastenbury Mountain, the location where Paula Welden disappeared.

On November 23, 1943, Carl Herrick and his cousin Henry Herrick went to West Townshend for deer hunting. At some point during the hunt, the Herricks got separated, and Carl never arrived at camp. Henry notified law enforcement almost immediately. In an unfortunate turn for searchers, snow started to fall the first night that Carl was missing.

The search for Carl continued for three days without finding any trace of the man. Late on that third day, Carl's cousin, Henry found Carl on the mountain lying on the ground, motionless. Henry walked to the body and found Carl's face black, with minor scratches on the arms and hands. There were some alleged *"huge"* bear tracks on the ground in the area. Carl's rifle was found leaning against a tree seventy feet away. There was one expended round lying on the ground near the rifle.

A November 27, 1943 article in the *Dunkirk Evening Observer* had the following: "Acting coroner Carlos Otis said the bear had cuffed (scratched) Herrick about the head but killed him by squeezing. The victim's lung was punctured."

Case Summary:

After conducting thousands of hours of research and reading countless documents about a person's cause of death, I have never read about a bear that squeezed an adult to death. Many of the articles surmised that Carl shot a bear, placed his rifle against a tree, and walked up to the body to find the bear still alive. All hunters are trained to keep their weapons with them, walk to the body, and touch the eye with the barrel to ensure the animal doesn't flinch. It's hard for me to believe that Carl placed his rifle against the tree and walked seventy feet to a downed bear.

Henry had told searchers that the pair were hunting deer, not bear. Even if Carl was charged by a bear, the likelihood of him shooting a huge bear only once and immediately dropping the animal would be minimal. A hunter would fire multiple times to ensure a wounded bear wasn't running around in the wild. If a bear charged Carl, I seriously doubt he'd lean his rifle against a tree just before his demise.

It's also extremely hard to believe that a bear would grab a person and try to squeeze him to death, especially black bears in the United States, which are not that large. If a bear grabbed a person, it would bite and claw him. There was not one mention on any report of a severe cut, bite or wound to Carl, only minor scratches and *no bite marks*. The coroner stated that Carl had a broken rib that punctured his lung. The force it takes to break a rib and puncture a lung is exceptional, and I don't believe that a black bear in North America could accomplish this on a grown adult male without inflicting severe parallel injuries that would make it clear it was a bear.

Carl left behind five small children.

Middie Rivers
Missing 11/12/45, Glastenbury Mountain, Bennington, Vermont
Age at Disappearance: 75 years

Middie Rivers lived almost his entire life in the Bennington area. He truly enjoyed the outdoor lifestyle and devoted every free minute of his time to hunting and fishing the area. Middie was lucky to blend a hobby into his job. He became a game guide.

On November 12, 1945, Middie was taking four hunters onto Glastenbury Mountain. They spent the day on the mountain and were on their way back down. Middie had made this trip hundreds of times; he knew this mountain like you know your backyard. As the group was returning, Middie got slightly ahead and somehow never arrived at their vehicles.

A search was conducted, and the path that the group took was retraced. The only item that searchers found was one bullet next to a creek along the path that Middie was traveling. The newspapers printed the following answer about the discovery of the bullet, "Middie leaned down to get a drink and it fell out of his pocket."

Searchers never found Middie, never found his supplies, rifle, coat, hat, nothing.

Case Summary:

Middie was the one individual in the Bennington area who would never get lost. The idea that searchers couldn't locate his body means that he was taken from the area; there is no other explanation.

Finding the bullet next to the creek could have one other explanation. Middie may have been walking near the creek, saw what appeared to be a threat, removed a bullet from his coat, and as he was trying to load his firearm, was overpowered.

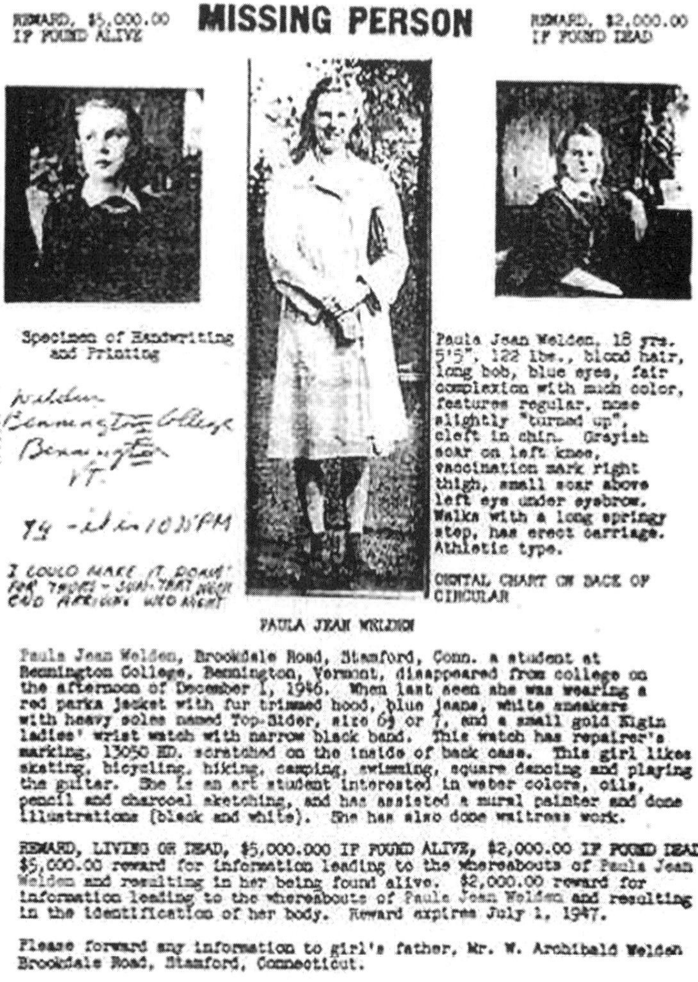

Paula Jean Welden
Missing 12/1/46, Glastonbury Mountain, Bennington, Vermont
Age at Disappearance: 18 years
5'5", 122 lbs

Bennington sits at the far southwestern portion of Vermont, two miles from the New York border and six miles from Massachusetts. Thick woods surround the city with the Green Mountain National Forest just to the northeast. Glastenbury Mountain is located just to the northeast of the main portion of Bennington and approximately an eight-mile drive up Highway 7. Somerset Reservoir sits just to the east of the mountain. Glastenbury Mountain has en elevation of approximately 3600 feet.

On December 1, 1946, Paula Welden was a sophomore at Bennington College. It was a Sunday, and Paula had worked the breakfast and lunch shifts at her dining hall. She went back to her dormitory room and told her roommate that she was going on a hike to Glastenbury Mountain. She put on blue jeans, sneakers, and took her red parka.

A motorist who was passing Paula picked her up and dropped her at Long Trail at the base of the mountain. Somewhere along this trail Paula met fate and was never seen again. Her roommate reported her as missing a day after Paula went to the mountain, hoping she would return. She never did.

Paula's father, W. Archibald Welden, was an industrial engineer in Glastenbury and her mother, Pamela, took care of the household duties. Once news came of Paula's disappearance, her parents responded to the campus and stayed onsite for almost two weeks while the search was conducted. There were many false leads and rumors that ensued during the fourteen days. In short, nothing was found, and no leads were developed. The police did find the person who gave Paula a ride to the mountain, and he did confirm he did give the ride. Police also found a person who was hiking down the mountain and who did see Paula at approximately 4:00 p.m. The man stated that Paula asked him how long it was to the top of the mountain. The man stated that he was slightly concerned because it got to be dusk at 5:00 p.m., and then it started to snow (three inches total the first night).

Searchers scoured the mountain until weather started to deteriorate. After two weeks, all SAR operations were terminated for 1946.

On May 26, 1947 there was an article in the *Meriden Daily Journal*. The article explained that another two-day search for Paula was conducted over twenty-four-square miles. The following statement appeared in the article:

Among spots investigated by searchers were Bickford Hollow area where a "strong odor" at first believed to be that of an animal or human body was detected Saturday and the swamp section in Manchester where screams of a young girl were reported on the night that Paula disappeared.

Law enforcement did have reports of a woman screaming in the swampy area that they were now searching again. The two days of search efforts did not produce any other positive results.

Hundreds of people participated in the search for Paula Welden. The search was touted as one of the largest ever conducted in the area.

Case Summary:

At the time of Paula's disappearance, there was not a state police department in Vermont, and this lack of a coordinated effort may have hindered the investigation. I do believe that Paula was murdered and/or abducted or she would have turned up somewhere by now. There was never an inkling that Paula was anything but a good student and a caring daughter.

A December 17, 1961 article in the *Sunday Herald* had an interview with the Vermont State Police, now an established law enforcement organization and still working the Welden case. The article stated that the Vermont investigators had come to some definitive conclusions about the Paula Welden case: "Paula was either dead somewhere in the white vastness of Glastenbury Mountain or she had been carried away and killed." The last part of the previous statement has me a bit perplexed: "Carried away and killed"—by what? A normal-sized man would have an extraordinarily difficult time carrying someone down off the mountain, let alone carrying her without being seen.

One portion of this investigation has me very concerned. Many people who have disappeared and were subsequently found were found in swampy areas. Law enforcement did state that a witness heard a female scream in the swampy area of Bickford Hollow the night Paula disappeared. Bickford Hollow is a location off Long Trail Road and probably a thousand feet from the end and to the north. The hollow is at the end of a long ridgeline that has its start near Glastenbury Mountain. The elevation at the hollow is 1500 feet. If we follow the evidence in many missing person cases listed in this book, there is a reasonably good likelihood that Paula Weldon is located in the swamp.

The last issue of concern is what Paula was wearing, a red coat. It would seem that the brighter the color of clothing the better the chance that searchers would find a missing person, almost the opposite is the case. It may be that the bright colors attract predators but it also seems that many people who have disappeared have been wearing red.

Paul Jepson
Missing: 10/12/50, City Dump, Bennington, Vermont
Age at Disappearance: 8 years

Nancy and Paul Jepson were schoolteachers in Schenectady, New York, when they decided they wanted a rural life for their family. Paul got a job as the local tax collector in Shaftsbury, and the family bought a ranch in that city. The Jepsons had two children, Nancy, seven years old, and Paul, Jr., eight years old.

The Jepson family was an energetic group who had several financial interests. While Paul took care of the family farm and the tax collections, Nancy was responsible for their sixty-five pigs that they left at the Bennington dump. Every day Nancy would go to the dump and relocate the pigs to a different plot at the site. The dump was located at the base of the Bald Mountains.

On October 12, 1950 Nancy took the family truck with Paul, Jr. in the front seat and drove to the dump as she usually did every day at 3:30 p.m. She parked the truck near the forest and adjacent to a ravine and started the thirty minute process of moving the pigs. At the end of the move, Nancy came back to the truck and found that Paul was missing. She ran to the woods calling Paul's name, then ran toward the ravine and looked into the gully. She didn't see the boy. She now went to the dump office and called her husband, who then called the sheriff. Inside of two hours, deputies and wardens had responded to the dump and were starting a search.

Paul Jepson felt his son might have gone into the woods because he had a fascination with the forest. There was also a concern that maybe there was a slight landslide in the dump and the boy was buried. That possibility was checked and confirmed it did not occur. The sheriff brought in a canine and attempted to track the boy's scent. The dog appeared to follow a scent down a road, onto another road, and then seemingly stopped. All of the homes along those roads were contacted, and nobody saw the boy.

On October 16, 1950 the *North Adams Transcript* ran the following paragraph: "Sheriff Maloney said today that he has discarded for the time being any theory that the boy might have met with foul play." As the search continued, a Coast Guard helicopter was brought to search the mountains for Paul. They did not have any luck in finding him. Professional and volunteer searchers looked for Paul Jepson, Jr. for almost two weeks, but they found nothing.

Case Summary:

The disappearance of Paul Jepson occurred sixteen days before the disappearance of Freida Langer. Langer and Jepson disappeared within miles of each other. Paul, Jr. disappeared at the base of the Bald Mountains. Alice was found on an old logging road between spruce and Bald Mountain. An investigator could not ignore the geographical similarities and timelines between these cases.

A very important similarity between the Baker, Weldon, Jepson, and Lange cases is that they disappeared in the woods. These people did not disappear on a city sidewalk. Paul Jepson believed his son wandered into the woods. This is where I would have focused my energies. Having knowledge of many missing children in the far northern portion of the U.S., my gut would tell me that Paul ended up high on Bald Mountain, somewhere, somehow.

Freida Langer
Missing 10/28/50, Somerset, Vermont
Age at Disappearance: 53 years

Mr. and Mrs. Langer left their residence in North Adams and proceeded to their hunting cabin in Somerset, Vermont, just four miles east of Bennington. Max and Freida brought their cousin Herbert Elsner with them to hunt. The group arrived at the cabin in the woods and unpacked their supplies. They were in an area that was known quite well to the Langers. They had owned and vacationed at this cabin for fourteen years.

On October 28, 1950, Max woke up with a very sore knee and told Freida and Herbert to go out and hunt and he'd stay behind at the camp.

Freida and Herbert got out of camp late and were walking for almost an hour when Freida tripped and fell into a small creek, getting wet. She told Herbert that she would get cold and wanted to walk back to camp to change clothes. The two walked in the direction of camp for several minutes and then decided to momentarily split up but later meet back in camp; it was now 3:50 p.m. An article in the *Lowell Sun* dated October 31, 1950 stated: "When last seen she (Freida Langer) was drenched from a fall in a brook and was within 150 yards of the woodland cabin she and her husband had owned for 14 years."

At 4:45 Herbert arrived back at camp and Freida had still not arrived. It was at this point that Max and Herbert decided to go out and search for Freida. The men were concerned because Freida knew the area very well; there was no way in their minds that she could have been lost, not this close to the cabin.

The men did not find Freida the first night and obtained assistance from wardens and law enforcement. A week-long search for Freida could not find the lady, and efforts were eventually suspended.

Nothing further was developed on the search for Freida until May 14, 1951. James Renton and Herman Lincoln were fishing in a spot three miles from the hunting cabin where Freida and Max were staying. This area had been thoroughly searched when Freida had initially disappeared. The men saw something in high weeds at the end of a swampy area near a flood dam. The men walked into the reeds and swamp and saw a body, the body of Freida Langer. A coroner's report indicated that Freida died from accidental drowning.

Case Summary:

In reading the articles associated with the Freida Langer case I was shocked that there was not an inquest into her death. The woman was 150 yards away from a cabin that she had owned for fourteen years. There is no way she was lost. This woman knew exactly where she was going. Something very bad happened to her.

The key to this and many other cases highlighted in this book is the location of the body. Freida was found in a swampy area in high weeds, a description very similar to many other locations where bodies in this book have been found. You cannot convince me that people seek out swamps to walk into and die. It makes no sense! Freida knew this area as well as Kory Kelly new northern Minnesota (See Chapter "Minnesota") when he disappeared, Kelly was found in almost an identical area as Freida. If a predator wanted to take a person into an area where they wouldn't be seen and a person wouldn't walk up on them, a swamp with high reeds would be ideal.

Chapter Summary

A time span of twenty-four years represented all of the missing people in Vermont that met the criteria for this book. From 1926–1950 seven people disappeared in Vermont and not another single disappearance in the wild—seems very odd. Something highly unusual was happening in southwest Vermont during those years, and it then appears to have moved on to Pennsylvania. Yes, there was significant activity in Pennsylvania before 1950, but from 1950–1957 there were five disappearances. There was a similar pattern of disappearances in New Jersey and New England.

The disappearances of Paul Jepson, Jr. and Freida Langer sixteen days apart cannot be ignored. Jepson, an eight-year old male, and Langer, a fifty-three-year-old female, both disappear in very rural settings and neither was ever found. Common sense dictates much about how an investigation is conducted. These dates are too close together and in too geographically close proximity to each other to think they are not somehow related.

The million-dollar question is, what changed in this region after 1950?

New Jersey Missing People

All of the people missing from New Jersey are males. Two of the three people missing in New Jersey were exactly six years old at the time of their disappearance.

Name	Date Missing•Age
Barofsky	07/01/1892•6
George "Billy" Dansey	10/08/19•30 MOS
Richard Peterson	11/05/82•6

Barofsky, Unknown First Name
Missing 7/1/1892, Bridgeton, New Jersey
Age at Disappearance: 6 years

Newspaper articles in the late 1800s and early 1900s usually didn't print the first names of young children who were missing or who were victims of crime. It was a rare occasion to find a child's first name; in this case no first name was listed in any article I found. The articles did indicate that the family did lose their "boy."

The Barofsky boy disappeared in a rural area where he lived in Carmel, New Jersey, three miles east of Bridgeton and four miles northwest of Millville. The area of the disappearance is rich with swamps and water and is just west of Union Lake.

Teams of searchers scoured the swamps for four days for Barofsky. There were heavy thunderstorms during these days that made the searchers face treacherous conditions. There are few facts surrounding how the boy disappeared, other than it was from the area of his residence. On the fourth day of searching, nearly everyone had given up finding the boy except a beehive hunter, David Carmen.

Mr. Carmen was over a mile from the Barofsky residence in very thick swamps when he heard a faint cry. The *Weekly Herald* had an article about the discovery of the boy in its July 8, 1892 edition:

The child was found hanging over a bush. There was at least two feet of water surrounding it. The bushes within the child's reach had been gnawed and eaten, and the clothes were torn from the little one, while blood streamed from the wounds and gashes on its body and legs. The skin and flesh on its legs were torn off, its hands badly lacerated and shrunken.

Doctors examined Barofsky and felt he may not survive because of pneumonia. There were no follow-up articles about his condition.

Case Summary:

All readers need to now reread the statement made in the article. The boy was found "Hanging over a bush." I doubt he thrust himself onto the bush to hang there. I doubt he placed himself in the middle of the swamp. It almost appears to me as though the boy was being carried through the swamp thickets being ripped and scratched. As searchers got closer, the boy was placed safely on the top of a bush, and the suspect escaped.

George William "Billy" Dansey
Missing 10/08/19, Unknown Time, Hammonton, New Jersey
Age at Disappearance: 30 months

In July of 1919 Hercules Dansey and his family moved to Hammonton from Pittsburgh, Pennsylvania. The family settled into a rural residence adjacent to a Dahlia Field and swamps.

On October 8, 1919, thirty-month-old George William (Billy) Dansey asked his mother if he and Jack could go into the yard to play. Jack was Billy's three-year-old fox terrier. The two were inseparable. Mrs. Dansey said they could go outside.

After a short time, Mrs. Dansey went into the yard and couldn't find Billy or Jack. She walked toward the dahlia field and the surrounding swamps but couldn't find the pair. It was at this time that Mrs. Dansey called Hercules and the local police.

Over the next several hours, police requested all available resources. From the start of the search, police were frustrated with the lack of clues or tracks. It wasn't until late on the first day that Jack walked back into the yard. The family took the dog back toward the dahlia field and swamp and asked, "Where is Billy?" The dog looked down and refused to move.

The first night of the search the weather started to turn bad and stayed bad off and on for many days. Several times rain fell very hard in the search area.

One of the searchers working in a remote area found one of Billy's toys that was described as "smashed." They also found an abandoned home deep in the woods where someone had been sleeping.

In the early days of the search, police made several statements that they believed Billy had been kidnapped. They stated that the evidence didn't add up, and they felt the boy had been taken. Posters printed about the boy were distributed throughout the United States indicating there was a $1400 reward for his location and return.

Police actually arrested an owner of a nearby farm in regards to Billy's disappearance. The theory behind why and how the man killed Billy didn't make a lot of sense, and it appeared as though that the police wanted a quick ending to a case that disturbed the community. The man was later released after the parents publicly stated that they doubted the police theory.

Police followed leads across the continent, some very frustrating. There were people who stated they had the boy, but they didn't. There were some very cruel hoaxes pulled on the Dansey family.

Six weeks after Billy disappeared, a hunter was deep in the swamps and came across what appeared to be a body. The hunter notified police, and they determined that Billy Dansey had been found. He was located in an area surrounded by one- to two-foot deep swamps in a very rough and thick location. Police immediately stated that Billy had been abducted and dumped at the location, as they did not feel he could get there under his own power.

Portions of Billy's clothes were hung on bushes near the body but he was essentially naked except for a shirt he was wearing. The body did not suffer bone fractures but the flesh had been eaten off the bones. The bones were in a formation showing that they had not been disturbed significantly from the time of death. A November 23, 1919 article in the *New York Times* had the following: "There was no blood found and on that account there can be no bacteriological tests made of any of the clothing. It is a pity that the corpse was not found earlier."

So, clothes were found off the body, and there was no blood on the clothing, meaning, the clothes had been removed prior to the body being ravaged by animals. Later in the same article is this:

Detective Wilson this afternoon told me that he was certain that the boy never got into the woods where he was found by himself, because it would have been necessary for him to force his way through the quagmire and underbrush, and it would have exhausted his physical strength. The boy in the judgment of Wilson was carried to the place where he met his death. Wilson has not found a mark or button which would be of assistance in unraveling this mystery.

On November 29 there was a coroner's inquest into the death of Billy Dansey. The inquest rehashed the points made by Detective Wilson and added one additional important point. The inquest revealed that it was known by the family that Billy could not undress himself. Billy's clothes were found inside out. He couldn't do this. It was also revealed that ten days before Billy disappeared, his dog had received some type of head injury while playing by itself. The exact cause of the injury could not be determined, but they did not know if it was related to the disappearance.

Case Summary:

The only difference in the Dansey case and dozens of others cited in this book is that detectives understood that the factual circumstances surrounding the disappearance were odd and didn't make sense. Billy was found in the middle of a swamp, like many other children in this book. Billy's clothes were removed, like many other children in this book. Billy died, like many other children cited in this book. Billy's clothes were removed by someone other than Billy, something that has happened to other children in this book but probably wasn't addressed by the press, search and rescue personnel, or law enforcement.

This case was very public, and the facts surrounding it caused many to be concerned. Police needed to solve the Dansey case and settle the community's concern, but the case was never solved. Communication in the early 1900s was not nearly what it is today. If law enforcement officials had known the number of children who had disappeared under frighteningly similar circumstances to Billy Dansey, this case would still be under investigation.

I would like every reader to put a book marker on this case and go back through each book and find the number of disappearances similar to Billy's. You will be shocked at the number.

There is one friend of Billy's that probably knows the entire story about his disappearance, Jack the fox terrier. Jack lost his best friend and probably harbored a horrific story.

Richard Peterson
Missing 11/5/82, 3:30 p.m., Delmont, New Jersey
Age at Disappearance: 6 years

On Friday, November 5, 1982, Richard and Bryan Peterson were visiting their grandparents' home in a rural area of Delmont, New Jersey. Delmont sits two miles north of Delaware Bay near the sloughs and less than one mile from the Heislerville Fish and Wildlife Management Area and one mile from Belleplain State Forest. There are very few homes in the area, and it sits in a region with acres of standing water. The entire area around Delmont is very wild and filled with open space and wildlife.

Richard and Bryan were playing in the yard at their grandparents' when the grandmother realized that both boys had disappeared. She did a cursory search of the yard and the immediate area and couldn't find either boy. Searchers started to arrive at the house at 4:00 p.m. and by 5:30, Bryan had been found one-half mile from the house in a wild and remote region. Searchers started to accumulate and expand the search without finding Richard. Over three hundred searchers had joined the hunt for Richard by Saturday morning. The searchers included soldiers from Fort Dix and surrounding armed forces bases.

Searchers were getting very concerned for Richard's welfare, as it was a very cold stretch of weather in New Jersey. On Sunday, a hunter, Frank Madden, decided he was going into the woods to check his hunting blinds. At 8:00 a.m., he thought he heard a slight moaning sound. Frank stopped and listened and heard nothing. He started walking again and then heard a sound similar to crying. Frank followed the sounds to an area near an abandoned sawmill and found Richard lying naked on the ground. A November 8, 1982 article in the *Philadelphia Daily News* had the following statement from Frank Madden:

He couldn't raise his head. I guess that's why he couldn't holler loud, Madden said. The boy was glassy eyed and weak and his pants and shoes were missing, Madden said. I tried to talk to him but he was, just staring way off. The only thing I could understand was, in the woods all night, or something like that.

Madden checked and found the boy did not have broken bones and then wrapped him in a blanket and carried him to the nearest home. The boy was transported to the hospital and placed in a warm bath to raise his body temperature.

Richard had scratches over his entire body, and his clothing was not found.

Case Summary:
Readers need to remember that this occurred in November in New Jersey, a very cold region at that time of year. The idea that Richard stripped himself of the clothing does not make sense. Richard was found in a daze, as many children are found in this same situation. It's an interesting scenario that both boys went missing simultaneously and that the articles do not state the condition of Bryan when found.

Chapter Summary
New Jersey was excluded from the New England section, but it could have been included. The only people missing in this section are three boys, all under age six.

LISTS

I am including two specific lists I used in evaluating the missing-person phenomena:

Children Under Ten Years
Master Missing Person List

I encourage all amateur sleuths to study the names, dates, and locations to see if you can identify trends.

Missing Children Under 10 Years

F-Katie Flynn	MI-----3--------06/1868-Unk
M-Eddie Prigley	IN-----3--------08/22/1874-Unk
M-Stephen Ford	PA-----9--------08/05/1880-Unk
M-Bachman	PA-----4M------06/10/1883-PM
M-James Vaughan	ID-----18M-----08/20/1883-10:00 a.m.
F-Davis	PA-----30M-----05/09/1888-Unk
M-Barofsky	NJ----- 6--------07/01/1892-Unk
F-Mary Sholtas	PA-----3--------04/21/1897-Unk
M-Augustus Staneker	PA----- 4--------04/21/1897-Unk
F-Simpson	PA-----3--------05/27/1901-Unk
M-Horace Marvin Jr.	DE---- 4---------05/04/1907-Unk
M-Roy Bilgrien	WI-----2---------10/21/1910-Unk
M-James Glass	PA-----4--------05/12/15-Unk
M-Edward Gately	MA----2---------10/27/17-10:30 a.m.
M-Abe Carroll Ramsay	GSM--3---------03/11/1919-3:15 p.m.
M-George Dansey	NJ-----30M-----10/08/1919-Unk
M-Eddie Hamilton	SASK-2---------07/06/28-Unk
F-Geraldine Markline	PA-----2---------10/26/29-Unk
M-Kenneth Swanson	CT-----2--------08/24/30-Noon
F-Cecilia Mitchell	CA-----3--------05/02/32-12:30 p.m.
M-Wesley Piatote	WA----7---------08/04/32-PM
M-Frank Lobears	ID-----7---------06/25/33-Unk
M-Alden Johnson	MA--- 4--------03/27/34-3:30 p.m.
F-Betty Wolfrum	MAN- 4--------05/15/34-Unk
M-Bobby Connor	NY----21M--07/13/34-6:00 p.m.
F-Claire Bensen	CT----21M---07/24/34-PM

F-Rita Lent	PA----3------11/22/34-Noon
F-Thelma Ann Wilke	WI----21M--05/03/35-PM
M-Jack Pike	MAN-5------09/05/35-Unk
M-Harold King	WI----3------09/07/36-Unk
M-Charles Warren	AR----2------12/20/36-PM
F-Alice Baker	VT----20M--08/16/37-PM
F-Florence Jackson	AR----4------09/06/37-PM
F-Marjorie West	PA----4------05/08/38-Unk
M-David Baumgarten	CA----2------05/11/38-Noon
M-Albert Beilhartz	CO----4------07/02/38-8:30 a.m.
M-Donald Farrington	NY----3------09/11/38-8:00 a.m.
M-Jerry Hays	AZ----5------11/10/38-Unk
M-Teddy Thompson	NCA--4------01/29/39-PM
F-Helen Chenoweth	IL-----3------03/28/40-6:00 p.m.
M-Simon Skogan	MAN-9------07/02/40-Unk
M-Ronald Rumbaugh	PA----2------09/15/40-2:00 p.m.
M-Rudy Kunchick	PA----4------10/21/40-Unk
M-Murray Upshaw, Jr.	GA----2------11/08/40-Noon
M-Eldridge Albright	PA----3------05/21/41-2:00 p.m.
F-Betty Bossier	PA-----3------06/25/41-10:30 a.m.
M-Joseph Prato	PA----19M---10/25/41-Unk
M-Ronald McGee	AZ----2------02/07/42-AM
M-Alvan Diggan	PA----3------05/30/42-Unk
M-Lloyd Hokit	OK----9------10/21/45-3:00 p.m.
M-Mike McDonald	AZ----2------10/30/45-AM
M-Dickie Suden	CA----3------11/01/45-9:00 a.m.
F-Katherine Van Alst	AR----8------06/16/46-2:30 p.m.
M-Eugene Shue	PA-----3------10/20/46-2:00 p.m.
M-Jimmy Senser	PA----4------04/06/47-5:00 p.m.
F-Greta Mary Gale	NCA--30M--06/29/47-10:00 a.m.
M-Wayne Bowers	CA----3------07/05/47-Unk
F-Carolyn Peterson	OH----20M--08/20/47-11:00 a.m.
M-Louis Dunton	NH----3------10/07/47-6:00 p.m.
M-Donald Collier	PA----23M--07/02/48-4:00 p.m.
M-Jerry Lee Hoffman	OH----3------08/05/48-6:00 p.m.
F-Janet Federer	WY----6-------09/29/48-1:00 p.m.
M-Rickey Tankersley	AL-----2-------02/16/49-4:30 p.m.

M-Billy Abbott	PA-----3-------02/18/49-4:30 p.m.	
M-Billy Clever	PA------3-------04/26/49-PM	
M-Daryl Webley	WA-----2-------04/30/49-4:00 p.m.	
M-Michael Fontaine	ME-----6-------05/30/49-Unk	
M-Larry Coleman	MN-----3-------08/20/49-Unk	
M-Otis T. Mason	MD----6-------10/11/49- 5:00 p.m.	
F-Anna Thorpe	PA------2-------05/05/50-Unk	
M-Jackie Copeland	PA------2-------05/14/50-1:00 p.m.	
F-Nicole Renaud	ME-----3-------06/03/50- 3:00 p.m.	
F-Susan Sweely	IL-------2-------08/09/50-7:00 p.m.	
F-Lorraine Smith	ALB---2-------09/02/50-5:00 p.m.	
M-Paul Jepson	VT-----8-------10/12/50-3:30 p.m.	
M-Larry McGee	NM-----7-------06/07/51-3:00 p.m.	
F-Janet McGee	NM-----5-------06/07/51-3:00 p.m.	
M-Steven Cross	NM-----3-------06/07/51-3:00 p.m.	
M-Raymond Hall	BC-----6-------06/09/51-Unk	
M-Keith Parkins	WA-----2-------04/10/52-Noon	
M-Joey Barkley	CA------2-------03/11/53-1:00 p.m.	
F-Patty Ann Mclean	MT-----3-------07/04/53-2:30 p.m.	
F-Geraldine Huggan	ONT----5-------07/05/53-10:00 a.m.	
F-Emma Bowers	PA------5-------07/22/53- Unk	
F-Shirley Sherman	WV-----3-------04/18/54-1:00 p.m.	
M-Gary Bailey	ME-----3-------07/17/54-Unk	
M-Jess Davis	OR-----2-------05/08/55-AM	
M-Fred Holmes	PA------23M---05/25/55-9:00 a.m.	
F-Ida May Curtis	MT-----2-------07/04/55-6:00 p.m.	
F-Nora Moore	AL-----7-------07/18/55-4:00 p.m.	
M-Ronnie Weitkamp	IN------3-------10/11/55-Noon	
F-Diane Abbott	ME-----2-------07/06/56-2:00 p.m.	
M-Tommy Bowman	SCA----8-------03/23/57-7:00 p.m.	
M-David Allen Scott	YOSE--2-------07/13/57-1:00 p.m.	
M-Richard Craig	WA-----5-------08/15/57-10:00 a.m.	
F-Candida Streeter	PA------2-------10/03/57-5:30 p.m.	
F-Minnie Haun	GSM---3-------10/08/57-1:00 p.m.	
F-Jill Hatch	CA------7-------11/02/57- 11:00 a.m.	
F-Shirley Ann Ramsburg	WV-----3-------12/27/57-5:00 p.m.	
M-John McKinney	WV-----5-------03/17/58-3:00 p.m.	

F-Brenda Jean Doud	NY-----5--------07/06/58-Unk
F-Mary Gay Bent	MT-----5--------07/13/58-3:00 p.m.
F-Debbie Ann Greenhill	KY------2--------08/09/58-8:00 p.m.
M-Kenneth Scott	MI------4--------09/28/58-2:00 p.m.
M-Willard E. Jones, Jr.	MO-----3--------01/17/59- Unk
F-Carol Van Hulla	MI------3--------06/28/59-6:00 p.m.
M-Richard Herman	WA-----6--------08/30/59-Noon
M-Randy Moy	OH------3--------01/08/60-3:30 p.m.
M-Martin Ryan	OR------8--------06/30/60/PM
M-Bruce Kremen	SCA----8--------07/13/60-Unk
F-Lisa Schackelford	IL-------3--------07/10/62-11:00 a.m.
M-Claude Goodwin	WA-----8--------06/16/63-Unk
M-Bobby Panknin	WA-----4--------08/03/63-Unk
M-Donald R. Griffen	YOSE--4--------08/22/63-8:30 a.m.
M-Dennis Lloyd Martin	GSM---7--------06/14/64-4:30 p.m.
M-Richard Spyglass	SASK--5--------08/05/64-7:00 p.m.
F-Bonnie Lee Edwards	NC-----9--------01/09/65-4:30 p.m.
F-Christine Woollett	WA-----2--------05/12/66-8:00 p.m.
M-Dennis Johnson	WY-----8--------07/12/66-1:30 p.m.
F-Diane Prevost	ONT----2--------09/17/66-Unk
M-Kenneth Coon	BC------2--------04/28/67-Unk
M-Danny Greenwood	AZ------5--------06/08/67-1:00 p.m.
M-Douglas C. Chapman	ME-----3--------06/02/71-10:30 a.m.
M-Douglass Legg	NY-----8--------07/10/71-Unk
M-Jimmy Duffy	WA-----2--------10/19/73-Unk
F-Jennifer Klein	UT------3--------05/25/74-Unk
M-Jeffrey Bratcher	WA-----7--------06/15/74-6:30 p.m.
M-Yehudi Prior	BC------2--------09/23/74-Unk
M-Kurt R. Newton	ME-----4--------09/01/75-Unk
F-Megan Ginevicz	MT-----2--------04/30/80-Unk
M-Larry D. Krebbs	OK------2--------06/30/80-5:30 p.m.
M-Richard Ray Barnett	WA-----2--------08/31/82-7:00 a.m.
M-Kevin Jay Ayotte	MN-----3--------09/30/82-PM
M-Richard Peterson	NJ------6--------11/05/82-3:30 p.m.
M-Tyler Inman	WA-----3--------12/21/82-Unk
F-Nyleen Kay Marshall	MT-----4--------06/25/83-4:00 p.m.
M-Michael E. Reel	GSM---8--------07/02/83-9:30 a.m.

M-Andrew Warburton	ME	9	07/01/86-Unk
F-Lynn Marie Hillier	BC	2	07/24/86-Unk
F-Colleen Tourtillott	WI	18M	07/03/88-6:00 p.m.
M-Nathan Madsen	OR	9	10/22/89-2:30 p.m.
M-Travis Zweig	CA	2	03/10/93-10:30 a.m.
M-Victor Shoemaker	WV	4	05/01/94-Noon
F-Ashley Krestianson	SASK	8	07/14/94-Unk
M-Bryce Herda	WA	4	04/09/95-Unk
M-Ruben David Felix	ID	2	02/23/97-Unk
M-Derrick Engebretson	OR	8	12/5/98-3:00 p.m.
M-Frank Downey	KY	4	08/16/99-8:30 p.m.
M-Jaryd Atadero	CO	3	10/02/99 Unk
F-Leeanna Warner	MN	5	06/14/03-4:30 p.m.
M-David Gonzales	CA	9	07/31/04-8:00 a.m.
M-David Tippen	GA	4	08/01/04-AM
M-Evan Thompson	CO	8	05/27/06-AM
M-Samuel Boehlke	OR	8	10/04/06-4:00 p.m.
F-Hannah Klamecki	IL	5	06/13/07-Unk
M-William Pilkenton	BC	7	02/15/08-10:00 a.m.
M-Wyatt Little Light	MT	2	12/23/08-Unk
M-Avery B. Blakeley	ID	2	03/26/09- 1:30 p.m.
M-Joshua Childers	MO	3	05/04/09-11:45 a.m.
F-Madyson Jamison	OK	5	10/08/09- 2:00 p.m.

Children Missing by Month

Jan–4
Feb–5
Mar–8
Apr–10
May–21
Jun–22
July–28
Aug–19
Sep–12
Oct–20
Nov–6
Dec–5
Total–160

By Hour of Day

7:00 a.m.–1
8:00 a.m.–2
9:00 a.m.–4
10:00 a.m.–6
11:00 a.m.–7
Noon–9
1:00 p.m.–8
2:00 p.m.–8
3:00 p.m.–12
4:00 p.m.–9
5:00 p.m.–9
6:00 p.m.–9
7:00 p.m.–4

8:00 p.m.–2
9:00 p.m.–1
Unk Time–53
PM hours–11
AM hours–5
**30 minutes after the hour posted on next hour.

Missing Children Under Ten Categorized by Age and Gender

Males Age/#	Females Age/#	
1–1	1–0	
2–30	2–17	
3–25	3–17	
4–18	4–3	
5–6	5–8	
6–6	6–1	
7–6	7–2	
8–11	8–2	
9–6	9–1	
109–Males	51–Females	160–Total

There is a significant bubble of missing males between the ages of two to four (73) with the closest female group being two to three years (34). It does seem odd that there is a significant increase in males missing at age eight, while the female numbers stay consistent from six to nine years old.

Odd Coincidences

West Virginia	Date Missing
Shirley Ann Ramsburg (3 years–Female)	12/27/57–5:00 p.m.
John Wayne McKinney (5 years–Male)	03/17/58–3:00 p.m.

How coincidental is it that—in one three-month time span, a boy and girl go missing in West Virginia in a two-hour time window?

F–Mary Sholtas	04/21/1897–Unk–3 years old
M–Augustus Staneker	04/21/1897–Unk–4 years old
F–Davis	05/09/1888–Unk–30 mos old
F–Simpson	05/27/1901–Unk–3 years old

The four cases above come directly from the missing list. It seems strange that four cases in the late 1800s to early 1900s all come from Pennsylvania.

M–NY–Bobby Connor	07/13/34–6:00 p.m.–21 mos old
F–CT–Claire Bensen	07/24/34–PM–21 mos old
F–PA–Rita Lent	11/22/34–Noon–3 years old
F–WI–Thelma Ann Wilke	05/03/35–PM–21 mos old

Each of the cases above occurred in the northern portion of the United States. All three cases involving females occurred within a span of less than ten months—as did the three cases involving victims who were exactly twenty-one months old. Very strange.

M–Rickey Tankersley   02/16/49–4:30 p.m.–2 years old (Alabama)
M–Billy Abbott   02/18/49–4:30 p.m.–3 years old (Pennsylvania)
M–Billy Clever   04/26/49–PM–3 years old (Pennsylvania)

The first two cases above went missing at exactly 4:30 p.m. two days apart. I would agree that Alabama is quite a distance from Pennsylvania, but the dates and times listed are too close to ignore. I think it's also quite coincidental that Abbott and Clever have the same first name.

Pennsylvania

M–Eldridge Albright   05/21/41–2:00 p.m.–3 years old
F–Betty Bossier   06/25/41–10:30 a.m.–3 years old
M–Joseph Prato   10/25/41–Unk–19 mos old

Again, another group of missing from Pennsylvania. All were within five months apart, and all were three years old or younger.

Pennsylvania

M–Stephen Ford   8/5/1880–Unk–9 years old

Ford disappeared five miles from Thorp and Bowers and twenty miles west of Collier and at essentially in the same location as Rumbaugh. What would be the statistical odds of this occurring if there wasn't the same perpetrator involved?

M–Ronald Rumbaugh   09/15/40–2:00 p.m.–2 years old
M–Donald Collier   07/02/48–4:00 p.m.–23 mos

Donald disappeared fifteen miles east of Bowers and twenty-five miles east of Thorp.

F–Anna Thorpe   05/05/50–Unk–2 years old
M–Jackie Copeland   05/14/50–1:00 p.m.–2 years old

One hundred and ten miles north of where Anna Thorpe disappeared, Jackie Copeland disappeared nine days later.

F–Emma Bowers   07/22/53– Unk–5 years old

Ten miles directly east of where Thorp disappeared, Bowers disappeared. This is one concise cluster in time and geography.

Twelve children ages twenty-three months to six years went missing in Pennsylvania from 1940 to 1949. No other state or province comes close to these numbers.

Twenty-nine children ten years old or younger went missing in Pennsylvania from 1880 to 1957. This is also the state that has the first child ever reported missing who fits the criteria in this book.

There are five groups of missing children who disappeared from Pennsylvania who are placed on the list in back-to-back scenarios all within a ten-year span, 1940–1950.

M–Ronald Rumbaugh–9/15/40
M– Rudy Kunchick–10/21/40
M–Eldridge Albright–05/21/41
F–Betty Bossier–06/25/41
M– Joseph Prato–10/25/41
M–Eugene Shue–10/20/46
M–Jimmy Sensor–04/06/47
M– Billy Abbott–02/18/49
M–Billy Clever–04/26/49
F–Anna Thorpe–05/05/50
M–Jackie Copeland–05/14/50

Washington–All Males

Claude Goodwin	06/16/63–Unk–8 years old
Bobby Panknin	08/03/63–Unk–4 years old
Jimmy Duffy	10/19/73–2:15 p.m.–2 years old
Jeffrey Bratcher	06/15/74–6:30 p.m.–7 years old

These are four cases of missing boys from Washington. Goodwin and Panknin cases occurred less than two months apart. The bottom two cases happened less than eight months apart.

Wesley Piatote and Bobby Panknin disappeared a mere 75 miles from each other, not much when you understand the amount of open space there is in Washington. I understand that there was thirty five years between incidents but Panknin disappeared in the Colville National Forest, a region that has had a long history of strange events.

Jimmy Duffy and Claude Goodwin disappeared just ten miles from each other, there was ten years between incidents. Goodwin went missing four miles from a location called *"The Devils Backbone"* and in a very rugged area of the Wenatchee National Forest. There is approximately one hundred and forty miles between each set of disappearances. In October of 1973 a deer hunter was walking through deep woods and found a human skull. Forensic testing on the skull confirmed it was Claude Goodwin, there are few other details available. Are these incidents a mere coincidence of time and space? Disappearances in Washington fitting the criteria of each book have not happened in this manner since.

Four groups of missing males and females on this list have disappeared in back-to-back scenarios. Although it may not appear that they are related based on the proximity of the disappearances, I do think it's quite odd that they are listed in this manner.

Bobby Connor–NY	07/13/34–6:00 p.m.
Claire Benson–CT	07/24/34–PM

Eldridge Albright–PA   05/21/41–2:00 p.m.
Betty Bossier–PA   06/25/41–10:30 a.m.

Anna Thorpe–PA   05/05/50–Unk
Jackie Copeland–PA   05/14/50–1:00 p.m.

Shirley Ramsburg–WV   12/27/57–5:00 p.m.
John McKinney–WV   03/17/58–3:00 p.m.

Date Anomalies–Males

Mike McDonald, Missing 10/30/45, a.m., Arizona, 2 years old
Dickie Suden, Missing 11/01/45, 9 a.m., Northern California, 3 years old

McDonald was missing while playing in the yard of his rural home in Arizona with his dog. Suden was missing from his rural home while playing in the yard with his dog.

McDonald is a male, age 2. Suden is a male, age 3.

The boys disappeared just one day apart from each other.

McDonald was found fifteen miles from his home, sleeping in a hole.
Suden was never found.

The FBI investigated the Suden case.

Arizona

There do seem to be patterns within several locations cited in the book. For example, the chart of missing at the beginning of the Arizona chapter shows that people disappear in two-to-three-year increments:

M-Jerry Hays-   11/10/38-Unk-5 years old
M-Ronald McGee   02/07/42- AM-2 years old

M-Mike McDonald   10/30/45-AM-2 years old
(22-year gap)
M-Danny Greenwood   06/08/67-1:00 p.m.-5 years old
M-Randy Parscale   01/13/69-Unk-10 years old

After 1969, the age dynamics of who went missing in Arizona drastically changes, but the two- to three-year cycle has continued. There hasn't been anyone under the age of thirty-two who has disappeared in Arizona since 1969.

M-William Sisco   06/12/94-PM-32 years old
M-Donald Shelenberger   07/03/94-Unk-35 years old
M-Abraham Kalaf   07/24/96-Unk -79 years old
F-Joan Shelton   02/07/04-Unk-65 years old
M-Jonathan Betts   10/20/06-4:00 p.m.-32 years old
M-Dwight Riggs   01/21/09-Unk-61 years old

Michigan

In Arizona, the age of the missing changed drastically after 1969. In Michigan, it changed after June 28, 1959. There also has not been another female reported missing since the identified date.

F-Katie Flynn   June 1868-3 years old
M-Raymond Maki   11/27/36-Unk-17 years old
M-Edward Woelfle   10/06/46-AM-15 years old
M-Kenneth Scott   09/28/58-2:00 p.m.- 4 years old
F-Carol Van Hulla   06/28/59-6:00 p.m.- 3 years old
F-Ida Porter   08/07/59-Unk-70 years old
(45-year gap)
M-Christopher Hallaxs   03/17/04-Unk-30 years old
M-Joe Clewley   07/13/08-Unk-73 years old
M-Derrick Hennegan   08/04/08-4:30 p.m.-35 years old

Gaps in Time With No Disappearances:

N. Sierras (CA)	11/01/45–08/04/71--26 years
Mt. Shasta (CA)	06/29/47–02/15/97--50 years
Colorado	10/09/49–06/29/82--33 years
West Virginia	03/17/58–05/01/94--36 years
Oklahoma/Arkansas	01/17/59–06/30-80- -21 years
New Mexico	02/16/60–09/13/82--22 years
S. California	07/13/60–03/10/93--33 years
Montana	11/14/60–04/30/80--19 years
Wyoming	07/12/66–04/17/89--22 years

The commonality of the above-listed states is that there were no disappearances meeting the criteria of the book from 7/1966–4/1989. Why?

There are a number of disappearances on this list in which four to five males go missing and then a female goes missing. Then three males go missing, and then a female goes missing. There are times on this list when there almost seems to be a consistent four to one or three to one ratio of boys to girls, evenly spaced by the sex of the person that goes missing.

If you study the list carefully, you will see that there almost seems to be a rotation to the location where children go missing. One to two children disappear on either coast, and then the pattern reverts back to the opposite coast.

I believe that it is very odd that the vast majority of the children on this list are Caucasian, with a handful of Native Americans, Hispanics, and Asians. It is also very rare that people on the master missing persons list have the same last name.

F-Katie Flynn	MI----3----------06/1868-Unk
M-Eddie Prigley	IN-----3----------08/22/1874
M-Stephen Ford	PA----9----------08/05/1880-Unk
M-Wolfe	PA----10---------07/08/1882-Unk
M-Bachman	PA----4M-------06/10/1883-PM
M-James Vaughan	ID-----18M-------08/20/1883-10:00 a.m.

F-Davis	PA----30M------05/09/1888-Unk
M-Barofsky	NJ----6---------07/01/1892-Unk
M-Alexis Bork	MT---Unk-------11/07/1896-PM
M-Frank Floyd	IA----Unk-------11/07/1897-Unk
F-Mary Sholtas	PA----3----------04/21/1897-Unk
M-Augustus Staneker	PA----4---------04/21/1897-Unk
F-Simpson	PA----3----------05/27/1901-Unk
M-Jack Wells	MT---Unk------11/05/1901-Unk
M-Riley Amsbaugh	OH----55--------07/25/1902-Unk
M-E. C. Jones	OH---Unk-------11/12/1903-Unk
M-Horace Marvin, Jr.	DE----4---------05/04/1907-Unk
M-J. Mitchell	ID----Unk-------01/11/1909-Unk
M-Johnnie Lembke	OH----15---------08/12/1910-Unk
M-Roy Bligrien	WI----2----------10/21/1910-Unk
M-B. B. Bakowski	OR----30--------02/22/1911-Unk
F-Elsie M. Davis	ME---24--------07/30/1911-Noon
M-James Glass	PA----4----------05/12/15-Unk
M-Edward Gately	MA---2----------10/27/17-10:30 a.m.
M-Edward Gerke	WI----Unk------06/11/18-Unk
M-Abe Carroll Ramsay	GSM--3------------03/11/1919-3:15 p.m.
M-George Dansey	NJ----30M------10/08/19-Unk
M-David Brown	ME---51---------11/18/22-Unk
M-Mertley Johnson	ME---24--------11/18/22-Unk
F-Bernice Price	CA----Unk-------03/22/23-Unk
M-Joseph Whitehead	MT----29--------08/24/24- Unk
M-William Whitehead	MT----32--------08/24/24-Unk
M-Alfred J. Bishop	VT----Unk-------11/03/26-Unk
M-Eddie Hamilton	SASK-2----------07/06/28-Unk
F-Geraldine Markline	PA-----2----------10/26/29-Unk
M-Kenneth Swanson	CT------2-------08/24/30-Noon
M-Emmet Mitchell	ID-------50------07/10/31-Unk
M-William Pitsenbarger	ID------61------08/07/31-Unk
F-Else Flothmeier	PA-------22------02/24/32-PM
F-Cecilia Mitchell	CA-------3-------05/02/32-12:30 p.m.
M-Wesley Piatote	WA-----7-------08/04/32-PM
M-Clarence Clark	NY-----62------10/17/32-Unk
M-Godfrey Wondrosek	YOSE--26------04/26/33-Unk

New Jersey Missing People | 297

M-Frank Lobears	WA-----7--------06/25/33-Unk
M-Joseph Halpern	CO------22------08/15/33-Unk
M-Alden Johnson	MA-----4-------03/27/34-3:30 p.m.
F-Betty Wolfrum	MAN---4-------05/15/34-Unk
M-Bobby Connor	NY------21M---07/13/34-6:00 p.m.
F-Claire Bensen	CT------21M---07/24/34-PM
M-Dr. Frederick Lumley	MT------Unk----08/13/34-Unk
F-Rita Lent	PA-------3-------11/22/34-Noon
M-Herbert Brown	OR------Unk----1935/Unk
F-Thelma Ann Wilke	WI------21M---05/03/35-PM
M-George Wanke	MAN---58------07/27/35-Unk
M-Jack Pike	MAN---5-------09/05/35-Unk
M-Raymond Maki	MI------17------01/27/36•Unk
M-Mr. Bell	MAN---62------08/31/36-Unk
M-Harold King	WI------3-------09/07/36-Unk
M-Charles Warren	AR------2-------12/20/36-PM
F-Alice Baker	VT------20M---08/16/37-PM
F-Florence Jackson	AR------4-------09/06/37-PM
F-Marjorie West	PA------4-------05/08/38-Unk
M-David Baumgarten	CA------2-------05/11/38-Noon
M-Richard McPherson	YOSE--10------05/26/38-Unk
M-Albert Beilhartz	CO------4-------07/02/38-8:30 a.m.
M-Donald Farrington	NY------3-------09/11/38-8:00 a.m.
M-Jerry Hays	AZ------5-------11/10/38-Unk
M-Teddy Thompson	NCA----4-------01/29/39-PM
F-Emma Steffy	PA------75------07/18/39-Unk
M-Billy Coleman	CA------14------01/01/40-4:00 p.m.
F-Helen Chenoweth	IL-------3-------03/28/40-6:00 p.m.
M-Simon Skogan	MAN---9-------07/02/40-Unk
M-Ronald Rumbaugh	PA------2------09/15/40-2:00 p.m.
M-Rudy Kunchick	PA------4------10/21/40-Unk
M-Murray Upshaw, Jr.	GA-----2------11/08/40-Noon
M-Eldridge Albright	PA------3------05/21/41-2:00 p.m.
F-Betty McCullough	OR-----10-----06/21/41-AM
F-Betty Bossier	PA------3------06/25/41-10:30 a.m.
M-Joseph Prato	PA------19M---10/25/41-Unk
M-Ronald McGee	AZ-----2------02/07/42-AM

M-Dewey Cook	WY-----25----03/02/42-Unk
M-Alvan Diggan	PA------3------05/30/42-Unk
M-Emerson Holt	YOSE--55-----07/18/43-2:00 p.m.
M-Ernest Polley	CO-----22-----07/23/43-Unk
F-Mrs. August Nelson	WI-----75-----07/28/43-Unk
M-Carl Herrick	VT------37-----11/26/43-Unk
M-C. H. Bordwell	MN----Unk---08/01/44-Unk
M-Lloyd Hokit	OK-----9------10/21/45-3:00 p.m.
M-Mike McDonald	AZ-----2------10/30/45-AM
M-Dickie Suden	CA-----3------11/01/45-9:00 a.m.
M-Al Owens	MT-----71-----11/07/45-Unk
M-Middie Rivers	VT------75-----11/12/45-3:00 p.m.
F-Katherine Van Alst	AR-----8------06/16/46-2:30 p.m.
M-Edward Woelfle	MI------15-----10/06/46-AM
M-Eugene Shue	PA------3------10/20/46-2:00 p.m.
F-Paula Welden	VT-----18-----12/01/46-4:00 p.m.
M-Jimmy Senser	PA------4------04/06/47-5:00 p.m.
F-Greta Mary Gale	NCA----30M--06/29/47-10:00 a.m.
M-Wayne Bowers	CA------3------07/05/47-Unk
F-Carolyn Peterson	OH-----20M--08/20/47-11:00 a.m.
M-Louis Dunton	NH-----3------10/07/47-6:00 p.m.
M-Donald Collier	PA------23M--07/02/48-4:00 p.m.
M-Jerry Lee Hoffman	OH-----3------08/05/48-6:00 p.m.
F-Janet Federer	WY-----6------09/29/48-1:00 p.m.
M-Rickey Tankersley	AL------2------02/16/49- 4:30 p.m.
M-Billy Abbott	PA------3------02/18/49-4:30 p.m.
M-Billy Clever	PA------3------04/26/49-PM
M-Daryl Webley	WA-----2------04/30/49-4:00 p.m.
M-Michael Fontaine	ME-----6------05/30/49-Unk
M-Larry Coleman	MN----3-------08/20/49-Unk
M-Frank Norris	WY-----46-----09/21/49-Unk
M-David Devitt	CO-----21------10/09/49-Unk
M-Bruce Gerling	CO-----20------10/09/49-Unk
M-Otis T. Mason	MD----6-------10/11/49- 5:00 p.m.
M-Donald McDonald	WA-----17------12/15/49-Unk
M-John Koza	MT-----50-60--04/26/50-Unk
F-Anna Thorpe	PA------2-------05/05/50-Unk

New Jersey Missing People | 299

M-Jackie Copeland	PA------2-------05/14/50-1:00 p.m.
F-Nicole Renaud	ME-----3--------06/03/50- 3:00 p.m.
F-Susan Sweely	IL------2-------08/09/50-7:00 p.m.
F-Lorraine Smith	ALB---2-------09/02/50-5:00 p.m.
M-Paul Jepson	VT-----8-------10/12/50-3:30 p.m.
F-Freida Langer	VT-----53------10/28/50-4:00 p.m.
M-Leroy Williams	IA------64------03/16/51-Unk
M-Larry McGee	NM----7-------06/07/51-3:00 p.m.
F-Janet McGee	NM-----5-------06/07/51-3:00 p.m.
M-Steven Cross	NM-----3-------06/07/51-3:00 p.m.
F-Evangeline Lorimer	GSM---21------06/08/51-Unk
F-Alma Hall	BC------28------06/09/51-Unk
M-Raymond Hall	BC------6-------06/09/51-Unk
M-Bobby Boatman	WA-----14------10/14/51-Unk
M-Keith Parkins	WA-----2-------04/10/52-Noon
M-David Feif	MA----85------07/06/52-Unk
M-Ralph Stutzman	IN------46------08/17/52-Unk
F-Catherine P. Maynard	WA-----38------01/19/53-Unk
M-Joey Barkley	CA-----2-------03/11/53-1:00 p.m.
F-Patty Ann Mclean	MT-----3-------07/04/53-2:30 p.m.
F-Geraldine Huggan	ONT----5-------07/05/53-10:00 a.m.
F-Emma Bowers	PA------5--------07/22/53-Unk
M-John Sweet	IL------Unk----10/26/53-Unk
F-Shirley Sherman	WV-----3-------04/18/54-1:00 p.m.
M-Gary Bailey	ME-----3-------07/17/54-Unk
M-Walter A. Gordon	YOSE--26------07/20/54-Unk
M- Orvar Von Laass	YOSE--30------10/09/54-Unk
M-Jess Davis	OR-----2-------05/08/55-AM
M-Fred Holmes	PA------23M----05/25/55-9:00 a.m.
F-Ida May Curtis	MT-----2------07/04/55-6:00 p.m.
F-Nora Moore	AL-----7------07/18/55-4:00 p.m.
M-Ronnie Weitkamp	IN------3------10/11/55-Noon
F-Diane Abbott	ME-----2-------07/06/56-2:00 p.m.
M-Louis Blair	ALB----26----08/05/56-Unk
M-Jerry Garcia	AZ-----Unk---08/12/56-Unk
M-John Davis	WA-----72-----08/26/56- Unk
F-Judy Rodencal	WI-----16-----10/30/56-7:30am

M-Tommy Bowman	SCA----8------03/23/57-7:00 p.m.
M-David Allen Scott	YOSE--2------07/13/57-1:00 p.m.
F-Rose Jewett	ID------95-----08/11/57-4:15 p.m.
M-Richard Craig	WA-----5------08/15/57-10:00 a.m.
F-Candida Streeter	PA------2------10/03/57-5:30 p.m.
F-Minnie Haun	GSM---3------10/08/57-1:00 p.m.
F-Jill Hatch	CA-----7------11/02/57- 11:00 a.m.
M-Earl Somerville	MN----48-----11/03/57-Unk
F-Shirley Ann Ramsburg	WV----3-------12/27/57-5:00 p.m.
M-John Wayne McKinney	WV-----5-------03/17/58-3:00 p.m.
F-Brenda Jean Doud	NY-----5------07/06/58-Unk
F-Mary Gay Bent	MT-----5------07/13/58-3:00 p.m.
F-Debbie Ann Greenhill	KY-----2------08/09/58-8:00 p.m.
M-Lawrence E. Prange	MT-----20-----08/14/58-Unk
M-Kenneth Scott	MI------4------09/28/58-2:00 p.m.
M-Willard Eugene Jones, Jr.	MO-----3------01/17/59- Unk
F-Carol Van Hulla	MI------3------06/28/59-6:00 p.m.
M-William Carmack	MT-----55-----07/22/59-Unk
M-Richard Herman	WA-----6------08/30/59-Noon
M-Meryl Newcombe	ONT----50-----10/29/59-Unk
M-George Weeden	ONT----63-----10/29/59-Unk
M-Arthur Jordan	MT-----59-----11/08/59-Unk
M-Randy Moy	OH-----3------01/08/60-3:30 p.m.
F-Fran Weaver	WY-----56-----02/01/60-Unk
M-Albert Cucupa	NM-----32-----02/16/60-Unk
M-Fernand Martin	ONT----36-----04/24/60-Unk
M-Martin Ryan	OR-----8------06/30/60/PM
M-Bruce Kremen	SCA----8------07/13/60-Unk
M-Sander Lingman	ONT----35-----11/01/60-Unk
M-Fritz Frey	MT-----65---11/14/60-Unk
F-Vanita Crook	WY-----25---05/03/61-Unk
M-James McCormick	OR------16---12/05/61-Unk
F-Lisa Schackelford	IL-------3-----07/10/62-11:00 a.m.
M-John Long	MN-----58---04/10/63-AM
M-Claude Goodwin	WA-----8----06/16/63-Unk
M-Lynn Olson	WY-----16---06/28/63-Unk
M-Bobby Panknin	WA-----4----08/03/63-Unk

M-Donald R. Griffen	YOSE--4----08/22/63-8:30 a.m.
M-Dennis Lloyd Martin	GSM---6----06/14/64-4:30 p.m.
M-Richard Spyglass	SASK---5----08/05/64-7:00 p.m.
F-Bonnie Lee Edwards	GSM---6----01/09/65-4:30 p.m.
M-Tom Garafalo	WY-----28---11/25/65-Unk
M-Frank Mean	WY-----55---04/21/66-Unk
F-Christine Woollett	WA-----2----05/12/66-8:00 p.m.
M-Dennis Johnson	WY-----8----07/12/66-1:30 p.m.
F-Mabel Moffitt	AK-----55---08/10/66-Unk
F-Diane Prevost	ONT----2----09/17/66-Unk
F-Annie Puglas	BC------43---04/19/67-Unk
M-Kenneth Coon	BC------5----04/28/67-Unk
M-Danny Greenwood	AZ------5----06/08/67-1:00 p.m.
M-John Gunn	YOSE--19---07/28/67-Unk
M-Kenneth Klein	YOSE--23---07/28/67-Unk
M-Tom Opperman	YOSE--21---08/08/67-Unk
F-Karen Cooney	PA------15---07/08/68-Unk
M-Lowell Smith	WA-----60---10/05/68-Unk
M-Randy Parscale	AZ-----10---01/13/69-Unk
F-Laura Flink	WA-----21---02/21/69-Unk
F-Marcelene Cummungs	WA-----54---07/14/69-Unk
M-Raymond Ewer	UT-----19---08/09/69-Noon
M-Louis Sandoval	ID------66---09/06/69-Unk
M-Robert Winters	OR------78---10/08/69-5:00 p.m.
M-Geoffrey Hague	GSM---16---02/07/70-3:20 p.m.
M-Douglas C. Chapman	ME-----3----06/02/71-10:30 a.m.
M-Douglass Legg	NY-----8----07/10/71-Unk
M-Dana Cooper	CA-----13---08/04/71-Unk
F-Elizabeth Kant	ONT----45---10/16/72-Unk
F-Joanne Burmer	CA------38----02/25/73-Unk
F-Leah Good	YOSE--49----04/30/73-Unk
F-Vital Vachon	ONT----56----05/01/73-Unk
M-Greg Lewellen	UT------66----08/03/73-Unk
F-Elizabeth Cardwell	ALB----31----09/16/73-Unk
M-Jimmy Duffy	WA-----2-----10/19/73-Unk
M-Brian Henry	ONT----21----05/05/74-Unk
F-Jennifer Klein	UT------3------05/25/74-Unk

M-Jeffrey Bratcher	WA-----7------06/15/74-6:30 p.m.
M-Yehudi Prior	BC------2------09/23/74-Unk
M-Mark Hanson	GSM---21----03/07/75-Unk
M-Edward Arcand	ALB---27----06/08/75-Unk
F-Milda D. Mcquillan	MN-----71----06/17/75-Unk
F-Jane Smith	ONT----20----08/09/75-Unk
M-Steve Martin	WA-----15----08/16/75-Noon
M-Kurt R. Newton	ME------4-----09/01/75-Unk
M-Raymond Juranitich	ONT---48----10/08/75-Unk
M-Harold Mott	PA------12----03/02/76-5:00 p.m.
M-Jeff Estes	YOSE--25----05/24/76-Unk
F-Trenny Lynn Gibson	GSM---16-----10/08/76-3:00 p.m.
M-Charles McCullar	OR------19-----10/14/76/Unk
M-Howard Booth	ALB---49----07/17/77-Unk
M-Edward Nye	OR------14----06/22/78-PM
M-Duane Scott	PA------31----07/27/78-Unk
F-Gayla C. Schaper	WA-----28----06/29/79-7:15 p.m.
M-James Caraley	ALB----22----07/18/79-Unk
F-Carol Laughlin	YOSE--19----09/09/79-Unk
M-Paul Fugate	AZ-----41-----01/03/80-2:00 p.m.
F-Megan Ginevicz	MT-----2------04/30/80-Unk
M-Larry D. Krebbs	OK-----2------06/30/80-5:30 p.m.
M-Foster Bezanson	ONT----64----10/25/80-Unk
M-Steve Maclaren	ALB----25----06/30/81-Unk
F-Stacey Anne Arras	YOSE--14----07/17/81-4:00 p.m.
F-Thelma Pauline Melton	GSM---58----09/25/81-4:15 p.m.
M-Jon Dabkowski	PA------11----01/14/82-5:30 p.m.
M-Greg Minarcin	PA------10----01/14/82-5:30 p.m.
M-Jay Charles Toney	GSM---17-----05/25/82-1:30 p.m.
M-Robert Baldeshwiler	CO-----12-----06/29/82-Unk
M-Richard Ray Barnett	WA-----2------08/31/82-7:00 a.m.
F-Ann Riffin	NM-----33-----09/13/82-Unk
M-Kevin Jay Ayotte	MN----3------09/30/82-PM
M-Richard Peterson	NJ------6------11/05/82-3:30 p.m.
F-Debra Manial	NCA---29-----12/12/82-3:00 p.m.
M-Tyler Inman	WA-----3------12/21/82-Unk
F-Shelly Bacsu	ALB---16-----05/03/83-Unk

New Jersey Missing People | 303

F-Nyleen Kay Marshall	MT-----4------06/25/83-4:00 p.m.
M-Michael E. Reel	GSM---8------07/02/83-9:30 a.m.
M-Larry Davenport	GSM---20-----07/17/83-PM
M-Gary Lee Chavoya	CA-----10-----07/30/83- Noon
M-Sharel Haresym	ALB----35-----09/04/84-Unk
M-Toivo Reinikanen	ONT----36-----09/26/84-Unk
M-Daniel Hilkey	OR------29-----01/22/85/Unk
M-David Jaramillo	UT------21-----06/13/85-Unk
M-Lloyd Reese	UT------13-----06/13/85-Unk
M-Emerson Carbaugh	PA------64-----11/11/85-6:00 p.m.
M-David Huckins	YOSE--21-----02/04/86-Unk
M-Edward Ludwig	ALB---27-----05/30/86-Unk
M-Andrew Warburton	ME-----9------07/01/86-Unk
F-Lynn Hillier	BC------2------07/24/86-Unk
M-Clayton McFaul	ONT----59-----08/15/86-Unk
M-Tom Klein	WA-----27-----09/08/86-Unk
F-Theresa Bier	YOSE--16-----06/01/87-Unk
F-Julie Ann Weflen	WA-----28-----09/16/87- 3:30 p.m.
M-John Clifford	ONT----65-----10/10/87-Unk
F-Tina Marie Finley	WA-----25-----03/07/88-2:00 a.m.
F-Colleen Tourtillott	WI-----18M---07/03/88-6:00 p.m.
M-Timothy Barnes	YOSE--24-----07/05/88-Unk
M-Nicolas Hibbert	ONT----66-----07/08/88-Unk
F-Kathleen Pehringer	WY-----41-----04/17/89-Unk
F-Ruth Jacobus	YOSE--76-----06/07/89-Noon
M-Nathan Madsen	OR------9------10/22/89-2:30 p.m.
F-Eloise Lindsay	GSM---22-----11/04/89-Unk
F-Elizabeth Bartholomew	YOSE--80-----01/08/91-Unk
F-Lillian Owens	ALB---46-----06/28/91-Unk
M-Dustin Rhodes	ONT----64-----07/06/91-Unk
M-William Caswell	ONT----52-----07/21/91-Unk
M-Brian Sines	ID------29---11/22/91-Unk
M-Corey Fay	OR------17---11/23/91-6:30 p.m.
M-Kenny Miller	YOSE--12----06/24/92-Unk
M-Travis Zweig	CA------2-----03/10/93-10:30 a.m.
M-Brad Lavies	GSM---13----03/28/93-Unk
M-Michael McIntyre	ONT----37----04/07/94-Unk
M-Victor Shoemaker	WV-----4-----05/01/94-Noon
M-William Sisco	AZ------32---06/12/94-PM

M-Wayne Powell	OR------39---06/18/94/Unk
M-Donald Shelenberger	AZ------35---07/03/94-Unk
F-Ashley Krestianson	SASK--8-----07/14/94-Unk
M-Donald Belliveau	ALB----28---01/27/95-Unk
M-Rhonda Runningbird	ALB----25---03/26/95-Unk
M-Bryce Herda	WA-----4----04/09/95-Unk
F-Jeanne Hesselschwerdt	YOSE--37---07/09/95-Unk
M-William Reed	ONT----69---08/01/95-Unk
M-Knut Thielemann	ALB----22---08/04/95-Unk
M-Daniel Edmonds	UT------22---08/22/95-Unk
M-Abraham Kalaf	AZ------79---07/24/96-Unk
M-Michael Madden	YOSE--20---08/10/96-Unk
M-Frank Szpak	ONT----69---09/23/96-Unk
M-Michael Malinoski	PA------37---10/24/96-Unk
F-Karen Mero	NCA----27---02/15/97-Unk
M-Ruben David Felix	ID------2----02/23/97-Unk
M-Melvin Hoel	ALB---64---03/12/97-Unk
M-Kenneth Churney	ONT----36---03/15/97-Unk
F-Hannah Zaccaglini	NCA----15---06/04/97-Unk
M-Bernard Champagne	ONT----80---07/10/97-Unk
F-Amy Bechtel	WY-----24---07/24/97-3:00 p.m.
M-David Crouch	WY-----27---09/07/97-Unk
M-Jonathan Aujay	SCA----38---06/11/98-Unk
M-Raymond Matlock	WA-----28---09/07/98-Unk
F-Emma Tresp	NM-----71---09/08/98-Unk
F-Joan Lawrence	ONT----77---09/23/98-Unk
M-Robert Bobo	OR------36---10/02/98/Unk
M-Derrick Engebretson	OR------8-----12/05/98/ 3:00 p.m.
M-Ernest Matthew Cook	OK------27---04/22/99-10:30 p.m.
M-Carl Landers	NCA----69---05/25/99-8:00 a.m.
M-Todd Lucchesi	NCA----28---05/31/99-Unk
M-Frank Downey	KY-----4----08/16/99-8:30 p.m.
M-Jaryd Atadero	CO------3----10/02/99 Unk
M-Joseph Moore	WV-----22---03/11/00-Unk
M-Kieran Burke	YOSE--45---04/05/00-Unk
F-Rosemary Kunst	NCA----70---08/18/00-4:00 p.m.
M-Patrick T. Whalen	MT-----33---11/02/00-Unk

M-Zbigniew Gajda	ONT----42---01/04/01-Unk
F-Gloria McDonald	AR-----68---01/26/01-2:00 p.m.
M-Michael Walsh	YOSE--56---03/01/01-Unk
M-Corwin Osborn	OR-----45---06/17/01/Unk
M-Jason Franks	OR------21---08/09/01/Unk
M-Chris Thompkins	GA-----20---01/25/02-1:30 p.m.
M-Raymond Tunnicliffe	SASK--79---08/26/02-Unk
F-Celia Barnes	OR-----53---09/01/02/Unk
F-Teresa Schmidt	CO-----53---09/06/02-3:00 p.m.
M-Walter Reinhard	YOSE--66---09/20/02-Unk
M-Jerry McKoen	NCA---48---09/21/02-Unk
F-Angela Fullmer	NCA----34---12/05/02-4:00 p.m.
F-Jennifer Dussaud	WA-----22---05/01/03-Unk
F-Leeanna Warner	MN-----5----06/14/03-4:30 p.m.
M-Michael Linklater	ONT----44---07/13/03-Unk
M-Fred Claasen	YOSE--46---08/01/03-Unk
M-Patric McCarthy	NH-----10---10/13/03-PM
M-Austin Sparks	NCA----15---01/04/04-AM
F-Joan Shelton	AZ-----65---02/07/04-Unk
M-Christopher Hallaxs	MI------30---03/17/04-Unk
M-David Gonzales	CA------9----07/31/04-8 a.m.
M-David Tippen	GA-----4----08/01/04-AM
M-Garrett Bardsley	UT------12---08/20/04-AM
M-Bart Schleyer	YUKN-49---09/14/04-Unk
M-Robert Springfield	MT-----49---09/19/04-4:00 p.m.
M-Doug Pearce	YOSE--86---04/21/05-Unk
M-Charles Beltz	PA------56---06/07/05-Unk
M-Michael Ficery	YOSE--51---06/15/05-Unk
M-Brennan Hawkins	UT-----11----06/17/05-5:30 p.m.
M-Gregory Brown	WA-----49---07/05/05-AM
F-Nita Mayo	YOSE--64---08/08/05-3:00 p.m.
M-Tom Howell	ALB---46---09/12/05-Unk
F-Michelle Vanek	CO-----35---09/24/05-1:30 p.m.
M-Wai Fan	ALB---43---09/28/05-Unk
M-Kenneth Schneider	UT------78---10/03/05-Unk
M-Roy Stephens	OR------48---11/16/05/PM
M-Christopher L. Jones	AR------37---04/05/06-Unk

M-Evan Thompson	CO-----8----05/27/06-AM
M-David Knowles	NCA---43---08/17/06-5:00 p.m.
F-Stephanie Stewart	ALB----70---08/26/06-Unk
M-Samuel Boehlke	OR------8----10/04/06/ 4:00 p.m.
M-Kory Kelly	MN-----38---10/16/06-7:00 p.m.
M-Jonathan Betts	AZ------32---10/20/06-4:00 p.m.
M-Jeremy Thomas	GA------22---02/16/07-2:20 p.m.
M-Michael Auberry	GSM---12---03/17/07-1:00 p.m.
M-Michael Bailey	ONT----38---04/20/07-Unk
M-Robert Neale	ALB----77---05/02/07-Unk
F-Hannah Klamecki	IL-------5-----06/13/07-Unk
M-Luciano Trinaistich	ONT----69---07/24/07-Unk
F-Christine Calayca	ONT----20---08/06/07-Unk
M-William Pilkenton	BC------7-----02/15/08-Unk
M-Joe Clewley	MI------73---07/13/08-Unk
M-Derrick Hennegan	MI------35---08/04/08-4:30 p.m.
M-Yi-Jien Hwa	MT------27---08/11/08-Unk
M-Michael Edwin Hearon	GSM---51----08/23/08-Unk
M-Ronald S. Gray	ID------62---09/19/08-Unk
M-Christopher Andrews	YOSE--42---10/03/08-3:00 p.m.
M-Wyatt Little Light	MT-----2----12/23/08-Unk
M-Dwight Riggs	AZ-----61---01/21/09-Unk
F-Nancy Moyer	WA-----36---03/06/09-7:00 p.m.
M-Avery B. Blakeley	ID------2----03/26/09- 1:30 p.m.
M-Joshua Childers	MO-----3----05/04/09-11:45 a.m.
F-Lindsey Baum	WA-----10---06/22/09-9:15 p.m.
M-Melvin Nadel	NM-----61---09/06/09-4:00 p.m.
F-Madyson Jamison	OK------5----10/08/09- 2:00 p.m.
F-Sherilynn Jamison	OK-----40---10/08/09-2:00 p.m.
M-Bobby Jamison	OK-----44---10/08/09-2:00 p.m.
M-Clinton Daines	UT-----35---10/16/09-Unk
M-Anthony Green, Jr.	YOSE--31---11/06/09-Unk
M-Michael Hinsperger	ONT---57---05/13/10-Unk

Males = 296
Females = 115
Total 411

This is the breakdown of missing people listed in both books by decade:

Decade	Males+Females=Total
1868–1879	1+1=2
1880–1889	4+1=5
1890–1897	4+1=5
1901–1909	5+1=6
1910–1919	8+1=9
1922–1929	6+2=8
1930–1939	24+10=34
1940–1949	37+9=46
1950–1959	35+26=61
1960–1969	28+11=39
1970–1979	21+11=32
1980–1989	30+15=45
1991–1999	36+9=45
2000–2009	56+17=73
2010	1+0=1
Totals	296+115=411

Most disappearances in
one year = 1949, 11, 11 males
2005, 11, 9 males, 2 females
1982, 10, 8 males, 2 females

There are several interesting aspects to the decade breakdown of the missing. In 1910 there is a significant increase in the number of males missing. In the early 1930s there is another major increase of men and women missing, with the escalation staying elevated until today.

It is possible that some increase in missing people could be the result of improvement in communications and reporting among newspapers and the advent of the Associated Press, United Press International, etc., I don't think, however, this can be the predominant factor. I did review current events for each decade listed and found nothing obvious that could account for these increases.

Something drastically changed in North America with the advent of the 1930–1939 decade. From 1922–1929, there were eight disappearances. From 1930–1939, there was a four-fold increase in disappearances to thirty-four.

CONCLUSIONS

Gaps in Time

Another unusual aspect of the missing people profiled in this book is the dates in which they disappear. I will readily admit that I have missed cases that fit the profile, but I believe the gaps in time will stand close to what is reported. In some of the chapters there is a gap in time where nobody goes missing. I am placing the twelve gaps in time that I have tracked:

Chapter	Time Gap with No Disappearances
Georgia	1940–1999
Colorado	1949–1982
Farmers	1956–1986
West Virginia	1958–1994
Kentucky	1958–1999
Oklahoma/ Arkansas	1959–1980
Michigan	1959–2004
New Mexico	1960–1982
Southern California	1960–1993
Montana	1960–1980
Illinois	1962–2007
Wyoming	1966–1989

When analyzing the gaps in time from the twelve sections listed above, the common years with no disappearances are 1966–1989, fourteen years in twelve states where there are no disappearances within the identified cluster. It would be interesting to understand what happened in North America during those years that caused disappearances to cease. I do not believe that disappearances randomly stopped in these clusters. There must be some rationale.

Acknowledgment
 I am the first to admit that there is no way I was able to glean all missing person cases in North America that fit the profile in this book. By the time you read this, I will have probably found a dozen

more cases or will have had additional cases forwarded to me for review. These additional cases will be posted on our website. This project could continue for years, and the information could and should continually evolve.

Danger in the Woods
The cases listed below identify an element of danger that was identified in the noted cases.

The cousin of Victor Shoemaker (Kirby, West Virginia) stated that the boy was grabbed by someone hiding behind a tree. Victor was never seen again and the suspect never identified.

Jackie Copeland (Pleasantville, Pennsylvania) saw someone or something peering at him from behind a tree. When it ran off, he followed it. The boy disappeared and was later found in a marshy area.

Florence Jackson (Berryville, Arkansas) stated that while she was missing in the woods, she slept in a tree and then met a family in the middle of the woods that allowed her to sleep in their house. After the single night she was allowed to sleep in the home, they told her to move on. Florence was carrying sheep sorrel and a tomato when searchers found her. Nobody had any idea where she obtained the sheep sorrel or tomato.

Eloise Lindsay (Seneca, South Carolina) was on a three-week hike when she disappeared. When found, the woman stated that she was chased for three weeks by several men that meant her harm. The men were never identified.

Karen Cooney (Corry, Pennsylvania) was hanging clothes in her backyard when her mother heard a scream. Karen disappeared and was later found by a helicopter. The girl stated that a "Big Man" chased her until she eventually fell asleep. Karen couldn't remember a majority of her missing time.

Cooney and Lindsay are claiming they were chased in the woods by men. The locations where these women were chased were extremely remote and locations where people routinely carry firearms. What type of man is lurking in the woods unafraid of being shot? I refer readers to the statement made by retired NPS Ranger Dwight McCarter in the Great Smoky Mountains section regarding

Dennis Martin. McCarter claims there are "wild men" living in the mountains who are known to commit crimes. Could these men be responsible for these incidents?

On the website Websleuth.com, an entry on the forum for February 14, 2005 (11:13 a.m.) stated the following:

My son was an avid hiker during high school and college. His dream was to hike the entire Appalachian Trail from Georgia to Maine before entering graduate school. The day after he graduated college he took off alone with plans to meet up at various points along the way with other hikers so none of them would ever be spending too many long periods hiking alone. Two weeks into the trip he called me to come pick him up in North Carolina after suffering an injury in a bad fall. Turns out he was injured after breaking camp in the middle of the night to evade several guys that appeared to be stalking him for several days.

On the same forum page entered on February 9, 2005 under "Tennessee" was the following:

I can tell you that I had a scary experience on one of the trails in the park one time that involved being closely followed. My hiking partner and I were frightened by these men. I believe that the only thing that saved us was that we spotted more hikers a few hundred feet away. I rather loudly said something to the effect of: "Hey, here come some more people." The men who were following us took off up the side of the mountain. We didn't stick around to see where they went.

What type of men leave an area by running uphill? People usually take the path of least resistance, downhill.

The entries on Websleuth.com are examples of incidents that occur on trails that the vast majority of the public will never hear about. I believe that these incidents may be occurring much more regularly than even I have documented. The idea that there is a group of men in the woods chasing, stalking, and following people seems initially absurd, but I doubt these stories are fictitious. When you read the statement by Dwight McCarter (Dennis Martin, Great Smoky Mountains) that there are wild men living in the mountains, this makes the stories of people being chased seem quite plausible.

Screams and Yells

The below listed cases represent an incident in which the children screamed or yelled and then disappeared. Think through this clearly. Children do not disappear; they do not run off and vanish—period. If children scream in conjunction with a disappearance, I think it's a rational assumption to believe they were confronted with something they could not overcome, and they were deathly afraid.

> *02/24/32*–Else Flothmeier (22 years), Fox Chase, Pennsylvania, walking in a park alone on edge of the wilderness. The girl disappears at the same time a woman in a nearby house hears a girl scream. Else is later found dead under suspicious circumstances.
>
> *09/05/35*–Jack Pike (5 years), St. Norbert, Manitoba, boy was with his family picking blueberries, parents hear a scream, and the boy disappears. Jack is found days later semiconscious, later dies.
>
> *05/21/41*–Eldridge Albright (3 years), Woodstock, Maryland, boy was playing in a creek behind his rural residence when his grandmother hears him scream. The mother runs into the backyard and hears two more screams further and further from the residence. Eldridge was found a day later in a swampy area with a bed made of leaves. The boy was asked how he got to the location and what happened; he couldn't remember.
>
> *12/01/46*–Paula Welden (18 years), Bennington, Vermont, taking a hike on Glastonbury Mountain and disappears. A woman nearby hears a girl scream near a swamp at the time Paula vanishes. Paula Welden is never found.
>
> *05/05/50*–Anna Pearl Thorpe (2 years), Dunbar, Pennsylvania, girl was playing in the yard of her residence

when her mother heard a scream. The mother rushed to the yard and could not locate Anna. Search parties found the girl on the other side of a ten-picket wire fence and two additional stone fences. Anna was found naked except for shoes she was wearing.

07/08/68–Karen Cooney (15 years), Corry, Pennsylvania, girl was hanging clothes in her rural backyard when her mother heard her scream. The mother ran to the backyard and could not locate the girl. A helicopter used in the search to find Karen located her. Karen later stated that she was chased by a "big man until I fell asleep." Karen could not remember much else about the incident.

Several of these individuals were missing from their yards or the area behind their residences. If a child wanted to run off or go to an area where he or she was not supposed to travel, the child wouldn't scream and sound an alert to parents. The child would stay quiet and meander away. In each of these incidents, the people screamed or yelled. Something caused them extreme angst. When children yell or scream, it is usually at a moment when they don't have the time or energy to call out with specifics. It is sometimes their last breath before they depart. It would appear that these young people confronted something drastic and immediate. It would appear from the list that Pennsylvania and Washington are hot spots for this type of activity. If you look at the list of missing from Pennsylvania, the group is heavily weighted with very young children in the early to mid 1900s, a disturbing scenario.

Bow Hunters

One of the most fascinating and unusual groups of missing people is bow hunters. The majority of these hunters that are highlighted in both books have never been found. The single person located was a most unusual find. Here is a list of bow hunters missing from both editions of Missing–411:

09/14/04–Bart Schleyer (49 years), Reid Lake, Yukon Territory, Canada. Schleyer was the one person in both books who was the most comfortable and experienced in the woods. He was bow hunting in a very remote region of the Yukon and disappeared. Parts of his body were located, but there were never answers as to what killed the man or the circumstances behind his death.

09/19/04–Robert Springfield (49 years), Bighorn Mountain, Montana. Springfield was bow hunting with relatives when he vanished. Several years later a few bones, boots, and his coat were located neatly placed next to a tree. A screeching crow directed another hunter to the find.

It seems very coincidental that Springfield disappeared five days after Schleyer and specifically participating in the exact same sport. Both men were exactly forty-nine years old, and their deaths are some of the most unexplainable in either edition of Missing–411. There are many coincidences listed in both books that seem almost odd that they exist.

09/12/05–Tom Howell (46 years), Limestone Mountain, Caroline, Alberta, Canada. Tom drove his ATV packed with supplies to an area at the base of a large mountain where he was going to bow hunt for Rocky Mountain sheep. He knew the area well and was an experienced hunter. Tom disappeared, and an extensive search was conducted without finding Tom or any of his supplies.

09/06/09–Melvin Nadel (61 years), Santa Fe National Forest, New Mexico. Melvin met friends at an area where he was leaving his vehicle and walking 100–150 yards to bow hunt. He told others that he wasn't going very far. He was never seen again. One of the largest searches ever conducted in this area failed to find Melvin or any of his supplies.

Bow hunting is intrinsically dangerous because of the proximity in which the hunter must get to the game. Non-hunters must understand that there are other predators in the woods that are also after the same game as the hunter. It's doubtful that Howell or Nadel met with a mountain lion or bear, as there would have been a large, gruesome scene of blood and torn clothing. This scenario was never found. In the Springfield case, it appears that something with advanced intelligence killed Robert, as his belt was found neatly rolled next to evidence of his remains, an unusual sight.

The Bart Schleyer case is very, very perplexing. I wish I could have been on that scene from the beginning and handled it like a crime scene, sealing the perimeter and collecting evidence from the outside moving in toward the center, preserving evidence (tracks, etc.) as you move toward the center. Each of these cases is quite unusual.

Scratches

There are many cases listed in both books where children are found with scratches listed over their entire body. Other cases describe childrens bodies "*torn*" with severe lacerations when they are found. I've never been one to believe that children will indiscriminately run through a thorny area ripping and scratching their body, that does not make sense. Many of these cases describe parents and law enforcement claiming the missing person was kidnapped. If the victim was taken against their will and the perpetrator didn't care about the welfare of the individual, maybe the victim was carried under the suspects arm as they ran from the scene, through the woods, through thorns and scratching the victims body. This scenario may explain the victim having scratches from head to toe.

National Park Service

There is one last issue regarding NPS and missing people that needs to be brought to the public's attention.

In 1984 the Missing Children's Assistance Act was passed, which established a national clearinghouse for missing and exploited children. On June 13, 1984 the National Center for Missing and Exploited Children was formally opened. Law enforcement agencies are now required to report all missing children to the national center (1-800-THE LOST).

During my search for missing people in the United States, I went to the National Center for Missing and Exploited Children and queried their database. I found limited data that could be gleaned from its search criteria, and I found few children listed as missing in the properties managed by the DOI. As I dug more deeply, I realized that there were several children I confirmed as still missing from a national park that the NPS had not listed in the national database:

Dennis Martin	7 years	Missing 06/14/69–Great Smoky Mtns
Dennis Johnson	7 years	Missing 07/12/77-- Yellowstone (Missing 411–Western U.S.)
Trenny Gibson	16 years	Missing 10/08/76–Great Smoky Mtns
Stacy Arras	14 years	Missing 07/17/81– Yosemite (Missing 411–Western U.S.)

Gaps in Time | 317

Top Row left to right; Dennis Johnson, Dennis Martin, Bottom Row Stacy Arras, Trenny Gibson.

I can guarantee for a fact that there are numerous people listed in the national database who went missing long before the required date of entry. The NPS is making a calculated decision not to place these missing children in the database. Whether the decision is to limit visibility of this issue to the public, laziness, or something else, the reality is that there is no downside to their entry, *none!* I personally find it reprehensible that these children are not in a database designed specifically for their cases.

The Interview

After speaking with dozens of SAR personnel over the last few years, I have realized that many conduct their missions in highly different ways. I am not going to pass judgment on their methods, but I would hope that every SAR team would start to implement the post-incident victim interview (PIVI).

Once the missing person is found, let him or her physically and emotionally stabilize to the point of being able to concentrate again. The SAR member doing this interview cannot wait weeks for the meeting—the closer to the time the person is recovered, the better. The amount of information that can be gleaned from an interview with the victim is extraordinary. We need to be doing this with all ages, male and female, under all circumstances. This information needs to be placed into a national database so SAR commanders can query the system and get a computer-assisted recommendation on where the missing person may be going based on the information gleaned from relatives and friends. A nationally standardized form should be implemented and used as a post-incident interview tool where it's legally mandated that it be completed.

I know that the FBI does not like to deal with missing people, but they seem to be the best federal law enforcement agency to manage information of this type. The agency managing this information needs to develop an easily understood form that can be completed by the victim with the assistance of the SAR member that can then be sent to the database for input. The database is only as good as the information it receives, and the more information the computer is given, the more successful future SARs.

It is probably a fact that many victims will not understand what path they took while they were missing. SAR members may need to take the victims back into the field and identify routes taken, uphill, downhill, crossing rivers, whatever they did. To gain a complete understanding of their path, it may be optimum to put the victims in a helicopter and fly the area with them to get an aerial view of the region. This process can be as important as the initial search for the victim.

DOI Recommendations

If someone goes missing in a national park, the park may take control of the SAR or it may relinquish control to the county sheriffs department. The same applies in the jurisdiction of the USFS.

If you are the missing person that the SAR team is operational, your life can be in the hands of the SAR commander and the decisions he or she makes. If commanders won't admit what they don't know and intend to learn through hands-on experience, you may not be found alive. This situation can occur in any jurisdiction and may occur during holidays when the experienced law enforcement SAR commanders are on vacation. Heck, they've earned the time off and deserve to be with their families. Holidays are a time when most people visit the woods, and many people go missing during those time periods.

The Department of the Interior, and its associated jurisdictions, controls a vast amount of the area where a person may go missing in the wild. Thousands of missing person reports, articles, and SAR statements show vast differences in the way SARs are managed and their subsequent effectiveness. It would be optimal if the DOI divided the United States into regions with each region having its own SAR Urgent Response Team with experts that do nothing during the high traffic months but train and learn the latest SAR methods. This team would immediately respond when a case reaches a level in which advanced expertise is needed. The cases that needed an expert team to assist would have been the cases of Stacy Arras (Yosemite), Dennis Martin and Trenny Gibson (Great Smoky Mountains), Dennis Johnson (Yellowstone), Samuel Boehlke (Crater Lake), among others. These are just examples. I would also recommend that an FBI agent be attached to each team and respond to monitor the search in the event the case turns criminal they could have their head in the game and contribute immediately.

People do not disappear into nothingness. When someone is missing and searchers are actively looking, there is a high degree of tension in the air. In many instances there is limited time to find the person based on the evaluation of how long he or she could live without additional assistance. If the assumption is that someone could live one week in the wild, the search may go ten days and then terminate, under the belief the person couldn't survive. I've had several sleepless nights thinking about the fear children listed in this book must have felt every night they were missing in the wild. The anxiety and horror that a parent feels under the conditions of losing a child are unfathomable. I can't imagine leaving the area where I lost a child and terminating the search effort and driving home. I know it would ruin me as a person as it has ruined many other parents in this book. I don't believe any human being could suffer a worse scenario.

I think that we as a society need to take a hard look at missing people, maybe missing children specifically. Perhaps we need a national study on the topic with peer review by world-renowned experts to develop a new paradigm on the search. If we absolutely know that a person is lost in the woods, should we really give up on finding the individual? With the advancement of technology, isn't there more we can do with satellites and tracking the possible locations of missing people? Can't we utilize the satellites that we employ to find terrorists—those same satellites that can read a license plate from space—can't we direct them to specific areas to search for children? Why can't the DOI borrow unmanned drones under a military contract to assist in searching large areas of forests with FLIR? Why can't the military loan the drones to the DOI or USFS to assist in searches? The public needs to voice its concern on these issues and get these changes implemented. The issue, nobody ever believes their family would be the victim of a missing person scenario; thus, they don't need to exude the energy on the topic.

FBI Involvement

As you've read through both books, you have seen the FBI become involved in cases that defy conventional kidnapping yet do point to abduction. The FBI has always been an agency that documents incidents very well. The agency is very thorough. The cases highlighted in both books show a pattern of missing people from the early 1900s with the FBI becoming involved during that same time period. The agency has a huge database of information to which we do not have access. The information this agency has accumulated allows it to make strategic decisions about when to be involved, when to back away, and when to sit on the sidelines and monitor.

The FBI Behavioral Analysis Unit is the profiling branch of the agency. Its agents use knowledge of past crimes and interviews of suspects and witnesses and apply that knowledge to ongoing cases to allow law enforcement officers a special view of the suspect they may be pursuing. This profile allows detectives to narrow their focus, using time-proven techniques that profilers employ.

Here is the definition of the FBI Behavioral Analysis Unit 2 and 3 directly from the FBI website:

Behavioral Analysis Unit 2 (crimes against adults): Resources are primarily focused on serial, spree, mass, and other murders; sexual assaults; kidnappings; missing person cases; and other violent crimes targeting adult victims. BAU 2 also provides assistance in potentially nonviolent investigations, such as white-collar crime, public corruption, organized crime, and civil rights matters.

Behavioral Analysis Unit 3 (crimes against children): Resources are focused on crimes perpetrated against child victims, including abductions, mysterious disappearances of children, homicides, and sexual victimization.

I immediately focused on Behavioral Analysis Unit 3 where it lists "mysterious disappearances of children." I believe that both books have many examples that exemplify many mysterious disappearances of children. The following is a list of cases in both books that indicated that the FBI was participating or monitoring at some level in the case:

Joseph and William Whitehead, missing August 24, 1924, Glacier National Park, Montana, Joseph was twenty-nine and William twenty-two years. Joseph and William were lost in the park while vacationing. There was no evidence ever found they were even hiking inside the park.

Bobby Connor, missing July 13, 1934, Greenburgh, New York, twenty-one months. Walking home and disappeared. Extensive search found the boy groggy and in brambles. Police believed he was abducted and later freed. Eleven days after this event and eighty miles north, Claire Benson, twenty-one months disappeared from her yard.

Albert Beilhartz, missing July 2, 1938, Rocky Mountain National Park, four years. Albert was in the park with his parents and disappeared. A witness saw a young boy high on a cliff sometime after the disappearance. Albert was never found.

Dickie Suden, missing November 1, 1945, northern California, Sierras, four years, missing from the yard of his parents' home in rural foothills. Glove found high on crag, extensive search could not find boy. Parents felt the possibility existed boy was abducted.

Greta Mary Gale, missing June 29, 1947, Lassen National Park, thirty months. Greta was vacationing with her grandfather who was a California congressman when she disappeared near their cabin. Two days after she disappeared, Greta was found high up a mountain, wearing only panties, one mile from the cabin.

Ronnie Weitkamp, missing October 11, 1955, Crane Depot, Indiana, three years. Ronnie disappeared in a rural area near his home located on a military installation. Every home on the base was searched as well as fields. He was eventually found deceased with his overalls removed from his body.

Minnie Haun, missing October 8, 1957, Wells Spring, Tennessee, three years. Minnie was with her mother and sister in the back of the family's rural home looking for walnuts. Minnie got separated and disappeared. Six days after Minnie vanished she was found on the top of a ridgeline missing shoes and clothing, deceased.

Debbie Ann Greenhill, missing August 9, 1958, Olive Hill, Kentucky, two years. Had just moved to new home near a reservoir. Extensive search initially didn't find anything. Eventually found in an area searched near reservoir.

Bobby Panknin, missing August 3, 1963, Stevens County, Washington, 4 years. Bobby was with his mother and other relatives looking at a waterfall off a logging road. Mrs. Panknin was no more then twenty feet from Bobby when he disappeared. Bobby was never found.

Dennis Martin, missing June 14, 1964, Great Smoky Mountains National Park, Tennessee, seven years. Dennis was in a field in the mountains being watched by his father and grandfather when he vanished. An extensive search never found the boy.

Dennis Johnson, missing July 12, 1966, Yellowstone National Park, eight years, disappeared from picnic spot in park just after sister momentarily went missing. After extensive search, parents felt boy was abducted. Dennis was never found.

Charles McCullar, missing January 30, 1975, Crater Lake National Park, Oregon, nineteen years. Charles traveled to Crater Lake to take photos when he disappeared. In October 1976, McCullar's remains were found deep in the wilderness under extremely strange circumstances. The FBI responded an Evidence Response Team because of the peculiarity of the findings.

Nyleen Kay Marshall, missing June 25, 1983, Helena National Forest, Montana, four years. Nyleen was walking ahead of her family on a trail in a national forest. When the family reached the end of the path, Nyleen was missing and has never been found.

Tina Marie Finley, missing March 7, 1988, Plummer, Idaho, twenty-five years. Finley was dropped at her rural residence by a friend and was never seen again. Her friend passed a polygraph and has no involvement. Tina matches the physical description of other females missing in the area.

Victor Shoemaker, missing May 1, 1994, Augusta, West Virginia, four years. Victor was playing in the woods with relatives when he decided to go back to his grandparents' cabin alone. He was never seen again. One of the boys who was with Victor at the time of the disappearance stated that somebody hiding behind a tree grabbed him. Victor has never been found.

Jeanne Hesselschwerdt, missing July 9, 1995, Glacier Point, Yosemite National Park, thirty-seven years. Jeanne and a boyfriend were visiting the park and stopped to take a short hike—she disappeared. In September 1995, two mountain climbers fishing in a very remote and rugged area found Jeanne's body in a creek. Nobody could account for how she arrived at the location where found.

Trenny Gibson, missing October 8, 1976, Great Smoky Mountains National Park, Tennessee, sixteen years. Trenny was with a class on a wilderness day hike near Clingman's Dome. Trenny was seen stepping off the trail and disappeared. An extensive search failed to find any clue that the girl had been in the woods. Trenny was never found.

Karen Mero, missing February 15, 1997, McCloud, California, twenty-seven years. Karen disappeared in McCloud, CA in the same time frame as Hannah Zaccaglini. Karen has never been found.

Hannah Zaccaglini, missing June 4, 1997, McCloud, California, fifteen years. Hannah disappeared in the rural community of McCloud near the base of Mt. Shasta. She has never been found.

Amy Bechtel, missing July 24, 1997, Shoshone National Forest, Wyoming, twenty-four years. Amy went to a small park to map a recreational run she was planning. Her car was found, but Amy disappeared. Six years after Amy disappeared, her Timex watch was found in the middle fork of a nearby river. Amy Bechtel was never found.

Jaryd Atadero, missing October 2, 1999, Comanche Peak Wilderness, Colorado, three years. Jaryd was walking a defined trail near a river with a group of people when he vanished. He was found four years later high up a mountainside. Only remnants of the boy were found.

Patric McCarthy, missing October 13, 2003, White Mountains, New Hampshire, ten years. Disappeared from an area near a ski resort. Was found deceased of hypothermia in mountains. His parents felt the boy had been attacked and abducted.

Garrett Bardsley, missing August 20, 2004, Cuberant Lake, Utah, twelve years. Garrett was fishing with his father when he got wet. He turned to walk back to camp and while in a woodsy area disappeared. Garrett's sock was found higher in elevation in a boulder field. He was never found.

Robert Springfield, missing September 19, 2004, Bighorn Mountain, Montana, forty-nine years. Robert was bow hunting with relatives when he vanished. An extensive search produced no evidence he was in the area. Thirteen months after Robert disappeared, small remnants of his bones were found, along with his belt and vest. The remainder of Robert's body has never been recovered.

Madyson, Sherilynn, and Bobby Jamison, missing October 8, 2004, Panola Mountain, Oklahoma, ages five, forty, and forty-four respectively. The Jamisons looked at mountain property for purchase and met the seller. After the meeting, the family stayed in the area and disappeared. They have never been found.

Samuel Boehlke, missing October 4, 2006, Crater Lake National Park, Oregon, eight years. Samuel was with his father driving the perimeter road of the lake when they stopped for the view. Samuel ran to the top of a small hill, yelled at his father and ran over the other side and was never seen again. A massive search failed to find the boy.

This is a confirmed list of twenty-six cases in which the FBI was on scene. Many times agents will not identify themselves or speak to the press, but local law enforcement officers will confirm that FBI agents are there. This is only a small list of cases in which we absolutely knew the FBI was there. I have no doubt that there are equally as many cases in which they were there and did monitor or read case reports.

Each time I file an FOIA with the FBI, I fail to receive all of the documents I request. The agency always refuses something. It's unclear to me how they can claim they cannot release documents regarding a dead body because they are concerned about the person's privacy.

The FBI is a group of very intelligent agents. Many of these law enforcement officers are not streetwise, but they are very intellectual and can connect the dots. I know that they have massive files on cases very similar to the cases I have presented, and they have come to conclusions about similarities in cases and possible relationships among different crime scenes. The number of children who have disappeared from a rural location with their dogs is something that is troubling. People in national parks who are chased and/or followed by unidentified men is also a troubling issue that I am sure the FBI understands and is tracking. I can guarantee that the NPS understands the issue of wild men living in their parks, one of their best retired rangers told us.

The number of children missing in national parks who are never found is also a troubling point that the FBI fully understands because they have participated by interviewing witnesses. There was one agent in the Knoxville office of the FBI who was heavily involved investigating several disappearances of children in the Tennessee mountains—Jim Rike. Agent Rike interviewed many people involved with several cases presented in this book and seemed to be well informed about the facts of each case. When I interviewed Mr.

Martin regarding his son's disappearance in the Smoky Mountains National Park, he specifically mentioned Agent Rike's name and felt that he knew a lot of the specifics of his son's case. Unfortunately Agent Rike is deceased, and we cannot question him. I can guarantee that everything Agent Rike did, every assumption he made, was documented and sent to headquarters. These reports still exist, but not under the victim's name. They are cross-referenced using special coding and names that behavioral analysts understand and can query. The public cannot get at these cases through an FOIA because private citizens don't know the codes or file names to ask for.

I personally believe that the FBI has a large case file with many of these incidents cataloged and well documented. The agency does not discuss cases with the media or usually share its intelligence with other law enforcement agencies unless asked specific questions. I have personally experienced this refusal numerous times. I have no doubt that the behavioral unit has many files of cases identical to the ones you've just read, along with its analysis of what occurred and how it occurred. However, recommendations by the agency for managing the media message have, no doubt, given many Supervising Special Agents heartache and anxiety over what they knew but could not say.

Next Steps

I know there are people with much more knowledge and many more facts on missing people than I. I am positive that the NPS has a treasure trove of information on missing people in its system that it does not release to the public. The NPS policy needs to change. It needs to start tracking missing people and releasing that data in its annual report for everyone to see. I do hope that this book acts as a catalyst for the public to start openly talking about the missing and then demanding disclosure and complete cooperation among various federal agencies. I spent three years researching these books. I could have easily continued for another ten. I would hope that some of the people who are harboring knowledge on this topic would step forward and add clarity and start the process of disclosure.

I ask readers to study the lists of missing children and adults attached at the end of this book. Look for similarities and comparative relationships, dates, times, ages, etc. There are clues to understanding the issues, and they are buried in these lists.

My prayers for a calming peace go out to each and every friend and relative of the missing.

You can reach me any time at: missing411@yahoo.com or visit the website at www.canammissing.com.

INDEX

Abbott, Billy 170, 195-197,
Abbott, Diane 233, 253,
Abduction 16, 87, 127, 140, 158, 176, 196, 199, 258,
Abitibi-De-Troyes Provincial Park 4,
Abitibi River, 4,
Abrams Creek, TN 105,
Ackworth, IA 31,
Acton, MT 23,
Acute Brain Syndrome 161,
Adirondack Mountains, NY 256,
Aiken Standard 134,
Air Force 125, 138,
   Eglin 258,
   Plattsburgh 256,
Air National Guard 139,
Alabama 95-97,
   Birmingham 96,
   Gardendale, AL 96,
   Map 95,
   Sylacauga 95,
Alaska
   Gilmore Creek 17-18,
Albany Herald 104,
Alberta, Canada 88,
   Provost 32,
Albright, Eldridge 188-189,
Alder, MT 22-23,
Allatoona Lake, GA 100,
Allegheny National Forest 184, 205, 213,
Altoona, PA 190,
Amsbaugh, Riley 28-29,
Appalachians 105,
Appalachian Trail 111, 116-117, 122-124, 133, 136,
Apple Orchard 216, 255,
Arcadia, MO 75,
Arizona
   Coconino County 23,
   Long Valley 23,
Arkansas 76-94,
   Berryville 78,
   Cadron Creek, AR 91,
   Devils Den State Park 82, 84,
   Holland 91-92,
   Hot Springs 77,
   Indian Creek 78,
   Little Rock 91, 141,
   Map 76,

   Mena 85,
   Oak Grove 77,
   Quachita National Forest 91,
   Queen Wilhelmina State Park, AR 89,
   State Parks 83,
   University of 84,
   Washington County 83,
Arkansas Times 83,
Army 118, 203,
   Camp Chaffee 81,
   Camp Maxey 81,
   Fort Bragg 158,
   Fort Leonard Wood 85,
   Third Army Headquarters 138,
   Soldiers 81,
Arras, Stacy 316,
   Photo 317,
Arrowheads 105,
Ashokan Indian Reservation, NY 203,
Atlanta Constitution 104, 155,
ATV 43, 54, 75, 128,
Auberry, Michael 106-109,
Augusta Motor Speedway 219,
Auroraville, WI 52,
Autopsy 29, 86, 179, 198, 242, 265,
   None Completed 110-111, 132,
Awhanee, CA 30,
Ayotte, Kevin Jay 36, 266,
   Photo 40,

Bache, OK 87,
Bachman, Unk First Name 172-173,
Bailey, Gary 8, 15, 233,
Bailey, Kenneth 15,
Bailey, Taylor 159,
Baker, Alice 265-267,
Baker, Howard 139,
Bald Eagle Mountain, PA 191-192,
Baldwin, Juanitta 156,
Barefoot
   Tracks 194,
Barnett, Dennis 154,
Barofsky, Unk First Name 277-278,

Battle Creek, MI 65,
Bayfield County, WI 13,
Bear 57-58, 90, 113, 115, 137, 143, 157, 173, 195, 251, 267,
   Black 49, 56, 252,
   Squeezed to Death by Bear 268,
Bear Creek Basin, ID 25,
Bear Creek, WI 29,
Bearden High School, TN 111,
Beaver 239, 241-242,
Bell, Mr. 28, 31,
Belt Buckle
   Unbuckled 121,
Beltz, Charles 171, 213-214,
Beltrami County, MN 40, 42-47,
Bench Creek, UT 25-26,
Bennington, VT 265-267, 273,
   Bickford Hollow 272,
   Dump 273,
Bennington College, VT 271,
Bensen, Claire 232, 233, 246-247, 263,
Berryville, AR 78,
Bezanson, Foster 2, 5,
Berries xv, 9-20, 28-29, 57, 59, 74, 135, 159-160, 175, 179, 202, 229-230, 249,
Berry Picker 174,
Biddeford Journal 240,
Bilgrien, Roy 48-50,
Birmingham, AL 96,
Bishop, Alfred J. 264-265,
Bitter Creek, WY 22,
Blackberry 159, 166, 179, 199,
Blancha, R.M. 182,
Bloodhounds xiii, 59,
   Can't Track Scent 14, 16-17, 19, 31, 37, 41, 52, 59, 62, 75, 103, 114, 154, 118, 135, 148, 159, 161, 183, 188, 190, 192, 194, 197, 200, 202, 204, 207, 229, 242, 243, 247, 256, 258, 260, 266-267, 274,
Blount County Sheriff, TN 128,
Blueberries 13-14, 19-20, 36, 249,
Blythe, Irma 129,
Blythe, Ken 129,

332 | Missing 411- Eastern United States

Bolton, Thaddeus 179,
Bordwell, C.H. 8, 14, 35,
Boston Globe 237, 240, 243,
Boulan Reef Mine 20,
Boulder Junction, WI 59,
Boulders 82, 183,
Bounds, Anita 113,
Bow Hunters 313-315,
Bowers, Emma 9, 185, 214,
Boy Scouts 14-15, 116-120, 138,
Braceville, IL 72,
Bradford Era 207,
Bramble Thicket 245,
Breeds, IL 70-71,
Brewer, Carson 143,
Briar Patches xv, 166, 168, 185, 192,
Briceville, TN 125,
Bridgeport Telegram 265,
Brightstone, MAN 12,
British Columbia, Canada
   Vancouver Island 18,
Broken Neck 29,
Broomsage 96,
Brown, David 232, 238-242,
Burbank, WA 24,
Burkhart, David 222,
Bureau of Indian Affairs
   (BOI) 25,
Busby, Claude 81,

Cadron Creek, AR 91,
C.A. McDougall 25,
California 256,
   Awhanee 30,
   Sierra Nevada Mountains 30,
Callaway State Wildlife
   Management Area, MN 40,
Camp Tree Farm, PA 208,
Campbell County, TN 126,
Campbell Mills, OH 28-29,
Canines xiii, *see*
   "Bloodhounds"
Cannon, Jack 153,
Cannon, Pauline 154,
Canton, IL 70,
Carbaugh, Emerson 171, 210-211,
Carbaugh, Ida 211,
Carey, Bob 158,
Cartersville, GA 98,
Carthage, TN 140,

Castle Rock Lake, WI 50,
Cat (Kitten) 72,
Catawissa Valley, PA 172,
Cattle 218,
Catskill Mountains 173, 203,
Cave 124, 141, 182,
Cemetary 86,
Champagne, Bernard 2, 6,
Chapman, Douglas C. 233, 254-255,
Charleston Gazette, 230,
Chased by Man/Men 133,
   Fell Asleep 205,
Chenoweth, Helen 70-71,
Chickens 204,
Chidester, John 122-124,
Childers, Joshua 74-75,
Children xiii
Chilhowee Lake, TN 128,
Chippewa County Sheriff 66,
Chippewa Hunting Post, MI 63,
Chisholm 41-42,
Civil Air Patrol 114,
Clark, Allen 70,
Clark, Clarence 28, 30, 233,
Clark, Gould 30,
Clayton County Reservoir, GA 104,
Clayton Peterson Logging
   Camp, MN 39,
Clever, Billy 170, 197,
Clewley, Joe 55, 63-65,
Clifford, John 2,
Clingmans Dome, TN 105, 111, 115,
Clothing
   Color (Yellow) 89, (red) 136, (Red) 194, (Red) 196, (Red) 271,
   Never Found 51, 161, 167, 178, 192, 218, 247, 254,
   Removed xv, 24, 38, 51-52, 75, 96, 101, 119, 172, 190, 191, 192, 218, 217, 228, 230, 248, 254, 266, 279,
   Torn to Shreds 50, 81, 190, 197, 277-278,
Clusters
   Lists xi-xii
Coal 73,
Coal City, IL 73,
Coast Guard 139, 274,
Cochrane, ONT 4-6,
Coconino County, AZ 23,
Coghill, Bobby 113-114,

Coeur D'Alene, ID 18,
Coleman, Kenneth 37,
Coleman, Larry 35, 37-38,
Colesville, MD 197-198,
Collier Lloyd 194,
Collier, Ronald 194-195, 214,
Colorado 22,
Columbia River 16-17,
Conclusions 309-329,
Connecticut
   Colebrook 242-243,
   Cromwell 246,
Connellsville General Hospital 186-187,
Connor, Bobby 232, 233, 244-246, 263,
Cook, Ernest Mathew 76, 87-88,
   Photo 87,
Cook, Dewey 21-22,
Cook, John 87,
Cooney, Karen 171, 205-206, 214,
Cooper, Robert 222,
Cooper Valeria 221,
Copeland, Jackie 200-201, 223,
Copper City, MI 58,
Copperheads 192,
Cornell Lookout, PA 193,
Cornfield 28-30, 32, 72, 167, 186-187, 225,
Coroner 21, 23, 29-30, 61, 110, 126, 182, 208, 234, 242, 268, 280,
Dentist 110,
Corry, PA 205-206,
Cows
   Milked 13,
Cox, Norman 18,
Crabtree, Ed 139,
Craig, Richard 8, 16-17,
Crane Depot, IN 226,
Crater Lake, OR 120,
Crookstown, MN 42,
Crown Game Preserve 4,
Crumley, Bill 158,
Cucupa, Albert 21, 25,
Cummings, Marcelene 8, 18,

Dabkowski, Jon 171, 210,
Daily Democrat 86,
Daily Herald 158,
Daily Middleboro 126,
Daily News 49, 215,

Index

Dansey, George "Billy" 277-281,
Davenport, Larry 106-107, 157, 161-162,
Davis Elsie M. 232, 235-237,
Davis, John 21, 24,
Davis, Unk First Name 173-174,
Davis, Millard 173-174,
Deaf-See "Disabled"
Deer 45, 67, 267,
Delaware 232,
  Kittshammock 233,
Delaware Lake 165,
Delaware Wilderness 165-166,
Delirious 51, 134,
Denman Mountain, NY 203,
Dentist 110,
Department of Interior (DOI) Recommendations 320-321,
Depatie, Marc 20,
Devils Den State Park, AR 82,
  Devils Den Dam 82, 84,
Dickinson County Picnic Grounds 61-63,
Dickson, Shane 91,
Diggan, Alvan 170, 191-192,
Dillon, MT 23,
Disabled xiv, 13, 91, 110, 206, 208,
  Blind 15,
  Deaf 172, 201-202,
  Diabetic 162,
  Odd Behavior 156,
  Hearing Impaired 40-41,
  Stroke 16,
Disappearances
  Unique Factors xiii-xvi
Dispatch 217,
Dogs xiii, 26, 44-45, 56, 58-59, 64, 72, 81, 93, 156, 166-167, 196, 206, 216, 231,
  Found Clean 99,
  Found in Septic Tank 198,
  Missing 95, 98, 167, 180, 189, 193, 196, 197-198, 206-207, 218, 231, 242, 278,
Doorknocker 130,
Doud, Brenda Jean 233, 253-254,
Doughton Park, NC 108,
Downey, Frank, 225-226, 230-231,
Drowned 74, 198, 217, 240,
Drummond, WI 13,
Dubois, ID 25,

Dubois, PA 213,
Duffy, Jimmy 11-12,
Duluth, MN 37,
Dunkirk Evening Observer 268,
Dunlap, Wayne 111,
Dunn Creek, TN 155,
Dunton, Louis 233, 247-249,
Dye Ranch, AZ 23,

Eastman, Quebec 249-250,
Edel, Monty 207,
Edmonton Sun 251,
Edwards, Bonnie Lee 106-107, 110-111,
Eglin Air Force Base 258,
Electrician 91,
Elizabethon Star 104,
Elkmont, TN 114,
Ellerslie, GA 101,
Ellyson, C.J. 222,
Elrose, Sask 9-11,
Ely, MN 39,
Elyria, OH 9,
Erie Railroad 175,
ESP Research Associates 141,
Evening Independent 187, 248,
Evening Telegram 9,
Exhaustion 235, 242, 250,
Exposure 61, 86, 100, 110, 168, 176, 179, 185, 188, 217, 242, 250,

Fargo, ND 40,
Farm/Farmer 12, 27-34, 50, 53, 73-74, 77, 100, 110, 157, 165-166, 172, 176, 177, 180-182, 185, 190, 203-204, 211, 218 (Dairy), 218, 231, 233, 241-243, 250, 255, 279,
Farrington, Donald 184-185,
Farrington, Emmett 184-185,
Fayetteville Daily 77,
FBI 93-94, 116, 120-121, 139-141, 143-147, 150-152, 262-263,
  On Scene 109 (Auberry), 114 (Gibson), 125 (Haun), 138 (Martin), 205 (Cooney), 222 (Shoemaker), 226-228 (Weitkamp), 229

(Greenhill), 246 (Connor),
  Involvement 322-328,
Feet
  Raw 202,
Feif, David 8, 14-15,
Fels Planetarium, PA 204,
Fever xiv, 179, 207, 236, 246,
Firearm 26, 46, 58,
Fish, Ben 122-124,
Flesh Eaten 279,
FLIR 65, 93, 108, 131, 220, 256,
Florence Morning News 110,
Florida
  Jacksonville 153,
  Panama City 63,
Flothmeier, Else 178-180,
Floyd, Frank 69,
Flynn, Katie 55-58,
Flynn, Henry 56,
Fontaine, Michael 233, 249-251,
Fontana Lake, NC 114, 139, 155,
Footprints 10, 60, 249,
Ford, John 9,
Ford, Stephen 8-9, 185, 188, 214,
Fort Benning, GA 138,
Fort Bragg 158,
Fort Campbell, KY 131,
Fort Dix 281,
Fort Devens, MA 256,
Fort Washita, TX 86,
Found
  Badly Scratched 56, 97, 99, 104, 119, 161, 166, 172, 178-179, 185, 199, 202, 216, 217, 228, 230, 244, 245, 249, 277-278, 282,
  Disoriented 109,
  Fell From Cliff 131,
  In Area Previously Searched 104, 159, 217, 234,
  In Creek/River Bed 53, 75, 96, 109, 123-124, 131, 162, 173, 185, 226, 216, 198,
  In Berry Patch 185, 199,
  In Tree 235-236,
  In Swamp 62, 200, 277, 279,
  Naked 54, 74, 78, 161, 163, 167, 179, 192, 199, 202, 237, 247, 248, 266, 281,
  Pants Pulled Down 119,
  Partially Clothed 75, 96, 119, 124, 178, 181, 199, 217, 235, 246, 247,

Semi Conscious/Groggy 75, 96, 161, 167, 168, 190, 205, 207, 216, 226, 235-236, 238, 243, 245, 281,
Unconscious 162, 191, 196,
With Nose Injury 99,
Four Town, MN 42-43,
Fox Chase, PA 178-180,
Fox News 109,
Frederick House River 5,
Free Lance Star Newspaper 221,
Freedom of Information Act (FOIA) 46, 111, 126, 136, 141, 143,
Fremont County, ID 25,
Fritz, Gabe 262,
Fritz, Noah 262,
Fronefield Farm 30,
Frye Mountain State Management Area, ME 15,

Gaddis, George W. 99,
Gadsden Times 255,
Gaines, PA 211-212,
Galatia Township 32,
Gallagher, Debbie 227,
Gallagher, Morris 264-265,
Game Warden 23, 38, 194, 238, 258,
Gaps in Time 294-295, 309,
Garbage Dump 273,
Garcia, Jerry 21, 24,
Gardendale, AL 96,
Gately, Edward 232, 237-238,
Gazette Mail 168,
Georgia 98-104
  Allatoona Lake 100,
  Cartersville 98,
  Clayton County Reservoir 104,
  Ellerslie 101,
  Fort Benning 138,
  List of Missing 98,
  Macon 102,
  Red Top Mountain State Park 100,
  Stockbridge 102,
  Tobesofkee Creek 102,
Gerke, Edward 28-29, 48,
Gettysburgh Times 187,
Gibson, Robert 115,
Gibson, Trenny Lynn 106-107, 111-116 162, 164, 316,

Photo 111, 317,
Similarities 116,
Trail Photo 112,
Gidlof, Andrew 13-14,
Gilmore Creek, Alaska 17-18,
Girard Manor, PA 172,
Glass, James 175,
Godwin, A.W. 78,
Gonzales, Elias 22,
Grahamsville, NY 203-204,
Grandparents Home Missing From 51,
Grangeville, ID 22,
Grapevines 231, 246,
Great Smoky Mountains National Park 90, 105-164, 237,
  Adams Creek 128, 130,
  Andrews Bald 111,
  Anthony Creek Trailhead 137,
  Big Creek 122,
  Boulevard Trail 118,
  Buck Fork Creek 124,
  Cades Cove 135, 137, 139, 142, 148, 150,
  Cataloochee Valley 148,
  Chapter Conclusions 163-164,
  Chilhowell Mountain 135,
  Clingmans Dome 105, 111, 115, 162,
  Deep Creek Trail 153, 155,
  Forney Creek Trail 114,
  Low Gap 122,
  Map 105,
  Mt. Chapman 124,
  Mt. Guyot 123,
  Mt. Leconte 131,
  Mt. Sterling 122,
  Newfound Gap 117-119,
  Rainbow Falls 131,
  Rowans Creek 137, 140-141, 144, 147, 150,
  Russell Field Shelter 136,
  Sea Branch Creek 137-138, 140, 144, 147, 150,
  Spence Field 136, 139, 144,
  Tricorner 122,
  Walker Camp Prong 118,
Greeley, PA 175-176,
Green Berets Search 119 (Hague), 121, 138, 147-148 (Martin), 150-152, 158 (Reel), 256 (Legg),
Green Mountain National Forest, NH 247,

Greenhill, Debbie Ann 225, 226, 228-230,
Greenhill, Earl 228,
Greenwood Lake, IN 226,
Grouse 39, 42,
Grubb, Ester 156,
Gudger, Trula 153,
Gulley, Cap 83,

Hague, Geoffrey Burns 106-107, 116-122,
Halifax, Nova Scotia 259,
  Beaver Bank 259,
  Tucker Lake 259,
Hallaxs, Christopher 55, 65-67, Photo 65,
Hamilton, Eddie 8-10,
Hammons, Bobby 231,
Hanover Bluff Nature Preserve, IL 71,
Hanover, PA 177,
Hanson, Mark 106-107, 122-125, 164,
Happy Valley, TN 127, 129,
Hardy, David M 126,
Harlan Daily 231,
Harrah, WA 17,
Hatfield, Glen 159,
Haun, Fran 125,
Haun, Minnie 106-107, 125-127,
Havelock, ONT 33,
Hawk 9,
Hayfield 72,
Hazleton, PA 174,
Hearon, Michael Edwin 106-107, 127-130, Photo 127,
Hearon, Sue 127,
Hearon, Verl 127,
Heber City, UT 25-26,
Hennegan, Derrick 55, 67,
Herald Examiner 227,
Herald Times 59,
Hermits 141,
Herrick, Carl 264-265, 267-268,
Hickey, John 119,
Hibbard Hunting Camp 58,
Higgins Lake, MI 63,
Hinton, Bobby 103,
Hitchcock, Alfred 186,
Hoaglin Township, OH 30,
Hokit, Floyd 76, 80-82,
Holland, AR 91-92,

Index | 335

Holland, NY 185-185,
Holman, William B 83,
Holmes, Fred 171, 203-204,
Holmes, Gertrude 203-204,
Holmes, Roderick 203,
Hooper Sheep Ranch, WA 24,
Hospital 54, 91, 96, 167-168, 182, 197, 238, 243,
Hot Springs, AR 77,
Howe Hill, ME 235,
Houghton County Sheriff, MI 58,
Huckleberries 11-12, 14, 16-17, 135,
Huffman, Jerry Lee 166-167,
Hulin, Hjalmar 37,
Hulla, Carol Van 55, 61-63,
Hunter 133, 210-211,
　Mysterious Death 264-265,
Hutchinson News 159,
Hypothermia 44-45, 262,

Idaho
　Coeur D'Alene, ID 18,
　Dubois 25,
　Elk River 15-16,
　Fremont County 25,
　Grangeville 22,
　Priest Lake 18,
　Salmon River Breaks 22,
Illinois 70-74
　Braceville 72,
　Breeds, IL 70-71,
　Canton, IL 73,
　Coal City 73,
　Galatia Township 32,
　Hanover Bluff Nature Preserve 71,
　Kankakee River 73,
　Lasalle Fish and Wildlife Area 73,
　List of Missing 70
　Momence 73,
　Pearl City 71-72,
　Wetlands Nature Preserve 73,
Indian
　Trackers 13,
Indian Creek, AR 78,
Indiana
　Crane Depot, IN 226-227,
　Crothersville 225,
　Greenwood Lake 226,
　Lagrange 31-32,
　Muscattatack River 225,

Interview 318-319,
Iowa 233,
　Ackworth 31,
　Atlantic City 69,
　Webster City 29,
　List of Missing 69,
Isett, Ralph 210-211,

Jackson, Arthur 77,
Jackson, Florence 76-80,
Jacksonville, FL 153,
Jamison
　Bobby 76, 92-94
　Madyson 76, 92-94
　Photo 92,
　Sherilynn 76, 92-94
Jepson, Nancy 273,
Jepson, Paul 273-274,
Jewett, Rose 8, 15-16,
Johnson, Alden 233, 243-244,
Johnson, Dennis 316
　Photo 317,
Johnson, Mertley 233, 238-242,
Jones, Christopher 76, 91-92,
　Photo 91,
Jones, E.C. 28-29,
Jones, Wilbert 85,
Jones, Willard Eugene 76, 85-86,
Joplin Globe 78,

Kankakee River, IL
Kansas City MO 82,
Kant, Elizabeth 2, 4,
Keewatin, ME 14,
Keewatin School 14,
Keeweenaw Woods, MI 58,
Kelly, Jan 44,
Kelly, Kory 36, 42-47, 276,
Kentucky
　Eastern Kentucky University 122,
　Fort Campbell 131,
　Louisville 229,
　Newport 122,
　Oakhill 225,
　Olive Hill 228-229,
　Scott County 230,
　Stamping Ground 225,
Keshena, WI 53,
Ketcherside Mountain Conservation Area 75,
Kettle Lake Provincial Park 6,

Key, Baxter 142, 144,
Key, Harold 137-138, 140, 142, 150,
Kiamichi Mountains, OK 80, 94,
Kidnapping (See also "Abduction") xiv, 71, 73, 88, 99, 158, 166, 174, 182, 187, 195, 205, 214, 219, 228, 229, 245, 251, 266-267, 272, 277-278, 279,
　Abduction 16, 79, 174, 176, 181, 184, 209 (Possible), 214, 227, 238, 242, 245,
　By Bear 49, 56, 58, 173-174, 175, 254,
　By Wolf 49,
King, Harold 48,
Kingsford, MI 62,
Klamecki, David 73-74,
Klamecki, Hannah 73-74,
Knoxville, Highway 98,
Koester, Robert 62,
Knox, ME 15,
Knoxville, TN 111, 114, 144, 162,
Knoxville Journal 142,
Knoxville News Sentinel 137, 143,
Kooser State Park, PA 194-195,
Koza, John 21, 23,
Krebbs, Dewayne 86,
Krebbs, Larry 76, 86-87,
　Photo 86,
Kunchick, Rudy 175, 188, 191,

La Crosse Tribune 51,
Lagrange, IN 31-32,
Lake Gibson, ONT 6,
Lake Placid, NY 256-257,
Lake Superior
　Chequamegon Bay 51,
　State Forest 66,
Lake Texoma, OK 86,
Langer, Freida 274-276,
Lansberg, Thomas 195,
Lansing, MI 63,
Lasalle Fish and Wildlife Area, IL 73,
Latimer County, OK 93,
Laureldale, PA 195-197,
Lavies, Brad 106-107, 131-133,
Lavies, Nancy 131,
Lavies, Randy 131,
Leader Post 36,

Lebanon, MO 85,
Legg, Douglass 233, 255-257,
Leisure Lake, PA 205,
Lembke, Johnnie 8-9,
Lent, Darrell 180,
Lent, Oliva 180-181,
Lent, Rita Margaret 180-182,
Lethbridge Herald 19, 260,
Lewellen, Greg 21, 26-26,
Lewiston Daily 236, 257, 258, 264,
Lewiston Evening Journal 194,
Lexington Herald 231,
Lightning 29,
Linahan, John 114,
Lincoln, Herman 275,
Lindsay, Eloise 106-107, 133-135, 206,
Lindsay, Gayle 134,
Linklater, Michael 2, 6-7,
Lists of Missing
  Alabama 95,
  Berry Pickers 8-9,
  Children Under 10 283-287,
  Odd Coincidences 289-293
  Date Anomalies-Males 293-294
  Gaps in Time 294-295
  Farmers 28,
  Georgia 98,
  Great Smoky Mountains 106-107
  Illinois 70,
  Iowa 69,
  Kentucky 225,
  Master 296-306,
  Missing by Decade 307,
  Michigan 55,
  Minnesota 35-36,
  New England 232-233,
  New Jersey 277,
  OK/AR 76-77,
  Ohio 165,
  Ontario (Central) 2,
  Pennsylvania 170-171,
  Sheepherders 21,
  Vermont 264,
  West Virginia 215,
  Wisconsin 48,
Logan, UT 22,
Logansport Press 201,
Loggers 105,
Loman, MN 39,
Long, John 35, 39,
Long, William 70,
Long Valley, AZ 23,

Loon Mountain Ski Resort 262,
Lorimer, Evangeline 106-107, 135-136,
Los Angeles Times 199,
Loss of Memory 109,
Lost Person Behavior 61-62,
Lost, A Rangers Journal 146, 155,
Lowell Sun 275,
L.U. Sheep Company 25,
Ludington Daily 56-57,

Mackinaw Wilderness, MI 66,
Macon, GA 102,
Maddox, John 114,
Maine 232,
  Aboconet Bog 240,
  Alfred 254-255,
  Bethel 235,
  Big Bog Dam 238,
  Chain of Ponds 249,
  Frye Mountain State Management Area 15,
  Greenville 240,
  Hebron 253,
  Howe Hill 235,
  Keewatin 14,
  Kennebec River 240,
  Kineo Station 239,
  Knox 15,
  Moosehead Lake 240,
  Natanis Point Campground 257,
  Portland 235,
  Somerset County 240,
  Spears Mountain 15,
Maki, Raymond 55,
Malinoski, Michael Joe 211-212,
Manheim, PA 192,
Manitoba 6, 12-13,
  St. Vital 36,
Maps
  Alabama 95
  Great Smoky Mountains 105,
  Michigan 55
  Minnesota 35,
  OK/AR 76
  Pennsylvania 169,
  West Virginia 215,
  Wisconsin 48
Marion, OH 165-166,
  County Sheriff 165,

Mark Twain National Forest, MO 75,
Markline, Geraldine 170, 177-178,
Marshburg, PA 183,
Marshfield Times 49,
Martin, Clyde 136,
Martin, Dennis Lloyd 106-107, 116, 136-153, 134, 159, 206, 257, 316,
  Photo 136, 317,
  Rowans Creek Photo, 142,
  Wanted Poster 149,
Martin, William 136-152,
Marvin Jr., Horace 232, 234-235,
Maryland
  Colesville 197-198,
  State Police 189,
  Woodstock 188,
Maryville, TN 127,
Maryville Alcoa Times 137,
Massachusetts
  Brighton 237-238,
  Chicopee Falls, MA 203,
  Fort Devens 256,
  North Rehoboth, MA 14-15, 243,
Mauston, WI 50-51,
Mayo, Nita 213,
McCarthy, Patric 232, 233, 262-263,
McCarter Dwight 118-119, 124, 135, 136, 140-141, 146, 155-156,
McClellan, Albert 50,
McCuller, Charles 120,
McDonald, Daniel 89,
McDonald, Gloria 76, 89-91,
  Photo 89,
McFaul, Clayton 2,
McGrady, NC 108,
McGregor, MN 37,
McGurk, J.J. 30,
McKenzie, Ann 101,
McKinney, Elizabeth 218,
McKinney, Johnny 215, 218-219, 224,
McKinney, Paul 218,
McMillan, WI 49-50,
McNeal, Lisa 132,
McQuillan, Milda 35,
Mean, Frank 21, 24,
Melton, Robert 155,
Melton, Thelma Pauline 90, 106-107, 153-155,
Melvin, Crandell 255,

Index | 337

Melvin Jr., Myron 255,
Mena, AR 85,
Mena Star 89,
Menominee County, MI
   County Sheriff 58,
   Indian Reservation, WI 53,
Mercersburg, PA 197,
Meriden Daily Journal 271,
Meriden Record 178, 246,
   266,
Michigan 55-68,
   Battle Creek 65,
   Chippewa County 66,
   Copper City 58,
   Keweenaw Woods 58,
   Kingsford 62,
   Higgins Lake, MI 63,
   Lake Superior State Forest
      66,
   Lansing 63,
   Mackinaw Wilderness 66,
   Map 48,
   Newberry 67,
   Norway Lake 60-63,
   Mohawk 58,
   Paradise 63, 65,
   State Police 64, 66,
   Tahquamenon State Park
      63, 66,
   Walhalla 56-58,
   Whitefish Township, MI
      63-64,
Mill Run, PA 201-202,
Milwaukee Journal 162,
Milwaukee Sentinel 61-62,
Minarcin, Gabriel 171, 210,
   Photo 210,
Minneapolis, MN 41,
Minnesota 12, 35-47, 276,
   Beltrami County 40, 43-47,
   Callaway State Wildlife
      Management Area 40,
   Chisholm 41-42,
   Crookstown 42,
   Ely 39,
   Four Town, 42-43,
   Loman 39,
   McGregor 37,
   Map 35,
   Minneapolis, MN 41,
   Moose River 39,
   New Brighton 37,
   Paul Bunyan State Forest
      40-41,
   Ponsford 39-40,
   Red Lakes Recreation Area
      40-41,

   Red Lakes Wilderness
      42-47,
   Sugar Bush 40-41,
Missing
   From Yard 98, 165, 167, 172,
      174-175, 177, 180, 184,
      186, 193-194, 197-198,
      202, 203-204, 205, 216,
      229, 237, 246, 247, 251,
      254, 253, 254,
   From Campsite 108,
   From Creek 189,
   From Inside Home 75, 87,
      103, 173, 277,
   From Grandparents 215-216
      (Sherman), 220 (Shoe-
      maker), 242 (Swanson),
      281 (Peterson),
Mississippi River 71-72,
Missouri 74-75,
   Arcadia 75,
   Fuson Conservation Area,
      MO 85,
   Ketcherside Mountain
      Conservation Area 75,
   Lebanon 85,
   Mark Twain National Forest
      75,
   Mitchell, J. 21-22,
   Moberly Monitor 83,
   Moffitt, Earl 17-18,
   Moffitt, Mabel 8, 17-18,
   Mohawk, Mi 58,
   Momence, IL 73,
   Monongahela National Forest
      224,
Montana
   Acton 23,
   Alder 22-23,
   Dillon 23,
   Duluth 37,
   Red Lodge 21,
   Ruby Lake 22-23,
Montgomery, PA 192,
Monument Mountain, WA 18,
Moon Madness 179,
Moore, Joseph 215, 223-224,
Moore, Nora 95-97,
Moose River, MN 39,
Moosonee, ONT 6,
Morgan, Tim 134,
Morse, Floyd 70-71,
Mott, Harold 206-208, 213,
Mount Adams, WA 16-17,
Mount Everest 121,
Mount Guyot, GSM Park 123
Mount Laurel, PA 195,

Mount Sterling, GSM Park
   122,
Moy, Randy 167-168,
Mulberries 74,
Muldoon, M.J. 237,
Murder 176,
Murty, Leon 52,
Muscattatack River, IN 225,
Mushroom 197,

Naked Body 24,
Natanis Point Campground,
   ME 257,
National Guard 37, 77, 110,
   147, 230,
National Park Service (NPS)
   111-115, 117, 120, 123,
   128, 131, 133, 145, 256,
   315,
Native Americans 183, 264,
Navy 227,
Neikin, Robert 209,
Nelson, August (Mrs.) 8,
   48-49,
Nelson, Dean 23,
Neprud, Jim 42-47,
Nespelem, WA 11-12,
Nevada 25,
Nevada State Journal 81,
Neversink Reservoir, NY 203,
New Brighton, MN 37,
New England 232, 282,
   List of Missing 232-233,
New Grenada Mountain, PA
   211,
New Hampshire 231, 255,
   Cheshire County Sheriff
      247,
   Fitzwilliam 247,
   Green Mountain National
      Forest 247,
   Loon Mountain Ski Resort
      262,
   White Mountains 262,
New Jersey 175, 277-282,
   Belleplain State Forest 281,
   Bridgeton 277-278,
   Carmel 277,
   Delaware Bay 281,
   Delmont 281,
   Hammonton 278,
   Heislerville Fish and
      Wildlife Area 281,
   List of Missing 277,
   Millville 277,

Union Lake 277,
New Mexico
  Nutria 25,
  Zuni 25,
New York 207, 232,
  Adirondack Mountains 256,
  Ashokan Indian Reservation 203,
  Boiceville 173-174,
  Catskill Mountains 203,
  Denman Mountain, NY 203,
  Eagle Pond 253,
  Grahamsville 203,
  Greenburgh 244,
  Hartsdale Manor 244,
  Hudson Falls, NY 265,
  Holland 184-185,
  Lake Placid 256-257,
  Neversink Reservoir 203,
  Newcomb 255,
  Palermo 30-31,
  Rondout Reservoir, NY 203,
  Schenectady 273,
  State Police 31,
  Syracuse 255,
  Titusville Mountain State Forest 253,
New York Times 1, 9, 58, 69, 172-173, 226, 279,
Newberry, MI 67,
Newcomb, NY 255,
Newcomb Lake, NY 255,
Newcombe, Meryl 2-4,
  Photo 3,
Newport, KY 122,
Newsome, Henry 110,
Newton, Jill 257,
Newton, Kurt R. 233, 249, 257-259,
Newton, Ronald 257,
Next Steps 328-329,
North Adams Transcript 274,
North Carolina 105, 136,
  Deep Creek Campground 153,
  Doughton Park, NC 108,
  Fontana Lake 114, 139, 155,
  McGrady 108,
  Pilot Mountain 110,
  Swain County 113-114, 153,
  Surry County 110,
Norway Lake, MI 60-63,
North Dakota
  Fargo 40,
Northwest Arkansas Times 79,
Nova Scotia
  Halifax 232, 259,

Nutria, NM 25,
NWA Online 90,

Oak Grove, AR 77,
Oconaluftee Indian Village 155,
Odor
  Strong 272,
Ohio
  Campbell Mills 28-29,
  Cincinnati 135,
  Delaware Lake 165,
  Delaware Wilderness 165
  Hoaglin Township 30,
  Marion 165-166,
  North Richmond Township 180,
  Ohio River 218,
  Philo 166,
  Vernon Township 167,
Ojibwe First Nation 4,
Oklahoma 76-94,
  Bache 87,
  Bureau of Investigation 93,
  Chelsea 77,
  Highway Patrol 81,
  Kiamichi Mountains 80, 94,
  Lake Texoma, OK 86,
  Mounds 163,
  Latimer County 93,
  Map 76,
  Panola Mountain 92,
  Zanesville 166,
Olympic Games 25-26,
Oneonta Star 203,
Ontario 39,
  Central 2,
  Havelock 33,
  Kirkland Lake 19,
  Talihina 80,
Oregon
  Crater Lake 120
Oshkosh, WI 51,
Otis, Carlos 268,
Ottawa Citizen 249, 260,
Overalls 43, 218, 228,
Owens, Al 21-23,
Ozark Mountains 85,
Ozark National Forest 94,

Paleo Indians 105,
Palermo, NY 30-31,
Panola Mountain, OK 92-93,

Paradise, MI 63, 65,
Parsons, Willis 239,
Pathologist 250,
Patterson, David 186,
Paul Bunyan State Forest, MN 40-41,
Pearl City, IL 71-72,
Pend Oreille 18,
Pennsylvania 12, 166, 169-214, 276,
  Allegheny National Forest 184, 205, 213,
  Allegheny Reservoir 207,
  Allegheny River 210,
  Altoona 190,
  Association of Retarded People 208,
  Bald Eagle Mountain 191-192,
  Bradford 183,
  Burholme Park 178,
  Catawissa Valley 172,
  Chapter Summary 213-214,
  Clear Creek State Park 213-214, 213,
  Cornell Lookout 193,
  Corydon Township 206-207,
  Corry 205-206,
  Cresco 175,
  Delaware River 178,
  Dubois 213,
  Dunbar 199,
  Fombell 208,
  Fox Chase, PA 178-180,
  Gaines 211-212,
  Girard Manor 172,
  Greeley 175-176,
  Hanover 177,
  Hazle Brook 174,
  Hazleton 174,
  Indian Creek Valley 199,
  Kooser Lake 199,
  Kooser State Park 194-195,
  Lake Pahagasco 177,
  Lancaster County 192,
  Laureldale 195-197,
  Leisure Lake 205,
  List of Missing 170,
  Manheim 192,
  Map 169,
  Marshburg 183,
  Mercersburg 197,
  Mill Run 203-204,
  Missing List by Month 171,
  Montgomery 192,
  Moshannon Creek 194,
  Mount Laurel 195,

Index | 339

New Grenada Mountain 211,
Philipsburg 193-194,
Pigeon Mountains 177,
Pike County 176,
Pine Creek Gorge 212,
Pine Tree Lodge 212,
Pitcairn 213,
Pleasantville 200-201, 223,
Pottstown 204,
Pottsville 172-173,
Robertsdale 210-211,
Robertsdale Mountain 211,
Scottdale 185-186,
Sheppton 175,
Somerset 194-195,
Spring Creek Township 213,
State Police 186, 202, 205, 211,
Susquehanna River 192,
Stroudsburg 175,
Tarentum 210,
Tioga County 212,
Tumbling Run Valley 173,
West Chester 212,
Williamsport 191,
Perry, Roland 260,
Peterson, Bryan 281,
Peterson, Carolyn 165-166,
Peterson, Charles 166,
Peterson, Richard 277, 281-282,
Philadelphia Daily News 282,
Philipsburg, PA 193-194,
Philo, OH 166,
Physicians xiv,
Piatote, Wesley 8, 11-12,
Pickens County, SC 134,
Pigs 32, 70, 273,
   Killed Man 69,
Pike, Jack 8, 12, 35-37,
Pike, Charles 36,
Pilot Mountain, NC 110,
Pinkerton Detectives 234,
Pisgah National Forest 158,
Pitcairn, PA 213,
Pitsenbarger, William 28, 30,
Pittsburgh, PA 9, 278,
Pittsburgh Post Gazette 177, 195,
Pittsburgh Press 70, 209,
Pittsburgh Times 99,
Plattsburgh Air Force Base 256,
Pleasant Valley, PA 9,
Pleasantville, PA 200-201, 223,
Poachers 239-240,
Pocahontas County Sun 29,

Poe, George 22,
Poison 182,
Polygraph 90, 195,
Ponsford, MN 39-40,
Pottstown, PA 204,
Pottsville, PA 172-173,
Prato, Joseph 170, 191-192,
Price, Bernice 28, 30,
Prigley, Eddie 225-226,
Priest Lake, ID 18,
Prior, Yehudi 8, 18,
Privation 234,
Prosser, W. O. 77,
Provost, Alberta 32-33,
Psychic 86, 114, 152, 207, 235,

Quachita National Forest, AR 91, 94,
Quarry 237,
Quebec, Canada 232,
   Bourg-La-Reine 251-252,
   Eastman 249-250,
Queen Wilhelmina State Park, AR 89,
Ququa Creek, OH 166,

Railroad 7, 202,
Rain 72, 78, 80, 98, 113, 122-123-124, 128, 138, 158, 162, 166, 202-203, 211, 220, 225, 229, 237, 243, 258, 277, 278,
Ramsay, Abe Carroll 106-107, 155-157,
Ramsay, John 156,
Ramsburg, Shirley Ann 215-218, 224,
Ranch 74,
Rapid River, MN 43,
Reading Eagle 179, 202,
Reading, PA 12,
Red Lakes Recreation Area, MN 40-41,
Red Lakes Wilderness, MN 42-47,
Red Lodge Creek, MT 21,
Red Top Mountain State Park, GA 100,
Reel, Michael Eugene 106-107, 157-160, 161,
Renaud, Lorenzo 251,
Renaud, Nicole 233, 251-253,
Renton, James 275,

Reterer, Leroy 165,
Rhinelander Daily 52,
Rhodes, Dustin 2, 5-6,
Rike, Jim 127, 139-140, 145, 151,
Ridgeline 82, 126,
Rioux, Edmond 249,
Rivers, Middie 269,
Roan Mountain State Park, NC 157, 161,
Rock Formation (w/stick) 221,
Robertsdale, PA 171, 210-211
Rock Hill Herald 150,
Rodencal, Judy 48,
Rondout Reservoir, NY 203,
Royal Canadian Mounted Police (RCMP) 10, 19, 31, 33, 260-261,
Ruby Lake, MT 22-23,
Rumbaugh, Ronald 185-186, 214,

Salmon River Breaks, ID 22,
San Antonio Express 181,
Salt Lake City, UT 25-26,
San Francisco 211,
San Jose Mercury News 99,
Sandoval, Louis 21,
Santa Fe New Mexican 84,
SAR xvi, 10-11, 19, 60, 75, 83, 108, 110, 120, 125, 149-151, 212, 216, 221, 249, 256,
Sarasota Herald 15,
Saskatoon 33,
Saskatoon Phoenix 10,
Saskatoon Star 249-250, 251,
Saw Mill
   Abandoned 78, 281,
Scent xiii
Schenectady Gazette 252,
Schenectady, NY 273,
Schmidt, Ronald 155,
Schnitzker, William 230,
Schroeder, Herman 23,
Scott, Duane 208-209,
Scott, Elmer 60-61,
Scott, Karen 209,
Scott, Kenneth 55,
Scottdale, PA 185-186,
Scratches 315,
Scream 36, 143, 312,
   For Help 123, 140, 189, 198, 205-206, 272,
Seattle, WA 119,

Semi-Conscious xiv, 75,
Senser, Jimmy 170, 193-194,
Senser, Sylvester 193-194,
Septic Tank
    Dog Found Inside 198,
Shackleford, Inex 72,
Shackleford, Lisa 72-73,
Sheepherders 21-26,
Sheep Sorel 78,
Shenandoah River, WV 217,
Sheppton, PA 175, 188,
Sherman, Harold 141,
Sherman, Shirley 215-216,
Shoemaker, Victor 215, 219-223,
    Photo 219,
Sholtas, Mary 174-175,
Short Mountain Wildlife Area, WV 219,
Sierra Nevada Mountains, CA 30,
Simpson, Frank 175,
Simpson, Robert 113, 115,
Simpson, Unk First Name 170, 175,
Skogan, Simon 8,
Sleeping Bag 88,
Smith, Eugene 117,
Snowstorm 50, 118, 120, 123, 218, 271,
Soldiers 13,
Soltes, Helen 179,
Sonora, CA 213,
South Carolina
    Pickens County 134,
    Table Rock State Park 133,
Somerville, Earl 35, 39,
Spears Mountain, ME 15,
Special Forces 138, 150,
Spokane, WA 18,
Spokesman Review 227,
Springfield, VT 264,
St. Joseph Press 182,
St. Norbert, MAN 12, 36,
St. Petersburg Times 99, 182,
St. Vital, MAN 36,
Staneker, Augustus 174-175,
Star News 158,
Stars and Stripes 254,
Starvation 176,
Steffy, Emma 8, 12,
Stevens Point Daily 52,
Stewart, Dwight 41,
Stewart, Stephanie 88,
Stockbridge, GA 103,
Strange Men 79,

Strawberry Mountain, WA 11-12,
Strawberry Patch 192,
Streeter, Candida 171, 204,
Streeter, John 204,
Stroudsburg, PA 175,
Sugar Bush, MN 40-41, 266,
Suicide 145, 152, 225,
Sullivan Lake 18,
Sullivan, Len 99,
Sunday Herald 272,
Surry County, NC 110,
Surveyor 101,
Susquehanna River 192,
Suttles, Charles 246,
Swain County, NC 113-114, 153,
Swamps/Bog xv, 14, 31, 38, 44-46, 51-53, 61-62, 72-73, 172, 176, 189, 193, 198, 200, 227-228, 234, 243-244, 247, 249, 250, 260, 272-273, 275, 277-278,
Swanson, Kenneth 233, 242,
Sweely, Susan 71-72,
Sweely, William 72,
Sylacauga, AL 95,
Syracuse Journal 133,
Syracuse Morning Herald 236,
Syracuse New York Times 30,
Szpak, Frank 8, 19,
    Photo 19,

Table Rock State Park, SC 133, 206,
Tahqua Trail, MI 64,
Tahquamenon State Park, MI 63, 66
    River 63,
Talihina, OK 80,
Tankersley, L.C. 96,
Tankersley, Rickey 95-96,
Tarentum, PA 210,
Taylor, Jack 31,
The Item 133,
Telegraph 266,
Telegraph Herald 71, 166, 189,
Temperature 50,
Temple University 179,
Tennessee 105, 136,
    Blount County Sheriff 128,
    Briceville 125,
    Campbell County Sheriff 126,

Carter County 158,
Carthage 140,
Chilhowee Lake, 128,
Cocke County 156,
Dunn Creek 155,
Elkmont 114,
Happy Valley 127, 129,
Knoxville 111, 162,
Maryville 127,
Mt. Chapman 124,
Pisgah National Forest 158,
Roan Mountain State Park 157,
Sevier County 156,
University of TN 132, 163,
Well Springs, TN 125,
Texas
    Fort Washita 86,
The Sun 62,
The Telegraph 234,
Thermopolis, WY 24,
Thomas, Jeremy 102-103,
Thompkins, Christopher 101-102
    Photo 101,
Thorpe, Anna Pearl 9, 171, 185, 198-199,
Throbbing Giant 201, 223,
Times 248,
Times Daily 131-132,
Timm, Edgar 52,
Timmins, ONT 2, 4-5, 21-22
Tippin, David 103-104
Tippin, Robert 103,
Titusville Herald 205,
Tobesofkee Creek, GA 102,
Toledo Blade 176,
Tomah, WI 29,
Tomaro Timber Company, MN 39,
Toney, Jay Charles 106-107, 162-163,
Tornado 122,
Tourtillott, Colleen, 48,
Tourtillott, Janelle 53
Tourtillott, Miles 53,
Tracked
    To River 217,
Trackers xiii,
Tracy Lake, SASK 18,
Trail 90,
    Trailhead 89,
Tri City Herald 229,
Trinastich, Luciano 9, 19-20,
Trout Creek, WA 17,
Trout Lake, WA 16-17,
Trout Lake Ranger Station 59,

Index | 341

Tunnicliffe, Raymond 9, 18-19,
Turkeys 210,
  Farm 243,
Turner, Richard 227,
Tuscaloosa News 136, 159,
Tyrone Daily Herald 209,

United States Forest Service
  (USFS) 16-17, 23, 161,
United States Secret Service
  234,
United States Senator 139,
University of TN 132,
Unsolved Disappearances
  in the Great Smoky
  Mountains 156,
Upshaw, Murray 98-100,
Utah
  Bench Creek 25-26,
  Heber City 25-26,
  Logan 22,
  Salt Lake City 25-26,
  Wasatch County 25-26,

Vachon, Vital 2, 4,
Val Cote, ONT 6,
Van Alst, Katherine 76, 82-85,
Vancouver Island, BC 18,
Vermillion River 9,
Vermont 264-276,
  Bald Mountain 265-266,
    274,
  Bennington 265-266, 269,
  Bennington College 271,
  Chapter Summary 276,
  Felchville 265,
  Glastenbury Mountain 264,
    267, 269-273,
  Green Mountain National
    Forest 270-272,
  Somerset Reservoir 271,
  Springfield 264,
  Reading 264-265,
  Rutland 265,
  Somerset 274,
  State Police 272,
  West Townshend 265,
    267-268,
Vernon Township, OH 167,
Virginia
  Leesburg 220,
  Martinsburg 219,
Vrholla, Paul 186,

Wailing 51,
Walhalla, MI 56-58,
Walla Walla Union 24,
Walnuts 125,
Wanke, George 8, 12,
Warburton, Andrew 233,
  259-262,
Warburton, Doreen 259,
Warburton, Tom 259,
Warner, Isaac 226,
Warner, Leeanna 36,
Warren, Charles 76-77,
Warren, Harold 77,
Wasatch County, UT 25-26,
Washburn, WI 51,
Washington 256,
  Burbank 24,
  Harrah 17,
  Monument Mountain 18,
  Mt. Adams 16-17,
  Seattle 119,
  Spokane 18,
  Trout Lake 16-17,
  Whatcom County 18,
Washington County, AR 83,
Washington Post 109,
Webster City IA 29,
Weeden, George 2-4,
  Photo 3,
Weeks, Charles 229,
Weitkamp, Lawrence 226-227,
Weitkamp, Ronnie 225-228,
Welden, Paula 270-273,
  Wanted Poster 270,
Welden, W. Archibald 271,
Wells, Jack 21,
Well Springs, TN 125,
Wellsville Daily 256,
Welsh Mountain Wilderness,
  PA 12,
Wenatchee Lake 11-12,
Wernberg, Beryl 43,
West, Dorothea 183,
West, Marjorie 170, 183-184,
  206, 207, 213,
  Photo 183,
West Townshend, VT 265,
  267-268,
West Virginia 215-224
  Augusta 219,
  Bureau of Criminal
    Identification 222,
  Chapter Summary 224,
  Charleston 223,
  Charles Town 216,
  Elk River 224,

Franklin 215-216,
Gallipolis 218,
Hampshire County 219,
List of Missing 215,
Map 215
Shenandoah River 217,
Short Mountain Wildlife
  Area 219,
State Trooper 222,
Will Run Creek 216,
Wetlands Nature Preserve,
  IL 73,
Weyakwin, SASK 18,
Whatcom County, WA 18,
Wheat 33,
Whitaker, Kaelin 41,
White Bear Hills 10,
White Bear Lake 10-11,
Whitefish Township, MI 64,
Whitney Lake, MI 60,
Wild Men 148,
Wildflowers 183,
Wilke, Thelma Ann 48,
Wilkes, Ray 38,
Willhoite, Billy 231,
Williams, Leroy 28, 31, 69,
Williamsport, PA 191,
Windsor Daily Star 13,
Winger, Keith 43,
Winnepeg 13, 31,
Winnepeg Free Press 11-12,
  260,
Wisconsin 48-54,
  Auroraville 52,
  Bear Creek 29,
  Boulder Junction 59,
  Castle Rock Lake 50,
  Drummond 13,
  Keshena 61,
  Mauston 50-51,
  McMillan 49-50,
  Map 48,
  Menominee Indian
    Reservation 53,
  Oshkosh 51,
  Tomah 29,
  Washburn 51,
  Waushara County 53,
  Whitney Lake 59,
  Whitney Lake, WI 59,
Witt, Floyd 26,
Woelfle, Edward 55, 59-60,
Woelfle, William 59,
Wolf
  Traps 59,
Wolfe, Unk First Name 170,
  172,

Wolfe, George 172,
Wolford, Oscar 220-221,
Wyoming
 Bitter Creek 22,
 Thermopolis 24,
Yosemite National Park, CA 105,
Young, Ralph 266,
Youngstown Vindicator 249,
Zanesville, OH 166,
Zuni, NM 25,
Zuni Tribal Police 25,